CURTAIN CALLS

BERNARD MILES
and
J. C. TREWIN

View of the Exterior of Drury Lane Theatre

LUTTERWORTH PRESS
Guildford Surrey England

First published 1981

To
JENNY OVERTON
for whose favours
both compilers are in fierce competition

31904

Selection of material, introduction, notes and linking
material, and programme note, copyright © 1981 by Bernard
Miles and J. C. Trewin.

ISBN 0-7188-2476-8

Set in 11/12 Bembo 270

Printed in Great Britain
by Butler & Tanner Ltd, Frome and London

SADLERS WELLS THEATRE.

Do they not maintaine bawdrie, insinuat foolery, and renue the remembrance of heathen ydolatrie? Do they not induce whordom and unclennes? Nay, are they not rather plaine devourers of maydenly virginitie and chastitie? For proof whereof but marke the flocking and running to Theaters and Curtens daylie and hourely, night and daye, tyme and tyde, to see Playes and Enterludes.

Philip Stubbes (1583)

NOTE

Many of the characters who appear in these pages play a part in more than one of the incidents here described. A reader whose interest is caught by any particular figure should consult the index of plays and players (pages 186–92) to discover what other appearances (if any) occur in this book.

At the head of each passage is a title (chosen by the compilers), the name of the author, the title of the original work, and the date of publication.

Footnotes appear only on the first instance of a source's being quoted.

The quotations on the second and last pages of this book are from Philip Stubbes's *Anatomie of Abuses* (1583).

ACKNOWLEDGMENTS

The compilers and the publishers thank Victor Gollancz Ltd for permission to quote the poem by V. C. Clinton-Baddeley (pages 96–7), taken from his novel *To Study a Long Silence*. They regret that they have been unable to trace the heirs of the late W. J. Lawrence, author of *The Life and Times of Gustavus Vaughan Brooke* (W. & G. Baird, 1892); the late James Lloyd, author of *My Circus Life* (Noel Douglas, 1925); the late Thomas Geering, author of *Our Sussex Parish* (Methuen, 1925); or the late Frank Hird, co-author of *The Romance of a Great Singer* (1910). They would welcome the opportunity to offer the customary acknowledgments in any future edition, in accordance with current recommended Society of Authors' practices.

One of Irving's interminable wires to me wound up with 'If convenient kindly call at Stratton Street tomorrow at twelve. Want to ask your advice.' Wondering what was 'up' now, of course, I duly obeyed the lengthy telegraphic summons. On my arrival I found that he had promised to appear at an Alhambra Charity Matinée, together with many other stars alike of the theatrical, musical and variety professions.

'I am going to make my debut in the London music-halls, you see,' said Irving. 'And the question has arisen whether I should precede or follow Mr Dan Leno. A very gifted droll, I have heard. I have never yet had the pleasure of seeing him at his work. I suppose,' he added, 'being, I may say, the chief star in this variety bill, I ought to follow Mr Leno!'

'I hope you will do nothing of the kind, Irving,' I replied. 'Dan Leno is not only the greatest comedian and greatest comic dancer in the music-halls, he is also a tremendous favourite in pantomime and at every theatre wherever he appears. If YOU follow HIM—even with a lighter kind of recitation than you usually give at charity matinées, you'll have the hardest job an actor ever had to make good! I've known Leno all his life—from his clog-dancing days,' I continued. 'I have worked with him and written for him, and I know what that wonderful little chap can do with an audience. You get on before him, or you'll fail at that matinée!'

'It was because I knew that you know Leno that I sent for you,' said Irving, 'and asked for your advice. Of course, I shall take that advice. Still, one would have thought that I, Henry Irving, would . . .' etc., etc.

Irving not only kept his promise to me and preceded dear, droll little Dan at that matinée, he also waited at the wings and saw Dan's 'turn'. Irving laughed till he cried at Leno's 'business', and when Dan came off Sir Henry introduced himself to Leno. 'An esteemed old friend of yours and mine, Chance Newton, my dear Mr Leno,' said Irving, 'strongly advised me not to follow your "turn". And now I'm damned glad I didn't. What a favourite! How gloriously funny! Come round to the club and let us have a chat—and a little crack!'

The larkish, lovable—and afterwards so sorely afflicted—little Dan afterwards told me of his huge delight and pride.

H. Chance Newton (1927)

IN ORDER OF APPEARANCE

INTRODUCTION

MR KEAN as MACBETH.

Why do we go on doing it despite the quarrels, the jealousies, the gossip, the ill temper? What keeps us going through the crises, the anxieties, the grinding circuit of agents and auditions and one-night stands?

This book began on the road. The greater part of it was collected whilst I was touring the provinces between 1950 and 1957. I was doing a single music-hall act, and once I had got over 'band call' on Monday, my pastime was to visit any abbeys, cathedrals, castles, and so on in the vicinity, but above all else, to explore the local antiquarian bookshops.

I bought an early edition of the Directory of Dealers in Secondhand and Antiquarian Books, published by Sheppard Press, and this was like a Bible to me, I kept it by my bed and tried to persuade the famous Cissie Williams of Moss Empires fame to book my tours in the towns and cities listed in its pages:

THE CASTLE BOOKSHOP, 37 North Hill, Colchester, Essex. Prop: A. B. Doncaster. TN: Colchester 77520. Est: 1947. Shop, no early closing. New, and medium to large sec. and antiq. stock. Spec: archaeology, topography of East Anglia, especially Essex. Cata: general, quarterly, free. NBL. BA. ABA.

J. STEVENS COX, Beaminster, Dorset. TA: Stevens-Cox, Beaminster. Est: 1930. Storeroom, appointment necessary. Very large sec. and antiq. stock; also maps, prints and paintings. Spec: archaeology, agriculture, history, Dorset and Somerset, world topography, English literature. Cata: all subjects, eight a year, and about forty small lists, 2s. 6d. per annum. ABA.

Thus, I could make straight for the local antiquarian bookshop, enjoy fine talk with the proprietor, and spend a happy afternoon among the books. Over the years I built up a considerable library of biographies, memoirs and so on, particularly from the late eighteenth and the nineteenth centuries. Reading them through between houses or in bed at night, I marked passages which especially appealed to me, and noted the page numbers on the flyleaf. Every time I returned from a tour, I got my secretary to make copies of the various passages. In the end my cherished books went the same way as Kean's letter (mentioned on page 178 of this book) and a great many more besides, sold to Ifan Kyrle Fletcher of Buckingham Gate or Andrew Block of Barter Street, to raise funds for the Mermaid Theatre. I wish now that I had signed and dated the volumes—I don't say that they would be of more value, but they would certainly be of great interest if brought together in a single collection once again.

In 1950, when these tours began, I bought in Aylesbury, for £40, a vast harvesters' table, built of elm. Eleven feet long and four feet wide, balanced on two mighty trestles, it had stood in a local farmyard for a couple of hundred years, and every autumn the great harvest supper was spread upon it. All the planning of the Mermaid Theatre was done on that table. It was so big that when our children left home and we moved to a smaller house, we couldn't get it in, so I bequeathed it to my son, who sold it for £1,500—I think the buyer was a Dutch farmer. Looking back, I wish I had fastened a brass plate to its underside. Holland has a great theatrical relic!

Although I sold my books and letters to fund the Mermaid, I kept the copies of my favourite passages in a huge box file, and they form the major part of this book. Hence the fact that it ends round about the turn of the century. I had not had the time to get further—besides, the later material was not always very interesting. Hence, too, the reason why, when it came to publication, I felt I must choose a collaborator: and who better than my old friend, John Trewin, one of the greatest and most ardent servants of the living theatre. A brief 'phone call, and all was arranged.

★   ★   ★

The words of Lear and Falstaff, of Major Barbara and Candida, of Tony Lumpkin and Lady Teazle, of Charley's Aunt and Polly Garter and Macheath and Joxer Daly, spring every night new-minted from the actor's mouth. Speaking them he re-enters the minds of their creators, he glows with the wit of Sheridan and Wilde, Coward and Lonsdale, he regularly partakes of something bigger than himself, he mingles with the immortals in a very special way and receives their nightly benediction.

But the actor does more. He passes the benediction on. He scatters bless-ings in his turn; he is part of the healing fraternity. For even at its worst, the stage is a solace, a cure for loneliness, a gathering together in the name of mankind. It is 'men speaking to men', a great laughter-spreader, it is love in action. It puts us into proportion, 'all to and fro but little heaps of dust', and yet 'in action how like angels, in apprehension how like gods'. Passion, warmth, wit, grace, precision, balance, co-ordination. 'What a piece of work is a man!'

Chaplin, Caruso, Sid Field, Edith Evans, Spike Milligan, Peter Sellers, Louis Armstrong, John Gielgud, The Carolis, Johnny Puleo, The Fratellinis, Ellen Terry, Larry Olivier, Robert Donat, Paul Scofield, Dan Leno, Beatrice Lillie, Wences, Edwige Feuillère, Flagstad, Eva Turner, Jean Louis Barrault, Harry Secombe—the list could go on for ever—all doctors, nurses and psychiatrists in their own humble or arrogant way, transporting us into worlds beyond our everyday selves, either by escape from reality (and what harm in that?) or by escape into a deeper reality; either helping us to forget or, if we can bear it, to remember.

More and more frequently, there steals over one the suspicion that the whole human story is a kind of play, a tragi-comedy in many episodes with script still being written in the wings, the mammoth cast under-rehearsed, imperfectly made up, unsure of their cues and dressed in the wrong clothes; the stage management either very inexperienced, inebriated or blatantly incompetent; and the Great Director tearing his hair in the stalls. To be of some minute assistance to Him in pulling the show together makes the whole thing seem abundantly worth while, and in any case I daresay it'll be all right on the night.

Bernard Miles

OVERTURE AND BEGINNERS

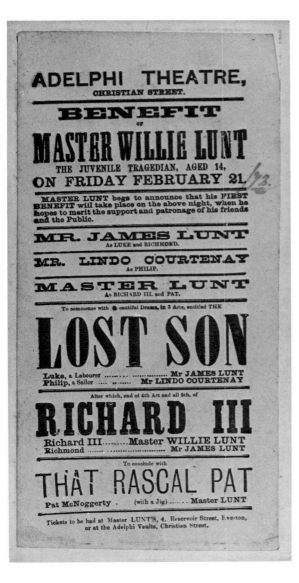

A playbill from the Adelphi, Liverpool, 1873, for the benefit night of juvenile tragedian, Master Willie Lunt. He was the last of a long line of child performers, often as young as six or seven. Starting with the famous Master William Henry West Betty (1791–1874), they were all the rage in the early nineteenth century. This bill is particularly precious to me as Willie Lunt was the grandfather of my old friend, that fine actor Milton Rosmer, and it was given to me as a parting gift a week or two before his death.

BY HIS MAJESTY'S COMPANY OF COMEDIANS
KILKENNY THEATRE ROYAL

(Positively the last night, because
the Company go tomorrow to Waterford)

ON SATURDAY, MAY 14th, 1793

will be performed, by desire and command
of several respectable people in this learned Metropolis
for the benefit of Mr Kearns the Manager

The Tragedy of
HAMLET THE PRINCE OF DENMARK

Originally written and composed by the celebrated Dan Hayes of Limerick,
and inserted in Shakespear's works.

Hamlet, by Mr Kearns (being his first appearance in that character), and who,
between the acts, will perform several solos on the patent bag-pipes, which
play two tunes at the same time.

Ophelia, by Mrs Prior who will introduce several favourite airs in character,
particularly 'The Lass of Richmond Hill' and 'We'll Be Unhappy Together',
from the Rev. Mr Dibden's oddities.

The parts of *the King and Queen*, by directions of the Rev. Father
O'Callaghan, will be omitted, as too immoral for any stage.

Polonius, the comical politician, by a young gentleman, being his first
appearance in public.

The Ghost, the Gravedigger, and *Laertes*, by Mr Sampson, the great London
Comedian.

The Characters to be dressed in Roman shapes.

To which shall be added an Interlude, in which will be introduced several
sleight-of-hand tricks, by the celebrated surveyor Hunt.

The whole to conclude with the farce of
MAHOMET THE IMPOSTER

Mahomet, by Mr Kearns

14

Tickets to be had of Mr Kearns, at the sign of the Goat's Beard, in Castle Street.

The value of the tickets, as usual, will be taken out (if required) in candles, bacon, soap, butter, cheese, potatoes, etc.; as Mr Kearns wishes, in every particular, to accommodate the public.

N.B. No smoking allowed. No person whatsoever will be admitted into the boxes without shoes or stockings.

GREAT IMPROVEMENT
W. T. Parke
Musical Memoirs (1830)

When I was at Oxford, a young Rhodes scholar, Alan Post, went to a performance of Hamlet. When asked what he thought of this great play, his comment was, 'Gee, he sure did talk back and forth a lot before slipping that old bird a dagger.' He might have preferred this performance by Mr Cubit, a subordinate actor and singer at Covent Garden in the early nineteenth century:

When, during one of his summer engagements at a provincial theatre, Cubit was announced to perform the character of Hamlet, he was 'seized with a sudden and serious illness in his dressing-room just before the play was going to begin. Whereupon the manager was constrained to request the audience to suffer them to go through with the play, omitting the character of Hamlet; which being complied with, it was afterwards considered by the bulk of the audience to be a great improvement.'

HAMLET HOTCH-POTCH
H. Chance Newton
Cues and Curtain Calls (1927)

From early youth up to not many years ago I used to see six Hamlets per week and five per night! This Hamlet hotch-potch occurred in the following manner: when at the 'Wells', the 'Brit.', the Standard, the Pavilion and the Effingham (Mile End), the Marylebone (off the Edgware Road), and the City of London Theatre, Norton Folgate, any striking week's attraction, especially of a Shakespearean kind, was felt to be needed, the management concerned used to select from the same company, or from other companies round about, six popular actors to play Hamlet one night apiece during that week.

The five-Hamlets-a-night group are to be accounted for thus: when one or other of these popular Hamlets used to have a benefit he got four others with himself to be a different Hamlet in each act!

The critic Bill Darlington (W. A. Darlington of the Daily Telegraph) told me that in a long and busy professional life, he had seen no fewer than 93 Hamlets, and that he inevitably carried into the theatre with him all too many vestiges of past performances. He confessed this to be an unavoidable handicap.

FROM LINKBOY TO LOON

Dutton Cook
A Book of the Play (1876)

In Foote's comedy of *The Minor* [1760], Shift, one of the characters, describes the changing scenes of his life. From a linkboy outside a travelling theatre he was promoted to employment within. 'I did the honours of the barn by sweeping the stage and clipping the candles. Here my skill and address was so conspicuous that it procured me the same office the ensuing winter, at Drury Lane, where I acquired intrepidity, the crown of all my virtues.... For I think, sir, he that dares stand the shot of the gallery, in lighting, snuffing, and sweeping, the first night of a new play, may bid defiance to the pillory with all its customary compliments.... But an unlucky crab-apple applied to my right eye by a patriot gingerbread baker from the Borough, who would not suffer three dances from Switzerland because he hated the French, forced me to a precipitate retreat.'

★ ★ ★

In small provincial or strolling companies it often becomes expedient to press every member of the establishment into the service of the stage. A useful property-man and scene-shifter was occasionally required to fill small parts, the 'cream-faced loon', for instance, in *Macbeth*. He thus explained his system of representation, admitting that from his other occupations he could rarely commit perfectly to memory the words he was required to utter:

'I tell you how I manage. I invariably contrives to get a reg'lar knowledge of the natur' of the *char-ac-ter*, and ginnerally gives the haudience words as near like the truth as need be. I seldom or never puts any of you out, and takes as much pains as anybody can expect for two-and-six a week extra, which is all I gets for doing such-like parts as mine. I find Shakespeare's parts worse to get into my head nor any other; he goes in and out so to tell a thing.

I should like to know how I was to say all that rigmarole about the wood coming; and I'm sure my telling Macbeth as Birnam Wood was a-walking three miles off the castle did very well.

'But some gen'lemen is sadly pertickler, and never considers circumstances.'

THE PLAYGOING TIME
Leigh Hunt
Autobiography (1850)

That is a pleasant time of life, the playgoing time in youth, when the coach is packed full to go to the theatre, and brothers and sisters, parents and lovers (none of whom, perhaps, go very often) are all wafted together in a flurry of expectation; when the only wish as they go (except with the lovers) is to go as fast as possible, and no sound is so delightful as the cry of 'Bill of the Play'; when the smell of links in the darkest and muddiest winter's night is charming; and the steps of the coach are let down; and a roar of hoarse voices round the door, and *mud-shine* on the pavement, are accompanied with the sight of the warm-looking lobby which is about to be entered; and then enter, and pay, and ascend the pleasant stairs, and begin to hear the *silence* of the house, perhaps the first jingle of the music; and the box is entered amidst some little awkwardness in descending to their places, and being looked at; and at length they sit, and are become used to by their neighbours, and shawls and smiles are adjusted, and the playbill is handed round, or pinned to the cushion, and the gods are a little noisy, and the music veritably commences, and at length the curtain is drawn up, and the first delightful syllables are heard:

'Ah, my dear Charles, when did you see the lovely Olivia?'

'Oh, my dear Sir George, talk not to me of Olivia. The cruel guardian—' etc.

Don't for a moment believe that this kind of excitement is outmoded. In the great cities of the north—Leeds, Bradford, Newcastle and others—the Christmas pantomime runs for four months, and is the mainstay of the theatre's yearly balance sheet, and the excitement is as intense today as ever.

ASTONISHING THE NATIVES
The Drama★ (*Vol. I, 1821*)

Little Newton, late of the Bristol Theatre, is at present manager of the theatre at the Isle of Man, where his daughter, about ten years of age, has astonished 'the natives' by her performance of Richard the Third.

★ *The Drama; or, Theatrical Pocket Magazine:* a periodical first issued in May, 1821; closed in December, 1825

On November 25th, 1805, Miss Mudie, called The Theatrical Phenomenon, a child apparently about eight years old, with but a comparatively diminutive figure even for that age, who in the preceding season had played the first-rate comic characters at Birmingham, Liverpool, Dublin, and other theatres, made her debut at Covent Garden as Miss Peggy in *The Country Girl*.

It is true, she repeated the words of the part correctly; her deportment was confident, unembarrassed, and sprightly; her voice, for her age, powerful; and her acting evinced intelligence and industry; in truth, considering her performance as that of an infant, it was surprising; but regarding it as a *dramatic personification*, it was contemptible. In the first scene the sense of the house was good-naturedly expressed, for when Moody promised to send her back into the country, the audience very cordially expressed their concurrence by loud applause. In the succeeding scenes they were less equivocal; for, when she came to be talked of as a *wife*, as a *mistress*, as *an object of love and jealousy*, the scene became so ridiculous that hissing and horse-laughing ensued.... In the third act, Miss Peggy is seen walking in the Park, dressed in boy's clothes under the care of her jealous guardian. Miss Mudie, instead of appearing a fine young man who ought to be 'shown the town', looked shorter than before, and even too little to be safely put in breeches. Yet [John] Brunton, as her lover Belville, pursued her and was transported to find her under this disguise; and Mr Murray, her pretended husband, was thrown into an agony of despair at the idea of another man taking her by the hand. The absurdity was now too great to be endured, and there was a burst of censure from all parts of the house. At last, Charles Kemble, as Harcourt, exclaimed, 'Let me introduce you, nephew; you should know each other, you are very like and of the same age.' The whole effect was so out of character, so very ludicrous, that the audience soon decided against Miss Mudie.

At first, they did not hiss when she was on the stage, from delicacy; but in her absence, they hissed the performance to stop the play, if possible. Yet, as she confidently persevered, they at length hissed her and called, vehemently, '*Off! Off!*' Miss Mudie was not, however, without a strong party of 'warm friends' to support her: and to such a degree did the noise increase, in the later scenes, that not a word could be heard; on which, Miss Mudie (who had, hitherto, appeared entirely occupied with the business of the scene, and whose energy had not in the least been damped by the marked disapprobation of the house), walked to the front of the stage with great confidence and composure, though not without some signs of indignation, and said: 'Ladies and gentlemen, I have done nothing to offend you; and as for those who are sent here to hiss me, I will be much obliged to you to turn them out.'

This bold speech, from such a baby, astonished the audience; some roared with laughter, some hissed, others again cried, '*Off! off!*' and many applauded. Miss Mudie did not appear to be in the slightest degree chagrined or embarrassed, but went on with the scene as if she had been completely successful. At the end of it the uproar was considerable; and a loud cry arising of '*Manager! Manager!*', Mr Kemble came forward and said:

'Gentlemen, the great applause with which Miss Mudie has been received at several provincial theatres, encouraged in her friends a hope that her merit might be such as to pass the tribunal of your judgement'—*violent hissing*—'Be assured, however, gentlemen, that the proprietors of this theatre by no means wish to press any species of entertainment upon you, which may not meet your approbation'—*loud applause*—'If therefore, you will permit Miss Mudie'—'*No! No!*'

Mr Kemble could not be heard for some time; but at last neatly resumed, 'The drama's laws the drama's patrons give! We hope, however, that as the play has proceeded so far, you will allow Miss Mudie to finish the character.'

'*No! No!*' was vociferated from various parts of the house. Finding this of no avail, Mr Kemble tried his success with the female part of the assemblage by saying, with emphasis: '*Ladies* and gentlemen, let me entreat that you will allow Miss Mudie to finish her part. Perhaps, when you are informed that after this night Miss Mudie will be withdrawn from the stage, you will be induced to comply.'

This last appeal seemed to produce the desired effect, but the calm was deceitful; for upon the next appearance of the child the uproar broke out with such violence that she was compelled to retire. Mr Murray then came forward, and requested to be heard for a few words, when he spoke as follows:

'Ladies and gentlemen, if you will have the kindness to allow me to trespass upon your patience for five minutes, Miss Searle, with your indulgence, will play Miss Mudie's part from the commencement of the fifth act.'

Order was again restored; but, upon the appearance of Miss Searle, hostilities were ungenerously renewed between the partisans of Miss Mudie and the Anti-Roscianites. All was noise and confusion. When it was found that any interference would but more embroil the fray, the remainder of the comedy was converted into pantomimic show, not a word being heard; and the curtain fell on the most imperfect performance ever witnessed on a London stage.

When asked if this eight-year-old wonder was really the child she appeared to be, John Philip Kemble replied sharply, 'Child! Why, sir, when I was a very young actor in the York company [c. 1778–80] that little creature kept an inn at Tadcaster, and had a large family of children.' Noël Coward himself couldn't have put it more neatly.

Frances Anne Kemble
Record of a Girlhood (1878)

First of the Infant Phenomena was Master William Betty, who appeared at Covent Garden and Drury Lane in 1804 aged thirteen. He played such parts as Norval in Home's Douglas, *and even Hamlet—Charles James Fox declared that in the latter role he was 'finer than Garrick'. Kemble and Mrs Siddons quietly withdrew from the stage during the Betty furore, and as quietly returned to it when the blaze of public interest dwindled away. A generation after Betty, but cast in the same mould, was Miss Davenport; born in 1829, she was a trying young woman who at eight years old played Richard III, Sir Peter Teazle and Shylock.... It is refreshing to turn instead to the delightful Fanny Kemble, who made her first appearance at the respectable age of nineteen, playing Juliet to William Abbot's Romeo, at Covent Garden, on October 5, 1829. Her actor-manager father, Charles Kemble, played Mercutio, and her mother, who had left the stage twenty years earlier, returned as Lady Capulet, to comfort and support her daughter through the ordeal. As a Kemble, Fanny belonged to a great theatre dynasty, like the Redgraves (who boast three famous youngsters to carry on the line) and my dear friend John Gielgud, in whom the brilliant Terry fire still burns:*

We drove to the theatre very early, indeed while the late autumn sunlight yet lingered in the sky; it shone into the carriage upon me, and as I screened my eyes from it, my mother said, 'Heaven smiles on you, my child.' My poor mother went to her dressing-room to get herself ready, and did not return to me for fear of increasing my agitation by her own. My dear aunt Dall and my maid and the theatre dresser performed my toilet for me, and at length I was placed in a chair, with my satin train carefully laid over the back of it; and there I sat, ready for execution, with the palms of my hands pressed convulsively together, and the tears I in vain endeavoured to repress welling up into my eyes and brimming slowly over, down my rouged cheeks—upon which my aunt, with a smile full of pity, renewed the colour as often as these heavy drops made unsightly streaks in it.

Once and again my father came to the door, and I heard his anxious 'How is she?' to which my aunt answered, sending him away with words of comforting cheer. At last 'Miss Kemble called for the stage, ma'am!' accompanied with a brisk tap at the door, started me upright on my feet, and I was led round to the side scene opposite to the one from which I saw my mother advance on the stage; and while the uproar of her reception filled me with terror, dear old Mrs Davenport, my nurse, and dear Mr Keeley, her Peter, and half the dramatis personæ of the play (but not my father, who had retreated, quite unable to endure the scene) stood round me as I lay, all but insensible, in my aunt's arms. 'Courage, courage, dear child! poor thing, poor thing!' reiterated Mrs Davenport. 'Never mind 'em, Miss Kemble!' urged Keeley, in that irresistibly comical, nervous, lachrymose voice of his, which I have never since heard without a thrill of anything but comical association; 'never mind 'em! don't think of 'em, any more than if they were so many rows of cabbages!' 'Nurse!' called my mother, and on waddled Mrs Davenport, and, turning back, called in her turn, 'Juliet!'

My aunt gave me an impulse forward, and I ran straight across the stage, stunned with the tremendous shout that greeted me, my eyes covered with mist, and the green baize flooring of the stage feeling as if it rose up against my feet; but I got hold of my mother, and stood like a terrified creature at bay, confronting the huge theatre full of gazing human beings. I do not think a word I uttered during this scene could have been audible; in the next, the ball-room, I began to forget myself; in the following one, the balcony scene, I had done so, and, for aught I knew, I was Juliet; the passion I was uttering sending hot waves of blushes all over my neck and shoulders while the poetry sounded like music to me as I spoke it, with no consciousness of anything before me, utterly transported into the imaginary existence of the play. After this I did not return into myself until all was over, and amid a tumultuous storm of applause, congratulation, tears, embraces, and a general joyous explosion of unutterable relief at the fortunate termination of my attempt, we went home. And so my life was determined, and I devoted myself to an avocation which I have never liked or honoured, and about the very nature of which I have never been able to come to any decided opinion ... a business which is incessant excitement and factitious emotion seems to me unworthy of a man; a business which is public exhibition, unworthy of a woman.

Fanny's success was the saving of her father, enabling him to pay off the theatre's massive debt of £13,000. To mark her first night, he laid by her plate at supper a little Geneva watch, the first she ever owned, encrusted with gold work and jewels. She christened it 'Romeo', and went blissfully to sleep with it under her pillow.

AN ACTOR'S DAUGHTER

Marie Bancroft
On and Off the Stage (1888)

Marie Effie Wilton (1839–1921), the wife of Squire Bancroft, was the daughter of provincial players and was on the stage as a child:

To show in what estimation country folk held the stage in my childhood days, I will tell what happened to me at an amateur entertainment which was given to aid a church-building fund. The programme was a varied one; my contribution of one or two recitations caused a flutter of admiration, especially among the ladies present, many of whom were district visitors, and expressed their approval loudly in such remarks as 'Wonderful!', '*Most* interesting!', 'Dear little thing!', 'How clever!' When the entertainment was over, these ladies asked to be allowed to speak to me. I was taken to them, and passed from one to another, undergoing meanwhile a kind of inspection; they kissed and petted me. 'What a sweet child!' said one; 'You must come some day to see Mama.' 'What lovely hair!' said another; the fuss they made about me was overpowering.

The gentleman who led me to them suggested to these ladies that they might subscribe a small sum to buy me a toy, as a souvenir of the occasion. They consented eagerly, and at once opened their clasped bags. While hunting for their purses, they asked with sweet smiles 'whose dear child I was'. When told that I was the daughter of an actor, the smiles vanished, and the expressions changed in a way to have turned even lemons sour. The bags were closed with a cold, relentless click, and the owners muttered between their teeth (for fear, doubtless, of breathing the same air as myself), 'Oh, gracious!', 'Horrid!', 'Oh, dear!', 'Unfortunate child!', and drew back from me as if plague-stricken. This scene dwelt upon my young mind, and I never forgot it. The poor ladies doubtless returned home scandalised and defiled; but the church did not suffer; the few bricks to which I subscribed have kept their places and have not quarrelled with the others on my account.

On September 2nd, 1642, all the theatres of London were closed by parliamentary decree and many a Puritan soul must at last have been set at rest. For fifty years or more the Puritans had been outraged by the existence of these 'gorgeous playing places' in their heathen splendour, staging 'beastly plays' which tempted servants and apprentices away from their proper work, snared the young with visions of an unreal world, provided a place of resort for layabouts and villains, and encouraged flirtations—and worse—among the spectators. But above all, they deplored the theatres' success. 'Will not a filthy play with the blast of a trumpet sooner call thither a thousand than an hour's tolling of a bell bring to the sermon a hundred?' cried a preacher at Paul's Cross in 1578. 'Reckoning with the least gain that is reaped of eight ordinary places in the city by playing but once a week (whereas many times they play twice or some times thrice) it amounteth to £2,000 by the year.' The theatres were to remain closed for some eighteen years: it was a long time before Times of Joy and Gladnesse were restored to this Nation.

II

IN FRONT

AN

ORDINANCE

OF BOTH HOVSES

OF

PARLIAMENT,

For the fuppreffing of Publike Stage-Playes throughout the
Kingdome, during thefe Calamitous Times.

Hereas the diftreffed Eftate of Ireland,
fteeped in her own Blood, and the
diftra&ted Eftate of England, threat-
ned with a Cloud of Blood, by a
Civill Warre; call for all poffible
meanes to appeafe and avert the
Wrath of God appearing in thefe
Iudgements; Amongft which, Fafting and Prayer having
bin often tryed to be very effe&tuall, have bin lately, and are
ftill enjoyned: And whereas publike Sports doe not well agree
with publike Calamities, nor publike Stage-Playes with the
Seafons of Humiliation, this being an Exercife of fad and pious
Solemnity, and the other being Spe&tacles of Pleafure, too
commonly expreffing lacivious Mirth and levitie: It is ther-
fore thought fit, and Ordeined by the Lords and Commons in
this Parliament Affembled, that while thefe fad Caufes and fet
times of Humiliation doe continue, publike Stage-playes fhall
ceafe, and bee forborne. Inftead of which, are recommended
to the people of this Land, the profitable and feafonable
Confiderations of Repentance, Reconciliation, and peace
with God, which probably may produce outward peace and
profperity, and bring againe Times of Joy and Gladneffe to
thefe Nations.

Die Veneris, Septemb. *the* 2. 1642.

Rdered *by the Lords and Commons Affembled in Parliament, that
this Ordinance concerning* Stage-Playes *be forthwith Printed and
Publifhed.*

John Browne Cler. Parliament.

Septemb.3.　　　London printed for Iohn Wright.　1642.

[*From the original Ordinance in the Poffeffion of* J. J. Cossart, *Efq.
of Clement's-lane, Lombard-ftreet.*]

When the theatres re-opened in 1660, they had no more ardent patron than Sam Pepys. Despite the near-penury of his early years, and the fact that there were only two theatres in London, he notched up 350 visits in the ten years covered by his diary—and always in the teeth of temptation, for he considered theatre-going an unwarranted extravagance which he had to combat with as much strength of will as he could muster:

JANUARY *28th, 1660* [61]   Thence to the Theatre, where I saw again *The Lost Lady* which do now please me better than before; and here I sitting behind in a dark place, a lady spit backward upon me by a mistake, but after seeing her to be a very pretty lady, I was not troubled by it at all.

SEPTEMBER *9th, 1661*   Thence to Salisbury Court playhouse, where was acted the first time *'Tis Pity She's a Whore*, a simple play and ill acted, only it was my fortune to sit by a most pretty and most ingenious lady, which pleased me much.

THE HUMBLE PETITION   *The Drama (Vol. IV, 1823)*

Ye Gods, who in the Gallery sit,
Above us mortals in the Pit
Who most submissively petition
That you will pity our condition,
And upon us throw no more
Your orange-peel and apple-core,
Nut-shells (and all that sort of thing),
Which on us you so often fling;
And we implore you not to spit
Your sacred phlegm into the Pit,
Which fills each mortal's soul with dread,
Lest it should light upon his head:
These favours grant, great Gods, and we
Will ever grateful be to thee.

HAT TRICKS

... A TANNER ONE   *The Drama (Vol. VII, 1825)*

On Friday night, during the performance of *Is He Jealous?* at the English Opera House, an individual in the side boxes, in the midst of the laughter excited by the admirable performance of Miss Kelly and Wrench, forgot to take care of his hat, and it fell into the pit. The moment he perceived the serious loss which he had sustained, considering generosity in that instance to be true policy, he called out aloud, 'I will give sixpence to any gentleman who will bring up my hat.' Such, however, is the state of affluence to which the country has arrived, that no gentleman sought to avail himself of this silver opportunity, and the owner was obliged to go down for it himself.

... A TWO-BOB ONE   James Smith

James Smith and his brother Horace achieved popular success with parodies of contemporary poets, purporting to have been written as entries for a prize offered by the management on the re-opening of Drury Lane, in October, 1812. These lines parody George Crabbe:

> Pat Jennings in the upper gallery sat,
> But, leaning forward, Jennings lost his hat:
> Down from the gallery the beaver flew,
> And spurn'd the one to settle in the two.
> How shall he act? Pay at the gallery-door
> Two shillings for what cost, when new, but four?
> Or till half-price, to save his shilling, wait,
> And gain his hat again at half-past eight?
> Now, while his fears anticipate a thief,
> John Mullins whispers, 'Take my handkerchief.'
> 'Thank you,' cries Pat; 'but one won't make a line.'
> 'Take mine,' cries Wilson; and cries Stokes, 'Take mine.'
> A motley cable soon Pat Jennings ties,
> Where Spitalfields with real India vies.
> Like Iris' bow, down darts the painted clue,
> Starr'd, strip'd and spotted, yellow, red and blue,
> Old calico, torn silk, and muslin new.
> George Green below, with palpitating hand,
> Loops the last 'kerchief to the beaver's band—
> Up soars the prize! The youth, with joy unfeign'd,
> Regain'd the felt, and felt what he regain'd;
> While to the applauding galleries grateful Pat
> Made a low bow, and touch'd the ransom'd hat.

SATAN'S GROUND   John Wesley

APR. 29, 1754 I preached at Sadler's Wells, in what was formerly a play-house. I am glad when it pleases God to take possession of what Satan esteemed his own ground. The place, though large, was extremely crowded, and deep attention sat on every face.

Wesley's gladness was premature. It took another, very different crusader, Samuel Phelps, to rescue the Wells (page 79) and the fruit born of his campaign to redeem it was not a meeting-house for the preaching of God's Word, but a well-conducted theatre staging the plays of Shakespeare. My own parents were strong Methodists and both suspected that I had embraced a non-productive profession. They lived long enough to begin to change their minds, but only just.

THE-A-TAR   Edward Stirling
                                                              Old Drury Lane (1881)

The 'Brown Bear' in Goodman's Fields next opened its claws to grasp my slender means. A Jew, one Ikey Solomons (lineally descended from Shylock), the landlord of the 'Bear', fitted up a dirty club-room with a few paltry scenes, and a ragged green baize curtain, and illuminated the floor with half-a-dozen oil-lamps. This Ikey called a 'The-a-tar to hact in', that is, if you could pay. Lord Lovell in *A New Way to Pay Old Debts* cost me two-and-sixpence, dress included. This at night, to my horror, I found to consist of my own frock-coat, russet boots, a torn scarf, and a bearskin grenadier's cap. It is said that dress makes the man, but it never made a 'lord' like this.

Ikey's room was filled with an uproarious assemblage: sailors and their female friends, Jews, lascars, workmen with their wives and families; pots of beer and 'goes' of gin, tobacco and pipes were in constant request, and went the round of the company to any amount, whilst Ikey Solomons' voice was always in the ascendant, crying out 'Give yer orders' and scolding his waiters, Moses and Aaron. I need not say our efforts on the stage could not be heard without some difficulty and under considerable disadvantage amid this universal din. Just at the critical moment when Lady Allworth, the rich widow, cries out as wicked Sir Giles Overreach draws his sword, and the audience are worked up to agony-point, Ikey bawled out in a tone more of sorrow than of anger, 'Aaron, there's that 'ere sailor, 'ad a go of rum, a-bolting without paying. Stan' afore the door.' Not another syllable was heard; the ragged baize dropped amidst yells of laughter, and cries of 'Go it, Ikey!' No more Brown, Black or White Bears for my money, depend upon it, reader, after this escapade!

A Victorian 'penny gaff', illustrated by Gustave Doré in London, A Pilgrimage

PENNY GAFF

Henry Mayhew
*London Labour and the
London Poor (1861)*

The 'penny gaff' was situated in a broad street near Smithfield; and for a great distance off, the jingling sound of music was heard, and the gas-light streamed out into the thick night air as from a dark lantern, glittering on the windows of the houses opposite, and lighting up the faces of the mob in the road, as on an illumination night. The front of a large shop had been entirely removed, and the entrance was decorated with paintings of the 'comic singers', in their most 'humorous' attitudes. On a table against the wall was perched the band, playing what the costers call 'dancing tunes' with great effect, for the hole at the money-taker's box was blocked up with the hands tendering the penny. The crowd without was so numerous, that a policeman was in attendance to preserve order, and push the boys off the pavement— the music having the effect of drawing them insensibly toward the festooned green-baize curtain.

The shop itself had been turned into a waiting-room, and was crowded even to the top of the stairs leading to the gallery on the first floor. The ceiling of this 'lobby' was painted blue, and spotted with whitewash clouds, to represent the heavens; the boards of the trap-door, and the laths that showed through the holes in the plaster, being all the same colour. A notice was here posted, over the canvas door leading into the theatre, to the effect that LADIES AND GENTLEMEN TO THE FRONT PLACES MUST PAY TWOPENCE.

To form the theatre, the first floor had been removed; the white-washed beams, however, still stretched from wall to wall. The lower room had evidently been the warehouse, while the upper apartment had been the sitting-room, for the paper was still on the walls. A gallery, with a canvas front, had been hurriedly built up, and it was so fragile that the boards bent under the weight of those above. The bricks in the warehouse were smeared over with red paint, and had a few black curtains daubed upon them. The coster-youths required no very great scenic embellishment, and indeed the stage—which was about eight feet square—could admit of none. Two jets of gas, like those outside a butcher's shop, were placed on each side of the proscenium, and proved very handy for the gentlemen whose pipes required lighting.

You cannot keep actors down. The booth, the fit-up and the penny gaff have their successors in today's fringe theatres, but with the essential difference that instead of aping the classics, they have now become in many ways the most vital part of the theatre.

ALL WORN BUT ONCE   John Ebers
                                        Seven Years of the
                                        King's Theatre (1828)

John Ebers became lessee of the King's Theatre in the Haymarket, in 1821. A seven-year career in management culminated in bankruptcy, and he returned to his earlier profession, bookselling.

On the morning after one of the performances I received a specimen of an epistle from a gentleman, who, having presented himself for admission at the pit door, in a pair of drab pantaloons, was, in accordance with a well-known and approved regulation, refused entrance as not being in dress. He was astonished, it seems, at this. 'For,' says his letter, 'I was dressed in a superfine blue coat with GOLD BUTTONS, a white waistcoat, fashionable tight drab pantaloons, white silk stockings, and dress shoes, ALL WORN BUT ONCE, A FEW DAYS BEFORE, AT A DRESS CONCERT AT THE CROWN AND ANCHOR TAVERN!' (The mark of admiration I beg to observe is the writer's own.) He proceeds to express his indignation at the idea of the manager presuming to 'enact sumptuary laws without the intervention of the legislature', with threats of legal proceedings, and an appeal to a British jury. 'I have mixed,' he continues, 'too much in genteel society, not to know that black breeches, or pantaloons, with black silk stockings, is a very prevailing full dress; and, why is it so? because it is convenient and economical, FOR YOU CAN WEAR A PAIR OF WHITE SILK STOCKINGS BUT ONCE WITHOUT WASHING, and a pair of black is frequently worn for weeks without ablution.' But the postscript is the cream: 'P.S. I have no objection to submit an inspection of my dress of the evening in question to you or any competent person you may appoint.'

SOOTY PATRONAGE   *The Morning Herald*

OCTOBER 28th, 1825 Astley's and the Coburg Theatres, it seems, are the only ones which admit chimney-sweepers in their working dress; in consequence of which, it is said, those places are sometimes honoured with this kind of sooty patronage to the extent of forty or fifty of a night.

Although a life-long radical, I think this was carrying democracy a little too far—an opinion borne out by the letter which an anonymous well-wisher wrote to Robert William Elliston, popular actor-manager of the Surrey Theatre, on August 10th, 1827—

I have, with my wife, been much in the habit of visiting the Surrey Theatre, and on three occasions we have been annoyed by these sweeps. People will not go, sir, where sweeps are; and you will find, sooner or later, these gentlemen will have the whole theatre to themselves, unless an alteration be made. I own, at some theatres, the managers are too particular in dress; those days are past, and the public have a right to go to theatrical entertainments in their morning costumes; but this ought not to include the sweeps. It is not a week ago since a lady in a nice white gown sat down on the very spot which a nasty sweep had just quitted, and, when she got up, the sight was most horrible, for she was a very heavy lady and had laughed a good deal during the performance; but it was no laughing matter to her when she got home.

SPECTRE IN FLAMES   *The Drama (Vol. VI, 1824)*

SURREY THEATRE, AUG. 26 During the performances of this evening, the audience was thrown into the most sensitive alarm, by an accident which took place on the stage, and which was likely to have ended fatally in its consequences. At the conclusion of the piece entitled *The Burning Bridge*, a

Spectre (performed by Mr Leslie) has to make its appearance surrounded by clouds, while seated in a car. In descending from the top of the stage, by some accident the machinery came in contact with some of the burning materials, and the trappings with which the young gentleman was surrounded caught fire. In a short period he was enveloped in flames, in which awful situation he remained for some time, the car being too elevated for him to leap out, and he seemed not to be aware of the danger that threatened him until the car was about eighteen feet from the floor of the stage.

The audience, on viewing the dreadful dilemma in which he was placed, expressed a feeling of horror, and several ladies fainted. The flames at length became so powerful, that Mr Leslie leaped from the car to the stage, and fell with considerable violence, in consequence of which he was dreadfully injured about the legs, &c. The curtain immediately dropped, and the unfortunate young gentleman was carried into the green-room, and a surgeon instantly procured. It was afterwards announced to the audience that he was not dangerously hurt, which seemed to appease their fears, as he was considered to be severely injured. He was conveyed home, and we understand that he is doing very well at present.

CAT-CALLS

W. R. Chetwood
*A General History of
the Stage (1749)*

I remember, above twenty years past, I was one of the audience at a new play. Before me sat a sea-officer with whom I had some acquaintance; on each hand of him a couple of sparks, both prepar'd with their offensive instruments vulgarly term'd CAT-CALLS, which they were often tuning before the play began.

The officer did not take any notice of them till the curtain drew up; but when they continued their sow-gelder's music (as he unpolitely call'd it) he begg'd they would not prevent his hearing the actors, tho' *they* might not care whether they heard or no; but they took little notice of his civil request, which he repeated again and again to no purpose. But at last one of them condescended to tell him if he did not like it, he might leave it alone. 'Why, really,' reply'd the sailor, 'I do not like it, and would have *you* let your noise alone. I have paid my money to see and hear the play, and your ridiculous noise not only hinders me, but a great many other people that are here, I believe, with the same design. Now, if you prevent us, you rob us of our money and our time; therefore I intreat you, as you look like gentlemen, to behave as such.' One of them seem'd mollify'd, and put his whistle in his pocket, but the other was incorrigible.

The blunt tar made him one speech more. 'Sir,' said he, 'I advise you once more to follow the example of this gentleman, and put up your pipe.' But the piper sneer'd in his face, and clapp'd his troublesome instrument to his mouth, with cheeks swell'd out like a trumpeter to give it a redoubl'd and louder noise; but, like the broken crow of a cock in a fright, the squeak was stopt in the middle by a blow from the officer which he gave him with so strong a will that his child's trumpet was struck thro' his cheek and his companion led him out to a surgeon. So that we had more room and less noise, and not one that saw or heard the affair but what were well pleas'd with his treatment.

Which of us has not longed for the chance to strike a blow for silence and the right to listen to the play in peace?—though not necessarily in such a dramatically effective way.

'MURDER!'   *Dramatic Table Talk (1825)*

In 1749, Garrick, having become manager of Drury Lane, employed the theatrical power with which he had just been vested, in bringing out Dr [Samuel] Johnson's tragedy of *Irene*, which had long been kept back; but in this benevolent purpose he met with no little difficulty from the temper of Johnson, who could not brook that a drama which he had formed with so much study and which he had been obliged to keep for more than the nine years of Horace, should be revised and altered at the pleasure of an actor; but Garrick knew that without several alterations it would be unfit for the stage.

A violent dispute having ensued between them, Garrick applied to the Rev. Dr Taylor to interpose. Johnson was at first very obstinate. 'Sir,' said he, 'the fellow wants me to make Mahomet run mad, that he may have an opportunity of tossing his hands and kicking his heels.' He was prevailed upon to comply with Garrick's wishes, and to permit a certain number of changes to be made, but still not enough to ensure its successful representation.

Before the curtain drew up [February 6, 1749] cat-calls were whistling, which alarmed some of Johnson's friends. The prologue, written in a manly strain, awed the audience by the extraordinary spirit and dignity displayed in some of its lines; and the play went smoothly until it approached the conclusion when Mrs Pritchard, the heroine, was to be strangled before the audience and had to speak two lines with the bow-string round her neck. The audience cried out 'Murder! Murder!' She attempted to speak, but in vain; and at last she quitted the stage alive.

The passage was afterwards expunged and she was carried off to suffer death behind the scenes, as the play now has it.

HAMLET'S HORNPIPE

H. Chance Newton
Cues and Curtain Calls (1927)

I have never forgotten playing on a platform slung between two destroyers, with a lively naval audience clinging to every available projection; and I daresay Sullivan's exchange with Jack Tar lived as long in his memory—

Barry Sullivan was giving this impersonation one night at Portsmouth to an audience largely composed of the breeziest of British sailors, who had been 'revelling' before arriving. After listening to the tragedy of *Hamlet* with commendably little interruption, suddenly, when Barry started 'To be or not to be' one of the Jack Tars in the gallery stopped him, and shouted, 'Hi, Barry, give us a hornpipe!'

Barry scowled, as only he could scowl, at the irreverent interrupter, and started to continue his soliloquy, when several other Jack Tars took up the cry and said, 'Yes, give us a hornpipe, Barry!' Then added a deep-voiced mariner, 'Mind as it's the sailor's one!'

This demand being repeated rather peremptorily, Barry felt it his duty to step down to the footlights and to reprove these dance demanders! Having done so, he returned to the throne chair and resumed the great soliloquy on Life and Death, when a Herculean tar from a corner of the gallery shouted, ''Ere, Barry! Are yer goin' to give me and my friends that 'ornpipe or am I to come down and make yer?'

Barry, by this time inwardly convulsed with laughter at this extraordinary joke, retorted: 'Gentlemen, as you insist upon my performing a Sailor's Hornpipe in the midst of this sublime tragedy, I will e'en do so.'

And Barry did it! And he did it well, for, like most of the tragedians of his time, from Phelps downwards, he had gone through the theatrical mill so much and had played Black-Eyed Susan's William so often that to dance a hornpipe at a moment's notice was the most natural thing in the world.

Having thus performed this famous dance to the tune of 'Jack Robinson', Barry Sullivan resumed his tragic and touching impersonation of Hamlet without further interruption.

Barry Sullivan was a giant of the nineteenth-century theatre. Sooner than be skinned alive by London landlords, he set off to tour Australia, Ireland, Scotland and the English provinces, and by sheer determination assured himself of a very handsome livelihood. As a boy Shaw saw him act and found him irresistible, particularly on one thrilling evening when Sullivan, as Macbeth, fought with such vigour that his sword-point snapped off, whizzed over the heads of the cowering playgoers in the pit, and buried itself deep in the dress circle. His private life was irreproachable but he burned himself out by the struggle to play the superhuman, six nights out of every seven, and died paralysed in 1891, leaving £25,000—the equivalent of more than half a million pounds today. He was one of the few actors to die truly rich.

'O WISE AND UPRIGHT JUDGE!'

Percy Fitzgerald
*A New History of the
English Stage (1882)*

In 1773, the veteran actor Charles Macklin, then in his seventies, appeared at the Haymarket under the management of George Colman the elder. Macklin was a robust, popular comedian, and a man of volcanic temper with a genius for making enemies. On November 18, when he was to appear as Shylock, a tailor named Leigh sent cronies round the alehouses to collect volunteers willing to attend the play and lead an outcry against 'a certain old villain of the name of Macklin'. The tavern troops knew nothing about Macklin, and cared less:

At these alehouses parties were collected, forty or fifty at one, and an equal number at another; such of the men as could read were given a paper to read; such of them that had eyes, and could see, were to take notice of a signal which was to be exhibited; such as had no eyes to see, and could only hear, were told that a whistle would be given, which they were to listen for. The commanders having given these orders among the very spirited corps of tailors, they were told that, besides all this comfortable preparation, they should each of them have a shilling apiece for the night's work, and after the work should be completed, and this old unknown villain of the name of Macklin should be driven to hell, these men should go to the Bedford Arms and have a supper.

On the appearance of Shylock a terrific uproar set in, and Colman was called for; and when the old actor advanced, in opposition to the general sense of the audience, on being desired to go off he peremptorily refused, and in the most insolent manner advanced to the orchestra and stamped with his feet, and continued on the stage.

The uproar intensified. Macklin was bombarded with apples and threatened with sticks brandished by the front rows. 'You're a villain, you're a rascal, you're a scoundrel; off, off!' they shouted. Colman was again called for:

Upon which Mr Colman went on and said, 'That ever since he and his fellow-proprietors had had the dominion in that theatre they had made it their study to please the public and obey their commands, as they would upon the present occasion.' Upon this there was a great applause; he then put the question, 'Is it your pleasure Mr Macklin should be discharged?' [Macklin] heard a great many ayes and he thought some noes.

Then Mr Colman said, 'Mr Macklin is discharged.'

Macklin brought an action against the leaders of the riot, conducting his own case before Lord Mansfield, the celebrated lord chief justice, whose judgement was as follows:

'Every man that is at the playhouse has a right to express his approbation or disapprobation instantaneously, according as he likes either the acting or piece; that is a right due to the theatre, an unalterable right—they must have that. The gist of the crime here is coming by conspiracy to ruin a particular man—to hiss if they were never so pleased—let him do never so well, they were to knock him down and hiss him off the stage. They did not come to approve or disapprove, as the sentiments of their mind might be, but they came with a black design, and that is the most ungenerous thing that can be. What a terrible condition is an actor upon the stage in with an enemy who makes part of the audience! It is ungenerous to take the advantage; and what makes the black part of the case is, it is all done with a conspiracy to ruin him; and if the Court were to imprison and fine every one of them, Mr Macklin may bring his action against them, and I am satisfied there is no jury that would not give considerable damages.'

To the alarm of the defendants, Mansfield awarded Macklin £600, plus expenses; but Macklin refused the sum, asking instead that the defendants should take £100-worth of tickets on three occasions: his own benefit night, his daughter's and, for the management's benefit, the night of his re-appearance. 'You have met with great applause today,' the judge said in reply; 'you never acted better.'
  I sent Mansfield's judgement to my old friend Tom Denning, the Master of the Rolls. This story delighted him. He had never heard it before.

CHILD'S PLAY

Thomas Moore
*Memoirs, Journals and
Correspondence (1853–56)*

One night when John [Philip] Kemble was performing, at some country theatre, one of his most favourite parts, he was much interrupted, from time to time, by the squalling of a young child in one of the galleries. At length, angered by this rival performance, Kemble walked with solemn step to the front of the stage, and, addressing the audience in his most tragic tones, said: 'Ladies and gentlemen, unless the play is stopped, the child cannot possibly go on.' The effect on the audience of this earnest interference, in favour of the child, can be easily conceived.

I have used this story on the music-halls and in cabaret, and it always gets a delighted laugh. Colleagues are welcome to borrow it!

'STOP THE PLAY!'

George Raymond
*Memoirs of Robert William Elliston,
Comedian* (*1846*)

An instance of accidental recognition occurred in North Britain in the year 1793, which was extremely curious. Mrs Cross, of Covent Garden Theatre, was acting in Glasgow, and on one occasion, the Provost being present, the lady had no sooner made her appearance on the stage than the agitated functionary exclaimed: 'Stop—stop the play! I would speak with that woman!'

Great was the consternation throughout the auditory at this highly dramatic cry, and the curtain being immediately lowered, the perturbed Provost made his way at once into the actress's dressing-room. After a few hurried words, he discovered her to be his own wife from whom he had been separated for nearly twenty years. Each had supposed the other dead, a *coup de théâtre* which would have turned the brain of Congreve himself. The magistrate, hereupon, bore off the lady, arm in arm, to his own house, and the next evening she took her place in the front of the theatre, amongst the patronesses of art, where she was quite as much of a heroine as when sustaining the woes of Calista★ herself.

FRESH HOWLINGS   *The Times*

MAY 13th 1796   Drury Lane Theatre has not experienced a riot so wild, and unappeasable, as that of Tuesday evening, since *The Blackamoor Washed White*, of famous memory. The Entertainments advertised for the night's amusements were three. *The Smugglers*, having nothing contraband on board, was not only suffered to pass, but was hailed with three cheers. *The Virgin Unmasked* had her admirers, but *The Deserter* was mauled most dreadfully—for Young Welsh had permitted a new Skirmish to make his debut, as Suett phrased it: and, being a miserable wretch, when the audience expressed a disapprobation, the Performers, to shorten the ridicule, shortened the scene, which on such occasions is usual, and prudent—but the curtain dropping at ten minutes past ten, created a violent burst of indignation. Kelly first attempted to enquire the wishes of John Bull, and expressed himself, in the name of the Performers, ignorant of how he was disobliged. All striving to be heard, none, of course, could be so, and he retired.

Uproar still increased, and, after near half an hour of this din, Suett made his appearance, and apologised for the badness of the stage-struck hero, but he was soon given to understand, that that was not the cause of the Row, but that the audience expected to have *The Deserter* played wholly over again. Mr S. after 'looking as queer as a quartern of soap after a week's wash'

★ Heroine of Rowe's *The Fair Penitent*

expressed his concern that many of the performers were gone, and the stage lights out, but this was the cause of fresh howlings, and as somebody cried out 'God save the King,' he promised to send as many of the Orchestra as could be found. In five minutes this popular hymn was received with acclamation. The curtain again dropt amid violent tumults which continued, and increased.

Again Mr Suett appeared, and declared 'how much hurt the Proprietors were at any part of the Performance being omitted: that it was without their concurrence, or even knowledge, and that such a circumstance should never happen again.' This rather mollified the audience, and many dispersed at a quarter past eleven. Almost the whole of the lights in the house had been long extinguished; and some of the benches were torn up.

Mr Suett's exhausting efforts to pacify the audience remind me how Charles Victor, stage director of the Birmingham Repertory Theatre in the 'thirties, was once caught napping. Worn out after a very wearying weekend of dress rehearsing and getting the show on, he was standing in the prompt corner, half asleep, with the prompt book open at the wrong page, when suddenly the play stopped. Someone had dried. He looked round the tormentors; five actors were gazing at him beseechingly—two of them even holding out their hands to collect a well-thrown prompt. He glanced at the prompt book, saw it was open at the wrong page, and spoke clearly and incisively to the floundering performers: 'Go back to Act 2, Scene 1.'

SUMMONED BACK   *The Sunday Times*

OCTOBER *14th 1866*   There were several first appearances last evening ... Mr Henry Irving, who played Doricourt [in *The Belle's Stratagem*] is an easy, gentlemanly, and to our own mind, thoroughly intelligent actor. He is a most valuable addition to the St James's Company, and we welcome him with all sincerity. Doricourt's feigned mad scene was most artistically played, and quite devoid of exaggeration. Mr Irving was summoned back on the stage in the middle of a scene to receive the congratulations of the audience.

SPEAK TENDERLY   Leigh Hunt
                                                    Critical Essays

Speak sparingly and tenderly of those who are to earn their living by their labours on the stage. I approve of their being told of faults which it would be for their interest to correct; but as I will not arraign them for defects with which nature has unalterably endowed them, I must be perfectly satisfied that correction is in their power before I move them to attempt it. As objects of our general censure they have no defence; as servants of the theatre exhibiting themselves on a stage for our amusement, they have no fastnesses to retreat to from our attack; they are at our mercy, and discouragement partakes of persecution. Until a performer shall offend against the respect due to his audience, great respect and lenity are due to his feelings. It is happy for an actor when nature has bestowed upon him an expressive countenance, but if he has it not by nature, he cannot make it such by art. Let him hear not of privations which he cannot supply; tell him only of such errors as he is able to correct.

Personally, and with the greatest possible respect to my distinguished collaborator, I have always found this an admirable principle to adopt when judging the critical profession—except the bit about their countenances!

NOT VERY GOOD   *The Players**

LYCEUM: *October 6th, 1860*   The novelty and great card of the evening was a new drama by Mr Tom Taylor entitled *The Brigand and his Banker*. We have seldom, if ever, witnessed such a miserable failure. We warn Mr Tom Taylor to write less, and more carefully. A few more such productions as the unfortunate *Brigand and his Banker*, and the greatest recommendation that a manager can give to a new piece will be to announce that it is *not* by Mr Tom Taylor. The plan of manufacturing dramas to order is most objectionable. . . .

Not only is the drama ridiculous, it is grossly vulgar. This is a strong term, and we use it reluctantly, but we should be failing in our public duty if we did not strongly censure such bad taste. . . .

Everything that could be done for this ridiculous drama was done. The landscapes, painted by Mr Callcott, were fully worthy of the loud applause which they called forth. The acting was also excellent in its way, and we only regret that such able artists had such poor materials to work with.

MIDNIGHT   Mary Howitt
Life (ed., Mgt Howitt; 1889)

Mrs Felicia Hemans, best known for *Casabianca* ['The boy stood on the burning deck'], wrote one play, *The Vespers of Palermo*. Produced at Covent Garden on December 12th, 1823, it was damned by all who saw it and immediately withdrawn. The author, who knew nothing of the world of the

★ A weekly journal (see page 152)

theatre, remained at home in Wales. Two days elapsed before news of the reception reached her at St Asaph. Her family, friends, and neighbours were wrought up to a pitch of excitement. Having ordered newspapers, they besieged the local post-office at midnight. The author's boys lay awake, waiting 'to hear about mama's play'; and perhaps her bitterest mortification came when she had to go up to their bedsides to announce that all their bright hopes had been dashed to the ground.

My five-year-old son John was hiding under the grand piano when my wife and I were having a blazing row about the accumulated deficit on our first Mermaid season. He suddenly appeared from his hiding-place, and, dangling a toy train with three coaches attached, walked with dignity to the door. As he made his exit he turned and gave us a parting shot: 'Nobody asked you to do it.'

TRANSFORMATION SCENE *The Era Almanack (1892)*

I shall never forget my astonishment when, having witnessed the first act of a four-act play at the Teatro Reale in Madrid, I saw the audience changing before my eyes. There was a little, short man in the stall next to me when the curtain fell on Act I and immediately a big, tall man took his place. The old lady who had been sitting in front of me was replaced by a young girl, and whichever way I looked I noticed a change in the audience. I was lost in bewilderment until an official came up to me and politely asked for my voucher. I showed him the one I came in with. 'That is for the first act, senor.' 'Eh?' I exclaimed. 'Is my ticket only good for one act, then?' 'Certainly, senor. If you wish to see the second act you must take a second ticket.' 'But I want to see the play through.' 'Then the senor should have taken four tickets on entering.'

I went out and purchased the tickets for the three remaining acts, and then I noticed that each ticket was a different colour. The first-act ticket had been white, the second was blue, the third was green and the fourth yellow. Between each act the audience was partially changed, and then the attendants came round and collected the tickets. I discovered afterwards that a Spaniard generally takes his dramatic fare in small doses, frequently seeing one act one night, another a few nights later, and so on. There is always a house waiting outside while the house 'inside' is having its 'turn'.

At some of the theatres a short opera will be played four times in one evening, and the audience will be completely changed each time. On Sundays, when there is a matinée, a piece is sometimes played eight times during the twelve hours. It was not until I appreciated this feature of Spanish theatrical entertainment that I could bring myself to believe a poster which announced the 716oth representation of *Le Gran Via*.

CLEARING THE HOUSE   Horace Smith

Miss Biffin [1784–1850] was a most accomplished person, who having been born without legs or arms, contrived to paint miniatures and cut watch-papers with her nose; the above feats I have seen her with mine own eyes perform at Croydon, where she was fairest of the fair. I can illustrate this account by an anecdote, equally true, which can be vouched for. Miss Biffin before her marriage—for married she is, if alive and even if dead—was taken to Covent Garden Theatre early in the evening before the performance began by the gentleman to whom she was afterwards united. He, having some other engagement, deposited his fair charge in the corner of the back seat of one of the upper front boxes, whereupon, aided by long drapery, such as children in arms wear, and a large shawl, she sat unmoved as immovable. The engagement, however, of her beau proved longer than the performance of the theatre. The audience retired, the lights were extinguished, and still Miss Biffin remained.

The box-keeper ventured to suggest that as all the company were out, and most of the lights were out too, it was necessary she should retire. Unwilling to discover her misfortune, and not at all knowing how far she might trust the box-keeper, she expressed great uneasiness that her friend had not arrived, as promised. 'We can't wait here for your friend, Miss—you really must go,' was the only reply she obtained.

At length Mr Brandon, then house-keeper and book-keeper, hearing the discussion, came to the spot, and insinuated the absolute necessity of Miss Biffin's departure, hinting something extremely ungallant about a constable. 'Sir,' said Miss Biffin, 'I would give the world to go, but I cannot go without my friend.' 'You can't have any friend here to-night, ma'am,' said Mr Brandon, 'for the doors are shut.' 'What shall I do, sir?' said the lady. 'If you will give me your arm, ma'am, I'll see you safe down to the stage door, where you can send for a coach.' 'Arm, sir,' said the lady, 'I wish I could; but I've got no arms.' 'Dear me!' said the box-, book- and house-keeper, 'how very odd! However, ma'am, if you will get on your legs—' 'I have not got any legs, sir.' Mr Brandon grew deadly pale, the box-keeper felt faint.

Just at that moment Miss Biffin's friend arrived via the stage door. He, perfectly alive to all the little peculiarities of his beloved, settled the affair in a moment by bundling her up, lifting her from her seat, and carrying her off upon his shoulders as a butcher's boy would transport a fillet of veal in his tray.

Engravings such as this one, showing actors and actresses in favourite roles, were immensely popular in the late eighteenth century, as familiar as picture postcards were in Edwardian days. I have thirty-two separate postcard studies of the beautiful Dare Sisters, Phyllis and Zena—including one of Zena as Peter Pan taken in 1922, autographed for me fifty years later when Graham Payn brought her to lunch at the Mermaid Theatre.

ON AND OFF STAGE

Act V. CARELESS HUSBAND. Sc M.

I.Taylor ad viv del et sculp.

M^{rs}. ABINGTON in the Character of
LADY BETTY MODISH.
How handsomely does he reproach me! But
I can't bear that he should think I know it.

Hostility to the theatre, especially from the Church—in whose arms the drama had been cradled—was common in the eighteenth century. In 1792, a Mr Garrod of Hull preached a sermon saying, 'No player, or any of his children, ought to be entitled to a Christian burial, or even to lie in a churchyard. Not one can be saved. Everyone who enters a playhouse is, with the players, equally certain of eternal damnation.' A century ago, in the issue of The Theatre *for July, 1888, F. W. Hawkins described a tragedy in eighteenth-century France, when players could not take Communion, nor be married or buried with religious rites:*

Prosper Dussieux, a youthful, enthusiastic, and educated member of the Bordeaux company, was to have played the young Brahmin in Lemierre's *Veuve de Malabar* at Toulouse. But on his way to Toulouse he became enamoured of a fair travelling companion, Mariamne Crussol, daughter of a woollen-draper there. For her sake he at once threw up his stigmatised profession, and believing that nobody in the town would recognise in him a certain M. Dennery from Bordeaux, obtained employment from her father as a sort of clerk. His affection for her was returned; M. and Mme. Crussol saw no objection to the match, and one morning the lovers presented themselves at the altar of the church of the Cordeliers to be married.

Suddenly the service was interrupted by the entrance of an unsuccessful pretender to the lady's hand, who gave a written paper to the priest. It was with a darkening countenance that the latter scanned it. 'Your name is Dennery?' he sternly said to the bridegroom. 'My name is Dussieux,' was the reply. 'No Christian woman's happiness,' continued the priest, 'can be entrusted to your hands. Imprudent parents, would you give your daughter to an actor?' In an instant the words were being repeated in tones of horror by most of the onlookers—'An actor!' 'Yes,' said the priest vehemently, 'an actor! And this man has dared to approach the altar—this child of perdition, on whom I invoke a curse instead of the intended benediction! Mariamne Crussol, my anathema be on your head, too, if you do not renounce all thought of this impious union. Leave the church,' he added to the player, 'and cease to profane this sacred place with your presence!' Dussieux, overwhelmed by the blow, fell to the ground insensible, and in this state was borne to a house well known as a resort for actors.

Mariamne displayed more fortitude; in a sort of stupor, without betraying any emotion, she went away with her parents. Her calmness seems to have marked a terrible resolution. In the dead of night she crept to Dussieux's lodging, taking with her some poisoned wine and food. Next morning, when one of Prosper's comrades entered the room, the lovers were found dead in each other's arms, Mariamne still in the bridal dress she had donned with so light a heart twenty-four hours before.

An English Bishop once asked the incomparable Garrick why the churches were so empty and the theatres so full. Garrick's reply was masterly. 'Because my Lord Bishop, you speak a truth as though it were a fiction, while we speak a fiction as though it were a truth.'

GOING TO WAR   Charlotte Charke
                                          A Narrative of the Life
                                  of Mrs Charlotte Charke (1775)

Mrs Charke was the youngest daughter of the actor-manager and dramatist Colley Cibber: an actress and an eccentric. Her charming sister-in-law Susannah, wife of her worthless brother Theophilus, was admired by Handel, and sang soprano in the first performance of The Messiah, *in Dublin in 1742. Charlotte herself liked to dress as a man and play masculine parts (she played Macheath at the Haymarket in 1744–5), and claimed to have been a sausage-seller, a publican, and even a valet, besides engaging in the threadbare life of a strolling player, which she described in her own emphatic style, liberally sprinkled with capital letters:*

I have seen an Emperor as drunk as a Lord, according to the old phrase, and a Lord as elegant as a Ticket-Porter: a Queen with one Ruffle on, and Lord Townly without shoes, or at least but an Apology for them.

This last Circumstance reminds me of the Queen in *The Spanish Fryar* once playing without Stockings; though I must do the Person Justice to say, it proceeded from an unprecedented Instance of even a Superfluity of good Nature, which was excited by her Majesty's observing Torrismond to have a dirty pair of Yarn Stockings, with above twenty Holes in Sight; and, as she thought her Legs not so much expos'd to View, kindly strips them of a fine pair of Cotton, and lends them to the Hero.

I played Lorenzo, and having no Business with the Queen, had a Mind to observe how she acquitted herself in her Part, being a Person I had known many Years, and was really anxious for her Success. I found she spoke sensibly, but, to my great Surprise, observed her to stoop extremely forward, on which I concluded she was seized with a sudden Fit of the Colic, but she satisfied me of the contrary; and on her next Appearance, I remarked that she sunk down very much on that Side I stood between the Scenes, on which I then conjectured her to be troubled with a Sciatic Pain in her Side, and made a second Enquiry, but was answered in the Negative on that Score:

upon which I desired to know the Reason of her bending forward, and sideling so. ·

She told me, 'twas a Trick she had got. 'Tis a very new one then, says I, for I never saw you do so before; but I began to suspect something was the Matter, and resolved to find it out. Presently the Royal Dame was obliged to descend from the Stage into the Dressing-Room, and made a Discovery, by tossing up her Hoop, of a Pair of naked Legs.

I own, I was both angry and pleased. I was concerned to find my Friend's Humanity had extended so far as to render herself ridiculous, besides the Hazard she ran of catching Cold: but must confess, I never saw so strong a Proof of good Nature, especially among Travelling Tragedizers; for, to speak Truth of them, they have but a small Share of that Principle subsisting amongst them.

The least Glimmering or Shade of Acting, in Man or Woman, is a sure Motive of Envy in the rest; and if their Malice can't persuade the Town's-People into a Dislike of their Performance, they'll cruelly endeavour to taint their Characters; so that I think going a-Strolling is engaging in a little, dirty Kind of War, in which I have been obliged to fight so many Battles, I have resolutely determined to throw down my Commission: and to say Truth, I am not only sick, but heartily ashamed of it, as I have had nine years Experience of its being a very contemptible Life; rendered so, through the impudent and ignorant Behaviours of the Generality of those who pursue it; and I think it would be more reputable to earn a Groat a Day in Cinder-sifting at Tottenham-Court, than to be concerned with them.

'Tis a Pity that so many, who have good Trades, should idly quit them, to become despicable Actors; which renders them useless to themselves, and very often Nuisances to others. Those who were bred up in the Profession, have the best Right to make it their Calling; but their Rights are horribly invaded by Barber Prentices, Tailors and Journeymen Weavers ... these Wretches very impudently style themselves Players; a Name, let me tell them, when properly applied, that is an Honour to an Undertaking, for none can deserve that Title, who labour under the Want of a very considerable Share of Sense.

FOOTE'S LEG

George Colman the Younger
Random Records (1830)

Samuel Foote (1720-1777) was an actor and dramatist whose satirical wit made all London smart. Even Garrick was known to give ground before him. Dr Johnson despised him and on meeting him at dinner resolved 'not to be pleased'; for the first part of the meal the Doctor managed to go on eating in grave and solemn silence, but

Foote was so comical that in the end he was obliged to lay down his knife and fork, throw himself back in his chair and laugh aloud. 'Sir, he was irresistible.'

The paradoxical celebrity which he maintain'd upon the Stage was very singular; his satirical sketches were scarcely dramas, and he could not be call'd a good legitimate performer. Yet there is no Shakespeare or Roscius upon record who, like Foote, supported a theatre [the Haymarket] for a series of years, by his own acting, in his own writings, and, for ten years of the time, upon a *wooden leg!*

This prop to his person I once saw standing by his bedside, ready dress'd in a handsome stocking, with a polish'd shoe and gold buckle, awaiting the owner's getting up; it had a kind of tragi-comical appearance; and I leave to inveterate wags the ingenuity of punning upon a Foote in bed, and a Leg out of it. The proxy for a limb thus decorated, though ludicrous, is too strong a reminder of amputation to be very laughable. His *undress'd* support was the common wooden leg, like a mere stick, which was not a little injurious to a well-kept pleasure-ground. I remember following him, after a shower of rain, upon a nicely roll'd terrace; in which he stump'd a deep round hole at every other step he took; till it appear'd as if the gardener had been there with his dibble, preparing (against all horticultural rule) to plant a long row of cabbages in a gravel walk.

PLAYER PUPPET   Charles Churchill
                                                The Rosciad (1761)

> Next Jackson came:—Observe that settled glare,
> That better speaks a puppet than a player:
> List to that voice! did ever discord hear
> Sounds so well fitted to her untuned ear?
> When to enforce some very tender part
> The right hand sleeps by instinct on the heart;
> His soul, of every other thought bereft,
> Is anxious only where to place the left.
> He sobs and pants to soothe his weeping spouse—
> To soothe his weeping mother turns and bows.
> Awkward, embarrass'd, stiff, without the skill
> Of moving gracefully, or standing still;
> One leg, as if suspicious of his brother,
> Desirous seems to run away from t'other....

The Rosciad satirized every prominent actor of the day but one: the glorious Garrick. Instead of merely declaiming his lines with a series of artificial gestures,

Garrick breathed life into his part. His pupil Jack Bannister said of him that in King
Lear *Garrick's very stick acted. Garrick trained Bannister for the part of the hero in
Voltaire's tragedy* Mahomet; *and when told later that his protégé now thought of
attempting comedy, shook his head: 'Eh, eh! Why, no, don't think of that, you may
humbug the town some time longer as a tragedian, but comedy is* a serious thing, *so
don't try it yet.'*

SPEAKING EYE   George Colman the Younger
                                                Random Records (1830)

[Garrick's] *Deaf-man's* eye (of which I once witnessed a specimen at Hamp-
ton) evinced his minuteness of observation and gift of execution. There is an
expression in the eye of deaf persons (I mean of such as have not lost all
perception of sound) which, difficult as it may be to exhibit in mimicry, it is
still more difficult to define in writing: it consists of a mixture of dullness and
vivacity in the organs of vision, indicating an anxiety to hear all, with a
pretending to hear more than is actually observed, and a disappointment in
having lost much; an embarrassed look between intelligence and something
approaching to stupidity—all this he conveyed admirably; and if I could
convey it in words one tithe as well, I should have made myself more
intelligible.

THE OTHER CORPS   *The Drama (Vol. VII, 1824)*

Before he went on the stage, Bensley [c. 1738-1817] was a captain in the
army. One day he met a Scotch officer who had been in the same regiment.
The latter was happy to meet an old messmate; but his Scotch blood made
him ashamed to be seen with a player. He therefore hurried Bensley into an
unfrequented coffee-house, where he asked him, very seriously, 'Hoo could
ye disgrace the corps, by turning play-actor?' Bensley replied 'that he by no
means considered it in that light; that, on the contrary, a respectable player,
who behaved with propriety, was looked upon in the best manner, and kept
the company of the best people.' 'And what maun,' said the other, 'do ye get
by this business of yours?' 'I now,' answered B., 'get about a thousand a
year.' 'A thousand a year!' exclaimed Sawney, astonished. 'Hae ye any
vacancies in your corps?'

BEAR HIM HENCE   Charles Mathews
                              Memoirs (ed., Eliza Mathews; 1839)

Embarrassed circumstances caused him [John Palmer] at one time to live in
his dressing-room in Drury Lane Theatre, and when the Haymarket re-
opened for the summer season, at which he was engaged, the fear of arrest
suggested the expedient of conveying him with a cart full of scenery, in one
of the cabinets used in *The Prize*, and in this manner he actually was removed
from one theatre to the other.

WALKING WITH MACKLIN   John O'Keeffe
                                          Recollections of the Life
                                          of John O'Keeffe (1826)

Charles Macklin, the actor, instructs his pupils, young Mr Glenville and Miss
Ambrose, in his Dublin garden, in about 1765:

In Macklin's garden there were three long parallel walks, and his method of
exercising voices was thus: his two young pupils with backboards (such as
they use in boarding schools) walked firmly, slow and well, up and down the
two side walks; Macklin himself paraded the centre walk. At the end of
every twelve paces he made them stop; and turning gracefully, the young
actor called out across the walk, 'How do you do, Miss Ambrose?' She
answered, 'Very well, I thank you, Mr Glenville!' They then took a few
more paces, and the next question was, 'Do you think it a very fine day, Mr
Glenville?' 'A very fine day indeed, Miss Ambrose!' was the answer. Their
walk continued; and then, 'How do you do, Mr Glenville?' 'Pretty well, I
thank you, Miss Ambrose!' And this exercise continued for an hour or so
(Macklin still keeping in the centre walk), in the full hearing of their religious
next-door neighbours. Such was Macklin's method of training the management of the voice; if too high, too low, a wrong accent, or a faulty inflection,
he immediately noticed it, and made them repeat the words twenty times till
all was right. Soon after this Mr Glenville played Antonio to his Shylock, in
The Merchant of Venice; and Miss Ambrose, Charlotte, in his own *Love à la*
Mode.

This reminds me that when I asked Edith Evans how she would describe the secret of
her miraculous speaking, she replied, with lower jaw dropped to its limit, 'I imagine a
silver thread stretched from the bottom of my top teeth to the very back of the gallery,
and on that I hang every single syllable according to its value.' Noël Coward summed
stagecraft up very succinctly: 'Speak clearly and don't bump into the furniture.'

In 1718 James Quin (1693–1766) took the title role in Cato *at Lincoln's Inn Fields Theatre. A Welsh actor named Williams was to play Decius, entering with the line 'Caesar sends health to Cato'; instead of the broad classical pronunciation which Quin expected, Williams pronounced the name 'Keeto'—at which Quin promptly exclaimed, 'Would he had sent a better messenger!' The fiery little Welshman was furious——*

Ten times in the short scene he had to repeat the name, and Quin nearly as often; but the latter gave it a broad sound, and delivered it with a significant look which almost shook the little actor off his feet, and did shake all the sides of the house with inextinguishable laughter. When they met in the green-room, the Welshman, triply armed by having just ground of complaint, assailed Quin for rendering him ridiculous in the eyes of the audience. Quin said it was in their ears, and would have laughed the matter off. But the soul of Williams would not stoop to such treatment, and after the play he lay in wait for Quin under the Piazza as Cato passed that way to take his punch. The older actor laughed as Williams drew his sword and bade Quin defend himself. The latter would have sustained defence with his cane, but the angry Welshman thrust so fiercely that the other was fain to draw his rapier, which speedily, but without malice or intention on the part of the wielder, passed clear through the poor player's body. Decius was stretched dead on the pavement, and Cato looked on bewildered. Here was a man slain, and all for the mispronunciation of a vowel! The tragedy brought Quin to the bar of the Old Bailey; but the catastrophe was laid rather to the fashion of wearing swords than to the drawing of them with evil purpose; and Quin was freed from censure, but not from sad memories.

WONDERFUL ANIMALS

Paul Bedford
*Recollections and
Wanderings (1864)*

Some years after, when Lord Byron bid adieu to his native land, and devoted his life and fortune to the Greeks (who had some slight difference of opinion with the Turks), he presented to his dramatic idol Edmund Kean, his pet lion, Nero—nursed and matured by his lordship from its infancy until it became as docile as a lamb. During the frequent visits of our hero to his lordship, the magnificent beast was always one of the party, and therefore was under the control of the actor as it had been of the lord—and frequently, on occasions of dinner parties, given in Clarges Street by the modern Roscius, he summoned this king of the woods to the presence-chamber, creating great terror among the assembled guests, some jumping on chairs, others rushing in dismay from the room.

'Don't be alarmed, my friends,' said the host; 'come back, and you shall see a performance that will astonish you'; and after going through all sorts of gambols rampant, the two wonderful animals would roll upon the carpet, to the surprise, terror and amazement of the beholders. The performance over, the noble creature, at the master's signal, would retire to his den as obediently as any pet dog of a lady's boudoir. When the master left Clarges Street, and was absent from town on a lengthened visit of provincial engagements, he sent his pet out to nurse, under the fostering care of Mr Cross of Exeter Change, who was the proprietor of that academy for the education of the four-footed children of the woods.

My own rather more modest pet is a ten-inch, green Amazona viridigena, *named Jack Sprat, who has done over a thousand performances of* Treasure Island, *perching on the shoulders of six successive Long John Silvers. She has travelled hundreds of miles with us on tour as a* bona fide *member of the cast.*

JO ATTWOOD   Squire and Marie Bancroft
                                    Recollections of Sixty Years (1909)

The carpenters of country theatres always dreaded Charles Kean's advent among them, for, in his earlier days on the stage, when he rehearsed he would steadily go through his own scenes just as at night. During this time silence was strictly ordered to be observed all over the theatre; a creaking boot, a cough, a sneeze, the knocking of a hammer, would distress the tragedian beyond measure. It was on pain of dismissal that any carpenter or other servant caused the smallest interruption during Mr Kean's scenes. This naturally caused much ill-humour among the men, and when it became known that 'Kean was coming', there would be various expressions of discontent. At one particular engagement these men formed a conspiracy among themselves. The opening play was *Hamlet*, and they conceived a plot by which the Royal Dane might be induced to cut short his long soliloquies. One particular man was to place himself at the back of the gallery, being quite hidden from sight, and just as Kean began his great soliloquy was to call out in a muffled voice to an imaginary fellow-workman. This was the result:

KEAN (in slow measured tones):

   To be or not *to be* (long pause)—*that is the question.*

VOICE (far off in front of house, calling): Jo Attwood!

49

KEAN (stopping and looking in the direction, then beginning again):
   To be—or not—to—be—that is the question.

VOICE: Jo Attwood!

KEAN (bewildered and annoyed): Will somebody find Mr Attwood?
   (A pause) *To be or not to be—that is the question.*

VOICE: Jo Attwood!

KEAN: Until Mr Attwood is found I cannot go on!

'Mr Attwood' could *not* be found, and the voice did not cease interrupting Kean, who, at last, gave up his attempt to rehearse and went home; upon which the carpenters rejoiced in a sort of triumphant war-dance.

REHEARSAL   William Charles Macready
                                 Reminiscences (ed., Pollock; 1875)

It was the custom [c. 1817] of London actors, especially the leading ones, to do little more at rehearsals than read or repeat the words of their parts, marking on them their entrances and exits, as settled by the stage-manager, and their respective places on the stage. To make any display of passion or energy would be to expose oneself to the ridicule or sneers of the green-room, and few could be more morbidly sensitive to this than myself. But the difficulty of attaining before an audience perfect self-possession, which only practice can give, made me resolve to rehearse with the same earnestness as I would act; reasoning with myself that if practice was of the value attributed to it, this would be a mode of multiplying its opportunities, of proving the effect of my performance, and of putting myself so much at ease in all I might intend to do, that the customary nervousness of a first night would fail to disturb or prevent the full development of my conceptions. Upon making the experiment I may quote Dryden's line, ''Tis easy said, but oh! how hardly tried!' I found it much more difficult to force myself to act in the morning with the cold responses and the composed looks of Miss [Eliza] O'Neill, [Charles Mayne] Young and the rest, than at night before the most crowded auditory.
   Frequently, in after years, when I have given certain directions to actors rehearsing, the answer has been: 'Sir, I can never act at rehearsal, but I will do it at night', to which I had only one reply: 'Sir, if you cannot do it in the morning, you cannot do it at night; you must then do *something* because you must go on, but what you cannot do now, or cannot learn to do, you will not be more able to do then.' The task I found a very hard one, but I fought successfully against my *mauvaise honte*, and went doggedly at it. By this means I acquired more ease in passing through the varieties of passion, con-

firming myself in the habit of acting to the scene alone, and, as it were, ignoring the presence of an audience, and thus came to wield at will what force of pathos I was master of.

In later years, when Macready played Shylock, he was in the custom of working himself into a violent passion before his entrance for the famous scene with Tubal by seizing the ladder to the 'flies', shaking it, and uttering language that made the stage-hands stare.

SOME BLOODY PASSION SHAKES HIS VERY FRAME

Frances Anne Kemble

FEBRUARY 23rd [*letters to Harriet St Leger, 1848*]   Macready is not pleasant to act with, as he keeps no specific time for his exits or entrances, comes on while one is in the middle of a soliloquy, and goes off while one is in the middle of a speech to him. He growls and prowls, and roams and foams, about the stage in every direction, like a tiger in his cage, so that I never know on what side of me he means to be: and keeps up a perpetual snarling and grumbling like the aforesaid tiger, so that I never feel quite sure that he *has done*, and that it is my turn to speak. I do not think fifty pounds a night would hire me to play another engagement with him. . . .

I do not know how Desdemona might have affected me under other circumstances, but my only feeling about acting it with Mr Macready is dread of his personal violence. I quail at the idea of his laying hold of me in those terrible, passionate scenes; for in *Macbeth* he pinched me black and blue, and almost tore the point lace from my head. I am sure my little finger will be rebroken, and as for that smothering in bed, 'Heaven have mercy upon me!' as poor Desdemona says. If that foolish creature wouldn't persist in *talking* long after she has been smothered and stabbed to death, one might escape by the off side of the bed, and leave the bolster to be questioned by Emilia, and apostrophised by Othello; but she *will* uplift her testimony after death to her husband's amiable treatment of her, and even the bolster wouldn't be stupid enough for that . . . He can't touch me tonight, that's one comfort, for I am Queen Katherine.

FEBRUARY 28th   I got through Desdemona very well, as far as my personal safety was concerned; for though I fell on the stage in real hysterics at the end of one of those horrible scenes with Othello, Macready was more considerate than I expected, did not rebreak my little finger, and did not really smother me in bed. . . . I really believe Macready cannot help being as odious as he is on the stage. He very nearly made me faint last night in *Macbeth* with crushing my broken finger, and, by way of apology, merely coolly observed that he really could not answer for himself in such a scene, and that I ought to wear a splint; and truly, if I act much more with him, I think I shall require several splints, for several broken limbs.

Like Fanny herself (page 20), Macready was put on the stage by an actor-manager father to prop up a collapsing company; and for him too, the play chosen was Romeo and Juliet. *His first appearance, as Romeo, was in 1810 at the age of seventeen. He had been taken from school when his father's fortunes failed and always resented the fact. For the rest of his life he felt that the stage was a very low profession, although he always defended it against attacks from outsiders. It was his delight to mix with cultivated men such as John Forster and Charles Dickens. When he retired it was to Sherborne in Dorset to live among respectably military folk, then to Cheltenham to die among even* more *respectably military folk. He had come to haven at last.*

LEAVING IT LATE
Michael Kelly
Reminiscences (1826)

The first night of Pizarro, *adapted by Richard Brinsley Sheridan from the German of Kotzebue, was given at Drury Lane on May 24th 1799. Kelly was the musical director.*

At the time the house was overflowing on the first night's performance, all that was written of the play was actually rehearsing, and, incredible as it may appear, until the end of the fourth act neither Mrs Siddons nor Charles Kemble nor Barrymore had all their speeches for the fifth. Mr Sheridan was upstairs in the prompter's room where he was writing the last part of the play, while the earlier parts were acting; and every ten minutes he brought down as much of the dialogue as he had done, piece-meal, into the green-room, abusing himself and his negligence, and making a thousand winning and soothing apologies for having kept the performers so long in such painful suspense.

One remarkable trait in Sheridan's character was his penetrating know-ledge of the human mind; for no man was more careful in his carelessness; he was quite aware of his power over the performers, and of the veneration in which they held his great talents; had he not been so, he would not have ventured to keep them (Mrs Siddons particularly) in the dreadful anxiety which they were suffering through the whole of the evening. Mrs Siddons told me that she was in an agony of fright; but Sheridan perfectly knew that Mrs Siddons, C. Kemble, and Barrymore were quicker in their study than any other performers concerned; and that he could trust them to be perfect in what they had to say, even at half an hour's notice. And the event proved that he was right; the play was received with the greatest approbation, and though brought out so late in the season was played thirty-one nights; and for years afterwards proved a mine of wealth to the Drury Lane treasury and, indeed, to all the theatres in the United Kingdom.

Such, however, were the delays during the first night's performance that the play did not end until within five minutes of midnight. The farce of *My Grandmother* was to follow, but the exhaustion of the audience was so complete that, when the after-piece commenced, only seventeen persons remained in the whole dress circle, and twenty-two in the pit.

Michael Kelly sang at the triumphant first night of Mozart's Marriage of Figaro *in Vienna in 1786. He took the conspicuous part of the stuttering judge. In the* sestetto, *which was the composer's favourite piece in the whole opera, Mozart asked him not to stutter, saying that if he did, it would spoil the music. Kelly respectfully disagreed and even said that unless he could perform the part with a stutter he would not perform it at all. Mozart yielded: Kelly stuttered: the Emperor cried 'Bravo', the audience roared its applause, and the whole piece was encored. Mozart, with great generosity, shook Kelly by both hands and said, 'Bravo! young man, I feel obliged to you; and acknowledge you to have been in the right and myself in the wrong.'*

'A—A—A DRY MAN!'   Frances Anne Kemble
                                         Record of a Girlhood (1878)

Elizabeth Inchbald (1753–1821) first tried to go on the stage when she was seventeen, but was turned down because of her stammer. Her charm and beauty were such, however, that she succeeded in becoming an actress and, later, a dramatist and writer.

Mrs Inchbald was a person of a very remarkable character, lovely, poor, with unusual mental powers and of irreproachable conduct. Her life was devoted to the care of some dependent relation who, from sickness, was incapable of self-support. Mrs Inchbald had a singular uprightness and unworldliness, and a childlike directness and simplicity of manner, which, combined with her personal loveliness and halting, broken utterance, gave to her conversation, which was both humorous and witty, a most peculiar and comical charm. Once, after travelling all day, in a pouring rain, on alighting at her inn, the coachman, dripping all over with wet, offered his arm to help her out of the coach when she exclaimed, to the great amusement of her fellow travellers: 'Oh, no, no! Y-y-you will give me m-my death of c-c-cold; do bring me a-a-a dry man!'

At the first reading of one of her pieces, a certain young lady, with a rather lean, lanky figure being proposed to her for the part of the heroine, she indignantly exclaimed: 'No, no, no: I-I-I won't have that s-s-stick of a girl. Do g-give me a-a-a girl with bumps!' Coming off the stage one evening, she was about to sit down by Mrs Siddons in the green-room when, suddenly looking at her magnificent neighbour, she said: 'N-n-no, I won't sit by you: you're t-t-too handsome!'—in which respect she certainly need have feared no competition, and less with my aunt than with anyone, their style of beauty being so absolutely dissimilar. Somebody speaking of having oysters for supper, much surprise was excited by Mrs Inchbald saying she had never eaten one. Questions and remonstrances, exclamations and astonishment, and earnest advice to enlarge her experience in that respect, assailed her from the whole green-room, when she finally delivered herself thus: 'Oh no, indeed! I-I-I never, never could! What! e-e-eat the eyes and th-the nose, the teeth a-a-and the toes, the a-a-all of a creature!'

On one occasion, when she was sitting by the fireplace in the green-room, waiting to be called upon the stage, she and Mrs Mellon (afterwards Mrs Coutts and Duchess of St Albans) were laughingly discussing male friends and acquaintances from the matrimonial point of view. My uncle John [John Philip Kemble], who was standing near, excessively amused, at last jestingly said to Mrs Inchbald who had been comically energetic in her declarations of who she could, or would, or never could or would, have married: 'Well, Mrs Inchbald, would you have had me?'

'Dear heart!' said the stammering beauty, turning her sweet, sunny face up to him, 'I'd have j-j-jumped at you!'

'SUPPOSE WE DON'T ...'   Frances Anne Kemble
                                      Record of a Girlhood (1878)

My objection to the dramatic profession on the score of its uselessness, reminds me of what my mother used to tell me of Miss [Louisa] Brunton, who afterwards [1807] became Lady Craven; a very eccentric as well as attractive and charming woman, who contrived, too, to be a very charming actress, in spite of a prosaical dislike to her business, which used to take the peculiar and rather alarming turn of suddenly, in the midst of a scene, saying aside to her fellow-actors, 'What nonsense all this is! Suppose we don't go on with it!' This singular expostulation my mother said she always expected to see followed up by the sudden exit of her lively companion, in the middle of her part. Miss Brunton, however, had self-command enough to go on acting till she became Countess of Craven, and left off the nonsense of the stage for the earnestness of high life.

On one occasion Edmund Kean agreed to appear at the Glasgow Theatre, in a benefit performance for his son Charles. The play was the tragedy Brutus, *performed on October 1, 1828. Kean and his son had quarrelled bitterly a year earlier, but were now reconciled. Embracing his son, Kean delivered Brutus's line 'Pity thy wretched* father', *moving the audience to tears; and promptly added under his breath, 'We're doing the trick, Charlie!'*

TOUCHÉ!

Mrs John Drew
Autobiographical Sketch (1899)

Mr [Thomas Abthorpe] Cooper was a very handsome man (the remains of one when I saw him), eminently gentlemanlike in appearance. In the company of the old Chestnut Street Theatre at this epoch was a young actor, Mr George Barrett, called generally 'Gentleman George'. He was a juvenile actor of great local repute in Philadelphia, and moved among all the young swells of that day. He was to play Laertes in *Hamlet* with Cooper, who arrived from Baltimore too late for rehearsal; so George went to his dressing-room in order to ascertain the arrangement of the fencing match in the last scene.

Mr Cooper was morose and said, 'Go to the prompter, sir, and find out!' When the fencing began, Barrett would not let Cooper disarm him, and the audience could see this fact and became excited. Finally Barrett, with sword down, stood quietly to be run through by Cooper. When the curtain fell Cooper started up in a towering passion and exclaimed to Barrett: 'What do you mean by your conduct, sir?' Drawing himself up to his full height, six feet two inches, Barrett replied: 'Go to the prompter, sir, and find out!'

FAMILY MATTER

Edward Stirling
Old Drury Lane (1881)

All the players but two were Jackmans [a Northampton company, 1827]. The family wrote plays, acted the best parts, delivered bills, painted scenery, in fact did all and everything. Jackman *père* played principal characters, to the great delight of the followers of St Crispin, Northampton's staple being shoemaking. In *Jobson and Nell* (a cobbler and his wife), when Jobson beat his turbulent wife with a strap, the 'gods' in the gallery applauded approvingly; it touched their feelings. On one occasion Cobbler Jobson had forgotten his strap, Nell's tongue going nineteen to the dozen; a long pause. An observant cordwainer jumped up in the gallery, calling out: 'Here, Master Jackman, take mine; leather her with this!' and he threw a strap on the stage.

The recent emphasis on the equality of women with their male counterparts made me hesitate about including the above—but my male-chauvinistic secretary insisted! And who was I to say her nay?

'MY NAME IS NORVAL'

W. Donaldson
Recollections of an Actor (1865)★

Home's Douglas, *first produced in 1756, rapidly became the best-known of all contemporary melodramas with its romantic story of a noble infant left to die by his wicked grandfather, but rescued and brought up by the shepherd Norval as his own son. Everybody played in it, everybody knew the key lines by heart, everybody waited for them—and when delivered with the right flourish, they were sure of a solid hand.*

Another aspirant for histrionic fame in Dublin felt a penchant for the drama, but this stripling was not so favoured with a kind indulgent parent; quite the reverse: his father was both fiery and irritable, and had the greatest horror of a theatre; in fact, he never entered one. His hopeful son arranged on the quiet to play Young Norval on an actor's benefit, and matters were so well managed that the old gentleman was kept in ignorance till the evening of the performance, and then by some unlucky chance it reached his ears. Instead of flying into a passion and marring the entertainment, he resolved to add to it. Accordingly, when the doors were opened, he took his seat in the stage box, enveloped in a cloak and armed with a stout horsewhip.

At length the curtain drew up, and the tragedy, that was soon to be a comedy, commenced. The youthful Norval appeared, and was received with the accustomed applause, and began the well-known address, 'My name is Norval.' The words were scarcely out of his mouth when the enraged father jumped up in the box and roared out, 'You lie, you rascal! it isn't—it's Mat Finnigan!' and, suiting the action to the word, jumped on the stage and seized the noble shepherd; when flourishing the whip over his head, Lord Randolph, who was a little in the rear, rushed forward to the rescue of his protégé, and received as hearty a horsewhipping as he could desire, while the house was convulsed with screams of laughter. The curtain dropped, and this proved the young gentleman's last appearance on any stage.

EDMUND KEAN'S FOCUS

John and Edward Coleman
Memoirs of Samuel Phelps (1886)

As a youth, Samuel Phelps (1804–78) acted for five nights at a provincial theatre with the great tragedian, Edmund Kean (c. 1787–1833):

PHELPS: He didn't come to rehearsal, and although Lee, his secretary, rehearsed carefully enough, I did not know where to find Kean at night, for he crossed here, there, and everywhere, and prowled about like a caged tiger. I never took my eyes off him. I

★ Re-issued as *Fifty Years of Green-Room Gossip* (1881)

dodged him up and down, crossed when he crossed, took up my cues, and got on pretty fairly, till he thoroughly flabbergasted me by hissing 'Get out of my focus, blast you!—get out of my focus!'

COLEMAN: What in the name of fate did he mean by his 'focus'?

PHELPS: I'll tell you. Next moment, Lee, who was at the wing, whispered, 'Higher up: stand higher up the stage!'

COLEMAN: I understand; his focus was the footlight.

PHELPS: Precisely; I had got between him and it, and so prevented the light from reaching his face. With the exception of this trifling hitch, the scene went like a whirlwind. When it was over he sent for me to his room, where he was, according to custom, imbibing copious libations of hot brandy and water. Anderton was with him. They were both more than half-seas over, as in fact they were during the whole of his visit. 'Have a glass of grog, young stick-in-the-mud,' says Kean pleasantly. 'You'll be an actor one of these days, sir; but mind, the next time you play with me, for God's sake steer clear of my focus.'

CONTRAST
Joseph Jefferson
Autobiography (1890)

I acted with Macready and [Junius Brutus] Booth during this season, and an anecdote of each will serve to illustrate their different characteristics. Macready was acting Werner. I was cast for a minor part. In one scene a number of characters had to rush off, bearing lighted torches, in search of some delinquent. At rehearsal the tragedian particularly requested that we should all be sure and make our exit at night at just the same time and place, so that we might not disturb the arrangement of the scene. All went well up to the time for making our hurried exit, when to my horror I found Werner standing exactly in line with the place of my exit at rehearsal. I presume that when he gave his directions in the morning he did not observe me. What was I to do? The cue was given, and there was no time for argument. I rushed past him, torch in hand. I heard his well-known groan; but as I flew by an unmistakable odour of burnt hair filled the atmosphere, and I knew that I had singed his wig. When the curtain fell I turned in horror to see the effect. The enraged Werner had torn his wig from his head, and stood gazing at it for a moment in helpless wonder.

Suddenly he made a rush in my direction; I saw he was on the warpath, and that I was his game. And now the chase began. I dodged him up and down the stage; then around the wings and over 'set' rocks and gauze waters. He never would have caught me but that in my excitement I ran head first into the stomach of a fat stage-carpenter. Here I was seized. The enraged Macready was so full of anger and so out of breath that he could only gasp and shake his burnt wig at me. Of course I was disgraced and not allowed to act again during his engagement. To make matters worse the whole affair got into the papers, and the next morning one of the critics remarked that he had never seen Macready act with so much fire! Now all of this could have been avoided if he had but moved six inches further up the stage when he saw me coming; but no, he had never shifted from that spot before, why should he do so now? I believe that if I had singed his very eyebrows he would have stood his ground.

Booth's whole nature was the reverse of Macready's. He would saunter into the theatre just a few minutes before the play began; robe himself, sometimes quite carelessly; converse freely upon local matters in a plain, practical way, or perhaps give some reminiscence of bygone years,—his memory was wonderful,—ending with an amusing anecdote, and in the next moment walk upon the stage in the full assumption of his character, over-awing the audience by the fire of his acting. The following incident will serve to show the wonderful manner in which Booth could drop his character and instantly resume it.

I was acting Sampson in *The Iron Chest* to his Sir Edward Mortimer. During the play he spoke to me of my grandfather's playing the same part with him when he (Booth) was a young man. He used, said he, to sing the original song; it ran thus—and assuming a comical expression he began to sing in an undertone:

'*A traveller stopped at a widow's gate—*'

At this moment his cue was given, and he rushed upon the stage, discovering Wilford at the chest. The scene is here very powerful, and I never saw him act it with more power. The audience was most enthusiastic, and as he rushed from the stage amid a storm of applause, he met me at the wing, and, reassuming the comic expression of his face, began the song just where he had left off, while the approbation of the audience was still ringing in his ears.

It must not be understood by this that Booth never became absorbed in his character; on the contrary, he sometimes carried his intensity in this respect to an extreme. It is only meant to show that he had also the power of dropping his character in the midst of his concentration, resuming it again at will. Macready had no such faculty whatever. The beam once kicked, the balance was destroyed beyond recovery.

A playbill from the Theatre Royal, starring Joseph Jefferson in Rip Van Winkle, *the highly successful dramatisation by Dion Boucicault of a favourite American story by Washington Irving, in which a hen-pecked husband falls asleep for twenty years, awakening to find his acid-tongued wife dead and gone, his house in ruins, and himself stranded in an unrecognisable world.*

THEATRE ROYAL, NEW ADELPHI.

SOLE PROPRIETOR AND MANAGER, MR. BENJAMIN WEBSTER.

THIS POPULAR THEATRE

NOW OPEN,

HAVING BEEN ENTIRELY

RE-PAINTED AND RE-EMBELLISHED,

AND THE

Seats throughout Re-Stuffed and Re-Covered in Costly Material,

in order to increase the Comfort and Accommodation of the numerous Patrons
of this Establishment,

Under the Superintendence of MR. T. IRELAND.

UNPARALLELED SUCCESS OF

MR. JEFFERSON

IN THE NEW DRAMA, CALLED

RIP VAN WINKLE;

Or, The Sleep of Twenty Years!

Written expressly for him by DION BOUCICAULT, Esq.

☞ *VIDE PUBLIC PRESS.*

Mr. FELIX ROGERS and Miss JENNY WILMORE
EVERY EVENING.

Mrs. ALFRED MELLON in GOOD FOR NOTHING.

MONDAY, SEPTEMBER 25th, 1865, & DURING THE WEEK,

The Performances will commence at SEVEN, with the COMIC DRAMA of

GOOD FOR NOTHING.

Tom Diddles,	—		Mr. FELIX ROGERS,
Harry,	Mr. BILLINGTON,	Charley,	Mr. W. H. EBURNE,
	Young Simpson, Mr. BRANSCOMBE,	Servant,	Mr. PAULO,
Nan,	—		Miss WOOLGAR, (Mrs. A. Mellon).

After which, AT EIGHT, the Highly Successful NEW DRAMA, in Three Acts, Written by
DION BOUCICAULT, Esq., with New and Striking Scenery, Dresses, Appointments
and Effects, entitled

RIP VAN WINKLE

OR,

THE SLEEP OF TWENTY YEARS!

The NEW SCENERY Designed and Executed by Mr. J. GATES & Assistants.
The Machinery by Mr. CHARKER & Assistants. The Appointments by Mr. T. IRELAND & Assistants.
The Dresses by Miss RAYNER and Mrs. PARSONS.
The Overture and Music Composed and Arranged by Mr. RIVIERE.

ACT I.—CHARACTERS.

RipVan Winkle,	—		Mr. JOSEPH JEFFERSON,
			(His Nineteenth Appearance in London.)
	Derrick,	—	Mr. R. PHILLIPS,
Nick Vedder,	—		Mr. PAUL BEDFORD,
	Hendrick, (a Boy, Son of Vedder)		Master CONRAN,
Cockles,	(Derrick's Nephew)	—	Mr. FELIX ROGERS,
	Rory, Mr. BRANSCOMBE,	Peters,	Mr. PAULO,
Gretchen,	—	(Rip Van Winkle's Wife)	— Mrs. BILLINGTON,
	Meenie, (a Child, Rip's Daughter)	—	Miss CONRAN.

★ ★ ★

The above illustrates a radical difference between members of the theatrical profession. It is a matter of temperament. The great dancer Karsavina describes in her book, Theatre Street, *how she would arrive at the theatre at least an hour before 'curtain up' in order to 'get the little motor going': yet other performers could plunge straight into a scene without preparation or warning. Jefferson's autobiography leads me to believe that he belonged to the former category. He was without the animal impetuosity of Kean or Booth, but a great performer nevertheless. I have heard a superb gramophone record (taken from an old phonograph cylinder) of him playing the scene from* Rip Van Winkle *in which he first sees the little subterranean creatures with whom he is to spend the next twenty years of his life.*

ROYAL VICTORIA THEATRE

IV

THE MANAGEMENT

Frodsham as Hamlet

A rare picture of Mr Bridge Frodsham (1734–68). Idol of York playgoers, it is clear from this that he could look the part—a satisfactory blend of the externals—but as Garrick realised, he had all too little of the true inner fire. However, his encounter with the great actor which follows gives us an opportunity of seeing Garrick unbuttoned—and who would not wish so to see all artists!

MR FRODSHAM OF YORK

Tate Wilkinson
Memoirs of his Own Life (1790)

Frodsham, besides his tragic abilities, acted some such parts as Lord Hardy, Young Bevil, Lord Townly, Sir George Airy, sung very tolerably, and was a very decent Macheath. About thirty-two years ago he obtained a fortnight for holidays, which occasioned great lamentations at York, for they were certain if Mr Garrick saw Frodsham it would be a woeful day for the York stage. He not only was young and vain, but self-opinionated to a super-abundant degree. When in London he left a card at Mr Garrick's house, 'Mr Frodsham of York', with the same ease and facility as if it had been the first gentleman from Yorkshire.

Mr Garrick judged this card of a country stroller very easy and very extraordinary, and from the sample wished to see the York actor, who had accordingly admittance the ensuing day; and after a slight conversation, during which Garrick was astonished at the young man's being so very free and affable, particularly on any subject pertaining to Shakespeare's plays, &c., and still with a procrastination that Garrick was not accustomed to, or by any means relished a compliance with, he delayed, every minute expecting that Frodsham would present his petition to be heard, and receive his commendation from Garrick's eye of favour. But this obsequious request not being made, Garrick urged present business, and presented the York Romeo with an order for the pit, desiring him that night to favour him with attendance to see him perform Sir John Brute*, accompanied with an invitation to breakfast the ensuing morning—at the same time asking him, 'Pray now, have you seen a play since your arrival in London?'

'O yes,' quickly answered Mr Frodsham, 'I saw you play Hamlet two nights ago'; to which he added it was his own favourite character. 'Well,' says Garrick, 'pray now, how did you approve, Frodsham? I hope I pleased you', for that night he had judged his performance a lucky hit. Frodsham replied, 'O yes, certainly, my dear Sir, vastly clever in several passages; but I cannot so far subjoin mine to the public opinion of London, as to say, I was equally struck with your whole performance in that part.' I do not conjecture that any actor who spoke to Garrick ever so amazed him—Garrick stammered and said, 'Why—why now, to be sure now, why I suppose you

---

* In Vanbrugh's *The Provok'd Wife*

in the country—Pray now, Mr Frodsham, what sort of a place do you act in in York? Is it a room, or riding-house, occasionally fitted up?' 'O no, Sir, a theatre upon my honour.' 'O sure, why my Lord Burlington has said that; why will—will you breakfast to-morrow, and we will have a trial of skill, and Mrs Garrick shall judge between us, ha, ha, ha, now, I say. Good day, Mr York, for I must be at the theatre, so now pray remember breakfast.'

Frodsham promised he would, and made his exit. And though Garrick himself told me the circumstances, and truly laughed then, yet I am certain at the time he had been greatly piqued, astonished, and surprised at so strange a visit from a country actor; yet wishing to satisfy his curiosity, had done it for once at the expense of his pride and dignity. The following day arrived the York hero at Palais Royale in Southampton Street, according to appointment—breakfast finished, with Madam Garrick as good superintendent waiting with impatience, and full of various conjectures why the poor man from the country did not take courage and prostrate before the foot of majesty humbly requesting a trial, engagement, &c. but as Frodsham did not, as expected, break the ice, Garrick did.

'Well, Mr Frodsham, why now, well, that is, I suppose you saw my Brute last night? Now no compliment, but tell Mrs Garrick; well now, was it right? Do you think it would have pleased at York? Now speak what you think!' 'O!' says Frodsham, 'certainly, and, upon my honour, without compliment, I never was so highly delighted and entertained—it was beyond my comprehension; but having seen you play Hamlet first, your Sir John Brute exceeded my belief; for I have been told Hamlet, Mr Garrick, is one of your first characters; but I must say, I flatter myself I play it almost as well; for comedy, my good Sir is your forte. But your Brute, damn it, Mr Garrick, your Brute was excellence itself! You stood on the stage in the drunken scene flourishing your sword; you placed yourself in an attitude—I am sure you saw me in the pit at the same time, and with your eyes you seemed to say "Damn it, Frodsham, did you ever see anything like that at York? Could you do that, Frodsham?"' (and it is possible that last remark was a just one.)

The latter part of this harangue of Frodsham's possibly went not so glibly down as the tea at breakfast; and the ease and familiarity with which it was accompanied and delivered, not only surprised, but mortified Garrick, who expected adulation and the bended knee.

Mr Garrick not only loved, but eagerly swallowed flattery with a conjuror's avidity, with, hey! pass and be gone; and had it daily served up not only by inferiors, equals, and dependents, but by persons of higher rank. Therefore to hear a country actor speak slightly 'touching his Lord Hamlet' was too much to bear, and as Sir Archy says, 'was vary new'. After much affectation of laughter, and seemingly approving all Frodsham had uttered— 'Well now, hey! for a taste of your quality—now a speech, Mr Frodsham, from Hamlet; and Mrs Garrick, "bear a wary eye".' Frodsham, with the utmost composure, spoke Hamlet's first soliloquy without any idea of fear or terror, or indeed allowing Garrick, as a tragedian, a better Hamlet, or superior to himself, Garrick all the while darting his fiery eyes into the soul of Frodsham, a custom of Garrick's to all whom he deemed subservient, as if he meant to alarm and convey from those eyes an idea of intelligence to the beholder of his own amazing intellects.

Garrick certainly possessed most extraordinary powers of eye, as they contained not only the fire and austerity he meant to convey, but his simplicity in Scrub, and archness of eye in Don John, was equally excellent and as various. On Frodsham, the eye of terror had no such effect; for if he had noticed and thought Mr Garrick's eyes were penetrating, he would inwardly have comforted himself his own were equally brilliant, if not superiorly so. When Frodsham had finished Hamlet's first speech, and without stop, 'To be or not to be', &c., Garrick said, 'Well, hey now! hey! you have a smattering, but you want a little of my forming; and really in some passages you have acquired tones I do not by any means approve.' Frodsham tartly replied, 'Tones, Mr Garrick! to be sure I have tones, but you are not familiarised to them. I have seen you act twice, Hamlet the first, and I thought you had odd tones, and Mrs Cibber strange tones, and they were not quite agreeable to me on the first hearing, but I dare say I should soon be reconciled to them.' 'Why now,' says the much astonished, wondering Garrick, 'nay, now, really Frodsham, you are a damned queer fellow—but for a fair and full trial of your genius my stage shall be open, and you shall act any part you please, and if you succeed we will then talk of terms.'

'O!' says Frodsham, in the same flighty flow of spirits, 'you are mistaken, my dear Mr Garrick, if you think I came here to solicit an engagement; I am a Roscius at my own quarters! I came to London purposely to see a few plays, and looking on myself as a man not destitute of talents, I judged it a proper compliment to wait on a brother genius: I thought it indispensable to see you, and have half an hour's conversation with you—I neither want nor wish for an engagement; for I would not abandon or relinquish the happiness I enjoy in Yorkshire for the first terms your great and grand city of London could afford'; and with a negligent wild bow he made his exit, and left the gazing Garrick following his shade, like Shakespeare's ghost, himself standing in an attitude of surprise, to ruminate and reflect, and to relate this account of the strangest mad actor he had ever seen, or ever did see.

LAST DELIVERY

W. Donaldson
Recollections of an Actor (1865)

The old managers were celebrated for their wit and humour. Thornton, of the Reading circuit, was not the least among them: he was an especial favourite with George III, as an actor. Thornton was particularly happy in getting through a character without knowing much of the words of the author; but, in consequence of being absent at times, he committed strange blunders in some of his tragic attempts. One night at Gosport, while representing Biron in the tragedy of *Isabella*, he died without giving the letter which unravels the plot; and as he lay prostrate in the last scene, one of the performers on the stage whispered to him, 'Mr Thornton, the letter—the letter!' Thornton then rose up, took the letter out of his bosom, and said, 'One thing I had forgot through a multiplicity of business. Give this letter to my father: it will explain all'; and lay down again in the arms of death.

My great friend Julius Gellner tells me a similar story about Max Reinhardt's famous production of Oscar Wilde's Salome. *In one of the first scenes a young soldier is killed, but has to lie on the stage as a corpse until the curtain comes down. On a certain day the very young actor playing this part had an appointment with his girl friend, and having been stabbed was trying to creep slowly off-stage to keep his tryst with her. But in the play there are four old Hebrews and they had a plan to nip the love affair in the bud (one of them was played by Ernst Lubitsch, later to be a famous Hollywood director). These old Hebrews prevented the young lover from creeping off, and indeed killed him again! Whereupon the lovesick young man tried desperately a third time, but they pulled him right into the middle of the stage and all four plunged their daggers into him whilst shouting, 'What! not dead yet?' So they succeeded in destroying a beautiful love affair....*

LOVE IS BLIND   *Wolverhampton Chronicle* (1792)

One Briscoe, the manager of a small theatrical company, now in Staffordshire, though stone blind, plays all the heroes in his tragedies and lovers in genteel comedies.

THE ESTIMABLE MRS BAKER   Dutton Cook
A Book of the Play (1876)

A famous provincial manager, or 'manageress', was one Mrs Baker, concerning whom curious particulars are related in the *Memoirs of Thomas Dibdin*, and in the *Life of Grimaldi, the Clown*. The lady owned theatres at Canterbury, Rochester, Maidstone, Tunbridge Wells, Faversham, Deal and other places, but was understood to have commenced her professional career in connection with a puppet-show, or even the homely entertainment of Punch and Judy. But her industry, energy, and enterprise were of an indomitable kind. She generally lived in her theatres, and rising early to accomplish her marketing and other household duties, she proceeded to take up her position in the box-office, with the box-book open before her, and resting upon it 'a massy silver inkstand, which, with a superb pair of silver trumpets, several cups, tankards and candlesticks of the same pure metal, it was her honest pride to say she had paid for with her own hard earnings'.

While awaiting the visits of those desirous to book their places for the evening, she arranged the programme of the entertainments. Her education was far from complete, however, for although she could read she was but an indifferent scribe. By the help of the scissors, needle, thread, and a bundle of old playbills, she achieved her purpose. She cut a play from one bill, an interlude from another, a farce from a third, and sewing the slips neatly together avoided the use of pen and ink. When the name of a new performer had to be introduced she left a blank to be filled up by the first of her actors she happened to encounter, presuming him to be equal to the use of a pen. She sometimes beat the drum, or tolled the bell behind the scenes, when the representation needed such embellishments, and occasionally fulfilled the duties of prompter. In this respect it was unavoidable that she should be now and then rather overtasked.

On one special evening she held the book during the performance of the old farce of *Who's the Dupe?* The part of Gradus was undertaken by her leading actor, one Gardner, and in the scene of Gradus's attempt to impose upon the gentleman of the story by affecting to speak Greek, the performer's memory unfortunately failed him. He glanced appealingly towards the prompt-side of the stage. Mrs Baker was mute, examining the play-book with a puzzled air. 'Give me the word, madam,' whispered the actor. 'It's a hard word, Jem,' the lady replied. 'Then give me the next.' 'That's harder.' The performer was at a stand-still, the situation was becoming desperate. 'The next,' cried Gardner, furiously. 'Harder still!' answered the prompter, and then, perplexed beyond bearing, she flung the book on the stage, and exclaimed aloud: 'There, now you have them all; take your choice.'

The lady's usual station was in front of the house, however. She was her own money-taker, and to this fact has been ascribed the great good fortune she enjoyed as a manager. . . .

A settled distrust of the Bank of England was one of Mrs Baker's most marked peculiarities. At the close of her performance she resigned the position she had occupied for some five hours as money-taker for pit, boxes and gallery, and retired to her chamber, carrying the receipts of the evening in a large front pocket. This money she added to a store contained in half a dozen large china punch-bowls, ranged upon the top shelf of an old bureau. For many years she carried her savings about with her from town to town, sometimes retaining on her person gold in rouleaux to a large amount. She is even said to have kept in her pocket for seven years a note for £200. At length her wealth became a positive embarrassment to her. She deposited sums in country banks and in the hands of respectable tradesmen, at three per cent, sometimes without receiving any interest whatever, but merely with a view to the safer custody of her resources. It was with exceeding difficulty that she was eventually persuaded to become a fundholder. She handed over her store of gold to her stockbroker with extraordinary trepidation. It is satisfactory to be assured that at last she accorded perfect confidence to the Old Lady in Threadneedle Street, increased her investments from time to time, and learned to find pleasure in visiting London half-yearly to receive her dividends.

Altogether Mrs Baker appears to have been a thoroughly estimable woman, cordially regarded by the considerate members of the theatrical profession with whom she had dealings.

The last sentence surely sums up Mrs Baker. Any manager who can win the unstinted devotion of the profession is deserving of all honour. Many a manager after long rehearsals and dedicated performances by his actors has gone missing overnight, abandoning the company, penniless, to pad the hoof all the way home—and this not in ancient times, but within the last forty years.

CORN *The Journal of Agriculture (c. 1854)*

J. DOBBS most respectfully informs his friends and the public, that having invented a machine to expedite the reaping of corn, etc., and having been unable to obtain the patent till too late to give it a general inspection in the field with safety, he is induced to take advantage of his theatrical profession, and make it known to his friends who have been anxious to see it, through that medium.

Part of the stage will be planted with wheat, etc., that the machine has cut and gathered where it grew, and the machine worked as exactly as in the field.

On Friday next, October 14th, will be presented the celebrated comedy of *A Bold Stroke for a Husband*. End of the play, Mr Dobbs will exhibit two machines of different powers and purposes, and explain the principles on which they are made and act. He will also show to what several uses they are designed, with reference to America and the Indies; concluding with an occasional address to his fellow townsmen, being the last time he shall have the honour of appearing before them in a public character.

To conclude with the celebrated farce of *Fortune's Frolic*.

The part of *Robin Roughead* by Mr Dobbs, in which he will work the machine in character, in an artificial field of wheat, planted as near as possible in the manner in which it grows.

67

ELBOW ROOM   W. R. Chetwood
                                  A General History of the Stage (1749)

Distinguished characters in bills were not formerly in fashion; they were
printed according to the order they stood in the drama, not regarding the
merit of the actor. For example, in *Macbeth*, 'Duncan King of Scotland'
appeared first in the bill, though acted by an insignificant person; and so
every other actor appeared according to his dramatic dignity, all of the same
sized letter. But latterly, I can assure my readers, I have found it a difficult
task to satisfy some ladies, as well as gentlemen, because I could not find
letters large enough to please them; and some were so fond of elbow room
that they would have shoved everybody out but themselves.

CURSED QUACKERY   Dutton Cook
                                       A Book of the Play (1876)

Garrick seems to have been the first actor honoured by capital letters of an
extra size in the playbills. *The Connoisseur*, in 1754, says:
    'The writer of the playbills deals out his capitals in so just a proportion that
you may tell the salary of each actor by the size of the letter in which his
name is printed. When the present manager of Drury Lane first came on the
stage a new set of types, two inches long, were cast on purpose to do honour
to his extraordinary merit.'
    These distinctions in the matter of printing occasioned endless jealousies
among the actors. Macklin made it an express charge against his manager,
Sheridan, the actor, that he was accustomed to print his own name in larger
type than was permitted to other performers. Kean threatened to throw up
his engagement at Drury Lane on account of his name having been printed in
capitals of a smaller size than usual. His engagement of 1818 contained a
condition: 'And also that his name shall be continued in the bills of performance in the same manner as it is at present,' viz., large letters.
    On the other hand, Dowton, the comedian, greatly objected to having his
name thus particularised, and expostulated with Elliston, his manager, on the
subject. 'I am sorry you have done this,' he wrote. 'You know well what I
mean. This cursed quackery. These big letters. There is a want of respectability about it, or rather a notoriety, which gives one the feeling of an
absconded felon, against whom a hue and cry is made public. Or if there be
really any advantage in it, why should I, or any single individual, take it over
the rest of our brethren? But it has a nasty disreputable look, and I have
fancied the whole day the finger of the town pointed at me, as much as to
say, "That is he! Now for the reward!" Leave this expedient to the police
officers, or to those who have a taste for it. I have none.'

Denis Matthews told me a wonderful story about a concert he gave in Lagos, Nigeria. The hall, the audience, the piano, the piano stool, were all above reproach. Only one thing was in doubt—he was billed as Mr Dennis Mathews, a member of the Worshipful Company of Muscians, who was to play the Sonote in C mior by Behoven. But what the hell, the whole thing went off with a bang, and who cares about billing when that happens! On second thoughts, no success, however great, would placate Mr G. Vining—

MR *GEORGE* VINING

25 St Paul's Road, Camden Town
December 5, 1858

MESSRS ROBSON AND EMDEN

Gentlemen—I perceive that my name is again put in the bills as Mr. G. Vining. I will come to business at once. My engagements are always made for Mr *George* Vining. For some years now I have been professionally known as Mr *George* Vining; I choose to be styled Mr *George* Vining and in truth I will not act unless I am called Mr *George* Vining, and if the name of Mr *George* Vining is disgraceful to the Olympic management Mr *George* Vining is willing to go: in a word you must please either restore the name of Mr *George* Vining or accept this as Mr *George* Vining's notice to leave, for Mr *George* Vining most positively and determinedly will not play but under the name of
Yours faithfully,
GEORGE VINING

December 6, 1858

Sir—We are sorry to say your note leaves no alternative but to accept the month's notice you have given for yourself and Mrs V.
I am, Sir, Yours obediently,
W. S. EMDEN and F. ROBSON

HERALD OF FAME   *The Drama (Vol. VI, 1824)*

Dramatic puffing has been carried to considerable perfection among us; but in this, as in several other of the fine arts, we are excelled by our neighbours. Nothing more will be required to establish the French claim than the following account of Mlle Georges. This actress is now travelling the departements, and exhibiting on the boards that rather extravagant mode of performing which is not always relished in the capital. She carries with her a kind of herald of her fame; and this person in one of the journals styles her as the 'queen of fine actresses—the most beautiful woman at present on the stage'. The following is the circular letter by which the manager of the theatre of Angers invited the chief persons of his district to attend the performances of this 'Queen of beautiful actresses':

Monsieur,—Mlle GEORGES, the first tragic performer of France, and of the two theatres of the capital, having been pleased to consent to appear on the stage, to which I endeavour to draw the honourable public, I dare hope that you will deign to encourage my efforts by a tribute of admiration in favour of the most beautiful woman in Europe—such a woman as has not her equal in all the pomp of her brilliancy, the pupil of TALMA and Mlle RAUCOURT, and, above all, of beneficent and generous Nature. In coming to see Mlle GEORGES you will at once see Nature, TALMA, and RAUCOURT. In the fine part of Semiramis she will appear with 100,000 crowns' worth of diamonds. All the ornaments which she wears in that tragedy are precious stones.

I present my humble respects, &c.

John Trewin recalls that one night in the autumn of 1927, a provincial manager spoke to him during the second interval of a Sensational Attraction. 'The curtain had fallen on the sight of a more than commonly insipid heroine bound and gagged in a chair over a trapdoor. The hero, threatened by several revolvers, fumed in a corner, and somebody's corpse lay well downstage. As a very young drama critic indeed, this seemed good enough to me, though I could not imagine at that moment how the hero would get clear. While I pondered, the manager whispered to me, without the slightest hint of irony: "Won't do. Won't do. Not enough incident".'

BENEFIT NIGHTS

... MADEMOISELLE GEORGES   Arsène Houssaye

When I see Mademoiselle Georges I seem to be beholding the ruins of Palmyra in motion. Age has played terrible havoc with her, still she is not less majestic, nor less coquettish. Coquetry in old age is like a rose in a grinning death's head. Mademoiselle Georges came to ask me yesterday to give a performance for her benefit.

'You'll save me from starving,' she said.

I looked at her in surprise, for she wore a magnificent hat and feathers and primrose kid gloves.

'You are thinking how well all this still becomes me, are you not, my dear Director?' she asked, smiling.

Thereupon she took a small glass from her pocket and looked at herself mincingly. I became thoroughly alarmed, for she looks seventy-five when she speaks and eighty when she smiles.

She proposed to me to edit her *Memoirs*. I took her at her word there and then, and tried to gather material for the chapters on Napoleon. 'Is it true that he sent for you long after midnight and that he forgot that you were there until morning, absorbed as he was in the map of Europe?'

'Pure slander,' she replied with dignity. 'He knew what was due to me and what was due to himself. His map of Europe! *I* was his map of Europe.'

... THE CELEBRATED MR COOKE   J. B. Howe
A Cosmopolitan Actor (1888)

The celebrated tragedian, Mr [George Frederick] Cooke, was always fond of a frolic on his benefit night, declaring he never took liberties with his friends at any other time.

It once happened during an engagement at Philadelphia that on such an occasion he was short of money and at a loss to know where to raise the wind for the accustomed breeze. In this dilemma he started up the town in a speculative mood, determined to inspirit himself in some way or other.

Having reached the corner of Callow Hill and Eighth Street he perceived one of those enticing signs of three golden balls. He turned the corner and entered the fatal door, and addressed the man behind the counter thus:

'My name is Cooke. This is my benefit night. The manager can't do without me. I am up for Richard III. I want something to eat. I have no money. Now I propose to pledge myself for ten dollars, and you may lay me upon one of your shelves.'

The joke was a queer one. The pawnbroker paid the ten dollars, and Cooke was laid up. The theatre that night was crowded, and at seven o'clock the manager came forward to apologise, stating that, with the permission of the audience, the performance would commence with a farce.

He had sent in different directions, but was unable to find Cooke in the city. He promised that the tragedian would be forthcoming in the course of half an hour.

As the manager retired, he was told that a boy wished to see him in the green-room. He found the boy, who presented a note, written in cypher, which he at length translated thus:

'My dear Jones, I am pawned for ten dollars; send and redeem me, or it will be impossible for Richard to be himself tonight. Yours, &c.'

The Manager started immediately after the fixed star, and found him nicely shelved with a plate of biscuits and cheese. In the buttonhole of his

71

coat was a piece of paper marked 'Number 1,473; pawned for ten dollars'.

The amount was paid, a cab called, and Mr Cooke and the manager returned to the theatre, where the former had just time to dress and commence '*Now is the winter of our discontent—*' It is said that he never acted better or received more applause.

ARGUMENT   William Charles Macready
                                              and Alfred Bunn

In April, 1836, the bland and ruthless vulgarian Alfred Bunn, manager of Drury Lane, announced a programme which would include the first three acts of Richard III *in the same bill as Planché's* The Jewess *and* Chevy Chase. *Bunn knew very well that William Charles Macready, the first tragedian of his day, who led the Drury Lane company, was at his best in the last act of* Richard; *hence his malicious choice of the truncated version (perhaps Cibber's?). Macready's journal records that this was more than he could bear:*

APRIL 29th, 1836   My spirits were so very much depressed, so overweighted by the situation in which I was placed, that I lay down to compose myself and thought over the part of Richard as well as I could. Went to the theatre, was tetchy and unhappy, but pushed through the part in a sort of desperate way as well as I could. It is not easy to describe the state of pent-up feeling, of anger, shame, and desperate passion that I endured. As I came off the stage, ending the third act of Richard, in passing by Bunn's door I opened it, and unfortunately he was there. I could not contain myself; I exclaimed, 'You damned scoundrel! How dare you use me in this manner?' And going up to him as he sat on the other side of the table, I struck him as he rose a back-handed slap across the face. I did not hear what he said, but I dug my fist into him as effectively as I could; he caught hold of me, and got at one time the little finger of my left hand in his mouth, and bit it. I exclaimed: 'You rascal! Would you bite?' He shouted out: 'Murder! Murder!' and, after some little time, several persons came into the room. I was then upon the sofa, the struggle having brought us right round the table. Willmott, the prompter, said to me: 'Sir, you had better go to your room, you had better go to your room.' I got up accordingly and walked away, whilst he, I believe—for I did not distinctly hear him—was speaking in abuse of me.

Four years later in 1840, Bunn published an account of this scene in his book The Stage: Both Before and Behind the Curtain:

On Friday, the 29th April, I was sitting at my desk, a few minutes before nine o'clock, and by the light of a lamp, so shaded as to reflect on the table, but obscure the room generally, I was examining bills and documents, previous to their payment on the following morning; when, without the slightest note of preparation, my door was opened, and after an ejaculation of 'There, you villain—take that—and that!' I was knocked down, one of my eyes completely closed up, the ankle of my left leg which I am in the habit of passing round the leg of the chair when writing, violently sprained, my person plentifully soiled with blood, lamp oil, and ink, the table upset, and Richard the Third holding me down. On my naturally inquiring if he meant to murder me, and on his replying in the affirmative, I made a struggle for it, threw him off, and got up on my one leg, holding him fast by the collar, and finally succeeded in getting him down on the sofa, where, mutilated as I was, I would have made him 'remember me', but for the interposition of the people who had soon filled the room. Had I had the remotest idea of the visit, I should have been prepared, but not particularly alarmed for the result ... but this was nothing more nor less than stabbing a man in the dark. If the provocation had been never so great, nothing could justify such a mode of resentment. But I maintain there was no provocation given—certainly none was intended.

Bunn brought an action for battery, and the whole business, with legal dues, cost Macready £150. I have never seen an actor strike a manager, though they have often had good cause. Forty-five years ago I recall rehearsing a revue called The Cresta Run. *A week before we were to open at the Fortune Theatre the manager disappeared and we never saw him again. We could all gladly have murdered him.*

COUNTING THE BRASS   George Vandenhoff
                                    Dramatic Reminiscences* (1860)

I had just finished breakfast at the hotel in Bolton, a small town in Lancashire, where I was playing a short engagement [in the winter of 1840] when the waiter told me that a gentleman wanted to speak with me. 'Who is it?' I asked.

'I don't know,' said the waiter; 'he's rather a strange-looking gentleman, sir.'

'How strange?'

'Well, sir, I can't exactly say; he looks queer, somehow; I think, sir, he must be one of the actor chaps—or else a gipsy.'

'Oh,' said I—a highly complimentary alternative, I thought to myself! 'Well,' I added, 'let me see this strange gentleman.'

'Yes, sir'; and the queer-looking chap was brought into my room.

A queer-looking chap he was indeed! A tall, gaunt, high-shouldered, raw-boned, bossy-faced, hook-nosed, sunburnt, and hollow-cheeked individual,

* Re-issued as *An Actor's Note-Book; or, The Green-Room and Stage* (1865)

with a pair of keen, restless, black eyes, deep set, under shaggy overhanging eyebrows; dressed in a faded frock-coat which had once been brown, but was now of no positive colour, and which—having formed part of the wardrobe of a smaller man than its present wearer, to whom by some freak of fortune it had lapsed—being too short for him in every way, showed his bare, bony wrists, innocent of wristbands; a dark double-breasted waistcoat, buttoned close across his chest, to conceal, perhaps, his bosom's secret (a scarcity of linen), a pair of trousers that, having probably been derived from the same source as the coat, presented the same exiguousness of length, and displayed the tops of a pair of very seedy and travel-worn high-lows, a fuzzy head of hair, so promiscuous and so indistinct of tint, from dryness, age, and the dust of the roads, that it was impossible to guess at its original shade,— such were the principal features of the strange-looking gentleman, who now, with a rusty, battered hat in his large, muscular hands, presented himself, bowing, to my notice.

'I am commissioned, sir,' he said, 'by Mr Parish, the manager of the Blackburn Theatre, to ask if your engagements will allow you to give us the aid of your splendid talents for a few, say three or more, nights; and if so, on what terms you would consent to visit us.'

Now, there was nothing in this address particularly outré in itself: it was the grandiloquent ambassadorial style of the man, coupled with his mean and wild appearance, that made it ludicrous. He had all the burlesque dignity, and self-importance, of a ragged plenipotentiary from Otaheite! 'I have not the pleasure,' I said, 'Mr Hall, of being acquainted with Mr Parish.'

'A highly respectable and responsible man, I assure you, sir: the soul of honour, sir,' quickly replied the ambassador, laying his hand on his breast.

'What plays are your company capable of performing, Mr Hall?'

'Any, sir, and all,' he answered, with a flourish. 'We are up in all the stock tragedies, and have an efficient company.'

'A good leading actress, Mr Hall?'

'An angel, sir! young, perfect, talented and amenable.' He laid particular stress on the last epithet.

'A rare assemblage of qualities,' I said: 'but let me order you some break-fast, Mr Hall; you seem fatigued. How did you come?'

'Walked, sir!'

'Walked!' I repeated; 'why it's twelve miles.'

'I know it, sir,' he replied; 'but exercise is good for me, and I preferred it to the coach: it will do me good.'

A good breakfast, thought I, would do you more good; and, the waiter just then coming into the room with a letter for me, 'Order a beefsteak for this gentleman,' I said. 'Tea or coffee, Mr Hall?'

'Why,' said that gentleman, 'you're very good, sir; but if you'll allow me, I'll take a little ale.'

'Bring some ale, waiter,' I said.

74

'Ale, sir? yes, sir'; and with a look of ill-concealed wonder, the waiter left the room.

In a few minutes the steak and ale were brought in. The strange gentleman fell to without ceremony, despatched them in a few minutes more. I turned towards him, as he rubbed his hands together, in token of the refreshment of his inner man; and he said, in a theatrical way, quoting from *The Merchant of Venice*—'Well, sir, shall I have your answer? Will you pleasure us?'

'Well, Mr Hall,' I replied, 'I am in your neighbourhood. I have three vacant nights next week, and I will come to you Monday, Wednesday, and Friday, for a clear half of the receipts, each night.'

'Those are very high terms, sir,' he replied, raising his eyebrows and screwing up his mouth. 'I am commissioned to offer you a clear third, and half a benefit. My power extends no further.'

'The value of a thing,' I answered, 'is that which it will bring, you know, Mr Hall. Allow me to ask how much money you play to ordinarily. What were the receipts of the house last night, for example? I trust to your honour.'

'Well, sir, last night was a bad night. We had not a great house last night.'

'Come, now; had you thirty shillings?'

'Oh yes, sir; we had thirty shillings.'

'Not much more, eh?'

'No, not much more,' said he, with a comic smile.

'Well, suppose I play to an average of twenty pounds nightly and you pay me half of it, if your ordinary business does not produce more than two pounds, you'll be a considerable gainer by the transaction.'

'Yes,' said he; 'if that were certain.'

'Nothing is certain,' I replied, 'in theatrical matters; but I have every right to expect it; and it is only on the terms I have mentioned that I can consent to visit you.'

'Well, sir,' said he, 'my instructions are to secure your services, and therefore I must accept your terms.'

The next week, on Monday, I reached Blackburn early in the morning, and about half past ten o'clock my strange negotiator was ushered into my room, accompanied by 'another spirit' almost as strange as himself; a very swarthy, powerful man, considerably over six feet high, with jet-black glossy hair, that hung on the sides of his cheeks in short ringlets. He was dressed in a velveteen suit, and had altogether a regular gipsy look and air. The last stranger was duly presented to me as 'Mr Gould; our stage manager, sir!'

They had called to show me to the theatre; and I got up and followed them, to the rather dingy back-street in which it was situated. The company was assembled, and we commenced the rehearsal of *Othello*. The tall Gould was the Iago, and my Desdemona was the 'angel' aforesaid, a well-looking young woman, who, without seeming particularly to understand them, was very perfect in the words of the text. My new friend the stage manager, barring occasional extraordinary, and hitherto undreamt of, readings, was pretty safe; and though there was a general air of seediness about the corps dramatique, they were all evidently desirous of doing their best, and we got through the rehearsal tolerably satisfactorily.

In the evening, I went rather early to the theatre, and was agreeably surprised by finding that a very good-sized room had been fitted up as my dressing-room, cleaned, carpeted, sofa'd, well lit with extra lights, and in every way made snug. This attention to my private comfort gave me better hopes of the appointments for the stage, about which I confess I had my doubts. But when we came to the Senate scene, I was pleased to find a respectable array of properties, with a Duke, who, though he had the snuffles in his utterance, was well-dressed, and correct in the text. Barring a few little contretemps, which did not seem to affect the enjoyment of the audience, if they did not even increase it (certainly they gave uproarious tokens of delight at the burlesque and Bombastes-Furioso death of Roderigo, who, in his agony, kept his leg quivering and shaking in the air as if he were galvanised, while Iago kept sticking his sword into him, and at every stick, a fresh kick), except this, and one or two other rather striking effects, the play went off with immense applause, and the actors were evidently highly satisfied with their own efforts in the Shakespearean Drama.

The house, as I had prophesied, was well filled; and after the performance, I had my first interview and settlement with the Manager: and a strange settlement it was. He walked into my room, as I had just finished my change of dress and washed off the last tint of Othello's swarthy hue; and said, with a strong Lancashire accent:—'Moy name's Parish, sir; Aw'm th' manager o' this cuncearn, and Aw've coomb to settle.'

'Good evening, Mr Parish; I hope you're pleased with the house to-night.'

'It's a foine house, sir; yaw've doon well: and every neet Aw expect yaw'll do better. Yaw've got th' stoof in yaw, and th' chaps loike yaw.'

I bowed—he went on: 'Aw don't knaw haw much is in th' 'ouse; Aw haven't counted th' brass'—money—'but Aw took it all mysen', and so there's no cheating here.'

With that, he turned his back to my dressing-table, and emptied out of his coat pockets as I looked on with wonder, a large quantity of silver and copper. Having turned his coat pockets thoroughly out, he next put his hand into his waistcoat pocket, and fished out a £5 note, which he laid down on the table; and lastly, he pulled from the pockets of his pants a couple of sovereigns; those also he deposited with the rest of the current coin of the realm, saying:—'Theere! theere it all is, just as Aw tak' it. Now th' bargain is auf and afe; pretty stiff terms, maister, but yaw've airnt it; so count away; and yaw tak auf and Aw'll tak afe; and then all' be straight 'twixt yaw and mysen'.'

So down we sat 'to count the brass'. During this interesting 'financial operation', not a word was spoken on either side; the piles being duly made up, it appeared on counting them, that there were twenty pounds ten shillings in silver, and two pounds and sixpence in copper; which, with the £5 note and the £2 in gold, amounted to twenty-nine pounds, ten shillings and sixpence; large receipts for a small country theatre, I can tell you! (I have seen less in a very large one, with a good company, and two or three London actors in the cast.)

Well, Mr Parish was evidently no Michael Cassio—no great arithmetician; but after some little difficulty, he gradually, after a good deal of puzzling and scratching of his head (there was no pen, pencil or paper in the room), satisfied himself that the half of £29 10s. 6d. was £14 15s. 3d.; whereupon, making an exact division, he said—

'Theere! theere's thy share, and here's moine; Aw've given thee th' gowd and th' flimsy, 'cause Aw 'pose yaw won't be wanting to carry th' copper; and Aw can pay it away to moy fowks at onest. So that's settled!' said he.

'And a very simple and straightforward settlement too, Mr Parish!'

'Whoy, yaw see, sir,' he replied, 'Aw'm not much i' th' littery loine; moine's mostly headwork; Aw don't do mooch wi' pen an' ink. Aw'm a scaffolder, Aw am!'

'A scaffolder, Mr Parish?'

'Aye; we're open-air chaps, we are; we play under canvas i' th' summer, and i' th' winter Aw'm forced to go into th' regular business, in walls; and it near ruins me. But yaw see, Aw mun keep my people togither agin th' summer time, or Aw should lose 'em. However, yaw'll find me aw reet, upreet and downreet. And now, sir, we mun ha'e a glass togither, if yaw please, just to wet th' first neet, and for luck for th' others.'

This was the system of settlement he followed every night; and, looking back on the many theatres I have played in since, and the many managers that have settled with me, I am inclined to think, that though it was not the most formal, or 'high-Roman fashion' of settlement, it was, perhaps, the fairest and honestest that I have ever been favoured with. The company was, in fact, a show-company—scaffolders—that played in booths in summer, and in winter betook themselves to small theatres, doing the best they could, and sharing the profits, if there were any.

My two other nights ('Rolla' and 'Hamlet') produced two excellent houses, and I took away from this petty place, as my share, about £40.

Vandenhoff's account reminds me of the sharing table used in all Elizabethan and Jacobean theatres. It was marked out like a checkerboard with the sharers' initials chalked in the various spaces. I myself never saw a scaffold company, but whilst working on the film Moby Dick *in Youghal, County Cork, I did meet a company of boothers, called Costello's Bohemians. The six actors had arrived the previous night and had set up their booth on the strand, a stretch of shelving beach leading down to the sea. The booth was a large marquee with rostrums lashed to the sides, giving an air of solidity to the tent-like structure. I ventured to ask Mr Costello if they would give us a bespeak. He asked what play we would choose and I said 'Could you get up* Othello?' *He hesitated. 'Ah now, that's quite a pill that one. There's a deal o' words in that. D'ye happen to have the words with ye?' I said not, but that we would send to Dublin for a copy of the book. The book duly arrived, and with my blue pencil I cut it to suit a gallant company of six. But Mr Costello shrank from taking the plunge, so we ended up with* Lost in London *and* The Wearing o' the Green, *followed by a full half-hour's variety show. The whole thing took four and a half hours including interval.*

MANAGING THE DUKE

James Henry Mapleson
The Mapleson Memoirs (1888)

One evening, when the opera of *Rigoletto* was being performed, with Mongini as the 'Duke', feeling tired, as I had been working in the theatre throughout the day, I went home just before the termination of the third act. I had been at home about three-quarters of an hour when my servant hurried up in a cab to inform me that the curtain had not yet risen for the final act, and that a dreadful disturbance was going on in consequence of some question with Mongini, who was brandishing a drawn sword and going to kill everybody. I immediately slipped on my clothes and went down to the theatre.

At the stage door, without her bonnet, I met the tenor's charming wife, the only person, as a rule, who could control him in any way; and she entreated me not to go near him, or there would be bloodshed. I insisted, however, on going to his room without delay, as the curtain was still down and the public was getting tumultuous. I took the precaution of buttoning my overcoat across my chest, and in I went, my first words being—'This time, Mongini, I hear you are right (*Questa volta sento che avete ragione*).'

With this preliminary we got into conversation, but he still remained walking up and down the room with nothing but his shirt on and a drawn sword in his hand. I saw that I had to proceed very slowly with him, and began talking on indifferent matters. At last I asked him the details of all the trouble. He thereupon explained to me that the master tailor, who had been requested by him in the morning to widen his overcoat by two inches, had misunderstood, and contracted it by two inches. I wished to have a look at the dress, which, however, was lying on the floor torn to pieces. I assured Mongini that the man should be cruelly punished, and he and his family put upon the streets to starve early the next morning.

He then got calmer, and I casually observed, 'Bye-the-bye, is the opera over yet, Mongini?' to which he replied, 'No, it is not.'

'Never mind that,' I continued; 'the public can wait. Everyone, by the way, is talking of the magnificent style in which you have been singing tonight.'

His eyes brightened and he said he should like to go on with the opera. 'Not at all a bad idea!' I remarked.

'But I have no dress,' said Mongini, rather sadly; 'it is destroyed.'

I suggested that he should wear the dress of the second act, putting on the breastplate and the steel gorget with the hat and feathers, and he would then be all right, and '*La Donna e Mobile*' would make amends for the delay. He dressed and followed me to the stage, when I made the sign for the stage manager to ring up the curtain, greatly to the astonishment of Mongini's wife, who was fully expecting to hear that I had been run through the body.

The next day at twelve o'clock, as per appointment, Mongini came to my office to be present at the punishment of the master tailor. I had taken the precaution to inform the tailor, who was a single man, that he had a wife and four children, and that he was to be sure and recollect this. I called him into my room in the presence of Mongini, and told him gravely that he and his wife and children must now starve. There was no alternative after the treatment Mongini had received the previous evening.

Mongini at once supplicated me not to let the children die in the gutter, as it might injure him with the public, and he ended by promising that if I would retain the tailor in my service he would sing an extra night for nothing.

PHELPS AT THE WELLS   John and Edward Coleman
Memoirs of Samuel Phelps (1886)

Living as we now do in Islington, my wife and I pass through Canonbury Square eight or ten times a week and we always give a little salute as we pass Number 8— the house which was once the home of Samuel Phelps. A few years ago we had an opportunity of buying it, but we found that we did not care for the inside as much as the outside with its bronze plaque on the wall, giving the great man's dates:

Samuel Phelps ★ 1804–1878 ★ Tragedian ★ Lived Here

It is difficult to know how good an actor Samuel Phelps was. I have the impression that he was very correct, vocally secure, but not greatly inspired. But he raised the status of our profession to heights hitherto unimagined, and prepared the ground for great performers like Irving and for great enterprises like the Old Vic.

During the early 1840s, Sadler's Wells Theatre at Islington was entirely delivered over to as ruffianly an audience as London could shake together. Without, the theatre by night was like the worst of the worst kind of fair in the worst kind of town. Within, it was a bear-garden, resounding with foul language, oaths, cat-call shrieks, yells, blasphemy, obscenity—a truly diaboli-cal clamour. Fights took place anywhere, at any period of the performance. The audience were, of course, directly addressed in the entertainments, and it was in the contemplation of the management to add the physical stimulus of a pint of porter to the moral refreshments offered to every purchaser of a pit ticket, when the management collapsed, and the theatre shut up.

At this crisis of the career of Mr Ketch and his pupils, Samuel Phelps conceived the desperate idea of changing the character of the dramatic entertainments presented at this den, from the lowest to the highest, and of utterly changing with it the character of the audience.

On the opening night [in 1844] the play was *Macbeth*. It was performed amidst the usual hideous medley of fights, foul language, cat-calls, shrieks, yells, oaths, blasphemy, obscenity, apples, oranges, nuts, biscuits, ginger-beer, porter, and pipes—pipes of every description were at work in the gallery, and pipes of all sorts and sizes were in full blast in the pit.

Cans of beer, each with a pint measure to drink from (for the convenience of gentlemen who had neglected the precaution of bringing their own pots in their bundles) were carried through the dense crowd at all stages of the tragedy. Sickly children in arms were squeezed out of shape in all parts of the house. Fish was fried at the entrance doors. Barricades of oyster-shells en-cumbered the pavement. Expectant half-price visitors to the gallery howled defiant impatience up the stairs, and danced a sort of carmagnole all round the building.

It being evident either that the attempt to humanise the place must be abandoned, or this uproar quelled, the manager made vigorous efforts for the victory.

The friers of fish, vendors of oysters, and other costermonger scum accu-mulated round the doors, were first got rid of. The noisy sellers of beer inside the theatre were next to be removed. They resisted, and offered a large weekly consideration 'for leave to sell and call'. The management was ob-durate and rooted them out. Children in arms were next to be expelled. Orders were given to the money-takers to refuse them admission, but these were found extremely difficult to be enforced as the women smuggled babies in under their shawls and aprons, and even rolled them up to look like cloaks. A little experience of such artifices led to their detection at the doors; and the play soon began to go on without the shrill interruptions consequent on the unrolling of dozens of these unfortunate little mummies every night. But the most intolerable defilement of the place remained. The outrageous language was unchecked; and while that lasted, any effectual purification of the audi-ence and establishment of decency was impossible.

Mr Phelps, not to be diverted from his object, routed out an old Act of Parliament, in which there was a clause visiting the use of bad language in any public place with a certain fine on proving the offence before a magis-trate. This clause he caused to be printed in great placards and posted up in various conspicuous parts of the theatre. He also had it printed in small handbills. To every person who went into the gallery, one of these handbills was given with his pass-ticket. He was seriously warned that the Act would be enforced, and it *was* enforced with such rigour that on several occasions Mr Phelps stopped the play to have an offender removed; on other occasions he went into the gallery, with a cloak over his theatrical dress, to point out some other offender who had escaped the vigilance of the police; on all occasions he kept his purpose, and his inflexible determination steadily to carry it out, before the vagabonds with whom he had to deal; on no occasion showed them fear or favour.

Within a month, the offenders, thoroughly disheartened and amazed, gave in; and not an interruption was heard from the beginning to the end of a five-act tragedy!

IN THE DOME   Margaret Halstan

Margaret Halstan (1879-1967) took her stage name from Halsetown in Cornwall, where Irving lived as a boy. She acted in London for over sixty years and played the Queen of Transylvania during the entire London run of My Fair Lady, *from 1958. In conversation with Wendy Trewin in 1961, she recalled the production of* Katharine and Petruchio, *Garrick's mishandling of* The Taming of the Shrew, *which Tree unaccountably resolved to stage at Her Majesty's in 1897:*

When Tree wrote, asking me to come round to see him and suggesting that I should play Bianca, the prospect delighted me. But though we discussed the part he said nothing at all about money. At last I summoned enough courage to say 'What about my salary?' 'Oh, yes,' he replied vaguely: 'salary, of course. Come to my office and you can look at my beautiful Japanese prints while we discuss it.' (It sounded alarmingly like the chestnut about etchings.) He had not yet fully furnished the Dome of Her Majesty's in which he was to spend a good deal of his time, but he already used one of the rooms as an office, and it was here, when we had looked at the pictures, that he put his arms round me. I stiffened like a ramrod, and the next thing I knew was that I had been sent bouncing against the opposite wall, and I heard Tree's guttural tones, 'Oh, my God! There is no thrill!' My shocked surprise evaporated, and I heard myself saying, in the most business-like fashion, 'But what about my salary, Mr Tree?'

'Oh, yes. How much do you want?'

'I'd like six pounds a week.'

'All right.' He opened the door, and we got into the lift and went down to the stage. Years later, when I had acted with him often and knew him better, I reminded him of this. A pause and we found ourselves laughing.

For my first entrance as Bianca, I led on two Great Danes, beautiful creatures but guaranteed scene-stealers. It was a short run; by the end of the autumn money was short as well. Wisely, he returned in the New Year to Shakespeare unexpurgated.

In 1840 an author declared that the first blow in the destruction of the great theatres was struck by the 'extraordinary increase' in the salaries demanded by the actors. The stars of a preceding generation had been content with their hire: Munden, £14 a week; Mathews, £17; John Philip Kemble, £36. In 1839 Macready was getting £25 a night; in 1840, Tyrone Power had £120 a week; and Miss Ellen Tree [who married Charles Kean two years later], content to play for £15 a week before her visit to America, now returned 'after this rustication' to demand, and get, £25 a night! Were it not for these outrageous demands, dramatists *might be better paid; and the writer looked back longingly to the days when Mrs Inchbald got £800 for* Wives as They Were, *and Colman £1,000 for* John Bull.

A prince of actors, and my dear friend, Robert Eddison, tells of his first encounter with Beatrice De Leon who, with her husband Jack, ran the tiny 'Q' theatre, way back in the thirties. Fresh from Cambridge and looking point devise the very man, he sat telling her of his ambitions and of what he expected the theatre to offer in return. Suddenly, a secretary put her head round the door and whispered to Mrs De Leon, 'It's Miss Jackson about the salary. What shall I say?' Quick as a cat and without a pause in her reply Mrs De Leon answered, 'She's worth ten she'll ask for twelve offer her four she'll take five.' The secretary closed the door and three or four minutes later came back to say that the deal had been concluded.

How fitting that Garrick's grave in Westminster Abbey should be at the foot of the Shakespeare memorial. During his long dominion of the London stage, Garrick produced some ten Shakespeare plays a year, revived people's interest in the original texts, and restored much of Macbeth, *which had been savaged by Restoration dramatists (one colleague innocently asked him where he had stolen all the wonderful new lines); one must admit that he also staged Nahum Tate's cannibalised* King Lear, *complete with happy ending, and that his acting version of* Hamlet *was so corrupt that he dared not put it into print, but in this he was in tune with his own and later ages, which preferred their Shakespeare predigested. In 1769 he staged a Shakespearean Jubilee at Stratford upon Avon. The heavens opened, the Avon burst its banks, the Jubilee marquee was washed out, and only half a line of Shakespeare was spoken in three drenching days (Garrick had to produce a Jubilee pageant at Drury Lane to recoup some at least of his losses): but even this disaster has a humour and gallantry appropriate to the Avon's Sweet Swan.*

V

SWEET SWAN OF AVON

DAVID GARRICK reciting the Shakespeare Ode at the Stratford Jubilee amid the musical performers:

> '*Still to thy native spot thy smiles extend,*
> *And, as thou gav'st it fame, that fame defend.*
>> *And may no sacrilegious hand*
>> *Near Avon's banks be found,*
>> *To dare to parcel out the land*
>> *And limit Shakespeare's hallow'd ground.*
> *For ages free, still be it unconfin'd*
> *As broad, and general, as thy boundless mind.*'

THESE OUR SERVANTS

In May 1603 King James I issued letters patent to Shakespeare's company under the Great Seal of England, whereby he declared that he did

—license and authorise these our servants, Lawrence Fletcher, William Shakespeare, Richard Burbage, Augustine Phillips, John Heminge, Henry Condell, William Sly, Robert Armin, Richard Cowley, and the rest of their associates, freely to use and exercise the art and faculty of playing comedies, tragedies, histories, interludes, morals, pastorals, stage plays, and such others like as they have already studied, or hereafter shall use or study, as well for the recreation of our loving subjects as for our solace and pleasure, when we shall think good to see them, during our pleasure; and the said comedies, tragedies, histories, interludes, morals, pastorals, stage plays and such like, to show and exercise publicly to their best commodity ... as well within their now usual house called the Globe, within our county of Surrey; as also within any town-halls, or moot-halls, or other convenient places within the liberties and freedom of any other city, university, town, or borough whatsoever, within our said realms and dominions. Willing and commanding you, and every of you, as you tender our pleasure, not only to permit and suffer them herein, without any your lets and hindrances, or molestations, during our said pleasure, but also to be aiding and assisting to them, if any wrong be to them offered, and to allow them such former courtesies as hath been given to men of their place and quality; and also what further favour you shall show to these our servants for our sakes, we shall take kindly at your hands.

Witness ourself, at Westminster, the nineteenth day of May.

In 1622, six years after Shakespeare's death, the King's Men were on a summer tour in the Midlands and came to Stratford, perhaps to see the portrait bust of their friend and fellow player, newly erected over his tomb in the parish church. The Puritan Council hastily forbade them to perform, and a note in the borough chamberlain's accounts reads with obstinate simplicity:

To the King's Players for not playing in the Hall, six shillings.

BREAD UPON THE WATERS
John and Edward Coleman
Memoirs of Samuel Phelps (1886)

Some years ago I [Samuel Phelps] took an obscure theatre in the north of London called Sadler's Wells, and nearly the whole of my brethren in the profession, and many out of it, said it would not last a fortnight. It lasted eighteen years, and my stock-in-trade chiefly consisted of the plays of Shakespeare. Now, I determined to act, if possible, the whole of Shakespeare's plays. I acted thirty-one of all sorts, 'from aged Lear to youthful Pericles', and the thought begotten in my mind latterly was, that if that theatre could be made to pay, as I did make it pay, not making a fortune certainly, but bringing up a large family and paying my way—well, ladies and gentlemen, I thought if I could do that for eighteen years, why could it not be done again? But, mark you, I found that about every five or six years I had fresh audiences, that plays would bear repeating again and again, and by a peculiar economic method of my own I was enabled to repeat them without any very great expense. Well, if that could be done by me as a humble individual, why could it not be done by the Government of this country? Why could not a subsidised theatre, upon a moderate scale of expense, be added to the late educational scheme, by which children are forced somehow or other into school?

I maintain, from the experience of eighteen years, that the perpetual iteration of Shakespeare's words, if nothing more, going on daily for so many months in the year, must and would produce a great effect upon the public mind. Moreover, I have at this moment in my possession hundreds of letters from men of all sorts and conditions who came to see me at Sadler's Wells as boys, and who have written to me as men to say that they received their first glimpse of education at that theatre.

If I could find any member of Parliament (which I fear is hopeless) I would willingly devote what little of life remains to me, to point out the way in which this could be done, and I would willingly give evidence in the House of Commons to prove the truth of Shakespeare's educating powers. I merely throw my bread upon the waters; it may float away and disappear for ever, but I throw out the hint in the earnest hope that it may gather strength and that it may come back after many days.

WHITE TIES
J. C. Trewin
Benson and the Bensonians (1960)

The Benson company, continuing its tour (1885), played at Cheltenham in the old Theatre Royal. It was also engaged to perform *Macbeth* in the hall of the Ladies' College. Dorothea Beale, who had been headmistress for nearly thirty years, was willing to let her pupils have the benefit of a Shakespeare play in action, but she felt impelled to protect them from the unhealthy lure of the theatre. There would be no scenery, no furniture, no make-up. The men would wear evening dress. If the words 'God' or 'Hell' appeared in the text, 'Heaven' or 'below' were to be substituted, thus:

> —Come, thick night,
> And pall thee in the dunnest smoke below

and

> Heaven, Heaven, forgive us all!

Moreover, the company was not to look at the audience, which consisted entirely of girls, with one clergyman in the middle of the front row, and no one must laugh on pain of instant execution. It was, on the whole, a distracting business. The Witches, in full evening dress and led by a sepulchral and bemused George Weir, walked solemnly round a chair while discussing swine-killing, sieve-sailing, and pilot's thumbs. Later, in the Cauldron scene, when Weir, looking like a conjuror at a children's party, cast in the poisoned entrails of a toad, the Armed Head, the Bloody Child, and the Crowned Child had to bob up in turn from a chair behind a screen, perplexing to an uninformed spectator who saw only three actors in white ties. Final horror came during the Sleep-walking. Just as Janet Achurch was in career with 'All the perfumes of Arabia will not sweeten this little hand', Miss Beale walked on the stage and said peremptorily, 'Pray wait a few minutes until the gas is lit.' Miss Achurch did so.

Robert Donat used to recall that, when he played in A Midsummer Night's Dream *with Benson during the nineteen-twenties, a Scarborough headmistress insisted that, at a matinée for her school, Bottom should be called 'Bothwell' throughout. And it was so.*

BETWEEN THE PARTS   *The Theatre (July, 1885)*

On April 16, 1767, at Worcester, Roger Kemble produced Dryden's and Davenant's curious and complicated re-writing of The Tempest *(an adaptation which was all but a century old). He had to present the comedy gratis because, under the Licensing Act of 1737, persons acting for 'hire, gain or reward' without license from the Lord Chamberlain were deemed to be rogues and vagabonds; he could, however, charge for entry to a 'Concert of Musick' and give the play, free of charge, during the interval. His daughter Sarah (later Mrs Siddons), then aged eleven, played Ariel. In this remarkable adaptation, Ariel is provided with a sweetheart, Milcha, and Caliban with a sister, Sycorax, instead of the hag mother of that name who is referred to in the original text.*

MR KEMBLE'S Company of Comedians

At the Theatre at the KING'S HEAD, on Monday evening next,
being the 20 of April instant, will be performed a
CONCERT OF MUSICK, to begin at exactly half an hour after
six o'clock. TICKETS to be had at the usual places.
Between the parts of the Concert will be presented *gratis*
a celebrated COMEDY called

THE TEMPEST, or THE ENCHANTED ISLAND

(as altered from Shakespeare by Mr Dryden and Sir W. D'Avenant)

With all the Scenery, Machinery, Musick, and other Decorations
proper to the piece, entirely new.

Alonso (Duke of Mantua) . . . . Mr Kemble
Hyppolito (a youth who never saw a woman) . . . Mr Siddons
Stephan (Master of the Duke's Ship) . . . . . Mr Kemble
Amphitrite . . . . Mrs Kemble
Ariel (the Chief Spirit) . . . . Miss Kemble
and
Milcha . . . . Miss F. Kemble

The performance will open with a representation of a tempestuous
sea (in perpetual agitation) and storm, in which the usurper's ship is
wrecked; the wreck ends with a beautiful shower of fire. And the
whole to conclude with a CALM AT SEA, in which appears
Neptune, Poetick God of the Ocean, and his Royal consort,
Amphitrite, in a chariot drawn by sea horses, accompanied with
Mermaids, Tritons, &c.

*To each age its own vision of the Enchanted Island! In a film version screened in
1980, the nuptial masque was represented by Miss Elisabeth Welch and a chorus line
of musical-comedy 'mariners', singing* Stormy Weather. . . .
*Two hundred years after Roger Kemble's ingenious side-stepping of the law,
Harold Fielding followed substantially the same course with his Sunday performances of 'Music for the Millions'. He put on what were, in essence, variety shows
containing sufficient musical items to qualify as concerts, thus slipping through the
loophole in the Sunday trading regulations. All performers had to appear without
make-up, stage costume or props. At one of these shows, ventriloquist Peter Brough
inadvertently broke the law by bringing on stage his famous dummy, Archie An-
drews. No sooner had he started his act than a couple of members of the Lord's Day
Observance Society came marching on to the stage and stopped the show with a*

loudly-voiced official announcement. Not to be out-done, comedian Eddie Gray promptly offered to take Archie's place. The offer was accepted, Archie was tossed into the wings, and the act proceeded with Eddie perched on Peter's knee and playing the dummy to admiration throughout. Exit the Lord's Day Observance Society with tail between legs.

THREE DEATHS

Leigh Hunt
The Tatler

SEPTEMBER 23rd, 1831   Kean always discriminates between the manner of death with reference to its cause. Richard, for instance, has fought five combats, and has traversed the field in a frenzy; when he meets Richmond, he is in a state of the highest excitement, smarting with wounds. How finely does Kean depict this as the contest concludes!—he is reduced to a state resembling the stupor of intoxication—he falls from exhaustion—and as loss of blood may be presumed to cool his frame and restore his sanity, so does he grow calmer and calmer through the dying speech, till his mighty heart is hushed for ever.

In *Othello*, death is occasioned by piercing himself to the heart with a poignard: can you not mark the frozen shudder, as the steel enters his frame, and the choking expression, with distended eyes and open mouth, the natural attendants of such an agony? Death by a heart wound is instantaneous. Thus does he portray it; he literally dies standing; it is the dead body only of Othello that falls, heavily and at once; there is no rebound, which speaks of vitality and of living muscles. It is the dull weight of clay seeking its kindred earth.

But the scene that actors admire most (perhaps, auditors from the remoteness least) is his death in *Hamlet*. The Prince does not die of a sword-wound, but from the poison impregnated in that wound; of course, from its rapidity in doing the work of death, it must have been a powerful mineral. What are the effects of such a poison? Intense internal pain, wandering vision, swelling veins in the temple. All this Kean details with awful reality: his eye dilates and then loses lustre; he gnaws his hand in the vain effort to repress emotion; the veins thicken in his forehead; his limbs shudder and quiver, and as life grows fainter, and his hand drops from between his stiffening lips, he utters a cry of expiring nature, so exquisite that I can only compare it to the stifled sob of a fainting woman, or the little wail of a suffering child.

I think we are far too prone to believe that acting began only last Wednesday week. Reading accounts of past performances I have been astonished to find Stanislavsky constantly foreshadowed by the great actors of the past. I have come to the conclusion that Stanislavsky's achievement was to wrap the whole thing up in a single grammar which, when adopted by the USA, became The Method.

88

KING RICHARD THE THIRD

... MONEY'S WORTH

Dutton Cook
A Book of the Play (1876)

Charles Mathews, the elder, an amateur actor, paid the manager of the Richmond Theatre seven guineas and a half for permission to undertake 'the inferior, insipid part of Richmond', who does not appear until the fifth act of *Richard the Third*. The Richard of the night was a brother amateur, equally enthusiastic, one Litchfield by name. 'I cared for nothing,' wrote Mathews, 'except the last scene of Richmond, but in that I was determined to have my full swing of carte and tierce. I had no notion of paying my seven guineas and a half without indulging my passion. In vain did he [Litchfield] give indications of exhaustion; I would not allow him to give in. I drove him by main force from any position convenient for his last dying speech. The audience laughed; I heeded them not. They shouted; I was deaf. Had they hooted I should have lunged on in my unconsciousness of their interruption. I was resolved to show them all my accomplishments. Litchfield frequently whispered "Enough!", but I thought with Macbeth, "Damned be he who first cries, Hold! Enough!" I kept him at it, and I believe we fought almost literally a long hour by Shrewsbury clock. To add to the merriment, a matter-of-fact fellow in the gallery, who in his innocence took everything for reality, and who was completely wrapt up and lost by the very cunning of the scene, at last shouted out, "Why don't he shoot him?"'

... FORCE OF HABIT

Alfred Bunn
The Stage: Both Before and
Behind the Curtain (1840)

Powell's faculty of retention in particular characters was so great that all the blunders of those with whom he happened to perform could never cause him to make a blunder himself. Whether he received a right cue from the speaker to whom he had to reply, or not, was to him a matter of perfect indifference—he would give the answer set down in the text, without deviating to the right or the left. This is carrying utility to a great extreme, no doubt, but it exemplifies how far the force of habit will go.

A curious instance of this occurred some years ago at the termination of the tragedy of *Richard the Third*. Mr Elliston was enacting the part of Richmond; and, having during the evening disobeyed the injunction which the King of Denmark lays down to his Queen, 'Gertrude, do not drink', he accosted Mr Powell, who was personating Lord Stanley (for the safety of whose son Richmond is naturally anxious) thus, on his entry after the issue of the battle:

ELLISTON (Richmond):	*Your son, George Stanley, is he dead?*
POWELL (Lord Stanley):	*He is, my Lord, and safe in Leicester town.*
ELLISTON (Richmond):	*I mean,—ah!—is he missing?*
POWELL (Lord Stanley):	*He is, my Lord, and safe in Leicester town.*

And it is but justice to the memory of this punctilious veteran to say that he would have made the same reply to any question which could, at that particular moment, have been put to him.

This reminds me of a famous story about Kean playing Iago to Pope's Othello and entering the great jealousy scene, very drunk. Iago opens his disguised attack with the words 'My noble lord—' *and when Othello answers* 'What does thou say, Iago?' *he begins to seed suspicion in the Moor's mind:* 'Did Michael Cassio, when you woo'd my lady, know of your love?'; *and thus the dialogue goes on. Kean duly opened with* 'My noble lord—', *but when Othello answered* 'What does thou say, Iago?', *said again, fluently,* 'My noble lord—'. *Pope countered with* 'What does thou say, Iago?' *Kean was persistent,* 'My noble lord—' *and so the exchange proceeded until the audience broke it up.*

OTHELLO THE MOOR OF VENICE

... NAME THIS CHILD   The Drama (Vol. VII, 1825)

Within these few days they performed *Othello* at Péronne; and, in the fifth act, an actress, who played Desdemona, took the liberty *de s'accoucher*, on the stage, of a fine boy. The young lady was only *grosse de sept mois;* Othello (for so the infant was named when baptised) is very strong and healthy.

... TWO GENNELMEN

Julian Charles Young
*A Memoir of Charles Mayne Young
with extracts from the Journal
of J. C. Young (1871)*

Last week I had my house full to repletion, it being the week of the Shakespeare Tercentenary at Stratford upon Avon [1864]. When my visitors had left me, as some return to my servants for their zeal and attention, I sent them in one night, and treated them to the theatre—a place they had none of them ever been in before. The play was *Othello.*

The next day I asked my butler, one of the most respectable and trustworthy of men, but staid and demure withal, how he had liked what he had seen, and all I could elicit from him, and this in the most cautious and deliberate manner, was the following tribute to the merits of the actors: 'Well—Sir—thank you, Sir, for the treat. The performers—performed—the performance—which they had to perform—excellent well—especially the female performers—in the performance.'

I then went to the stables and asked my coachman, an honest, simple creature, but not over-burdened with imagination, how he had been impressed with what he had seen. Grinning from ear to ear with pleasurable reminiscence, he replied, with infinitely more alacrity than his predecessor— ' 'Twas really beautiful, Sir. I liked it onaccountable!'

The cheerful face clouded over as I asked him what it was about.

'I don't exactly know, Sir.'

'Do you mean to say that you saw the play of *Othello*, and can't tell me what it was about?'

'Well, Sir, if you'll believe me, I don't rightly know the meaning on't; but it was very pretty—that it were.' (Then, after a moment's reflection, as if he had recalled the thread of the tragic tale)—'Oh! I know, Sir, now; I know. It ran upon *sweethearting*. Aye that it did—and there were two gennelmen, one was in white, and the other was in black; and, what was more, both of these gents was sweet on the same gal!'

Way back in 1941 I played Iago to the Othello of a magnificent Czech actor, Frederick Valk, of whom James Agate wrote 'The Moor at last.' Arriving in Burnley, we invited our landlady to come and see the performance, and for her benefit gave of our very best. The show over, we walked home together wondering what Mrs Mayhew had thought of it. We sat ourselves down at the supper table and she came in with a rabbit pie, giving us both fine big helpings, but making no comment on the play. At last Freddy could contain himself no longer. 'Well, Mrs Mayhew,' he said, 'what did you think of it?' Mrs Mayhew paused, weighed things up very carefully in her mind, then pronounced her verdict in a forthright Lancashire accent: 'Well, sir, it certainly makes your own troubles look very, very light.'

MACBETH

... ENTER MESSENGER

Dutton Cook
A Book of the Play (1876)

A famous Lady Macbeth, starring in America, had been accidentally detained on her journey to a remote theatre. She arrived in time only to change her dress rapidly and hurry on the scene. The performers were all strangers to her. At the conclusion of her first soliloquy, a messenger should have entered to announce the coming of King Duncan. But what was her amazement to hear, in answer to her demand, 'What is your tidings?', not the usual reply,

'The King comes here tonight,' but the whisper, spoken from behind a Scotch bonnet, upheld to prevent the words reaching the ears of the audience, 'Hush, I'm Macbeth! We've cut the messenger out—go on, please!'

... ENTER PORTER   Charles Dickens (Editor)
                                                              The Life of
                                                 Charles James Mathews (1879)

Once during her engagement, the evening being hot, Mrs Siddons was tempted by a torturing thirst to avail herself of the only relief to be obtained at the moment. Her dresser, therefore, despatched a boy in great haste to 'fetch a pint of beer for Mrs Siddons'. Meanwhile the play proceeded, and on the boy's return with the frothed pitcher, he looked about for the person who had sent him on his errand, and not seeing her, inquired, 'Where is Mrs Siddons?' The scene-shifter whom he questioned, pointing his finger to the stage where she was performing the sleeping scene of Lady Macbeth, replied, 'There she is.' To the horror of the performers, the boy promptly walked on to the stage close up to Mrs Siddons, and with a total unconsciousness of any impropriety, presented the porter! Her distress may be imagined; she waved the boy away in her grand manner several times without effect. At last the people behind the scenes, by dint of beckoning, stamping, &c., succeeded in getting him off with the beer, while the audience were in an uproar of laughter, which the dignity of the actress was unable to quell for several minutes.

... STAR-CROSSED   Mrs John Drew
                                               Autobiographical Sketch (1899)

Mr Macready was a terribly nervous actor; any little thing which happened unexpectedly irritated him beyond endurance. Once, at the Park, New York, *Macbeth* was the play. Mrs Sloman, an old-fashioned actress, dressed Lady Macbeth in the manner which prevailed in her early life—in black velvet, point lace and pearl beads. In the murder scene part of Macready's dress caught on the tassels of her pearl girdle; the string broke, the beads fell on the floor, softly, with a pretty rhythmic sound, distinctly heard through the intense silence of the scene. This so exasperated Mr Macready that he was almost frantic, until, with the final line of the scene, 'Wake Duncan with thy knocking! I would thou couldst!', he threw Mrs Sloman off the stage, with words which I hope were unheard by the public.

... 'HOLD, ENOUGH!'   Edward Stirling
                                                   Old Drury Lane (*1881*)

Another of Neville's Theatres, in this case a real one. *Macbeth* acted without
Macduff; Neville played Macbeth and Hecate (in a cloak), singing well. His
family doctor kindly fought the tyrant in the absence of the Thane of Fife, at
Manchester. Neville spoke his own part and Macduff's, addressing the astonished medical gentleman:

'You would say, then' (Shakespeare's words), 'you're not of woman
born.' He seized the trembling actor (a very old one). 'Damn'd be you if you
call out "enough".'

An awful fight, on Neville's side. Macduff cautiously held up his sword, to
protect his gray head.

*I am reminded of a tolerant stage-hand who had once to take over the part of King
Duncan. He had been well-coached in his lines and survived the opening scenes.
However, when they came to Duncan's entry as Macbeth's honoured guest, with the
King's courteous greeting to his host,* 'This castle hath a pleasant seat; the air
nimbly and sweetly recommends itself unto our gentle senses,' *memory failed
the poor man. He filled in bravely, getting the sense if not the words:* 'You've got a
lovely place 'ere, guvnor.'

HANDFULS OF WORDS   Dutton Cook
                                                   A Book of the Play (*1876*)

'What's the use of bothering about a handful of words?' demanded a veteran
stroller. 'I never stick. I always say something and get on, and no one has
hissed me yet!' It was probably this performer who, during his impersonation of Macbeth, finding himself at a loss as to the text soon after the
commencement of his second scene with Lady Macbeth, coolly observed:
'Let us retire, dearest chuck, and con this matter over in a more sequestered
spot, far from the busy haunts of men. Here the walls and doors are spies, and
our every word is echoed far and near. Come, then, let's away. False heart
must hide, you know, what false heart dare not show.'

A prompter could be of little service to a gentleman so fertile in resources.
He may be left to pair off with that provincial Montano who modernised his
speech in reference to Cassio:

> *And 'tis great pity that the noble Moor*
> *Should hazard such a place as his own second*
> *With one of an ingraft infirmity:*
> *It were an honest action to say*
> *So to the Moor—*

into: 'It's a pity, don't you think, that Othello should place such a man in such an office. Hadn't we better tell him so, sir?'

MACBETH MENU

Bernard Miles
Mermaid Theatre programme

Present grace spoken by Banquo

Slab gruel
Marrowless bones tied to stake
Grilled paddock
Unseamed chaps (twice done and then done double)
Roast benison lapped in proof

Great Nature's second course

Careless trifles
Macduff
Temple-haunting tartlets with kerns and whey

Gallowglasses of porter
Drugged posset (natural ruby)

Indissoluble ties (knitted) will be worn with borrowed robes
Rugged looks will be sleek'd o'er

TUNING HER PIPES

Benjamin Robert Haydon

Haydon records in his journal an evening spent at Mrs Siddons's house at the upper end of Baker Street. She was then sixty-five. To entertain her guests, who included the portrait painter Sir Thomas Lawrence, she read Macbeth.

MARCH 10th, 1821 She acts Macbeth herself better than either Kemble or Kean. It is extraordinary the awe this wonderful woman inspires. After her first reading the men retired to tea. While we were all eating toast and tinkling cups and saucers, she began again. It was like the effect of a Mass bell at Madrid. All noise ceased; we slunk to our seats like boors, two or three of the most distinguished men of the day, with the very toast in their mouths, afraid to bite. It was curious to see Lawrence in this predicament, to hear him bite by degrees, and then stop for fear of making too much crackle, his eyes full of water from the constraint; and at the same time to hear Mrs Siddons's 'eye of newt and toe of frog', and then to see Lawrence give a sly bite, and then look awed and pretend to be listening. I went away highly gratified, and as I stood on the landing-place to get cool I overheard my own servant in the hall say: 'What! Is that the old lady making such a noise?' 'Yes.' 'Why, she makes as much noise as ever!' 'Yes,' was the answer, 'she tunes her pipes as well as ever she did.'

RELICS   *The Drama (Vol. I, 1821)*

STRATFORD UPON AVON   Mrs Hornby, the Authoress, who styles herself a lineal descendant of SHAKESPEARE, and who till lately occupied the house in which he was born, has lately been ejected by the owner. She circulated handbills on the occasion, stating her rent having been raised from £10 to £40 per annum, she was obliged to quit; but that she had taken up her residence in an opposite house, carrying with her the relics of her great ancestor, and hoped therefore to be still favoured with visits from the curious. The poet's house is now occupied by a butcher, who is on the look out for a new collection of relics, and attends all the sales of furniture that occur, in order to meet with a set to his mind.

John Forster gave Henry Irving an old dinner knife which was discovered in the foundations of Shakespeare's home in Stratford when the floor was being relaid. This knife came down to Sir Henry's grandson, Laurence, who passed it on to me (along with a pair of press-cutting scissors). I have looked in vain for the scratched letters WS on the knife's bone handle.... Clubs such as The Garrick in London and The Players in New York are loaded with relics—scripts, playbills and programmes, brooches, rings and buckles, daggers and swords, boots, shoes and slippers, helmets and tiaras, all the insignia of stage royalty, all the clutter of the dressing-room. I suppose that knowing their profession to be so essentially transient, actors seek thus to substantiate their reality.

ALL THE PERFUMES   *The London Shakespeare Tercentenary*
OF ARABIA   *Festival official programme (1864)*

THE BARD OF AVON'S PERFUME

In a neat box, with a Photograph of the Poet,
and appropriate quotations. Price 2s. 6d.

The Shakespeare Tercentenary was celebrated at Stratford by the renovation of the town, in readiness for hordes of visitors who never arrived, and by the building of a lavishly decorated Grand Pavilion. Prospero's speech, The cloud-capp'd towers, *was inscribed round the pavilion and proved to be sadly appropriate; the scenery and furnishings had to be sold off at knock-down prices, leaving not a rack behind. In London the Great National Festival was marked by a straggling procession to Primrose Hill, where Samuel Phelps was to plant 'the people's oak in honour of the people's poet'. Queen Victoria sent from Windsor a fine young oak which professional gardeners planted early on Festival morning; Mr Phelps 'planted' it again and made a short, graceful speech; a lady sprinkled the tree with Avon water and christened it* The Shakespeare Oak; *and an ode was recited, written by Miss Eliza Cook for the occasion. A hundred years later in April, 1964, there was to be another festival, another oak, another poem:*

AN ENGLISH OAK   V. C. Clinton-Baddeley

'Nor marble, nor the gilded monuments
Of Princes, shall outlive this powerful rhyme'—
The boast was courtly, but (as happened) true:
Your lightest words, good sir, yield not to Time.

The marble's chipped, the gold is smeared with grey,
The broken canopy conceals the bone,
Yours, surely, was a modest claim, good sir:
An English oak lasts longer than the stone.

The oak that sheltered Edward's Parliament;
The Abbot's tree; the Reformation Oak;
That ancient tree from which Glendower watched
While Harry Hotspur fought with Bolingbroke,

All these were old when you were born, good sir—
And live, great oaks from Saxon acorns sprung;
And even now, new-green in Arden stand
Oaks that were inches-high when you were young.

An oak, 'unwedgeable' (your word, good sir)
Is liker you than any mason's skill:
And so, our tribute on this famous day,
We plant an oak upon this famous hill.

Recklessly once you said your words would last
'So long as men can breathe or eye can see'—
Lend us a little of your humour, sir,
That just so long may last this English tree.

Seen here are some of the finest Shakespearean players of the past. What a company! From left to right, top to bottom, they are: THOMAS BETTERTON (?1635–1710), whose Hamlet was portrayed with such intensity that the audience, seeing the Ghost through his eyes, trembled at the sight; the supreme and unparalleled DAVID GARRICK (1717–1779); CHARLES MACKLIN (?1697–1797), first to insist on playing Shylock as a true-life character instead of the Restoration's buffoon; MRS PRITCHARD (1711–1768), one of Garrick's leading ladies, and the greatest Lady Macbeth of her day; SARAH SIDDONS (1755–1831), so stately an off-stage matron, so passionate and tender an actress; GEORGE FREDERICK COOKE (1807–1863), whose short, abrupt and savage utterance gave extraordinary conviction to his Iago, Shylock and Richard III; JOHN HENDERSON (1747–1785), once regarded as the heir to Garrick's mantle, killed tragically young when his wife accidentally gave him an overdose of a sleeping potion; and lastly JOHN PHILIP KEMBLE (1757–1823), who with his sister Sarah was to reign supreme in London for more than a quarter of a century.

As children in their father's troupe of strolling players, Sarah Kemble (later to be Mrs Siddons), her brothers John Philip, Stephen and Charles, and the rest of Roger Kemble's brood, trudged the highways and byways of England. Like all the great stars of the eighteenth- and nineteenth-century theatre, they learned their craft the hard way. They and their fellows kept the theatre alive and kicking through hard times, and our debt to them is inestimable.

VI

THE POMPING FOLK

EMINENT BY-GONE PERFORMERS
OF
SHAKSPEARE'S CHARACTERS.

Strolling is the life-blood of the theatre. To be on the move, ready to meet the unexpected—the cat-calls, the rotten apples, the eggs—the bountiful landladies, the suppers of sausages and beer—tucked up in a double bed-sitter with a benevolent female partner—setting out next day to pad the hoof for cheese and buttermilk—what more has life to offer?

One of the greatest troupers I have ever known, perhaps the greatest ever born, was May Hallatt, a splendid actress who was well past pensionable age when World War II broke out. She packed her traps and set off to follow the army. Her ship was torpedoed on the voyage out, her belongings lost, but for two years this unquenchable woman, then in her seventies, marched across Africa in the army's wake, hitching lifts on lorries, sleeping on the sand, entertaining the troops night after night. She came home with nothing but the clothes on her back and a yakskin overcoat from the Caucasus. She was the sum and total of all the race of strolling players—and I daresay she would have risen triumphant even above Mr Chetwood's fatal rum-punch——

AN UNBLESSED COMPANY

W. R. Chetwood
*A General History of
the Stage* (1749)

Our plantations in America have been voluntarily visited by some itinerants, Jamaica in particular. I had an account from a gentleman who was possessed of a large estate in the island that a company in the year 1733 came there and cleared a large sum of money. They received 370 pistoles the first night of *The Beggar's Opera*, but within the space of two months they buried their third Polly and two of their men. The gentlemen of the island for some time took their turns upon the stage to keep up the diversion; but this did not hold long; for in two months more there were but one old man, a boy, and a woman of the company left. The rest died either with the country distemper, or the common beverage of the place, the noble spirit of rum-punch, which is generally fatal to new-comers. The shattered remains, with upwards of 2,000 pistoles in bank, embarked for Carolina to join another company at Charlestown, but were cast away in the voyage. Had the Company been more blessed with the virtue of sobriety, &c., they might perhaps have lived to carry home the liberality of those generous islanders.

THE STROLLING TRIBE

Charles Churchill
The Apology (1761)

The strolling tribe—a despicable race!—
Like wandering Arabs, shift from place to place.
Vagrants by law, to justice, open laid,
They tremble, of the beadle's lash afraid,
And fawning, cringe for wretched means of life
To madam Mayoress, or his Worship's wife.
The mighty monarch, in theatric sack,
Carries his whole regalia at his back;
His royal consort heads the female band,
And leads the heir apparent in her hand.

In shabby state they strut, and tatter'd robe,
The scene a blanket, and a barn the globe;
No high conceits their moderate wishes raise,
Content with humble profit, humble praise.
Let dowdies simper, and let bumpkins stare,
The strolling pageant hero treads in air:
Pleased, for his hour he to mankind gives law,
And snores the next out on a truss of straw.

PROFLIGACY IN ROMFORD

Edward Stirling
Old Drury Lane (1881)

Applying to a local magistrate (period 1830) for permission to perform a few nights in the Town Hall of Romford during a London vacation, the ruling Dogberry met my humble request in this fashion:

'What, sir! bring your beggarly actors into this town to demoralise the people? No, sir; I'll have no such profligacy here in Romford; poor people shall not be wheedled out of their money by your tomfooleries. The first player that comes here I'll clap him in the stocks as a rogue and vagabond. Good morning, sir!', motioning his servant to usher me out.

WAR-WHOOP

William Dunlap

George Frederick Cooke, a great figure in the early nineteenth-century theatre, was a man of culture, originality and physical power. He was one of the first British actors to find fame in America (witness pages 71 and 125). A glorious story told of him—

and probably a true one—describes how he arrived forty minutes late for a performance in Liverpool. The angry audience shouted, 'Apologise, Cooke! Apologise!
Apologise!' Cooke stalked to the front of the stage. 'Apologise be damned!' he said.
'There is not a single stone in your blasted city that is not cemented with the blood of a
slave!' and he walked out of the theatre. Do they come like that these days?

In his memoir of Cooke, issued in 1813, Dunlap quotes Ryley's account of an
exhibition of scalping given on stage by a supposed Red Indian, when Cooke was
playing in Stephen Kemble's company:

The bills of the day announced that, between the acts of the play, Prince
Anamaboo would give a lively representation of the *scalping operation;* he
would likewise give the Indian war-whoop, in all its various tones, the
tomahawk exercise, and the mode of feasting at an Abyssinian banquet.. . .
At the end of the third act his *highness* walked forward with dignified step,
flourishing his tomahawk, and cut the air, exclaiming 'Ha, ha! Ho, ho!' Next
entered a man with his face blacked, and a piece of bladder fastened to his
head with gum; the *prince*, with a large carving knife, commenced the
scalping operation, which he performed in a manner truly *imperial*, holding
up the skin in token of triumph. Next came the war-whoop, which was a
combination of dreadful and discordant sounds; and lastly the Abyssinian
banquet, consisting of raw beefsteaks; these he made into rolls as large as his
mouth would admit, and devoured them in a *princely* and dignified manner.
Having completed his cannibal repast, he flourished his tomahawk in an
exulting manner, exclaimed 'Ha, ha! Ho, ho!' and made his exit.. . .
The property man's bill explains by the following item who it was that
was scalped: *Goin on myself to be scalp 2s. 6d.*

I once owned one half of Cooke's diary, written in Appleby Gaol, where he was
apprehended when trying to escape from Manchester to Scotland without paying his
landlady. When I read Dunlap's life of Cooke, I found that he confirmed the
existence of the diary. He gave the whereabouts of the first half but said that the
second half had disappeared—'No one knows where it is.' I wrote in the margin of
my copy, 'No, because I have it!' But eventually I sold it to Harvard University
Library, as I did most of my theatrical collection, when the Mermaid Theatre put the
family into financial straits.

PADDING THE HOOF   John and Edward Coleman
                                    Memoirs of Samuel Phelps (1886)

One day, while hanging about the Harp, I [Samuel Phelps] came across a
fellow of the name of Hay, who afterwards became a famous comedian at
Exeter and Plymouth. Over a glass of beer he told me that he was then on his

way to an engagement at Brighton. The day before he had left Abbott's Company in Lincolnshire. They were located at Gainsboro', and he was quite sure that they wanted a sharp young fellow like myself.

'Cut this game,' said he, 'you'll never get an engagement here to the day of judgment—make the best of your way to Gainsboro'. Stay. I'll give you a line.' And he wrote me an introduction to the manager, there and then. 'Now, hook it at once, and if you can't manage the coach fare, get on to the Great North Road, pad the hoof for twenty or thirty miles, till the mail overtakes you, and ten to one they'll give you a lift the rest of the way for a few shillings. Goodbye, and good luck to you.'

When I got home of course *she* wouldn't hear of my proposed journey. We had never been parted since our marriage, and she was convinced I should be robbed and murdered on the highway. I soothed her down and pointed out what a desirable opening it would be. Of course we couldn't doubt that I should be immediately snapped up by the manager, that I should take the provincial public by storm, &c. She was even more convinced than I was that I had only to be seen to be appreciated; so at length she yielded to my arguments, and it was settled that I was to start on Monday morning.

It was then Thursday, and the first thing was to hold a consultation over our finances, which were very low indeed. I couldn't take an engagement without my 'props', and I had to ascertain how few I could do with, and how much, or rather how little, I had to pay for them. In this emergency, I bethought me of my new acquaintance, and returned to the Harp to consult him.

As luck would have it, he had been playing the interesting heroes, and was now going into low comedy. He sold me a handful of valuable things, including a ringlet wig, for which he had no further use, for a crown. Then he accompanied me to Vinegar Yard, where we picked up a pair of russet boots, a pair of sandals, a pair of fleshings, a pair of worsted tights, an old sword, and a few other odds and ends, for thirty shillings.

Bidding my kind friend once more 'Goodbye', I trotted home with my purchases, as proud as a dog with two tails. The time 'twixt Thursday night and Monday morning was passed in alternate fits of hope and despondency, with intervals of experiments in making lace collars, cuffs and ruffles, ballet shirts, and other little nicknacks.

When we came to cast up accounts, at the last moment, we found we had barely two pounds left. Of course, *she* wanted me to take it all, but on this point I was inflexible. I took ten shillings, and left her the rest, and so, having previously arranged that I would send for her as soon as I got to Gainsborough, with aching hearts and tearful eyes we parted on that memorable winter morning.

It was a sharp frost, and bitterly cold. There was one comfort, I was well wrapped up; in fact, she tied round my neck the muffler which she had herself knitted for the occasion. I stuck my sword (which was covered with brown paper for decency's sake) through the handle of my carpet-bag, slung it over my shoulder, and away I trudged in the dark.

At first this precious bag seemed light as a feather, but after I had walked twenty miles or more, and there was no sign of the coach, the infernal thing had become a load for a pack-horse. I struggled on a few miles further, and then giving it up as a bad job, came to anchor on a heap of stones by the roadside, where I lighted my pipe and awaited the coach.

Half-an-hour, an hour, another half-hour. Blame the coach! Would it never come? At last I heard the tantara of the guard's horn and the sound of wheels; the next moment she came rattling over the summit of the hill with the horses in a lather.

Up sprang I on the heap of stones. 'Holloa! Holloa!' I shouted. I might as well have shouted to the dead, for neither the driver nor the guard deigned to take the slightest notice of my existence. The passengers did, though, and no wonder, for in my rage I started back and fell heels over head into the ditch behind. Fortunately for me, it was a dry one. The unfeeling ruffians positively roared with laughter as they dashed by, and I was left with my head in the ditch and my heels in the air.

The passing glimpse I caught of the coach, however, enabled me to distinguish that it was packed inside and out, which accounted for the lordly disdain of guard and driver. There was nothing for it but to limp on to the next town, where I resolved to stay for the night, and try my luck with the next coach the following day.

After another drag of seven or eight miles I reached my destination footsore and weary. Of course my resources would not admit of my putting up at the hotel where the coach stopped, so after hunting about for another half-an-hour I found a fourth-rate public house called The Three Jolly Beggars, where I secured a bed for sixpence. Then I made friends with the mistress, a great ample-breasted jolly woman of fifty, with black eyes and hair, and red cheeks. This honest soul gave me a capital supper of tea, new bread, bacon and eggs for another sixpence.

I soothed myself with a pipe before I turned in to roost, where, thinking of my poor lass, and wishing that her dear arms were around my neck, I fell fast asleep, and never woke till the landlady came and shook me up at nine to tell me that breakfast was ready. I was out of bed like a shot. Finding myself rather stiff in the fetlocks, I improvised a tub as well as I could, and sluiced myself from head to foot. That freshened me up a bit. Then more tea, more new bread, more bacon and eggs, and they freshened me up still more.

I had to brush my own shoes, but that didn't hurt me. When I came to settle up I made myself free of The Three Jolly Beggars for two bob. That didn't hurt me either, especially as my good landlady threw me in a lunch in the shape of a couple of hard-boiled eggs, a slice of fat bacon, a huge chunk of brown bread, and a pint bottle of beer. Then, bless her heart, with all sorts of kind wishes, she put me on the way, and at twelve o'clock I set off again

John Liston (1776–1846), schoolmaster turned actor, was a particular favourite with George IV. His acting career opened with The Heir-at-Law *at Weymouth, an all-time flop, but he did better on the Newcastle circuit, and eventually became a highly successful and well paid comedian, and gifted dancer. His greatest triumph was at the Haymarket in 1825, when he played the title role in* Paul Pry.

with my sword, and my carpet-bag.

The day was fine, though frosty; and as I had no particular occasion for haste I strolled leisurely along until the coach overtook me, when I was delighted to find there were very few passengers. As soon as I hailed the driver he stopped. The guard leapt down, and we soon struck a bargain. Five bob for the lift, and a bob apiece for the guard and driver, would leave me a solitary 'Roberto' at the end of the journey.

Up I jumped and took my seat on the box. The coachy was a smart, intelligent old fellow, and better still, a great playgoer. He beguiled the time by talking about Mrs Siddons, the Kembles, Charles Young, Kean, Incledon, Macready, Elliston, Liston, and Mathews; and, above all, of John Emery, who was an acquaintance of his.

When I mentioned my business at Gainsborough, he became very communicative, told me that my manager (for, of course, I had made up my mind that Mr Abbott was to be my manager!) was a man of great probity, and much respected in the district, that the company were eminently respectable people, and that some of them were very clever.

The drive was exhilarating, and by about four o'clock, when we stopped to change horses and refresh ourselves, I was as hungry as a hunter, so I said I would walk on a bit, which I did, and pitched into my luncheon. I had put it out of sight long before the coach overtook me. I don't mean to say I ate it all but I stowed one half away in my stomach, and the other half in my pocket in reserve for an emergency.

At last, about nine, we got to Gainsboro', and off I trotted to look out for lodgings. I soon got a couple of snug little rooms at a widow's, a Mrs Wilkinson, for three bob a week, and went to bed after making a hearty supper on the remains of my lunch.

In the early 'thirties I was touring in Once in a Lifetime, *the brilliant comedy by Moss Hart and George Kaufman (recently—and too soon!—revived in London). My companion was Eric Barker, later famous for his radio work. In Birmingham we found lodgings—or 'digs' as they are called by theatricals—with a Mrs Pellew, living in one of the humbler parts of the city. She showed us the double bed-sitter. The room was clean, the bed comfortable, and Mrs Pellew as rosy and plump and amiable as Samuel Phelps's hostess. We struck a bargain with her: 35 shillings a week, we to buy in our own provisions, she to do the cooking. She said, 'Well, I'll leave you to get unpacked, then', and made to leave us, but turned in the doorway and said, 'One last thing. Should you have occasion to use the chamber pot, kindly* don't *put it back under the bed. The steam rusts the springs.'*

FOUR-POSTER   Dutton Cook
                                              A Book of the Play (1876)

A strolling company, performing in Wales, had for theatre a bedroom and for stage a large four-post bed. The spaces on either side were concealed from the audience by curtains, and formed the tiring-rooms of the ladies and gentlemen of the troupe. On this very curious stage the comedian afterwards famous as Little Knight, but then new to his profession, appeared as Acres in *The Rivals*, and won great applause.

ON THE ROAD

James Lloyd
My Circus Life (1925)

Among the strolling players, who could forget the tenting folk of the circus, making the most of every casual encounter. G. K. Chesterton thought so highly of the little book from which this brief scene is taken that he wrote a preface for it, saying that circus folk, though humble, were never to be despised.

The show was travelling one Sunday to Limerick. On the road I met a gentleman riding a beautiful red and white horse. I stopped him, and asked if he would sell it. He replied: 'I would talk about it, if it was not Sunday.' I said, 'Now, supposing it was not Sunday, would you sell it?' He said: 'Supposing it was not Sunday, I would.' I said: 'Supposing it was not Sunday, what do you ask for the horse?' 'Supposing it was not Sunday, I would take thirty-five pounds.' I said: 'Now, supposing it was not Sunday, I will give you twenty-eight pounds.' He said: 'My last words. If it was not Sunday I would take thirty pounds.' I said: 'Supposing it was not Sunday, I will give you that sum.' 'Supposing it was not Sunday' I bought the horse. I named it 'Supposition.'

LIVING VAN

Sam Wild
*Old Wild's: a Nursery
of Strolling Players* (1888)

In the various towns and villages at which we stayed during our yearly peregrinations, I had for some time past experienced difficulty in obtaining lodgings for my family. It was a large one now, and required considerable attention; besides which we carried a private wardrobe of more than ordinary dimensions, and bed and bedding specially for the younger children. Hence the difficulty in meeting with the necessary accommodation will readily be perceived. Under these circumstances I decided to have a van built, and, like other travellers I was constantly meeting with, be always at home wherever I went. I broached the subject to Mr James Bedford, at Halifax, during the fair, in June 1858, and he engaged to carry out my requirements. I also agreed with him to make me another van for the scenery, etc. During the progress of the work I came over to Halifax several times, but it was not until the Easter of 1859, and while my company was at Blackburn, that the vans were completed, and that was the time, too, when I came over to fetch them. They were capitally made things, both of them.

The living van was considered by competent judges to be the handsomest ever turned out. It was sixteen feet long by eight feet six inches wide, and full of cornices and carved work. The outside panels were painted bird's eye maple, and stood out in bold relief against a groundwork of ultramarine blue. Inside, the van was oak-grained throughout. It was divided into two compartments, bedroom and sitting-, or more properly living-, room. In the first were two large shelves, which, with the help of mattresses and blankets, were converted nightly into two beds. The shelves, being attached by hinges to the side of the van, were capable of being lowered or raised at pleasure. This arrangement enabled us to keep tidy, and, in a sense, enlarged our sleeping apartment during the daytime, when a large curtain effectually concealed our little berths from view. Then there was other shelving in the room, also a nest of drawers, a locker, and a couple or so of chairs. The windows were partly of coloured glass, were large and of oblong shape, with venetian blinds before them. The living-room contained two small fire-places, each boasting a chimneypiece of its own, and over one of these was a large handsome gilt mirror. There were several lockers in this room, more shelving, two—I believe three—tiny chiffoniers, a side table, a rocking-chair, an easy chair, and of smaller chairs a few. Full of business though I generally was, I always contrived to get into that rocking-chair whenever I wished to have a good think about anything. Then we had gas fittings in both rooms, handsome brackets, and cheery-looking globes; but these, of course, could only serve us, except for ornament, when we were located where gas was procurable. Then we had—in fine, we had well nigh every comfort we required; certainly every convenience that a van of this description is capable of affording.

The living van, and the scenery, or as I afterwards called it, the 'colossal' van, cost me, inclusive of furniture for the former, over £150.

For real luxury, though, I turn to Lillie Langtry's description of the railway car built for her when she was travelling in America. She christened it 'Lalee' (from an Indian word for 'flirt'). There were ten rooms, including a saloon complete with piano, a bathroom with silver fittings, and a maid's room equipped with a sewing-machine; hangings of green silk brocade, curtains of rose silk and Brussels lace; a pantry, a kitchen, and ice chests each big enough to accommodate a whole stag. The exterior was painted blue, emblazoned with wreaths of lilies, the roof white, the fitments of brass wrought into lily designs, and the platforms of teak brought from India for the purpose. The whole contraption was so heavy that Lillie was more than once officially warned to avoid insecure bridges. I am reminded of Queen Victoria and Prince Albert making their first train journey from Windsor to Paddington in 1842. 'Not so fast next time, Mr Conductor,' said the Prince when the train reached twenty miles an hour. It is said that on a later journey, to the north, orders were given that the blinds should be drawn as the train approached Birmingham, and not raised again until it passed Wolverhampton, so that Her Majesty should not gaze upon the giants who, stripped to the waist, amid smoke and flame, were hammering out girders, bridges, railway lines, piers, all the wealth of an industrial Empire.

John Richardson's stage and fittings were at first of a very rude character. The first floor of a public-house was turned into a theatre, and the platform or parade, which was fitted up outside the window, formed an arch over the stalls of the sellers of gingerbread nuts and fried fish, which stood below. The audience had to reach the theatre by means of a ladder, communicating from the platform to the fair. Twenty-one times a day were the unlucky performers called upon to go through their parts. The audiences were not very fastidious, and as long as they had a broadsword combat and a ghost, the actors were at liberty to play all sorts of tricks with the drama. The length of the performance was indeed usually regulated by the number of people waiting to enter the show. When it was thought that there was a sufficient quantity of visitors outside to form another audience, some one would be sent in to inquire in a loud voice if John Audley was there. This was a signal to the actors to cut the part short; and to abridge a performance is very commonly called to 'John Audley' it. This trick was first practised by Shuter at his booth in 1759.

Richardson's show became one of the principal features of many of the fairs of the kingdom—Bartlemy and Greenwich being his headquarters—but it was not until after many years, and many hardships, that he was enabled to give his show that appearance of splendour which we were accustomed to associate with it in our younger days.

I once did fourteen Treasure Islands *in a week—again, in order to get the Mermaid Theatre out of trouble; and my old friend and teacher Baliol Holloway did six different plays in one week at a theatre in the Midlands, but that was in the days when you were expected to have by heart a stock range of plays—lines and moves together—the positions on stage being established by tradition and learned as one with the script.*

STAGE ARMY   John and Edward Coleman
Memoirs of Samuel Phelps (1886)

On his arrival at Gainsboro' (described on pages 102–106), Samuel Phelps applied to join Mr Abbott's company:

I was engaged there and then, at a salary of a guinea a week, and it was arranged that I was to open on the following night in the Third Witch, King Duncan, the First Murderer, Ross, one of the Apparitions, one of the witches' solos, the Physician, and the 'cream-faced loon', in *Macbeth*. Yes, and I did 'em too, my boy, or I suppose I did for 'em. Anyhow, I spoke the words, or something like them.

I don't think I distinguished myself very highly. The fact is, I had only one wig for the Witch and Duncan, and as I did not know much about the art of making up, I couldn't get the beastly stuff off my face in time for my changes. So there was a family likeness between the weird sister, Duncan, the Physician, and the unfortunate 'cream-faced loon'. I got through Ross's great scene with Macduff, with only about half-a-dozen sticks. I even struggled through the Physician with but an occasional break-down, but when I came to form part of Macbeth's valiant army in the one scene, and of Macduff's yet more valiant army in the other—when I found myself coming off in one entrance as a 'first officer', and rushing on in the next as the 'cream-faced loon'—I got so helplessly mixed, that I completely 'corpsed' poor Hamilton, our leading man, a great strapping fellow he was—six feet high or more. The eagle's feather in his Scotch bonnet touched the border lights, which singed the tip of it. When he bade 'the devil damn me black' for a 'cream-faced loon', and inquired 'Where got'st thou that goose look?', I ingenuously responded, 'My lord, there are ten thousand geese without', which effectually took the wind out of his sails in that situation. Next moment I came rushing on and gasped—and gasped—deuce a word could I articulate. He glared at me and hissed through his teeth—'Now then, stupid, spit it out!' Thus encouraged, in trembling accents I volunteered the information that—

> *As I did stand my watch upon the hill,*
> *I look'd toward Birnam, and anon methought*
> *The wood began to move upon its head—*

The bold Macbeth didn't wait to hear any more, but rushed at me, and half strangled me. He let me have 'Liar and slave!' and the rest of it with a vengeance, and literally flung me off the stage, landing me in a heap in the prompt corner.

Under other circumstances, of course, I should have resented this rough-and-ready punishment for my stupidity, but I was so hopelessly demoralised by my incapacity, and so conscious of my own shortcomings, that I submitted to it like a lamb; in fact, I rather fancied that I deserved all, and more, than I got.

When Macbeth made his exit, a minute afterwards, avowing his intention to 'die with harness on his back', he went for me, sword in hand, and I think if he had got at me my professional career would have ended there and then. Fortunately, however, I had nothing more to do with him, so I kept out of the way until the play was over, and he had simmered down a bit, when I made my excuses in the best way I could. Although a little hot-headed, he was a fine, large-hearted fellow, and not half a bad actor. My apologies were graciously accepted, and soon after we became sworn chums.

BARNSTORMING

Joseph Jefferson
Autobiography (1890)

That fine actor Joseph Jefferson (1829-1905) looked back from the heights of a theatrical career which brought him fame and success on both sides of the Atlantic to the time when he was little more than a boy, with a company of strolling players in the Southern States. The America he knew then, vast, bountiful, its forests full of game, its plains covered with herds of buffalo, vanished within a generation. The wild pigeons he shot for the company's dinner were passenger pigeons, two or three times the size of today's ring-doves. Millions of these beautiful birds, rare examples of Nature's handiwork, were massacred by shotgun enthusiasts, and they are now extinct.

Upon our return to Nashville it was time to think of going South, as most of the company had engagements in New Orleans, Mobile, and Texas, but the Cumberland River had fallen so low that no steamboat could navigate it. In this dilemma there was but one course left: the company must come together, buy a barge, fit up a cabin, caboose, and sleeping-apartments. This was done. Where the money came from to pay for the boat and the lumber I cannot tell, but this floating camp was put together, and we all departed down the river in the queerest-looking craft that ever carried a legitimate stock company of the old school. To a boy of my age this was heaven. To stand my watch at night gave me that manly feeling that a youngster, just before he grows his beard, enjoys beyond everything.

The whole of this trip was to me delightful. It was in that rich and mellow season when the foliage seems to change from day to day. The river was full of ducks, which I could sometimes shoot from the deck of the flatboat; great flocks of wild pigeons filled the air for days together, so that I could supply our table well with game. There was a small set of scenery on board that had been brought in case of an emergency. We had used it only in Clarksville so far, but now the time came when it could be displayed and utilised in a manner 'never before attempted in the annals of the stage'.

When we reached the Ohio the river widened out, and some stretches were from five to six miles in length; so, if we had a fair wind blowing downstream, by hoisting one of the scenes for a sail we could increase our speed from two to three miles an hour. A hickory pole was cut from the shore, and a drop-scene, with a wood painted on one side and a palace on the other, was unfurled to the breeze. The wonder-stricken farmers and their wives and children would run out of their log-cabins and, standing on the river bank, gaze with amazement at our curious craft. It was delightful to watch the steamboats as they went by. The passengers would crowd the deck and look with wonder at us. For a bit of sport the captain and I would vary the picture, and as a boat steamed past we would first show them the wood scene, and then suddenly swing the sail around, exhibiting the gorgeous palace. Adding to this sport, our leading man and the low comedian would sometimes get a couple of old-fashioned broadswords and fight a melo-dramatic combat on the deck. There is no doubt that at times our barge was taken for a floating lunatic asylum.

The company sailed south to Cairo, where the Ohio River joins the Mississippi, and thence to Memphis, where they quitted the barge and went on by steamboat to New Orleans.

We now entered upon a course of the most primitive acting, going from town to town and giving entertainments in the dining-rooms of the hotels. As there were no papers published in these small villages, there were no printing-offices, consequently no bills; so flaming announcements of our arrival in a bold handwriting were displayed in the three important points of the town, viz., the hotel, the post office and the barber shop. It fell to my duty, being an adept with the brush, to write, or rather paint, these advertise-ments. The plays were acted in costume, but without scenery or curtain. The nightly receipts were small—just about enough to get us from place to place.

Our objective point was the town of Liberty, Mississippi; but there was some difficulty in getting there, as the distance was greater than we could accomplish in a day. A farmer who had been to the theatre the night before for the first time in his life was so struck by the performance that he proposed to have his teams brought in and take us to his farmhouse, about twenty-five miles distant. According to his suggestion we were to rest for a day, give an entertainment in his barn, and so go on to Liberty.

'But,' said my brother, 'you tell me there is no other house there but your own. What shall we do for an audience?'

'Well,' said the farmer, 'all my family will come, to begin with, and there's a dozen or more on 'em; then there's eight or ten farmhouses close by, and if one of your men will drive there with my son and blow the horn they will all come, for there ain't one on 'em ever seen a play before. I'll insure you a full house.'

So the matter was settled, and we actually played in a barn, the house that we staid in being the only one in sight. It seemed in vain to look for an audience in such a lonely place, but the farmer was right. Soon after the sun had gone down the full harvest moon rose, and by its dim light we could faintly see family groups of people, two and sometimes three on a horse, coming from all directions over the hill—now a wagon with a great load. Some of them walked, but all were quiet and serious, and apparently won-dering what they were going to see.

Those who have travelled through the Southern States will perhaps re-member the kind of barn we acted in: there were two log-houses joined together with an opening between them which was floored and covered in.

The seats were arranged outside in the open air—benches, chairs, and logs. The double barn on each side was used for dressing-rooms, and for making entrances and exits, while the opening was devoted to the stage. The open air was well filled, containing an audience of about sixty persons. Our enthusiastic admirer, the farmer, collected the admission fee, a dollar being charged and freely given. The plays were *The Lady of Lyons* and *The Spectre Bridegroom*. The farmer had supplied us liberally with candles, so that the early part of the entertainment was brilliantly illuminated, but the evening breeze had fanned the lights so fiercely that by the time the farce began the footlights were gone. The little 'flaming ministers' had all sputtered out, so *The Spectre Bridegroom* was acted in the moonlight.

It was curious to watch the effect of a strong emotional play like *The Lady of Lyons* upon an audience that had never seen a drama before: they not only were much interested, but they became excited over the trials of the hero and heroine; they talked freely among themselves, and, at times, to the actors. One old lady insisted that the lovers should be 'allowed their own way', and a stalwart young farmer warned the villain not to interfere again 'if he knew what was best for him'.

In 1941 I was touring as Iago to the Othello of Frederick Valk (page 91). In Act IV, Scene ii, Desdemona (played by Hermione Hannen) sends for Iago and goes on her knees to him, begging him to use his influence to restrain her husband's fury. The scene ends with Iago reassuring her and saying 'All things shall be well.' As I spoke these words, the director, Julius Gellner, had me place my hand gently on Desdemona's head. At this moment during a performance at Stoke on Trent, a woman sitting four or five rows back said in a fierce whisper, 'You bugger.' There was not so much as a shiver of laughter from the audience.

POOR PLAYER'S EXIT

Thomas Geering
Our Sussex Parish (1925)

The first Church schoolmaster whom we have any reliable information about is Francis Howlett. His advent here [Horsham] was somewhat remarkable. Being one of a party of strolling players who arrived in the place on a professional tour, he gave up the buskin and settled down to quiet domestic life, married a wife from the neighbourhood, and ultimately became factotum of the parish. At that time it was no uncommon event for a party of players to arrive in the town, and they were always welcomed. The south coast then was a camp—the military outnumbering the fixed population. Diversion was necessary, and willingly paid for. If accommodation could not be had at the inn, a barn was speedily improvised into a theatre. The opening would be announced in the street by beat of drum, and tragedy, comedy, and farce were kept up according to patronage bestowed. If a party could manage to hit the public taste, and become popular, they would maintain their hold for weeks, it might be months, but the end was too often, financially, failure.

The break-up of such a party is well described by a local writer of the time. The 'Man of the Rocks', the Rev. Richard Mitchel, vicar of East Dean, in a letter to the *Lewes Journal*—Lee's old paper, now the *Sussex Advertiser*—says: 'This morning a wagon passed the door conveying from a barn in the last town to a malthouse in the next the wardrobe of a company of strolling players, their thunder and lightning, pasteboard crowns, wooden sceptres, poisoned bowls, daggers, &c., &c., in short, the whole theatrical apparatus and stock in trade, excepting only a few articles which, in consequence of a want of due taste for such exhibitions in the inhabitants of the place, had been left in pawn. In front of the carriage sat a tragedy-queen or two, and at a respectful distance behind a mute candle-snuffer and train-bearer. The greater part of the dramatic troupe followed on foot. Hamlet's ghost and one of the witches in *Macbeth* brought up the rear, with a large bundle under each arm.'

This is, without doubt, though a little cynical, a true picture of the poor player's exit—camp and baggage; and it was from a similar party that our schoolmaster separated himself; giving up the boards and the footlights, and settling down for life in our town, and it must have been with a pang of sorrow that he parted from his companions. I have great sympathy with players. I hold them to be closely allied to some of the best instincts of our nature, and to be a much maligned people; but they need no apology, their being, next to the priesthood, an ever-enduring profession. They are Nature's children, and we cannot do without them.

POMPING FOLK   J. C. Trewin

Pomping folk! What a wonderful phrase. I had never heard it before, but John Trewin assures me that it is genuine South Cornish. It reminds me of Mistress Quickly's description of Falstaff on his death-bed—'His nose was as sharp as a pen on a table of green fields'—and the famous gloss made by the eighteenth-century critic Lewis Theobald, who amended the last words to read, 'and a-babbled of green fields'. Myself, I suspect that a coverlet embroidered with a rural scene was drawn up under the nose of the dying man ... but who would not wish to accept Theobald's emendation? And who would not wish to accept John Trewin's inspiration—if such it be?

A heron stood by the Helford tide
When the pomping folk looked back,
The green reeds pliant in their hands,
And the royalty of all the lands
Secure within their pack.

They had come down to the river
By teased and thorny ways
In the height of the budding summer,
The sky in a summer haze;
But who would hear their plays?

Only the fishing heron;
Squirrel, badger, mole;
No stir else by the Helford tide,
The shelving oaks of the riverside;
Never a sound, never a soul.

They stared at the water's vacant glass;
Weary, they turned to go.

Cracking the twigs in the knotted grass,
Sadly they went, and slow.

Pomping folk from the market square,
The night, the booth, the torches' flare,
Hamlet, Ophelia, Romeo, turning in silence back.
Only the reeds limp in their hands,
And the royalty of all the lands
Secure within their pack.

In 1730, John Rich began to raise subscriptions in the hope of erecting a new theatre in Bow Street, Covent Garden, following his stupendously successful production of Gay's Beggar's Opera (refused by Cibber at Drury Lane, but accepted by Rich at Lincoln's Inn Fields, where it was to make 'Gay rich and Rich gay'). The house opened triumphantly in 1732, and did well; there was a particularly profitable season in 1746, with Garrick as star performer, when the box office took some £8,500. Thereafter, however, came a sad decline. Garrick went into management on his own account at Drury Lane, and Rich, who died in 1761, was succeeded as manager by a son-in-law, John Beard, who evidently lacked his own theatrical flair. This is a particularly interesting print because it includes a map showing the out-of-town playgoer just where to find his evening's entertainment.

VII

STAGE EFFECTS

The illustration shows the repertoire at the New Theatre, Covent Garden, from January to May 1733. The theatre had opened on December 7, 1732. The highly successful revival of The Beggar's Opera ran from the 1st to the 10th January, being given twenty times. Thereafter, as you will see, the repertoire was mostly made up of classics—Volpone, Measure for Measure, Othello, The Plain Dealer, The Way of the World, Macbeth, and so on. Gay's posthumous opera Achilles was given for the first time on February 10 and played successfully for eighteen nights. I think this list is written in Manager John Rich's own hand.

I also have another slip of paper—same size, same hand, with instructions to the bill poster:

St James's, 4 sheets,
do Piccadilly,
do Islington,
do Improvements

—and so on, very homely and personal.

When John Rich founded his New Theatre in Covent Garden in 1732 he did so on the basis of eighteen years' success as manager of the Lincoln's Inn Fields Theatre, which he had inherited from his father, Christopher Rich, in 1714.

In 1688 Christopher Rich had purchased a share in the management of the Theatre Royal in Drury Lane, and with his training as an attorney at his back, set out on an endless succession of lawsuits with the actors, his fellow proprietors and even the Lord Chamberlain. As Manager, he was Autocracy personified. He cut the actors' pay, interfered with their benefit nights, refused to commit himself to written agreements with them, and loftily ignored any approaches from his fellow proprietors. In 1709 the actors were driven into applying to the Lord Chamberlain for redress; he supported their cause, and when Rich would not yield, issued a Silence Order. Rich was ousted by an alliance of the actors, led by Colley Cibber (actor, playwright, and eventually, in 1730, to become Poet Laureate), Robert Wilks (an actor remarkable for his diligence), and Thomas Doggett (of Coat and Badge fame, author of The Country Wake in which, by royal command, he took the leading role of Hob).

Rich promptly stripped the theatre of everything moveable, so that the new company started out with no props and no costumes. Nevertheless, as may be seen from the engagingly spelt bills and dockets (quoted by Fitzgerald in his New History of the English Stage) they always managed to put on a show——

'For silk to face the sleaves, 1s. 8d. for *Jane Shore*—For making a manto and a flounced petticoat, 18s.—For binding, bone buttons, and lupes, 3s.—Mrs Willis, jun., £4 13s. 4d.—For emptying dust-hold, 1s.—Mending a gold braslet, 5d.—Cotton for lamps, 1s. 8d.—Sand, whiting, brick-dust, 1d.'

'For Mr Cox, for *The Libertin*: For making a flounced manto, lined with scarlet, 5s.—For stuffe for a false taile, 2s. 6d.—For silk for face, &c.'

'September 22, 1714: Soldiers*, 18s. 6d., £1 14s. Ye double boxes, which were kept for the Prince and Princess, and their attendants, will hold twenty people; at single prices, make £4 a night; twenty more nights at £4 per night, makes £166, and extra-ordinary charges, soldiers, &c., £49 11s.—total £168 11s. Also books of plays at 3s.'

'Tuning the harpsichord, 5s.—Painter's bill for painting Appollo's chariot in gold, four horses, a glory, a bench of rushes, a sea, and Dafne turned to a tree, £7†.—The timber, boards, screwes, &c., small nayles to nayle the cloth on. For the brass enstrooment that Appollo carys in his hand, four carpinders work, £3.—Dew to the scavingers at Christmas last past, one quarter, £1 7s. 6d.—Dew to the watch, detto, 7s. 6d.'

---

* Soldiers were always placed at the corner of the stage, underneath the royal box, on the occasion of the royal visits, which appear to have been continued for many nights. From October 1713 to April 1714, the item 'for soldiers' cost nearly £50

† The Managers gave him £6

[For *What D'Ye Call It*] 'Paid for ye hire of a couple of houndes from Knightsbridge, 4s.—For a paper of vermilion used on the stage, 2d.'

[For *Oronooko*] 'For blood, 2d.—And 8 ounces of pomatum for Mr Booth and Mr Mills, 1s.'

'A sham child, dressed, at 5s.—The use of a surgeon's box, 6d.—In *The Relapse*, two great looking glasses, cost 2s.—A sedan, 1s.—An ice cake, 2d.—For oranges and aples for Mr Bicknall, 6d.—The use of a cobbler's bench and tools, 6d.—And making 12 wiskers of hair, 2s.—Due for a ring lost by Mr Powil, 7s. 6d.'

A GARRET VILE   Robert Lloyd
                                                  The Actor (1762)

> High o'er the stage there lies a rambling frame,
> Which men a garret vile, but players the tire-room name:
> Here all their stores (a merry medley) sleep
> Without distinction, huddled in a heap.
> Hung on the self-same peg, in union rest
> Young Tarquin's trousers and Lucretia's vest,
> Whilst, without pulling coifs, Roxana lays
> Close by Satira's petticoat, her stays....
> Here Iris bends her various-painted arch,
> There artificial clouds in sullen order march;
> Here stands a crown upon a rack, and there
> A witch's broomstick by great Hector's spear;
> Here stands a throne, and there the cynic's tub,
> Here Bullock's cudgel, there Alcides' club.
> Beards, plumes, and spangles in confusion rise,
> Whilst rocks of Cornish diamonds reach the skies;
> Crests, corslets, all the pomp of battle join
> In one effulgence, one promiscuous shine.
> Hence all the drama's decorations rise,
> Hence gods descend majestic from the skies,
> Hence playhouse chiefs, to grace some antique tale,
> Buckle their coward limbs in warlike mail.

To see the kind of scene Robert Lloyd describes, turn to Hogarth's superb picture of a company of strolling actresses in a barn, getting ready for a performance.

SWEET BIRDS SANG

Joseph Addison
The Spectator (1711)

As I was walking in the streets about a fortnight ago, I saw an ordinary fellow carrying a cage full of little birds upon his shoulder; and, as I was wondering with myself what use he would put them to, he was met very luckily by an acquaintance, who had the same curiosity. Upon his asking what he had upon his shoulder, he told him that he had been buying sparrows for the opera. 'Sparrows for the opera,' says his friend, licking his lips; 'what! are they to be roasted?'—'No, no,' says the other, 'they are to enter towards the end of the first act, and to fly about the stage.'

This strange dialogue awakened my curiosity so far, that I immediately bought the opera, by which means I perceived the sparrows were to act the part of singing birds in a delightful grove; though upon a nearer inquiry I found the sparrows put the same trick upon the audience that Sir Martin Mar-all practised upon his mistress; for though they flew in sight, the music proceeded from a concert of flageolets and bird-calls, which were planted behind the scenes. . . .

There have been so many flights of them let loose in this opera that it is to be feared the house will never get rid of them; and that in other plays they may make their entrance in very wrong and improper scenes, so as to be seen flying in a lady's bedchamber, or perching upon a king's throne; besides the inconveniences which the heads of the audience may sometimes suffer.

FLAMING AMAZEMENT

... RED FIRE

The Drama (1824)

The beautiful Red Fire, which is now so frequently used in the theatres, is composed of the following ingredients: 40 parts of dry nitrate of strontian, 13 parts of finely powdered sulphur, 5 parts of chlorate of potash, and 4 parts of sulphuret of antimony. The chlorate of potash and sulphuret of antimony should be powdered separately in a mortar and then mixed together on paper; after which they may be added to the other ingredients previously powdered and mixed. This fire was originally invented by a musician of Astley's Amphitheatre.

... COLOURED FLAMES

The Drama (1825)

Add a little boracic acid to a spoonful of alcohol, and stir them together in a saucer or cup, then set them on fire, and the flame will be of a beautiful green colour. If strontites in powder be added to alcohol, it burns with a carmine flame; if barytes be added, the flame is yellow; if the alcohol contains muriate of magnesia, it burns with a reddish-yellow flame.

... BLUE FIRE   *The Flying Dutchman (1827)*

Stage direction:
    Vanderdecken, amid blue fire, appears from the waves.

INSUBSTANTIAL PAGEANT   John William Cole
*The Life and Theatrical Times
of Charles Kean, F.S.A. (1859)*

In 1857, Charles Kean staged The Tempest *at the Princess's Theatre, as part of his series of Shakespeare revivals:*

One of the most strikingly original conceptions was the entire execution of the music (with the exception of the duet in the masque) by an invisible choir, led by Miss Poole, whose mellow voice sounded with the rich, full clearness of a bell in the midst of, and above, the accompanying melody. . . .

      Come unto these yellow sands,
        And then take hands:
      Court'sied when you have and kiss'd,—
        The wild waves whist,—
      Foot it featly here and there;
      And, sweet sprites, the burden bear.

We were really presented with a 'delicate spirit', Ariel at one moment descending in a ball of fire; at another, rising gently from a tuft of flowers; again, sailing on the smooth waters on the back of a dolphin; then gliding noiselessly over the sands, as a water nymph; and ever and anon, perched on the summit of a rock, riding on a bat, or cleaving mid-air with the velocity of lightning. The powers of modern stage mechanism are almost as marvellous as the gift ascribed to the magic wand and book of Prospero.

I still think that the production of The Tempest *designed by Walter Hodges and Michael Stringer, with which we opened at* The Mermaid *in 1951, was one of the loveliest ever staged. Dressed in a skin-tight leotard thickly sewn with pale blue feathers, Ariel descended from the heavens on a nylon cord. In the banquet scene, the feast was spread on a special table, whose overhanging table cloth concealed a large* canvas bag under its hinged top. As Ariel clapped his wings over the table, he pressed a pedal with his foot; the two halves of the table top folded inwards, and the entire banquet slid into the bag—golden plates and goblets, forks and spoons, food and wine and so on; the table top sprang up into place, and when Ariel raised his wings, the cloth was smooth, bare, empty.

The shipwreck, too, was brilliantly contrived. Running rigging, ratlines, etc., hung from the roof, swinging wildly to and fro as the boatswain bellowed his orders. At the fearful shout 'We split, we split!', there came a flash of lightning, a roar of thunder, and an unbearable rending of timber as the ship struck. In the darkness the rigging was cut loose from the roof and crashed into an open trap, while long branches luxuriant with fronds and tropical flowers were pulled round from the sides—and when the lights went up, there was the magic island.

BETTER THAN VERDI

James Henry Mapleson
The Mapleson Memoirs (1888)

James Henry Mapleson was a London opera manager at Her Majesty's (page 131). Opera lovers should buy his two-volume autobiography and commit it to memory. They will be rewarded with a unique vision of nineteenth-century music, and get many laughs in the process. Antonio Giuglini was a temperamental tenor.

Giuglini now informed me that he had written a better cantata than Verdi's, and that unless I performed it I could no longer rely upon his services; if, however, his work were given he would remain faithful to me for the future. The work was duly delivered, in which I remember there was a lugubrious character destined for Mademoiselle Titiens, called *Una madre Italiana*. Giuglini further required 120 windows on the stage, from each of which, at a given signal, the Italian flag was to appear; and no smaller number than 120 would satisfy him. We were at our wits' end. But the difficulty was met by arranging the scene in perspective; grown-up people being at the windows nearest the public, then children at those farther removed, until in the far distance little dolls were used. At a given signal, when the orchestra struck up the Garibaldi hymn, these were all to appear.

I need hardly say that the cantata was given but for one night.

WARDROBE

Elizabethan and Jacobean theatres were referred to as 'gorgeous painted playing places', and the actors must surely have matched them. Every company of players was under the special patronage of the Court, or the Lord Chamberlain, or one of the nobility—the Admiral's Company, the Earl of Derby's Men, Lord Strange's Men, and so on. The players wore their patron's livery, and naturally he saw to it that when on stage they did justice to his name and social status.

... THE KING'S COAT

Thomas Shepherd Munden
Memoirs of Joseph Shepherd Munden,
Comedian: By his Son (1844)

Munden always provided his own costume, wearing nothing that belonged to the theatre, and gave large sums for any dress that suited his fancy. Among the suits which formed his wardrobe was a black velvet coat, &c., which had belonged to George II, of the richest Genoa velvet; and another, made for Francis, Duke of Bedford, at Paris, on the occasion of the Prince of Wales's marriage, which is said to have cost £1000. The coat had originally been fringed with precious stones, of which the sockets only remained when it came into the hands of the 'fripier', but in its dilapidated state Munden gave £40 for it.

... VERY SPECIAL OCCASIONS

Sam Wild
Old Wild's (1888)

The drama selected for performance on Colonel Haliday's patronage night was *Belphegor*, in which were introduced 'the court-dresses of Louis Philippe, late King of the French'. These dresses were first purchased by Mr Edwin Hughes in Paris on July 27th, 1846, and at the sale of his stock in London on November 4th, 1847, were bought by my mother. They were of a most magnificent description, and I need hardly say, were only mounted by our company on very special occasions.

... THE HAT

Eric Barker and
Bernard Miles

Lloyd and Churchill, Trewin and Clinton-Baddeley—why should they be the only poets represented in this collection? (Did I say 'poets'?) The lines that follow were written by my good friend Eric Barker and myself. When we were touring in Once in a Lifetime, *as I mentioned earlier (page 106), we went down to the wardrobe to rig ourselves out to play the two electricians. This involved sorting through a basketful of assorted hats. Later, when the tour was over and we had gone our various ways, we still kept in touch by letter, and created jointly the following jeu d'esprit, Barker supplying the first four lines and myself the second stanza. Never before has this been published!*

I found a hat that must have been
Discarded for its age,
A scurvy felt that might have seen
The crowning of a sage.

Its brim was battered out of true,
All dented was its crown.
Said I, 'The head where once that grew
Must now be very far from new,
But Fame is fickle, Friends are few,
And rotten is Renown.'

RENOUNCING THE VEIL   *The Drama (1825)*

Doth the first appearance of Baker in breeches yet linger in the public
memory? Can those slender pins, which she exhibited in *Giovanni* at the
Olympic, ever be forgotten? She came on in white shapes, red morocco
boots, and blue upper garments, looking like an azure sylph mounted upon
two tobacco pipes with waxed tips. How the women giggled! Baker long
enjoyed the credit of having a handsome leg; she should never have withdrawn the veil. Her clean and clever ankle gave us hopes of the existence of a
lovely calf, delicately reposing on it. Above her flounces, all was shadowy
mystery—a bourn from which no traveller had returned; her knee had never
visited the glimpses of a London float-light; and imagination painted two
Parian pillars springing from those pretty pedestals. The sad reality has at
length stalked gaunt before us. Baker has published her legs, and our dreams
are gone!

'LEND ME YOUR SKULL'   'Corin' [Mr Lind]
                                       The Truth about the Stage (1885)

*The great Edmund Kean was an ardent disciple of George Frederick Cooke (page
101); it is said that when he was in New York, he went to visit Cooke's grave, had
the tragedian's coffin opened, and removed from the skeleton the fore-finger which
Cooke had extended slowly, dramatically, in his celebrated delivery of the rolling line
'In the deep bosom of the ocean ...' Kean brought his treasured relic home to
London, meaning to hang it over the mantelpiece of his house in Clarges Street, but
his wife did not approve, and seizing it, threw it out of the window. The recent press
reports saying that Cooke's doctor buried the body but kept the actor's skull for
experimentation may well be true; in 1980, an American company proposed to*

borrow the skull from the Pennsylvanian medical school in whose custody it was, and carry it on stage as poor Yorick in Hamlet. *I remember being told that in the mid-thirties the former Old Vic director, Andrew Leigh bequeathed his skull to the theatre for this purpose, at the minimum Equity salary—then about £3 a week. . . . But I fancy this story is apocryphal.*

Tom Saunders, the property man at the Coaltown Theatre, was a clever artisan; he could make anything, from a fiddle to a string of sausages. He was an admirable modeller, and quite competent to mould in papier-mâché a skull that would deceive the eye of any sawbones who chanced to be in front. But Tom had a serious failing, he was fond of 'twos of Irish', and on the day in question he had been twoing it a little too-too. Of course, he 'knowed the piece backwards, sir', but he forgot all about the skull, and the rascal's neglect was not discovered before the end of the third act [of *Hamlet*].

The theatre was crammed. The elite of Coaltown were present, and the performance was under the 'distinguished' patronage of the mayor, Mr Ferram, the great colliery proprietor. The guilty Claudius was just rushing off, howling for 'Lights, lights', when Jackson, the stage manager, dashed into my dressing-room and, with a look of disgust upon his face, exclaimed, 'That beast Saunders is tight again, and he's forgotten the skull. You've finished as the Player King, and you've nothing more to do, have you?'

'No, sir.'

'Run to the nearest barber's and borrow a wig-block.'

I finished dressing, rushed out of the theatre, and hurried to the principal hairdresser's shop. To my dismay, I found it closed. There was a bell at the private door, which I rang furiously. A stupid-looking girl appeared.

'Where's your master?'

'He be gone to the theayter to see Hamlick.'

'Have you got a wig-block you could lend me?'

'Eh?'

'A wig-block. I saw one yesterday in the shop-window with some golden ringlets on it. Take off the curls and give it to me at once. I'll make it all right with your master tomorrow morning.'

'I'll give yer in charge if yer doant be orf.' So saying, she slammed the door in my face.

After muttering a few words which were anything but complimentary to the fair sex of Coaltown, and barber's servants in particular, I hailed an empty cab which was passing. 'Drive me to the doctor's,' I shouted to the cabby, as I leaped into the fly.

'Which on 'em, sir?'

'I don't care a hang, whichever you like, only be quick.'

'All right, sir. I s'pose Doctor Coffin 'll do for yer?'

In two minutes the cab stopped at Doctor Coffin's door. A sleepy-looking pageboy answered my vigorous pull at the bell. 'Doctor Coffin at home?'

'No, sir, he's gone to the play with the mayor.'

'Confound it, all Coaltown is at the show. Here, cabby, take me to another doctor—the nearest.'

'Doctor Vomer, sir?'

'All right. I'll pay you double fare if you'll stir up that old screw of yours.'

The promise of a good tip acted like magic upon man and beast, and away we rattled towards the High Street.

Doctor Vomer was at home. The servant led me into the surgery, and a dapper little man, with a shining pate fringed with a few snowy white hairs, smiled blandly as he entered the room.

'Doctor,' I exclaimed excitedly, 'will you lend me your skull?'

'My skull, sir, my skull! Oh, I see. Pray, be calm, my dear sir, rest yourself a bit, and then we will discuss your case.'

He evidently concluded that I was an escaped lunatic.

'Pray do not misunderstand me. I thought you might have a skull.'

'Indeed I have, sir.'

'Will you favour me with the loan of it for half an hour—only half an hour?'

'I should be most happy to oblige you, but'—looking at his watch—'it is almost supper-time, and when one sups one's skull is indispensable.'

'You have a skeleton, sir?'

'True.'

'Do you mind disconnecting the skull? I am an actor, sir. We are playing *Hamlet* tonight. It is the mayor's bespeak; and the performance will come to an untimely end unless I can borrow your skull for the graveyard scene.'

'Oh, I begin to understand,' said the little man, laughing heartily. 'Certainly, if you will take care of it.' And, going to his osteological cabinet, he handed me the coveted article.

'A thousand thanks,' I exclaimed, as I opened the street-door and rushed to the cab.

I arrived at the theatre with my ghastly burden just as the prompter was ready to ring up. The treasure was deposited in Ophelia's grave, and mixed with a shovelful of mould and a few beef and mutton bones obtained for an 'order' at the cook-shop next door.

The gravedigger, when he saw the skull, exclaimed, 'What a beauty!' The drop ascended, and the fifth act began. When Hamlet picked up the head of the Jester there was a murmur of admiration from the audience. Yorick's skull was a great success.

Tom Saunders was lucky—he got away with it, unlike the property man in Stephen Kemble's company. The play was Othello, *the place was Glasgow, the performance had reached the last scene, and the stage was being made ready with Desdemona's bed handsomely arranged, curtains, pillows, wedding sheets and all. The property man was a new hand, very keen; it was all to look right and proper, befitting a honey-*

moon. *He had thought of everything—even a chamberpot, discreetly placed and hidden by a deep valance. Desdemona took her place and disposed herself for sleep, the curtain was drawn up, and Kemble entered as Othello, candle in hand, with the great soliloquy:*

> It is the cause, it is the cause, my soul—
> Let me not name it to you, you chaste stars—

As he stooped over his sleeping bride, his foot struck the chamberpot with a resounding ping—a sound the audience instantly recognised from many a sleepy blundering search of their own. They began to titter, then to laugh, then to rock in their seats. Kemble seized the pot, rushed off-stage, and with a shout of 'Villain! Villain!' belaboured the unhappy property man with it, as murderous as if he had Iago at his sword's end.

ENTER . . . EXIT

Stage direction   *Ramah Droog (Cobb, 1798)*

Enter the Rajah on the elephant, returning from hunting the tiger, preceded by his hircarrahs or military messengers and his state palanquin. The Vizier on another elephant. The Princess in a gaurie, drawn by buffaloes. The Rajah is attended by his Fakeer or soothsayer, his officer of state, and by an ambassador from Tippoo Sultan in a palanquin, also by Nairs or soldiers from the South of India—Poligars, or inhabitants of the hilly districts, with their hunting dogs—other Indians carrying a dead tiger, and young tigers in the cage—a number of sepoys—musicians on camels and on foot—dancing girls, etc.

Stage direction   *The Vampire (Planché, 1820)*

A Thunderbolt strikes Ruthven to the ground, who immediately vanishes.

VIII

GRAND OPERA

The glorious MARIA MALIBRAN (1808-36), one of a famous trio. Her younger sister was the great mezzo-soprano, Pauline Viardot, mistress of Turgenev; her brother Manuel Garcia, New York's first Figaro, inventor of the laryngoscope, long survived her, living on until 1905.

Malibran's tempestuous career exemplified all that was wildest and most reckless in the artistic life. Europe flocked to hear her. She was indisputably the most exciting singer of her time. Macready worshipped her from afar. Like so many other singers, she had a tragic death. Riding in Regent's Park in April 1836, she was thrown from her horse and suffered a concussion, but insisted on keeping her summer engagements; she collapsed in Manchester that September after a performance in oratorio. The wife of Sir George Smart, organist of the Chapel Royal, cut off a lock of her hair as she lay in her coffin, and an elderly opera lover sent it to me in 1955, together with an engraving of the singer. These form an indissoluble link with this great artist.

When people heard, back in 1950, that I had persuaded Kirsten Flagstad to sing Dido in Dido and Aeneas, *to launch the Mermaid Theatre in our St John's Wood home, for a pint of oatmeal stout per performance, they said, 'How charming, how original.' But like so much in my life, the idea was cribbed! I remembered Alfred Bunn's description in his autobiography (1840) of how he had sustained Malibran through the desert scene in* The Maid of Artois, *at Drury Lane, 1836, and thus won an encore from the great singer: and I thought this would make an excellent publicity stunt. At the time of the performance described by Bunn, Malibran was suffering the after-effects of her concussion. Four months later, she was dead.*

If to have been the humble medium of introducing to the public an entertainment of so delightful a nature, of bringing before them, in all the splendour of her unrivalled powers, such an extraordinary creature as this artiste, be the proudest and the brightest recollection of far-departed years of memory, during a long theatrical career, the knowledge that the Maid of Artois was the first and unhappily the last original character portrayed by the enchantress on this stage, and the last character she performed on any stage, presents a sorrowful contrast.

It may be, therefore, an acceptable diversion to record a humorous incident which led to the thrilling, the more than brilliant, the not-to-be-forgotten execution, by Madame Malibran, of the finale to this opera. I had occasion, during its last rehearsal but one, to express myself in strong terms at her leaving the stage for more than an hour and a half, to go and gain £25 at a morning concert. Neither the concerted pieces of music, nor the situations of the drama in which she was involved, could possibly be proceeded with, and the great stake we were then contending for was likely to be placed in jeopardy by an unworthy grasp at a few pounds, to the prejudice of a theatre paying her nightly five times as much. She knew she had done wrong, and she atoned for it by her genius, while her pride would not have permitted her to do so. She had borne along the two first acts on the first night of performance in such a flood of triumph, that she was bent, by some almost superhuman effort, to continue its glory to the final fall of the curtain.

I went into her dressing-room previous to the third act, to ask how she felt, and she replied, 'Very tired but' (and here her eye of fire suddenly lighted up) 'you angry devil, if you will contrive to get me a pint of porter in the desert scene, you shall have an encore to your finale.'

Had I been dealing with any other performer, I should perhaps have hesitated in complying with a request that might have been dangerous in its application at the moment; but to check *her* powers was to annihilate them. I therefore arranged that, behind the pile of drifted sand on which she falls in a state of exhaustion, towards the close of the desert scene, a small aperture should be made in the stage; and it is a fact that, from underneath the stage through that aperture, a pewter pint of porter was conveyed to the parched lips of this rare child of song, which so revived her, after the terrible exertion the scene led to, that she electrified the audience, and had strength to repeat the charm, with the finale to *The Maid of Artois*. The novelty of the circumstance so tickled her fancy, and the draught itself was so extremely refreshing, that it was arranged, during the subsequent run of the opera, for the Negro slave, at the head of the governor's procession, to have in the gourd suspended to his neck the same quantity of the same beverage, to be applied to her lips, on his first beholding the apparently dying Isoline.

'VERY BADLY INDEED'   James Henry Mapleson
                                       The Mapleson Memoirs (1888)

The Mapleson Memoirs are required reading for all true lovers of opera. James Henry Mapleson (1830–1901) was a military man with a flair for showbiz. In 1862 he took a twenty-one-year lease of what was then Her Majesty's Opera House (on the same site as the present theatre). Here he weathered all the hazards inseparable from the mad world of theatrical management. It was he who mounted the first London production of Gounod's Faust. *He picked the famous baritone Charles Santley to sing the part of Valentin. At Santley's request, Gounod agreed to write him a special aria: the result was one of the war-horses of the baritone repertoire,* Avant de quitter ces lieux. *Mapleson had heard* Faust *in Paris and resolved that London must hear it too, but visiting the box office three or four days before the first night, June 11, 1863, he found that a mere handful of seats had been sold and there was only £30 in the till.*

He was not to be defeated:

I had set my mind upon a brilliant success. I told Mr Nugent [the box-office manager] in the first place that I had decided to announce *Faust* for four nights in succession. He thought I must be mad, and assured me that one night's performance would be more than enough, and that to persist in offering to the public a work in which it took no interest was surely a deplorable mistake.

I told him that not only should the opera be played for four nights in succession, but that for the first three out of these four not one place was to be sold beyond those already disposed of. That there might be no mistake about the matter, I had all the remaining tickets for the three nights in question collected and put away in several carpet bags, which I took home with me that I might distribute them far and wide throughout the Metropolis and the Metropolitan suburbs. At last, after a prodigious outlay in envelopes, and above all postage stamps, nearly the whole mass of tickets for the three nights had been carefully given away.

I at the same time advertised in *The Times* that in consequence of a death in the family, two stalls secured for the first representation of *Faust*—the opera which was exciting so much interest that all places for the first three representations had been bought up—could be had at twenty-five shillings each, being but a small advance on the box-office prices. The stalls thus liberally offered were on sale at the shop of Mr Phillips, the jeweller, in Cockspur Street, and I told Mr Phillips that if he succeeded in selling them I would present him with three for the use of his own family. Mr Phillips sold them three times over, and a like success was achieved by Mr Baxter, the stationer, also in Cockspur Street.

Meanwhile demands had been made at the box-office for places and when the would-be purchasers were told that 'everything had gone', they went away and repeated it to their friends, who, in their turn, came to see whether it was quite impossible to obtain seats for the first performances of an opera which was now beginning to be seriously talked about. As the day of production approached the inquiries became more and more numerous.

'If not for the first night, there must surely be places somewhere for the second,' was the cry.

Mr Nugent and his assistants had, however, but one answer, 'Everything had been sold, not only for the first night, but also for the two following ones.'

The second night *Faust* was received more warmly than on the first, and at each succeeding representation it gained additional favour, until after the third performance the paying public, burning with desire to see a work from which they had hitherto been debarred, filled the theatre night after night. No further device was necessary for stimulating its curiosity; and the work was now to please and delight successive audiences by its own incontestable merit. It was given for ten nights in succession, and was constantly repeated until the termination of the season.

SHIPWRECK

James Henry Mapleson
The Mapleson Memoirs (1888)

A rather startling event occurred during the first act [of *The Flying Dutch-man*] on the arrival of the Phantom Ship, which, after sweeping gracefully round, broadside to the audience, suddenly capsized, casting the Dutchman and his crew promiscuously on to the stage, the masts going straight across the occupants of the stalls and the sails covering Arditi, who was then at the desk.

At this juncture loud screams were heard. They came from the wife of the principal baritone [Galassi] who, witnessing the accident, had fears for her husband's safety. The choristers, who were thrown pell-mell into the water, and onto their stomachs, began with a great deal of tact to strike out as if swimming, until—as soon as possible—the curtains were lowered. The ship was soon set on its keel again, but nothing could induce Galassi to board the vessel.

AT A STROKE

The Times

MAY *9th, 1796*   The stage at the Opera is so crowded that Madame Rose, in throwing up her fine muscular arm into a graceful attitude, inadvertently levelled three men of the first quality at a stroke.

EVERY POSSIBLE CARE

John Ebers
*Seven Years of the
King's Theatre (1828)*

In 1826 John Ebers of the King's Theatre in the Haymarket (later to become Her Majesty's) concluded an agreement with De Valabrègue, husband of the singer Angelica Catalani (1780–1849). He gave a literal translation of this unique docu-ment in his memoirs. A précis is given below. When I tell you that Malibran's terms were even more rapacious, you will have some idea of what Bunn, Mapleson and their fellow managers had to cope with. Catalani was famous for the size of her voice—and big voices are always in demand.

1. Every box and every admission shall be considered as belonging to the management. The free admissions shall be given with paper orders, and differently shaped from the paid tickets. Their number shall be limited. The manager, as well as Madame Catalani, shall each have a good box.

2. Madame Catalani shall choose and direct the operas in which she is to sing; she shall likewise have the choice of the performers in them; she will have no orders to receive from anyone; she will find all her own dresses.

3. Madame Catalani shall have two benefits, to be divided with the manager; Madame Catalani's share shall be free; she will fix her own days.

4. Madame Catalani and her husband shall have a right to superintend the receipts.

5. Every six weeks Madame Catalani shall receive the payment of her share of the receipts and of the subscription.

6. Madame Catalani shall sing at no other place but the King's Theatre, during the season; in the Concerts or Oratorios, where she may sing, she will be entitled to no other share but that specified as under.

7. During the season, Madame Catalani shall be at liberty to go to Bath, Oxford, or Cambridge.

8. Madame Catalani shall not sing oftener than her health will allow her. She promises to contribute to the utmost of her power to the good of the Theatre. On his side, Mr Ebers engages to treat Madame Catalani with every possible care.

9. This engagement and these conditions will be binding for this season, which will begin ... and end ..., and continue during all the seasons that the Theatre shall be under the management of Mr Ebers, unless Madame Catalani's health, or the state of her voice, shall not allow her to continue.

10. Madame Catalani, in return for the conditions above mentioned, shall receive the half part of the amount of all the receipts which shall be made in the course of the season, including the subscription to the boxes, the amount of those sold separately, the monies received at the doors of the Theatre, and of the Concert-room; in short, the said half part of the general receipts of the Theatre for the season.

11. It is well understood that Madame Catalani's share shall be free from every kind of deduction, it being granted her in lieu of salary. It is likewise well understood that every expense of the Theatre during the season shall be Mr Ebers's, such as the rent of the Theatre, the performers' salaries, the trades-people's bills; in short, every possible expense, and Madame Catalani shall be entirely exonerated from any one charge.

This engagement shall be translated into English, taking care that the conditions shall remain precisely as in the original, and shall be so worded as to stipulate that Madame Catalani, on receiving her share of the receipts of the Theatre, shall in no ways whatever be considered as partner of the manager of the establishment.

12. The present engagement being made with the full approbation of both parties, Mr Ebers and M. de Valabrègue pledge their word of honour to fulfil it in every one of its parts.

Catalani makes a superb 'guest appearance' in Benjamin Lumley's Reminiscences of the Opera *(1864). As a young woman full of high spirits she was singing at Lisbon. For a wager, she accepted a challenge to run a foot-race against one of the young English attachés there. There was a mighty struggle between the fleet-footed young man and the singer with her magnificent lungs, and she would have won but—alas!—she tore her drawers and down they came, entangling her feet. Another glimpse of the wild world of the opera before it was, tragically, gone for ever.*

TWO INCHES   Sutherland Edwards
                                         History of the Opera (1862)

As for Catalani's husband, Valabrègue, he appears to have been mean, officious, conceited (of his wife's talent!) and generally stupid. M. Castil Blaze solemnly affirms that when Madame Catalani was rehearsing at the Italian Opera of Paris an air which she was to sing in the evening to a pianoforte accompaniment, she found the instrument too high, and told Valabrègue to see that it was lowered; upon which (declares M. Blaze) Valabrègue called for a carpenter and caused the unfortunate piano's feet to be amputated!
    'Still too high?' cried Madame Catalani's husband when he was accused in the evening of having neglected her orders. 'Why, how much did you lower it, Charles?' addressing the carpenter.
    'Two inches, Sir,' was the reply.
    The historian calls Tamburini, Lablache, and Tadolini, as well as Rossini and Berryer, the celebrated advocate, to witness that the mutilated instrument had afterwards four knobs of wood glued to its legs by the same Charles who executed in so faithful a manner M. Valabrègue's absurd behest. It continued to wear these pattens until its existence was terminated in the fire of 1838.

MODESTY   Anon. [John Edmund Cox]
                                    *Musical Recollections of the
                                       Last Half-Century (1872)*

Rosamunda Benedetta Pisaroni (1793–1872) was a magnificent singer but unfortunately her face was pockmarked:

Without exception Madame Pisaroni was the most ugly woman that was ever seen on the opera-stage; her appearance indeed was almost revolting. Besides the plainness of her face, she also limped, her figure was distorted, and her stature was short and squat. So well aware was she of her want of personal attraction, that when she was applied to by the management of the Italian Opera to sing at Paris, she sent her picture, accompanied by an explanation that she was even uglier than that made her to appear. The moment, however, that she opened her lips, the feeling, that was little short of disgust at these imperfections, at once vanished.

This reminds me of Madame Guimard, star dancer at the French Court in the late eighteenth century. She too was marked by smallpox, but was so slender and graceful, with such elegant features, that, according to Walpole, at forty-five she danced like a girl of fifteen. Having captivated the Parisian public for many years, she at last retired, but the King begged her to make one final appearance in the tiny Court theatre. To this she agreed only on condition that the curtain be lowered sufficiently to conceal her face which she said had grown wrinkled and old, though her legs and arms retained all their grace and fluency.

THE MANAGER REMEMBERS

James Henry Mapleson
The Mapleson Memoirs (1888)

... VIA HULL

Ilma de Murska was punctual with a punctuality which put one out quite as much as utter inability to keep an appointment would have done. She was sure to turn up on the very evening, and at the very hour, when she was wanted for a representation. But she had a horror of rehearsals, and never thought it worth while, when she was travelling from some distant place on the Continent, to announce that she had started, or to give any idea as to when she might really be expected.

Her geographical knowledge, too, was often at fault, and some of the routes—'short cuts' she called them—by which she reached London from Vienna, were of the most extraordinary kind. She had taken a dislike to the railway station at Cologne, where she declared that a German officer had once spoken to her without being introduced; and on one occasion, partly to avoid the station of which she preserved so painful a recollection, partly in order to get to London by a new and expeditious route, she travelled from Vienna to St Petersburg, and from St Petersburg took a boat to Hull, where she arrived just in time to join my Opera company at the representations I was then giving in Edinburgh. We had not heard of her for weeks, and she came into the dressing-room to find Madame Van Zandt already attired for the part Mademoiselle de Murska was to have played, that of Lucia. She argued, with some truth, that she was in time for the performance, and declared, moreover, that in entrusting the part of Lucia to another singer she could see a desire on my part to get rid of her.

... 'MAY I INTRODUCE—?'

During the three or four years that Madame Patti was with me in America she never once appeared at a rehearsal. When I was producing *La Gazza Ladra*, an opera which contains an unusually large number of parts, there were several members of the cast who did not even know Madame Patti by sight. Under such circumstances all idea of a perfect ensemble was, of course, out of the question. It was only on the night of performance, and in presence of the public, that the concerted pieces were tried for the first time with the soprano voice. The unfortunate contralto, Mademoiselle Vianelli, had never in her life seen Madame Patti, with whom, on this occasion, she had to sing duets full of concerted passages. At such rehearsal as she could obtain, Arditi did his best to replace the absent prima donna, whistling the soprano part so as at least to give the much-tried contralto some idea of the effect.

★ ★ ★

The public are under the impression that the closest intimacies are contracted between vocalists in consequence of their appearing constantly together in the same works. Under the new system, by which the prima donna stipulates that she shall not be called upon to appear at any rehearsal, this possible source of excessive friendship ceases to exist. It now frequently happens that the prima donna is not even personally acquainted with the singers who are to take part with her in the same opera; and on one occasion, when *Il Trovatore* was being performed, I remember the baritone soliciting the honour of an introduction to Madame Patti at the very moment when he was singing in the trio of the first act. The Manrico of the evening was exceedingly polite, and managed without scandalizing the audience to effect the introduction by singing it as if it were a portion of his role.

... COUNTING THE COST

In a letter to the papers an American mathematician stated that by carefully counting the notes in the part of *Semiramide*, and dividing the result by the sum paid nightly to Patti for singing that part, he discovered that she received exactly $42\frac{5}{8}$ cents for each of the notes that issued from her throat. This was found to be just $7\frac{1}{10}$ cents per note more than Rossini got for writing the whole opera.

Amongst the numberless enquiries at the box office several were made as to how long Madame Patti remained on the stage in each of the different operas; and the newspapers busied themselves as to the number of notes she sang in each particular work; larger demands for seats being made on those evenings when she sang more notes. *La Traviata* generally carried off the palm, perhaps because of one journal having calculated the interest of the money accruing on her diamonds, whilst she was singing in that work.

A party of amateurs would buy a ticket between them, each one taking twenty minutes of the ticket and returning with the pass-out check to the next. Lots were drawn to decide who was to go in first; and in the event of anyone overstaying his twenty minutes he had to pay for the whole ticket; correctness of time being the essence of the arrangement.

'AH, VIENS!'   Mrs Godfrey Pearse and Frank Hird
                                         The Romance of a Great Singer
                                                          (*1910*)

Giovanni Mario (1810–1883) was the most celebrated tenor of the mid-nineteenth century—and is said to have been the inventor of elastic-sided boots! He and his wife, Giulia Grisi, were a famous operatic duo. They were once nearly killed when singing in Les Huguenots *in Paris: to make the scene more realistic, some guardsmen had been engaged to play Charles IX's troopers and when given the order to fire obeyed it literally, taking deliberate aim at Mario and Grisi who were, in consequence, covered with gunpowder. Grisi's muslin gown was nearly set alight. She and her husband cried out 'It all be fun, why blow guns at us?', but the soldiers were greatly surprised and said they were merely obeying orders. Despite this painful experience, Mario was greatly addicted to smoking cigars; Spanish audiences, sympathising with this taste, even encouraged him to smoke on stage, where he would puff happily away as Edgardo while his Lucia was in full operatic flood.*

The first time Mario and Grisi were in America it was a terribly hard winter. The theatre at Washington was bitterly cold and part of the roof having given way under the weight of a heavy fall of snow, the heat of the gas melted the frozen snow and it streamed down through the aperture upon the unfortunate singers. The opera was *Norma* and Grisi, instead of appearing in her traditional white robes with heavy folds, was compelled to come upon the stage huddled up almost to her eyes in a great fur cloak; but the audience only perceived that something was wrong when Mario entered holding a coachman's umbrella over his head. The house burst into roars of laughter as Pallione and Norma had their tragic meeting under this prosaic safeguard. Mario held the umbrella over both of them while they sang the great duet.

A curious incident, showing the fascination Mario exercised over his listeners occurred once at a concert. He was singing Alary's charming romance, *La Chanson de l'Amoureux*, which in those days was very popular. As he sang the second verse with passionate feeling—

> '*Ah, viens au bois, folle maîtresse;*
> *Au bois, sombre et mystérieux;*
> *Ah, viens au bois!*'

a young lady rose from her seat and in a dreamy ecstatic voice exclaimed, 'Je viens, je viens!'

ALL FOR LOVE or THE STAGE WELL LOST

James Henry Mapleson
The Mapleson Memoirs (1888)

In July 1875, one of the most charming vocalists that it has been my pleasure to know, a lady who as regards voice, talent, grace, and style was alike perfect, and who was as estimable by her womanly qualities as by her purely artistic ones, made her first appearance at my temporary Operatic home, Drury Lane, as Rosina, in *Il Barbiere*. This was Mademoiselle Marguerite Chapuy, and no sooner had the news of her success been proclaimed than Adelina Patti came, not once, but twice running, to hear her.

At the first performance Mademoiselle Chapuy made such an impression on the public that in the scene of the music lesson she was encored no less than four times; Sir Michael Costa hated encores, but on this occasion he departed willingly from his usual rule.

Marguerite Chapuy charmed everyone she came near; among others a young French sergeant, a gentleman, that is to say, who had enlisted in the French army, and was now a non-commissioned officer. Her parents, however, did not look upon the young man as a fit husband for such a prima donna as their daughter, and it was true that no vocalist on the stage seemed to have a brighter future before her. Mademoiselle Chapuy remained meanwhile at Drury Lane, and the success of her first season was fully renewed when in the second she appeared as Violetta in *La Traviata*. A more refined impersonation of a character which requires very delicate treatment, had never been seen.

It struck me after a time that my new Violetta was not wasting away in the fourth act of *La Traviata* alone. She seemed to be really perishing of some malady hard to understand; and when the most eminent physicians in London were called in, they all regarded the case as a difficult one to deal with since there was nothing definite the matter with the patient. Gradually, however, she was fading away.

There would be no thought of her appearing now on the stage; and at her own desire, as well as that of her father and mother, who were naturally most anxious about her, she was removed to France. No signs of improvement, however, manifested themselves. She got weaker and weaker, and when she was seemingly on the point of death her hard-hearted parents consented to her marriage with the young sergeant. My consent had also to be given, and I naturally did not withhold it.

Mademoiselle Chapuy had signed an engagement with me for several years. But everyone said that the unhappy vocalist was doomed; and such was beyond doubt the belief of her parents, or they never would have consented to her throwing herself away on an honourable young man who was serving his country for something less than a franc a day, when she might so easily have captured an aged banker or a ruined Count.

Shortly afterwards I met her in Paris looking remarkably well. She told me that her husband had received his commission soon after their marriage, and that he now held some local command at Angoulême. As I had not released her from her engagement, I suggested to her, and even entreated, that she should fulfil it. Her husband, however, would not hear of such a thing. He preferred that they should live quietly on the £120 a year which he was now receiving from the Government. I offered as much as £200 a night, but without effect.

There are two ways of judging a singer—by the vocalist's artistic merits, and by the effect of his or her singing on the receipts. In the first place I judge for myself by the former process. But when an appearance has once been made I fall back, as every manager is bound to do, on the commercial method of judgment, and calculate whether the amount of money drawn by the singer is enough to justify the outlay I am making for that singer's services.

Referring to my books, I find with great satisfaction that the charming artist, whom I admired quite as much before she had sung a note at my theatre as I did afterwards when she had fairly captivated the public, drew at her first performance £488, and at her second £538; this in addition to an average nightly subscription of £600.

Thus Mademoiselle Chapuy made her mark from the first.

CONCUSSION

R. M. Levey and J. O'Rorke
*Annals of the Theatre Royal,
Dublin (1880)*

Marietta Alboni (1823–94) was one of the most celebrated contraltos of the mid-nineteenth century. In her later years Rossini called her 'the elephant that swallowed a nightingale'.

The enormous size of Alboni rendered the appearance of Zerlina [in *Don Giovanni*] peculiar. The transposition of the song *'Batti, batti'* a full tone below the original considerably marred the effect, as the violincello obbligato is thereby spoiled. However, the change becomes necessary with contralto vocalists. The appeal to Masetto during the song was, on this occasion, rather forcible; he was in person the reverse of muscular or powerful; and the sudden concussion with such an immense body of animated matter as Zerlina presented was well-nigh causing a curious scene, for if one 'gave way' the other would have followed. However, by a little artistic management on Zerlina's part, matters righted themselves and a little sensation in the pit was the only result.

ENGAGEMENT

Ernest Newman
Birmingham Daily Post

OCTOBER, 1915   The curate sitting near me at the last Leeds Festival was a touching example of the music-lover who doesn't know but who is anxious to learn. When Miss Edyth Walker and Mr John Coates had finished the great duet from the first act of *Götterdämmerung*, the curate said to the lady next to him: 'Was Siegfried *engaged* to Brünnhilde?' I could hardly be restrained from rushing up to this priceless person with open arms. I wanted to take him home with me and keep him as a pet.

'I'VE GOT IT!'

TO THE EDITOR,
   THE THEATRE

August 1st, 1888

Dear Sir,
   When Titiens was singing one evening at a performance of *Norma*, I was sitting behind two dear old ladies who took the deepest interest in all that went on, though they much lamented their inability to 'hear the words'. Their speculations as to the meaning of the various scenes much amused me, but the crowning point arrived at the end of the act when Norma discovers the faithlessness of Pollione. The Adalgisa of the night was some lady far smaller and younger than Titiens. When Norma turned on Pollione with the celebrated *'Oh non tremare! oh perfido!'* delivered with all the fire of the great prima donna, one of my old ladies turned to the other and exclaimed: *'Now* I've got it, my dear, 'e must be that little gal's young man, and she's been telling 'er ma about 'im, and the old gal won't 'ave 'im at any price, and Lor! ain't 'e gittin' it 'ot, that's all!'
   Your obedient servant, GALLERY

141

THE LAST ROSE
OF SUMMER

R. M. Levey and J. O'Rorke
Annals of the Theatre Royal,
Dublin (1880)

It was clearly common for nineteenth-century audiences to interrupt performances and insist that the leading singer deliver one of their favourite ballads, regardless of the sense of the plot. Among the favourites were 'Robin Adair', 'Home Sweet Home', and 'The Last Rose of Summer'.

A slight inconsistency occurred on the last occasion but one of the performance of *Oberon*. It was for the benefit of Titiens. At the forcible request—indeed, the continued and boisterous command—of the members of the upper gallery, immediately following 'Ocean, thou mighty monster', a pianoforte had to be carried on the stage (the waters of said ocean supposed to be running thereon) that poor Titiens should sing 'The Last Rose of Summer'! This she did with her (on this occasion) too yielding kindness and good nature, notwithstanding her dishevelled hair and sea-like appearance. The pianoforte, on being rolled off the stage, unfortunately rolled over, creating shouts of laughter.

LAST WORDS

The Musical Times

MAY, 1891   The *Menestrel* is responsible for the following curious fact—if it be a fact—about the late Miss Emma Abbott, which may interest our readers: 'She was well-known in her own country, as well as in England, not only for her talent, but also for her eccentricities. . . . It was she whose uncompromising and grotesque puritanism transformed, to suit her taste, the character of Verdi's *Traviata*. Violetta was no longer the Marguerite Gautier who made the name of Alexandre Dumas famous in twenty-four hours. Miss Abbott converted her into a pure girl of platonic affections, who, after being mortally stricken with consumption, expires singing, not *"Addio del passato"*, but the hymn "Nearer my God to Thee".'

LAST NIGHT

James Henry Mapleson
The Mapleson Memoirs (1888)

Our last night was indeed a gala night. The most brilliant audience of the whole season filled every corner of the theatre, so great was the curiosity of the public to see Madame Patti and Madame Scalchi together in the same opera. About five o'clock the crowd outside the Academy was already immense, and it was not until seven that we opened the doors. The rush was great, and a sad incident now took place. An old lady in the crowd who had purchased her ticket beforehand was taken up from the bottom of the staircase to the top, though she died before reaching the first landing from disease of the heart, rendered fatal by the excitement. Borne upwards by the dense crowd she did not fall till she reached the gallery. Fearing the alarm this occurrence might cause, the servants, in order that I should not hear of it, had placed the lady on the floor of a little top private box, where she remained during the whole of the performance; her body not being removed by her friends until the next morning.

FLIGHTS OF ANGELS   *Theatrical Anecdotes (1882)*

Elizabeth Billington (c. 1765–1818) was an English singer with a voice of remark-able sweetness. When travelling in Italy she was engaged to sing at Naples, through the good offices of the English ambassador, Sir William Hamilton: Vesuvius promptly erupted, and some of the Neapolitans declared that God was expressing His displeasure at the advancement of a Protestant prima donna. No such misfortune marred her appearance in Dublin, where an Irishman bawled from the gallery 'Heaven bless ye! Ye've surely got a nest o' nightingales in your belly.'

Haydn was an enthusiastic admirer of the singer Mrs Billington; and one day, calling on Sir Joshua Reynolds, he found her sitting for her portrait in the character of St Cecilia, listening to the celestial music. Haydn, having looked for some moments attentively at the portrait, said, 'It is fery like—a fery fine likeness; but dere is a strange mistook.'

'What is that?' said Sir Joshua, hastily.

Haydn answered, 'You haf painted Mrs Billington listening to der angels; you should haf painted der angels listening to Mrs Billington.'

A theatre lease these days would run to thirty or forty pages and be the subject of long, long correspondence between lawyers, in order to cover every possible eventuality of default by the lessee. This is a particularly interesting document, signed by Henry Loveday and Bram Stoker, for many years Irving's stage manager and theatre manager, as well as being signed by Irving himself. The fourth signatory, M. L. Mayer, a French impresario, sub-leased the Lyceum in July, 1889, to stage the first London performance of Verdi's Otello.

Irving had become lessee and manager of the Lyceum, where he and Ellen Terry were to reign supreme, some ten years earlier. One of his most loyal supporters was the great Victorian benefactress Angela Burdett-Coutts, who invited him to join a yachting party in the Mediterranean so that he might study costume and scenic effects for his opening production, The Merchant of Venice, *in 1879. People who bank at Coutts will know that even in a harsher financial climate, they retain the dignified courtesy of that more leisurely time.*

IX

FROM FANS AND OTHERS

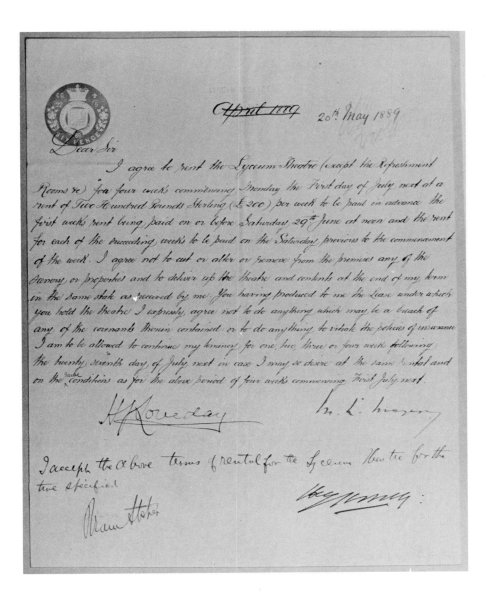

Most fan mail is as fleeting as the performances which call it forth, but I treasure still a letter sent to me in 1948. It seems to me to express the warmth, the affection, and the sympathy which may be created between actor and audience——

> *Pardon me writing to you but I should like to say how much I admire your acting, which is always a most enjoyable pleasure in watching you, your brogue and also your mannerisms, which are a great delight, when you was in the Forge in* Great Expectations *it brought back many joys of my childhood, when I was 12 years of age I spent my holidays with a great Uncle who kept a Forge and a great Farm House attached where large Victoria plums grew all over the wall and round the bedroom window when Windy the apples use to fall plonk in the night you know how that sounds. The very best of good luck to you and your Family, may you live many years to entertain your Public, you love the country and I love the country so we have something in common when you read this I can see your eyes sparkle and a real hearty chuckle well cheerio your admirer——*

The address was merely 'Hammersmith', the signature merely initials; he asked for nothing in return. Truly, a pearl among fans.

SUSPENSE

TO MR GEORGE COLMAN, SENR.   [early 1773]
    MANAGER, COVENT GARDEN

Dear Sir,

I entreat you'll relieve me from that state of suspense in which I have been kept for a long time. Whatever objections you have made, or shall make, to my play, I will endeavour to remove, and not argue about them. To bring in any new judges of its merits or faults I can never submit to. Upon a former occasion, when my other play was before Mr Garrick, he offered to bring me before Mr Whitehead's tribunal, but I refused the proposal with indignation; I hope I shall not experience as hard a treatment from you as from him. I have, as you know, a large sum of money to make up shortly; by accepting my play, I can readily satisfy my creditors that way; at any rate, I must look about to some certainty to be prepared. For God's sake take the play, and let us make the best of it; and let me have the same measures, at least, which you have given as bad plays as mine.

I am, your Friend and Servant,
OLIVER GOLDSMITH

The play was She Stoops to Conquer, *and Mr Colman had despaired of it. It was staged at last on March 15, 1773, thanks largely to the efforts of Dr Johnson, and has long been recognised as one of the classic English comedies. Goldsmith died a year later, penniless and owing some £2,000; had he been on the most modest of present-day royalties, 6% rising to 7½% rising to 10%, he could have lived out the short time remaining to him in security and comfort, and left his kinsfolk well provided.*

THE PIVY'S PRAISE

TO MR DAVID GARRICK
Twickenham,
June 23rd, 1776

In the height of the public admiration for you, when you were never mentioned with any other appellation but the Garrick, the charming man, the fine fellow, the delightful creature, both by men and ladies; when they were admiring everything you did and everything you scribbled, at this very time, I, *the Pivy*, was a living witness that they did not know, nor could they be sensible, of half your perfections. I have seen you, with lamb-like patience, endeavouring to make them comprehend you; and I have seen you when that could not be done. I have seen your lamb turned into a lion; by this your great labour and pains the public was entertained; they thought they all acted very fine—they did not see you pull the wires.

There are people now on the stage to whom you gave their consequence; they think themselves very great; now let them go on in their new parts without your leading-strings, and they will soon convince the world what their genius is. I have always said this to everybody, even when your horses and mine were in their highest prancing. While I was under your control I did not say half the fine things I thought of you, because it looked like flattery, and you know your Pivy was always proud; besides, I thought you did not like me then, but now I am sure you do, which makes me send you this letter.

KITTY CLIVE

Kitty Clive [1711-85] who acted so long with Garrick at Drury Lane, wrote this on his retirement in 1776. They had frequently quarrelled, but this last letter meant much to Garrick, who preserved it with the inscription My Pivy—excellent. *'Clivy-Pivy' had been his familiar name for her.*

KILLING WITH KINDNESS

TO MRS ELIZABETH MACKLIN,
   Tavystock Row,
   Covent Garden,   Dublin
   London   Friday, May 20th, 1785

My Dear Bess,

This night, Mr Anthony Perry, nephew to our Friend Frank Perry, sets out for London,—I suppose, as the wind is fair, that he will be in Holyhead tomorrow morning, in Chester on Sunday night, & be in London on Tuesday night, or on Wednesday night at farthest. Pray be ready to receive him, and treat him with all Kindness that your Friendship and hospitality can show him—let him lie in your room and provide him with meat, drink, washing & Lodging.

Let our Boy, John, attend on him constantly, wherever he goes, and show him the town, & tell him the names of every thing he sees, & of the Places, etc.—upon no account must he take any money of him—I have charged Mr Anthony not to offer him any, nor must Judy or any of our people take any money from him—

I long to be at home very much indeed—for the eating & drinking here is most inviting, provoking, and, to me, most troublesome—I shall be killed with kindness—I shall not stay to play so many nights as I intended—for I can not drink, study, and act—I shall not, nay indeed I can not play above five or six nights,—

God bless you—my compliments to everybody—
    Yours whilst——
Let our boy John go to the Golden Cross to await the Coach coming in—to show Mr Perry the way to our house in a coach.
      CHARLES MACKLIN

I have by blowing thro a red-hot pipe melted the wax of this letter & by that means opened it on purpose to desire you to send me your Recipe for the worms,—for my Landlady's Daughter four years old—pray be very clear & particular how much she must take at a time—how often—and what time must elapse between each dose—& how she must proceed till the cure is performed, and how to act should they return at any time.

Charles Macklin was no ordinary homespun actor. He had successfully won his case against the hired bullies who disrupted his performance as Shylock at the Haymarket in 1773 (page 33) and was to make a last stage appearance in this, his most famous role, when in his ninetieth year (page 167). The author of two very successful plays in which he wrote star parts for himself—as Sir Archy MacSarcasm in Love `a la

Mode *and Sir Pertinax MacSycophant in* The Man of the World—*he was a life-long rival of the great David Garrick. As young men, Davy Garrick and Sam Johnson had journeyed from Lichfield to London to seek their fortunes, sharing one nag between them, ride and tie (my editor claims that though I did not know this expression, it is a familiar one . . .), and they remained dear friends. On one occasion, when Macklin was of the company, Dr Johnson was, as usual, laying down the law. His theme was the importance of a classical education—'No man may claim to be civilised,' he said, 'who is not familiar with one or both of the ancient languages.' Thereupon Macklin let loose a stream of pure eloquence—not Latin, not Greek, but Gaelic—which laid the Doctor flat. Touché!*

RISING SCALE

TO MR RICHARD PEAKE,
    TREASURER,
    DRURY LANE

[Autumn, 1800]
Tuesday, half-past Five

My dear Peake,

It is now two days since my necessity made me send to you for Sixty Pounds. My Request has been treated with a Disregard that I am at a loss how to account for.

I certainly shall go, and act my Part tonight—but unless you send me One hundred pounds before Thursday, I will not act on Thursday—and if you make me come a-begging again, it will be for Two hundred pounds before I set my Foot in the Theatre.

    I am, dear Peake, your

        J. P. KEMBLE

John Philip Kemble was not a man to be lightly disregarded. It is said that when living in Lausanne he used to feel jealous of Mont Blanc; he disliked to hear people always asking 'How does Mont Blanc look this morning?'

DEAR MR YATES

The following letters, written to the actor Frederick Henry Yates (1797–1842) in the eighteen-thirties, when he was in management at the Adelphi Theatre in the Strand, were quoted by his son Edmund Yates in his Recollections and Experiences, *published in 1884:*

149

Dear Yates,

Can I have my usual box tonight? I stay in London but a couple of days, and it will be an indulgence. I detest mixing with the canaille. *I like the public's money, but despise them.*

Yours truly, EDMUND KEAN

From Jane Porter, author of The Scottish Chiefs, *an appeal for a protégée:*

... a person in whom I am greatly interested. She was a leading comic actress in a small but respectable company which used to come annually to Thames Ditton, and perform there during five or six years of our residence in the neighbourhood. My venerable mother, and other most excellent heads of the families about, always patronised the company because of the Worthiness of character as individuals. My protégée is now a middle-aged woman, of a slight, airy form, a quick and pleasing countenance, though not handsome, a pleasant and clear voice, and genteel enunciation. She would be capable to undertake all old or elderly female characters in comedy, or, indeed, from the still juvenile appearance of her figure and lively countenance, chamber-maids and the like would not come amiss to her. She could also lead choruses of peasantry, etc.

From the writer Mary Russell Mitford, author of Our Village:

What would be the remuneration for a drama such as you wish? ... Supposing we agree as to terms, would the enclosed Incendiary story answer for the serious part of a piece? I think it would; that is to say, I think it might admit of some good scenes for Mrs Yates, whom I have never had the pleasure of seeing perform, but who is said by everyone to be a sweet, affecting and natural actress. ... I saw a part of the *Wreck Ashore* at Reading, but could not sit it out. I was so terribly nervous that the motion of the latch and Grampus's face through the window seemed to me like house-breaking, of which I have great dread. I have an equal aversion to guns and explosions of all kinds, which may account for my never having been to any small theatre except the Haymarket. ...

NAMESAKE

This letter was quoted by its recipient, Alfred Bunn, in his book The Stage: Both Before and Behind the Curtain *(1840):*

Sir,

I am induced to address you, from information that you are a gentleman not to be prejudiced by others, but always judging for yourself. I saw you at the Lyceum, where I lately made my debut as the representative of my namesake of immortal memory, in a dramatic trifle which I had sketched merely for the purpose of my introduction to the London public. It may perhaps be called a bold, if not impudent attempt, from a tyro, but as the audience expressed their approbation (and Mr Sheridan Knowles and yourself were amongst the number who did me that honour) I thought I had gained the point proposed, for I then knew nothing about newspaper reports. But the pot-house critics of the Sunday press (the gin-and-water comates of the actors, who felt indignant at having to perform indifferent parts to one whom they kindly termed an ill-clad strolling vagabond) thought otherwise, and I have been abused by them with a rancour that has thrown me upon a sick-bed.

You witnessed my performance—you have experienced judgement, unwarped by prejudice—will you allow me an opportunity in the young Shakespearean characters? Romeo, Orlando, Benedict, or in others more melodramatic and operatic—Gambia in *The Slave*, Daran in *The Exile*, at the re-opening of Drury Lane?

I am, with respect, Sir, your humble servant,
    W. WALTON SHAKESPEARE

Humble servant or not, young Mr Shakespeare did not appear at Drury Lane. Bunn thought he had some talent, but held that 'the assumption of so sacred a name might have rendered all his exertions, as I fear they have done, abortive'. I am reminded of another young actor who approached me with cheerful confidence many years ago—

Dear Mr Miles,
Unfortunately you say in your letter you would like to see some of my TV film or theatre work. Well there's a very quick answer to that question. Impossible because you see I have only acted on the stage and you couldn't see me Act on the stage for the simple reason right now I have no stage to Act on. These last two lines sound like something out of a play. But then I suppose I always was one for Acting and I think a darn good one. So what do I do? Well first of all I think what experience of Acting outside Amateur shows I've had nothing except at the local School of Drama at which I won the Bronze Medal not much I agree but my teacher said I should go straight in for the Gold. But I hesitated think about this for a few days I said even weeks. No! I finally made up my mind I shall

try the Playhouse so I do and I get a small part in Hindle Wakes *then I land another part in* Night Must Fall *but I couldn't get taken on as a student as they had enough students so when* Night Must Fall *finished I finished. I do stand a chance of getting there as a student if someone leaves. But then what happens I get small parts and so on and so on and so on but it's such a waste of time! Given a good part in a Film I could become a Star inside a year why should I think such a thing simple I can Act and I defy every rule in the book about years and years and years of Rep Experience because I believe what the great Hollywood Director Sam Goldwyn said Stars are born. And I was born Mr Miles—*

Such would-be stars hunger after West End success, their names in lights on Broadway, their faces familiar to millions who have seen them on the cinema or television screen. Hazlitt knew better. Nothing, he said, could be more intoxicating than 'unlooked-for success in a barn'; and that is as true of our weekly 'reps' today as it was of his country farmyards or the Elizabethan taverns, or even, perhaps, the Balls Pond theatre curtly dismissed by the Editor of The Players *in the next item.*

ANSWERS TO CORRESPONDENTS

The following replies are taken from the correspondence columns of The Players, *a weekly dramatic, musical and literary journal, published in London, in 1860:*

JULIA complains that in a tragedy she recently saw at a London theatre, one of the actors—the name we suppress—wore natural whiskers which she thinks spoilt his performance, and asks, 'Do you not think he ought to be compelled to shave them off, as it seems quite out of place for an actor to wear whiskers unless they are sham ones.' We really cannot see why an actor should be required to be more barefaced than other people.

SILLY BILLY has adopted a very appropriate cognomen.

FRANK MOSS.—We sent a gentleman to the performance of the Gloster Amateur Society at the Garrick Theatre, but he states that the noise and disturbance was so great that it was perfectly impossible to hear whether the actors played well or ill; indeed such language was indulged in at one part of the evening, in the box in which he sat, accompanied by a lady, that he was compelled to leave the house before the performance was half over. This was much to be regretted, the more especially as the fault did not at all rest with the actors, but with the audience. We trust that the Gloster Society will take precautions to keep out of the theatre all persons who do not know how to conduct themselves properly, the next time they give a performance.

J. ALLEN.—We do not believe in a 'young man in full health, of good natural ability, and a very superior education', being without money unless he hates industry. With the qualifications you mention, the stage is open to you; but without you have an ardent love for the art, do not attempt it.

JAMES JOHNSTONE.—We never heard of the Balls' Pond Theatre.

H. SMITH should give up all hopes of the stage; a man who writes 'Amlet' is not likely to act Hamlet.

APEMANTUS—Surely our irate correspondent did not expect that we could insert his letter, so full as it is of the most slanderous attacks upon the moral characters of actors and actresses, without one word of proof to substantiate the charges. The style of his letter betrays clearly the tone of his mind.

SQUEEZED

TO THE EDITOR,   January 16th, 1861
    THE PLAYERS

Sir,
    A short time since, on visiting the Adelphi Theatre, I was astonished and mortified to find that the seat allotted to me in the balcony stalls was contracted to that degree that it was with the greatest difficulty I could squeeze myself into the narrow space between the back of my seat and the railing in front of the balcony. Hitherto I had looked on the Adelphi as the *ne plus ultra* of comfort, and I had distinct visions of having lounged but a few months ago in the very seat in which I was now so tightly wedged and jammed up that I could scarcely turn round to ascertain the cause of this strange metamorphosis. A slight glance, however, revealed the fact that into the space formerly occupied by *two* rows of stalls were now crammed three, with scarcely room enough between them for a person to pass along to his seat. To enable this change to be carried out, a small slice had been coolly cut off from the 'family boxes', the occupants of which were, of course, as much inconvenienced by the change as the visitors in the stalls themselves. Now, Mr Editor, is this not a breach of faith deliberately committed by the manager against the public?
        I remain,
            Your obedient servant,
            AN OLD PLAYGOER

CLAIMING THE RIGHT

Samuel Phelps was outraged when the Stratford upon Avon Tercentenary Festival Committee invited Charles Albert Fechter, a Frenchman of German descent, to play the Tercentenary Hamlet.

TO THE REV. J. M. BELLEW,   January 21st, 1864
    Corresponding Secretary in London,
    Stratford upon Avon Tercentenary Committee

My dear Sir,
    I *claim the right*, upon the following ground, to be considered the foremost man in my profession in a demonstration meant to honour Shakespeare. I have produced worthily thirty-four of his plays, which no individual manager ever did before. They were acted in my theatre four thousand times, during a period extending over eighteen years. I acted to the satisfaction of a large *English* public all his heroes—tragic and comic—and to that public I shall appeal, and publish this correspondence. The Stratford Committee have insulted me by asking any man in this country to play *Hamlet* on such an occasion without having first offered a choice of characters to
        Yours faithfully,
           S. PHELPS

In the event, Fechter withdrew, and there was no Hamlet *at all.*

IT IS A GOOD PLAY

The following letters were addressed to Edward Stirling at Drury Lane in about 1869, and were quoted by him in Old Drury Lane: Fifty Years' Recollections of Author, Actor and Manager (*1881*):

TO MUSTER STIRLING
    manger
    dury lane playhouse   No 35 blomsbry stret
    London   Wolverampton

dear sir i wright these few lines to ask you if you can oblige me With a place in the Stage i can play ither comick or sentinental but cant dance it is years since i played first in Wolverampton i ave been Burmingham Nottinam Liverpool an Scotlan the last time i played Was With Mr Dillon in hamlet a month ago Sir i ave ritten a play out of my own ead 3 acts an 7 seams i call it ellin brouke the betrayed it is a good play if you will exept it you shall ave it

on condition that i take ellin in it please Wright an say if you can oblige me or no—an i Wil Wright an say—Ill send it an my cart i remain
yours obedient servant nelly lyn

Stirling replied—'The offer was too inviting to lose'—and in response Nelly sent him her carte and the plot of her play:

dear sir, you ask me for a plot ofe my play i sent it you first seam a sittin rom With fire an gas ned sitting in a cheer talken to himself mr thorymore a neglected luvyer ofe ellins enters the rom bob blackthorne a villin ellin With her true luv arther Wood—at a glass doare florence a ladys companion enter—there is a tuzzle With ned she nocks ned down—bob carry ellin ofe—one act.

second act a forrest with a river an rocks ellin lying on the grounded With mr thorymore an bob a stairin over her—she asks for Water mr thorymore go's for it, bob goes and stanins by a tree florence Wanders in finds ellin there is a talk—with bob and florence in Wich she pushes bob into the river, then return ellin, they are startled by a Great noys they make byined—a number of Wild injuns rush in dancin round un ellin crying and grown—they all run ofe bar mary more a lying there ellin speach

third act—seam a churchyard With graves enter ned then gos too sleep. ellin an flo enter—speach then go. Seam a gardin With a gate ellin flo With ellin leaving on her arm flo leave ellin buy the gate an finds arthur an brings him to nell—speach then go.

4 seam—same sittin room as the fust ned lyin on a sofa a nock at dor—artur an ellin an florence the forgiveness an end—if a reception i sings ome sweet ome.

dear sir if this is the way you mean pleas tell me as i dont know any other Way—pleas send me Word if you think it will do an Wen i can come an Wat the Wages are i has sent you a cart ofe myself as i played in hamlet as a page last Witsuntide.
nelly lyn

caracters   ned brown ellins father   mr thorymore a neglected luvyer
            ellin brown   bob blackthorne a villin
            florence   arther Wood ellens tru luv

            an a number of Wild injuns—praps you could put more seams
            in it—not very short

            a bad Writer   but good Worder

'Could there exist a doubt, poor girl, of her powers of composition?' wrote Stirling. 'Writing plays puzzles many wiser heads than Nelly Lynn's.'

MONEY IN IT!

This letter was received by Cyril Maude when in management and was quoted by him in his memoir, The Haymarket Theatre *(1903)*

Dear Sir,

I have written a play, and for some weeks I was unable to decide whether to send it to you or to Mr Tree. Finally, however, as I hope you will be glad to hear, I decided on you.

It is a naval play, and I was well qualified to write it, having been a surgeon in the navy, addicted to writing, a keen amateur actor, and a persistent playgoer.

The leading part (your part) is that of a naval officer, who is supposed to be the son of a bishop by a woman who had been in the ballet. But nothing is definitely known. Anyhow, your two characteristics are, a passion for practical joking, and fitful moments of religious devotion. In Act I, owing to one of your jokes, a midshipman is killed, which so works on you that you resign your commission and in an ecstasy of religious enthusiasm enter a monastery. Here all goes well for a time, but eventually your inbred love of practical joking reasserts itself, and in a sudden fit you play pranks in the monastery, and again accidentally kill a young monk. It now transpires that you are the son of the Father Superior, and you learn this in a highly dramatic scene. 'Who then,' you demand, 'is my mother?' Upon this the Mother Superior (hitherto of unsuspected virtue) comes forward and says 'I am.' (*Sensation*)

This, of course, alters things, and your child (you have a young illegitimate son) appears on the scene, and the action becomes both exciting and involved.

This is only a crude character sketch, but if you *feel* the idea, will you kindly suggest what fees I should receive?

The writing is—if I may say so—of extraordinary brilliance, and in the words of the company manager, 'There's money in it'—

Yours faithfully. . . .

Theatre managers receive offers of this kind three or four times a week, not only from authors, but also from actors offering their services in the most glowing terms. I must have received hundreds in my time, on the following lines:

> *dear mr Miles, please read all my letter as it has an alternitave. I know that I am tallanted as an actress but tallant can never excell itself without proffessionall expearience you see I am an artist I want to creeate sincear beauty because I love truth. I had a very good training. During hollidays I studyed costume makeing millinry stage jewellry props and I can allso paint sceanery. I have develloped these sidelines for begginning when*

*walkons are heardly proffittable or on the odd week I am not needed I can
be very usefull else where. Allthough I have no proffessionall expearience
I have lived intensly in exsticy dispair fear lonelyness and love allso I
have lived and travalled in other countrys and all walks of life surely this
attones for my lack of proffessionall expearience because a lot of emmo-
tionall knowlege other people gain from expearience I have* lived *so I
know what they only gess allso I have studyed people I can annallise any
caracter accuratly on introduction—RUBBISH?—no* true. *I need only
15 minuts out of your life 5 to summon me and ten to talk to me so I can
proove real acting ableity and true understanding I am not in any way
accademmic. 15 minuts is no great loss even if I was no use evryone must
start some where and I can offer my sidelines as compenseation to start
with, yours sincearly LILIAN CASHFORTH*

I sometimes wish I had had time to invest a few minutes in Lilian's sidelines. But I
was up to my ears getting the Mermaid Theatre built and feared she might prove a
responsibility.

I WANT WORK

TO SIR HENRY IRVING

10 Belvedere Crescent,
Lambeth, S.E.
Wednesday, 15th, '96

Dear Sir,
    I have been about thirty years on the Stage, playing High, Low, Jack &
The Game—seldom the latter, generally the penultimate (as pedants say) and
never the first—said I wasn't funny enough. *Can* you give me a part, however
small (salary duly apportioned) in *Cymbeline* on tour? *With* understudy preferred—also Comedy, Comedy Character, Old Man, Servants—'Green
Man'—there are few old pros know that term—or anything? I am simply,
literally starving but for some aid from my dear old managers Messrs Chas
Wyndham and Hawtrey, whose professional servant I have been all my life,
on and off; I was Principal Comedian with Mr C. W. who, I think, knew
you not very long before he opened with Miss Patty Oliver at the redesigned Royalty.
    I've also tried to support Phelps, Dillon, Barry Sullivan, Miss Marriott,
Henry Lorraine, etc.
    Do give me an engagement and let me rehearse at once, however small
(super?) or I've only the workhouse.
    I am so hungry (this is private). I'm a most conscientious Shakespearean
student and actor, as dear Lewis Bell was, but I hope not so pedantic.

157

I'm in very low water—you should see my cupboard—Mr C. W. & Mr C. H. & Mr A. B. F. have all helped me.

I want *work*—not compassion. Reason why I've been so long hors de la scène—Rheumatism—been playing it till *almost* rotten perfect. Can write no more—so weak, what with weather, food, etc. But I *never* felt better in my life! All rheumatism gone, thank God! PLEASE SEE ME at your very earliest convenience.

I'm 'sans this-sans that' etc. But not like Old Gobbo. I wish you'd see me—I'm as big a worshipper of the Master, perhaps, as *you* and will yield to no one in fealty and loyalty.

I've watched nearly all the great men's rise in our beloved profession. Well: DO SEE ME. I'll read you my last play if you like—there's a part for you and another for the greatest little actress on the stage, that I think would fascinate you both. I had you both in my eye; but it wants difficult special engagements. It's not a *star* piece.

Do write at once to yr humble servant

FREDERIC BOND

Laurence Irving, Sir Henry's grandson, gave me this letter. Fred Bond was one of the legion of dutiful supporting actors, 'table-legs' as Gordon Craig has so aptly called them, who lived and died in the service of our glittering, glamorous, treacherous bitch of a profession. I should like to know when and where he made his final exit.

A YOUNG LOT

TO SIR HENRY IRVING

Swan Hotel,
Maesteg, Bridgend,
Glamorgan, S. Wales

March 24th 1905

Dear Sir,

We are as amuteures taking on a Play & as we are not accustomed to the stage we kindly Ask your advice of the Play to take & also where to buy it. The princepal caracttiers in the Play we want is the villaness and the villan. We are a young lot taking it on. I am the oldest of the Girls & I am only 16 years of age, but we are considered more because we are tall. We have read that you are retireing off the stage so if it will give you no trouble we will be much obliged with your advice. We are all the company having our photographs taking in a Group & will, if you will accept, send you one on. I hope you will help us. If so you will oblige

MINNIE DEAVINE

P.S. Hoping you are in good health.

This letter was endorsed in Irving's own hand: 'The Lady of Lyons'—best wishes. *In another hand was written:* Sent April 20th 1905. *Irving died at Bradford on October 13, that year. 'A young lot' would need all the best wishes they could muster, to tackle* The Lady of Lyons.

AN IRISHMAN'S ANSWER

Andrew Cherry was an actor and dramatist, born in Limerick in 1762. As a young strolling player in Ireland, he nearly starved; but eventually he made his name, crossed to England, and played in the major provincial cities and at Drury Lane. After his success in London, he was invited to return to Dublin by a theatre manager who had previously broken faith with him. Cherry's reply was succinct:

Sir,

    I am not so great a fool as you take me for. I have been bitten once by you, and I will never give you an opportunity of making two bites of
    A. Cherry

OLYMPIC THEATRE.

One of Edmund Kean's greatest successes was as Sir Giles Overreach in the comedy A New Way to Pay Old Debts, written by the Jacobean playwright, Philip Massinger, and first published in 1633. It remained a very popular piece with its forceful characterisation of the rapacious Sir Giles, who seizes the property of his heedless nephew Frank Wellborn and tries to force his daughter Margaret into marriage with Lord Lovell. Helped by Lovell and a rich widow, Lady Allworth, Margaret wins her true love; Wellborn wins back his property; the lord marries the lady; and Sir Giles, having lost daughter and ducats together, is driven mad and carried off to Bedlam—a fine comic ending! Kean's portrayal of this part was so powerful that on his first performance, January 12, 1816, the pit rose as one man, and his fellow actors, 'in common with an astonished Public, were overcome with the irresistible power of his Genius.'

X

RINGING DOWN

EDMUND KEAN, 1787–1833, the greatest actor of his time, was a man of incandescent temper and theatrical genius. Coleridge said that to see him act was like reading Shakespeare by flashes of lightning.

It's been going on for a long time. In 1483, when the play of Noah was staged at Hull, a Yorkshire actor named Robert Brown was paid sixpence for acting the part of God. A fine British name, a good strong role, and a fair wage! But the theatre was already centuries old. Two hundred years before Robert Brown's performance, a great audience gathered to watch a mystery play at Beverley Minster:

It befell one summer day that the masked players played and acted, after their wont, a certain play of the Lord's Resurrection within the churchyard of St John. Thither were gathered together a great multitude of both sexes, moved by divers causes; some for pleasure, some for wonder, and some for the holy purpose of arousing devotion. In this dense crowd that gathered round the players, there were many (and especially of small stature) who failed to gain the access which they desired; wherefore very many entered into the church, either to pray or to look at the pictures or to beguile the weariness of this day by some kind of recreation and solace.

Certain youths, therefore, entering the church precincts, found by chance a half-opened door leading to the stairs which ascend to the top of the walls. Thither they hastened with boyish levity, and began to climb, step by step, to the stone vault of the church, intending either to peep through the lofty loopholes of the turrets, or through any holes they might find in the glass windows, that thus they might see more clearly the dress and gestures of the actors, and hear their dialogues with greater distinctness; wherein they imitated Zacchaeus, who, because he was little of stature, climbed up into a sycamore tree to see Jesus. But behold! men told the custodians what these youths were doing; and they (fearing lest the boys should break or in some way harm the glass windows in their eagerness to see the performances in this miracle play) followed swiftly after them and rebuking their temerity, buffeted them soundly with the palms of their hands and drove them down again.

Meanwhile one of the boys, beholding how ill his fellows fared and fearing to fall into the pursuers' hands, ran aside among the upper parts of the church, until he had come in his hasty course to a spot beyond the great cross, which then stood by St Martin's altar. Standing there and looking down, he rashly set foot upon a certain squared stone which broke away from the wall and fell down with a crash to the stone pavement, with such a force that, notwithstanding its hardness, it was dashed to a thousand pieces. The youth, lacking all support, and struck with fear and horror, fell also, lying there as one dead for some time afterwards. A crowd gathered round, sighing grievously and wailing miserably over this misfortune and venting their grief with gushing tears. His parents shrieked and tore their hair, while frequent sobs interrupted their cries of sorrow; for they knew not that their mourning was destined soon to be turned to laughter, and their sadness to joy, by God's good providence. For the Lord suffered not that the church, built in His honour and in that of His confessor, St John of Beverley, should be polluted as with a man's death; but, desiring it to be held in even greater reverence for the future, and desiring also to give a testimonial of veracity to that representation of His own resurrection which was meanwhile being played, He raised up in the sight of all men safe and sound, that youth who was believed to be dead, so that no hurt whatever could be found in his whole body.

PREMATURE REPORT   W. R. Chetwood
                                                A General History of
                                                  the Stage (1749)

I cannot avoid mentioning a passage in the life of this truly good comedian [Robert Wetherilt: 1708–1743]. While he and his family belonged to the Theatre Royal in Drury-lane, after the company had finished the season of playing in London (which generally is at the end of May) he, with his father and mother, went, for the summer season, to play at several towns in Lincolnshire (the custom of many of both established theatres). When the company were summoned to meet in London at the usual time (the latter end of August) to begin the winter season, I received the following short letter:

> Sir—Mr Wetherilt and his wife, beg you will excuse them to Mr Wilks; their son is at the point of death. They beg an answer. Be pleased to direct to your humble servant R. Stukely, apothecary, in Grantham, Lincoln-shire.

The meaning why I mention this letter is, that the son, the very night this letter was written, in all appearance expired, was stripped and washed, the bed taken away, and he laid stretched on a mat, with a basin of salt (a common custom in England) placed on his stomach, the inconsolable parents removed to another house, the coffin brought to the son's chamber, and the windows all open. About eight at night a person was sent with a light to watch the corpse. When she opened the door, the first object she perceived was poor Bob (as he was generally called by his familiars) sitting up, with his teeth trembling in his head (and well they might) with cold. The woman, in her fright, dropped the candle and screamed out, 'The devil! the devil!' This fright alarmed the woman below, who ran upstairs to see what was the matter. In the meantime Bob, with much ado, had made a shift to get from the bed; and taking up the candle, which lay upon the floor unextinguished, was creeping to the door to call for assistance, as naked as from the womb of his mother; which the two women perceiving, with joint voices repeated again, 'A ghost! a ghost! The devil! the devil!'

The master of the house, hearing this uproar, ran himself to know the reason; where poor Bob, the supposed devil, and he, soon came to a right understanding. He was put into a warm bed, to the unspeakable joy of his desponding parents, and in ten days after in London (viva voce) told me the whole story of his death.

Medical friends assure me that the alarming experiences of young Mr Wetherilt, and of the old bill poster whose story follows below, must have been duplicated a thousand times in past centuries, so rudimentary were the means of deciding death. The compilers of this book are both taking suitable precautions. . . .

TRANCE   *The Drama (Vol. V, 1824)*

A man named Christopher Lowe was for many years bill distributor to the theatre at Chester, and died in 1801, aged ninety-two. When in his fiftieth year, he was afflicted with a severe fever, of which he apparently expired. He was laid out, shrouded, and coffined; and nearly three days after his supposed demise, being carried on four men's shoulders to the grave, he suddenly knocked off the lid of the coffin. To the ineffable amazement of the carriers and attendants, on opening it they found honest Christopher in a complete state of resuscitation. For many years after he used to amuse and astonish his neighbours and friends with 'the wonderful things he saw in his trance'.

NIGHT OF THE EXECUTION   *The Cork Remembrancer (1760)*

Patrick Redmond, the Tailor, was executed at Gallows Green on September 10th for robbing the dwelling-house of John Griffin. Glover the Player who was then in Cork, took an active part in this man's restoration; after he hung nine minutes, and was cut down, he was perfectly restored to life, by the dint of friction and fumigation. He afterwards made his escape, got drunk, went to the Playhouse door (the night of his execution) to return Mr Glover thanks, and put the whole audience in terror and consternation.

A PRIMA DONNA STILL

James Henry Mapleson
The Mapleson Memoirs (1888)

Patti honoured the performance with her presence in a private box and a somewhat indiscreet gentleman, Dr Nassau, paid her a visit to remind her that it was over twenty-nine years since she had sung under his direction at the old Mozart Hall, 'Coming through the Rye', 'The Last Rose of Summer', Eckert's 'Echo Song', and 'Home, Sweet Home'. He substantiated his statements by one of the original programmes which he had brought purposely to show her. She received him coldly.

CUZZONI'S MELANCHOLY END

Sutherland Edwards
History of the Opera (1862)

Cuzzoni returned to London in 1734 and sang at the Opera in Lincoln's Inn Fields, established under the direction of Porpora, in opposition to Handel. She visited London a third time in 1750, when a concert was given for her benefit; but the poor little siren was now old and infirm; she had lost her voice, and even the enemies of Faustina [her rival] would not come to applaud her.

This stage queen had a most melancholy end. From England she went to Holland, where she was imprisoned for debt, being allowed, however, to go out in the evenings (doubtless under the guardianship of a jailer) and sing at the theatres, by which means she gained enough money to obtain her liberation. Having quite lost her voice, she is said to have maintained herself for some time at Bologna by button-making.

PASTA'S FAREWELL

Henry F. Chorley
Thirty Years' Musical Recollections (1862)

In 1850, when she was fifty-two, Pasta emerged from retirement, seduced into giving one performance at Her Majesty's Theatre, and into singing in a concert for the Italian cause at the Royal Italian Opera, the chosen opera being Donizetti's Anna Bolena:

Nothing more inadvised could have been dreamed of. Madame Pasta had long ago thrown off the stage and all its belongings; and any other public than those who have made their boatmen linger on the lake of Como, hard beneath the garden walls of her villa, with the hope of catching a glimpse of one who in her prime had enthralled so many.

Her voice, which at its best had required ceaseless watching and practice, had been long ago given up by her. Its state of utter ruin on the night in question passes description. She had been neglected by those who, at least, should have presented her person to the best advantage admitted by Time. Her queenly robes (she was to sing some scenes from *Anna Bolena*) in no-wise suited or disguised her figure. Her hairdresser had done some tremendous thing or other with her head—or rather, had left everything undone.

A more painful and disastrous spectacle could hardly be looked on. There were artists present who had then, for the first time, to derive some impression of a renowned artist—perhaps with the natural feeling that her reputation had been exaggerated. Among these was Rachel—whose bitter ridicule of the entire sad show made itself heard throughout the whole theatre, and drew attention to the place where she sat—one might even say, sarcastically enjoying the scene.

Among the audience, however, was another gifted woman, who might far more legitimately have been shocked at the utter wreck of every musical means of expression in the singer—who might have been more naturally forgiven if some humour of self-glorification had made her severely just—not worse—to an old prima donna; I mean Madame Viardot. Then, and not till then, she was hearing Madame Pasta. But Truth will always answer to the appeal of Truth. Dismal as was the spectacle—broken, hoarse and destroyed as was the voice—the great style of the singer spoke to the great singer. The first scene was Anne Boleyn's duet with Jane Seymour. The old spirit was heard and seen in Madame Pasta's '*Sorgi!*' and the gesture with which she signed to her penitent rival to rise. Later, she attempted the final mad scene of the opera—that most complicated and brilliant among the mad scenes on the modern musical stage—with its two cantabile movements, its snatches of recitative, and its bravura of despair, which may be appealed to as an example of vocal display, till then unparagoned, when turned to the account of frenzy, not frivolity—perhaps as such commissioned by the superb creative artist. By that time, tired, unprepared, in ruin as she was, she had rallied a little.

When—on Anne Boleyn's hearing the coronation music for her rival, the heroine searches for her own crown on her brow—Madame Pasta wildly turned in the direction of the festive sounds, the old irresistible charm broke out; nay, even in the final song, with its roulades, and its scales of shakes, ascending by a semitone, the consummate vocalist and tragedian, able to combine form with meaning—the moment of the situation with such personal and musical display as form part, an integral part, of operatic art—was indicated: at least to the apprehension of a younger artist.

'You are right!' was Madame Viardot's quick and heartfelt response (her eyes full of tears) to a friend beside her—'you are right! It is like Leonardo's 'Last Supper' at Milan—a wreck of a picture, but the picture was the greatest in the world!'

There is a last glimpse of Pasta in John Edmund Cox's Musical Recollections. *On an August evening in 1861, he was a passenger on the steamboat plying between Colico and the town of Como, across the Lake. An old woman armed with a stick was driving a string of turkeys along the lake-shore, urging them home to their roosting-place. It was Pasta herself.* Quantum mutata ab illa! *he thought. What a fall was there....*

'OLD MEN FORGET'

James Boaden
Life of Mrs Jordan (1831)

The great excellence of the veteran Macklin drew considerable audiences whenever he appeared at Covent Garden Theatre, and he had been announced to perform Shylock on the tenth of January 1788, at the extraordinary age of eighty-nine. I went there to compare his performance with that of my friend Henderson, whose loss I even still regret; and with some anxiety, and much veneration, secured a station in the pit.

... Macklin got through the first act with spirit and vigour, and except to a very verbal critic, without material imperfection. In the second, he became confused, and sensible of his confusion. With his usual manliness, and waiting for no admonition from others, he advanced to the front of the stage, and with a solemnity in his manner that became extremely touching, thus addressed his audience:

'Ladies and gentlemen, within these few hours I have been seized with a terror of mind I never in my life felt before; it has totally destroyed my corporeal as well as mental faculties. I must, therefore, request your patience this night—a request which an old man of eighty-nine years of age may hope is not unreasonable. Should it be granted, unless my health is totally re-established, you may depend upon it this will be the last night of my ever appearing before you in so ridiculous a situation.'

Thus dignified, even in his wreck, was that great man, whom Pope had immortalised by a compliment*, and whose humanity Lord Mansfield had pronounced to be at least equal to his skill as an actor [see page 34]. He recovered with the general applause of the audience, and got through the play by great attention from the prompter and his assistant.

MUNDEN'S BENEFIT

Joseph Shepherd Munden was born in 1758 and in his teens ran away from the sober life of a stationer's apprentice to join the strolling players. He specialised in playing old men and was particularly pleased by an unwitting compliment which he received in his early days on the stage. 'When I was very young,' he said, 'and looking still

---

* 'This is the Jew, That Shakespeare drew'

younger, I performed the part of Old Philpot in The Citizen *to a respectable audience at Brighton, with great success; and it chanced on the next evening, being disengaged from any professional duty, I was introduced by the gentleman who principally patronised me, as Mr Munden, into a club-room full of company. On hearing my name announced, a nice, snug-looking, good-humoured personage laid down his pipe, and taking up his glass, said: "Here is to your health, young sir, and to your father's health. I saw him perform last night, and a very nice, clever old gentleman he is".'*

A career of over fifty years came to its end on May 31, 1824, when at his farewell performance he played Sir Robert Bramble in Colman's Poor Gentleman *and Old Dozey, one of his greatest roles, in Dibdin's* Past Ten o'Clock and a Rainy Night.

... GROG FOR A SAILOR   *The London Magazine*

JULY, 1824   The regular playgoers ought to put on mourning, for the kind of broad comedy is dead to the drama! Alas!—Munden is no more!—'Give sorrow vent!' He may yet walk the town—pace the pavement in a seeming existence—eat, drink, and nod to his friends in all the affection of life—but Munden—*the* Munden! Munden, with the bunch of countenances—the banquet of faces,—is gone for ever from the lamps; and as far as comedy is concerned, is as dead as Garrick!—When an actor retires, (we will put the suicide as mild as possible), how many worthy persons perish with him! With Munden, Sir Peter Teazle must experience a shock—Sir Robert Bramble gives up the ghost; Crack ceases to breathe. Without Munden, what becomes of Dozey? Where shall we seek Jemmy Jumps? Nipperkin and a thousand of such admirable fooleries fall to nothing—and the departure, therefore, of such an actor as Munden is a dramatic calamity.

On the night that this inestimable humourist took farewell of the public, he also took his benefit;—a benefit in which the public assuredly did not participate! The play was Colman's *Poor Gentleman*, with Tom Dibdin's farce of *Past Ten o'Clock*. Reader, we all know Munden as Sir Robert Bramble, and old tobacco-complexioned Dozey; we have all seen the old hearty baronet in his light sky-blue coat and genteel cocked hat; and we have all seen the weather-beaten old pensioner, dear old Dozey, tacking about the stage in that intenser blue sea-livery—drunk as heart could wish, and right valorous in memory. On this night Munden seemed, like the gladiator, 'to rally life's whole energies to die'...

The house was full—*full*! Pshaw! that's an empty word—the house was stuffed—crammed with people—crammed from the swing-door of the pit to the back seat in the banished one-shilling. A quart of audience may be said (vintner-like may it be said) to have been squeezed into a pint of theatre. Every hearty playgoing Londoner, who remembered Munden years agone,

Mr. MUNDEN as AUTOLICUS.

Joseph Shepherd Munden playing in A Winter's Tale. *Immortalised in an affectionate and illuminating essay by 'Elia', Charles Lamb ('He is not one, but legion. Not so much a comedian, as a company'), Munden was a perennial favourite with Londoners. The report of his last performance, printed in the* London Magazine *and quoted on the facing page, was not by 'Elia', but Lamb was present on this sad occasion (see overleaf) and according to his friend Talfourd, it was the last time he took any real interest in the daily scenes of life. 'His real stage henceforth only spread itself out in the selectest chambers of his memory.'*

mustered up his courage and his money for this benefit, and middle-aged people were, therefore, by no means scarce. The comedy chosen for the occasion is one that travels a long way without a guard;—it is not until the third or fourth act, we rather think, that Sir Robert Bramble appears on the stage. When he entered, his reception was earnest,—noisy,—outrageous,— waving of hats and handkerchiefs, deafening shouts, clamorous beating of sticks; all the various ways in which the heart is accustomed to manifest its joy were had recourse to on this occasion.... The old performer—the veteran, as he appropriately called himself in the farewell speech,—was plainly overcome; he pressed his hands together—he planted one solidly on his breast—he bowed—he sidled—he cried! When the noise subsided (which it invariably does at last), the comedy proceeded—and Munden gave an admirable picture of the rich, eccentric, charitable old bachelor baronet.

In the farce he became richer and richer. Old Dozey is a plant from Greenwich. The bronzed face—and neck to match—the long curtain of a coat—the straggling white hair—the propensity, the determined attachment to grog—are all from Greenwich. Munden, as Dozey, seems never to have been out of action, sun, and drink. He looks (alas! he *looked*) fire-proof. His face and throat were dried like a raisin—and his legs walked under the rum and water with all the indecision which that inestimable beverage usually inspires. It is truly tacking, not walking. He *steers* at a table, and the tide of grog now and then bears him off the point. On this night he seemed to us to be doomed to fall in action, and we, therefore, looked upon him as some of the Victory's crew are said to have gazed upon Nelson, with a consciousness that his ardour and his uniform were worn for the last time.

... AND STOUT FOR A FRIEND   Thomas Noon Talfourd

Charles Lamb had long been an admirer of Munden and was anxious to attend the farewell performance, but he was too late to get a box and too frail to fight his way into the pit on so uproarious a night. When Munden heard of Lamb's disappointment, he secured places for the great essayist and his sister in a corner of the orchestra, as a way of thanking Lamb for his praise and regard:

The play of *The Poor Gentleman*, in which Munden played Sir Robert Bramble, had concluded, and the audience were impatiently waiting for the farce, in which the great comedian was to delight them for the last time, when my attention was suddenly called to Lamb by Miss Kelly, who sat with my party far withdrawn into the obscurity of one of the upper boxes, but overlooking the radiant hollow which waved below us, to our friend. In his hand, directly below the line of stage lights, glistened a huge pewter pot, which he was draining, while the broad face of old Munden was seen thrust out from the door by which the musicians enter, watching the close of the

170

draught, when he might receive and hide the portentous beaker from the gaze of admiring beholders. Some unknown benefactor had sent four pots of stout to keep up the veteran's heart during the last trial; and, not able to drink them all, he bethought him of Lamb, and, without considering the wonder which would be excited in the brilliant crowd who surrounded him, conveyed himself the cordial chalice to Lamb's lips.

A BROKEN HEART   *Dramatic Table Talk (1825)*

John Palmer (1742-98), son of a Drury Lane pit doorkeeper, was the first actor to play Joseph Surface in The School for Scandal. *Sheridan's name for him was 'Plausible Jack'.*

The last engagement of the eminent actor, John Palmer, was at Liverpool; and on the morning of the day on which he was to have performed *The Stranger*, he received, for the first time, the distressing intelligence of the death of his second son, a youth in whom his tenderest hopes were centred, and whose amiable manners had brought into action the tenderest affections of a parent. The play, in consequence of this, was deferred, and during the interval he had in vain endeavoured to calm the agitation of his mind. The success with which he performed the part called for a second representation (August 2nd, 1798) in which he fell a sacrifice to the poignancy of his own feelings, and when the audience were doomed to witness a catastrophe which was truly melancholy.

In the fourth act Baron Steinfort obtains an interview with the Stranger whom he discovers to be his old friend. He prevails on him to relate the cause of his seclusion from the world: in this relation, the feelings of Mr Palmer were visibly much agitated, and at the moment he mentioned his wife and children, having uttered (as in the character) '*There is another and a better world*', he fell lifeless on the stage.

The audience supposed for a moment that his fall was nothing more than a studied addition to the part; but on seeing him carried off in deadly stiffness, the utmost astonishment and terror became depicted in every countenance. Hamerton, Callan, and Mara were the persons who conveyed the lifeless corpse from the stage into the green-room. Medical assistance was immediately procured; his veins were opened, but they yielded not a single drop of blood; and every other means of resuscitation were had recourse to, without effect.

The gentlemen of the faculty, finding every endeavour ineffectual, formally announced his death. Surgical operations upon the body continued about an hour; after which, all hopes of recovery having vanished, he was carried home to his lodgings on a bier, where a regular inventory was taken of his property. Mr Aickman, the manager, came on the stage to announce the melancholy event to the audience, but was so completely overcome with grief as to be incapable of uttering a sentence, and was at length forced to retire, without being able to make himself understood. He was bathed in tears, and, for the moment, sunk under the generous feelings of his manly nature. Incledon then came forward and mastered sufficient resolution to communicate the dreadful circumstances. The house was instantly evacuated in mournful silence.

THE TRAGEDIAN'S END

W. J. Lawrence
*The Life of Gustavus Vaughan Brooke,
Tragedian (1892)*

Gustavus Vaughan Brooke, the much-applauded, Irish-born tragedian (1818–66), was reputed to have the biggest voice of his time—a quality not always appreciated by his fellow actors. Both in London and in New York he gravely damaged his career by his extravagance and insobriety. Resolved to redeem himself, he sailed for Australia in January, 1866, in the S.S. London, his sister accompanying him. A terrible gale blew up in the Bay of Biscay. The lifeboats were washed away, and water poured into the engine-room, silencing the massive machinery for ever.

It needs no great powers of imagination to picture the anguish and agony of suspense suffered by the passengers at this terrible juncture. Albeit the hatches had been nailed down five or six hours previously, the deck-water found its way into the state cabins with alarming persistency, and had now accumulated to such an extent that the bedding in the lower bunks on the starboard side was being washed from the berths. Terrified by the sight, all the first-class passengers assembled in the saloon where the Rev. D. J. Draper, a Wesleyan divine, strove fervently to administer spiritual consolation to those who felt unprepared to meet their Maker. A knot of earnest women gathered around reading Bibles with the children; and now and again all would unite zealously in prayer. Powerful, indeed, was the effect of the good minister's exhortations, for soon the epidemic of calm resignation cast its spells over the anxious, maintaining its sway until the last dread moment.

Although something like a score of the crew were lying below, ill or hurt (many of the foreign element skulking to their berths and refusing to work), hopes of saving the vessel had not yet been abandoned. With the putting out of the engine-room fires, Angel, the third officer, summoned most of the male passengers on deck to assist in covering the gap made by the carrying away of the skylight. Sails were brought up and with difficulty nailed over the opening. Mattresses and other bulky objects were piled on top as additional security. But all to no purpose. Nothing could have withstood the seas which kept pouring over the vessel with alarming violence and persistency. Observing how fruitless were their efforts, many of the passengers went below and, with a determination born of despair, spent hours at a stretch, in attempting to bale out the lower saloon by passing up buckets of water.

Meanwhile, God in his mercy had cut short the suspense of at least one of the passengers. Troubled with heart failure, Miss Brooke's vitality proved too weak to resist the shock. Watching over her tenderly to the last, Gustavus lost all grip of the world—all desire for self-preservation—with the closing of her eyes for ever. Giving no thought to himself, he rushed on deck to do what he could for the others. Owing to the washing out of the [engine-room] fires, no use could be made of the powerful engine pumps; but the ordinary deck pumps had been rigged without delay. It was a difficult and highly dangerous task to work these in the face of the violence of the elements, and volunteers were none too plentiful. Brooke, of his own free will, at once decided to lend a hand. Bareheaded and barefooted, attired only in a red Crimean shirt and trousers, with his braces fastened belt-like around him, he laboured untiringly at the pumps, and time after time revived the drooping spirits of his companions by the almost superhuman energy with which he applied himself to his task.

All through the night of January 10/11, those aboard struggled to keep the vessel afloat, but the water continued to pour into the ship, and at five o'clock that morning, the stern ports were driven in, the sea swept into the lower saloon, and the ship rolled helplessly, completely disabled.

When daylight came Captain Martin ordered the remaining boats to be cleared, and by nine o'clock the starboard pinnace, capable of holding fifty persons, was swung outboard. Six of the crew got in, but the boat was lowered unevenly, and a heavy sea coming to leeward filled her as she hung in the davits. Hence when released she shot her bow under the ship and sank like a stone, the occupants scrambling up again into the *London*, aided partly by the ropes hanging alongside and partly by the advent of a heavy sea. A few of the sailors then endeavoured to clear away the port iron-boat, but getting little help from the others, who deemed the task hopeless, had to abandon their efforts. Finally, the port cutter was provisioned with bread, water, brandy and champagne, and lowered without mishap a few minutes before two o'clock in the afternoon. Sixteen of the crew and three passengers eventually got in. Happily there was little disposition to overcrowd the boat, the sinking of the pinnace having acted as a wholesome corrective. Revolvers were freely displayed by many of the passengers remaining on board, most of whom declared their intention to shoot themselves rather than meet their death in the manner imminent.

Everything now being prepared in the boat, one of the sailors hailed the captain as he walked meditatively up and down the poop deck, and asked whether he intended to accompany them. 'No, King, I do not,' he replied; 'I am going to remain on board.' And then, with considerable forethought, he gave them their course—'E.N.E. for Brest, 190 miles; the nearest land.'

And Brooke? Just as they were pushing off, Gardiner, the assistant steward, observed him leaning with stern composure against the half-door of the companion-way. Here he stood calmly surveying the scene, with his chin resting on his hands as they grasped the top of the door, which swayed slowly to and fro under the pressure. 'Will you come with us, Mr Brooke?' shouted Gardiner, pity welling up in his heart for the man who had toiled so bravely. 'No! no!' replied Brooke. 'Goodbye. Should you survive, give my last farewell to the people of Melbourne.'

As the cutter rowed slowly away, many of the passengers, anxious that someone should survive to tell the tale, waved their handkerchiefs and cheered as best they could. Straining their eyes back eagerly as the distance grew greater, the men saw that the ill-fated vessel was sinking rapidly by the stern. In fact, the stem rose so high out of the water three minutes after their departure that the keel was visible for a moment as far as the foremast. Then the cutter went down into the trough of the sea, and when she climbed a hill of water, Olympus high, no trace of the *London* or of the remnants of her living freight was to be seen; nothing but an awful gulf of dark whirling water.

BEQUEST   Sutherland Edwards
                                   History of the Opera (1862)

Banti died at Bologna in 1806, bequeathing her larynx (of extraordinary size) to the town, the municipality of which caused it to be duly preserved in a glass bottle. Poor woman! she had by this time dissipated the whole of her fortune, and had nothing else to leave.

This treasured bequest, said to have been preserved in alcohol, has apparently disappeared. . . .

FAREWELL KISS   Hannah More

On February 2, 1779, Hannah More wrote to her sister, describing the funeral of David Garrick in Westminster Abbey:

Just at three the great doors burst open with a noise that shook the roof: the organ struck up, and the whole choir, in strains only less solemn than the archangel's trump, began Handel's fine anthem. The whole choir advanced to the grave, in hoods and surplices, singing all the way; then Sheridan as chief mourner; then the body—alas! whose body? with ten noblemen and gentlemen, pall bearers; then the rest of the friends and mourners; hardly a dry eye—the very players, bred to the trade of counterfeiting, shed genuine tears.

As soon as the body was let down, the bishop began the service, which was read in a low but solemn and devout manner. Such an awful stillness reigned that every word was audible. How I felt it! Judge if my heart did not assent to the hope that the soul of our dear brother now departed was in peace. And this is all of Garrick! Yet a very little while, and he shall 'say to the worm, thou art my brother: and to corruption, thou art my mother and my sister.' So passes away the fashion of this world. And the very night he was buried the playhouses were as full, and the Pantheon was as crowded, as if no such thing had happened; nay, the very mourners of the day partook of the revelries of the night—the same night, too! ...

On Wednesday night we came to the Adelphi—to this house! She [Mrs Garrick] bore it with great tranquillity, but what was my surprise to see her go alone into the chamber and bed in which he had died that day fortnight. She had a delight in it beyond expression. I asked her the next day how she went through it? She told me, very well; that she first prayed with great composure, then went and kissed the dear bed, and got into it with a sad pleasure.

Mrs Garrick lived on for another forty-three years. She died in 1822, at the magnificent age of ninety-eight, and was buried beside her husband. Not until Sir Henry Irving's death, in 1905, was another actor granted the honour of an Abbey funeral. An application to bury Kean in the Abbey, close to Garrick, was refused because of 'financial difficulty'.

THE LAST ACT

... 'PRAY YOU NOW, FORGET AND FORGIVE'

'Barry Cornwall'
[Bryan Waller Procter]
The Life of Edmund Kean (1835)

In February, 1833, Edmund Kean was playing Othello at Covent Garden, to his son Charles's Iago. He was taken ill during the performance, and by Act III he could scarcely walk:

He held up, however, until the celebrated 'farewell' which he uttered with all his former pathos, but on concluding it, after making one or two feeble steps towards his son (who took care to be near him) and attempting the speech 'Villain, be sure', &c., his head sank on his son's shoulder, and the tragedian's acting was at an end.

He was able to groan out a few words in Charles's ear—'I'm dying—speak to them for me'; after which (the audience refusing, in kindness, to hear any apology), he was borne from the stage. His son, assisted by other persons, carried him to his dressing-room, and laid him on the sofa. He was as cold as ice; his pulse was scarcely perceptible and he was unconscious of all that was going on around him. In this state he remained some time, when the remedies which were applied having restored him to his senses, he was taken to the Wrekin tavern near the theatre, and Messrs Carpue and Duchez (the surgeons) were sent for.

From the 'Wrekin' he was, after a week's stay, removed to Richmond, still very weak and ill, but without any apprehensions being entertained of immediate danger. At Richmond, he continued to improve a little in health, and was even enabled to go out in his carriage. One day, however, having stayed out longer than usual and the weather being unusually cold, he came home exceedingly ill. He said that he had got his death-blow; asked for brandy, which he drank (saying, however, that it made him colder), and went to bed. This was the last time that he left the house. He grew gradually worse, reviving at times, however, sufficiently to speak of old times, and to talk on the subject of acting. In one of these intervals he wrote the following letter to his wife:

> My dear Mary,
>   Let us be no longer fools. Come home. Forget and forgive. If I have erred, it was my head, not my heart, and most severely have I suffered from it. My future life shall be employed in contributing to your happiness; and you, I trust, will return that feeling by a total obliteration of the past. Your wild, but really affectionate husband,
>   EDMUND KEAN

Mrs Kean answered this appeal by proceeding at once to Richmond. She saw her husband once more, after seven years of estrangement, and the most complete forgiveness and reconciliation followed. She went again to him repeatedly, and the best understanding prevailed between them. All this was the work of their son.

Kean was now in an alarming state. He was very weak, from refusing food. At times he grew delirious; at others, he lapsed into apathy:

In his better intervals, however (for he had a few), his mind still recurred to the subject of acting and actors; and he remembered—not without pleasure—his former triumphs. With his bed always covered with books— Shakespeare, Gibbon, Rollin, an Atlas, &c., and (under the others) his Bible and a Missal—he would still turn back to the stage and show his son how Garrick and Barry had acted Lear. (Sir George Beaumont had formerly explained their manner of playing to him.) And then he would give, in his own fashion, that tenderest of all tender passages: '*Pray, do not mock me—*', &c., where Lear, awakening from his madness, recognises at last his true Cordelia. Nothing could exceed the effect of this, recited as it was under such circumstances.

This, it may be said, was the last act of the actor's life. He grew rapidly worse; although he had his ebbs and flows and was tenacious of life to the end. At one time he was given over; his pulse announced speedy death; but he rallied a little, drank brandy, and (in the absence of those who watched him) crawled out of bed, covered himself with a racoon's skin and, by some extraordinary efforts, dragged himself into the next room. He was found there drinking, and attempting to smoke a cigar, and was prevailed upon to return to his bed from which he never afterwards rose. During the last hours of his existence he was almost insensible; and on the fifteenth day of May, 1833, he quitted the stage of life without consciousness or pain.

... 'A LONG FAREWELL'   Paul Bedford
                                   Recollections and Wanderings (1864)

Bedford was among those granted a last look at the body of Edmund Kean as it lay on a humble couch, awaiting the post mortem:

On looking upon the remains of the dear departed, I observed on the left knee a large blackened bruise. Inquiring of my friend Lee the cause of that blemish, he said that, having attended the bedside of the suffering one for many an anxious night, and being on one occasion overcome by sleep, he was awakened by hearing him utter the well-known passage from the tent scene in *Richard*—'A horse! a horse! my kingdom for a horse!'—and at that moment he sprang off the couch, falling on his knees, which produced the discoloration of the limb. That event occurred about two hours before the final moment. It was the farewell dream of his earthly greatness.

Richmond was crowded for Kean's funeral, which took place ten days later. 'Respectable tradesmen' volunteered to act as special constables, assisting the local police. By their exertions, order and 'a decent aspect of grief' were maintained as Kean was carried to his last resting-place in Richmond Church.

In 1933, on the anniversary of Kean's death, my old friend Sir Seymour Hicks and the dramatic critic Philip Page resolved to walk from Drury Lane to Richmond, carrying a laurel wreath to lay on Kean's grave. When they arrived, the grave was not to be found, nor could the vicar help them. At last, they discovered a stone sarcophagus, half hidden under a wall of the church, into which it had been built.

Whether it was indeed Kean's actual tomb, I can't say, but there, on the protruding stone slab, they laid their wreath of laurels.

Seymour gave me a magnificent letter of Kean's, which I afterwards sold, along with letters from Mrs Siddons, Rachel, and others, in order to pay the debts incurred by the first Mermaid Theatre season. He also presented me with a pair of boots which Kean was said to have worn as Coriolanus. There are many of these relics flying around—ours is an ephemeral profession, which treasures such things. I believe John Gielgud gave Larry Olivier the sword Kean used in Richard the Third; and stage jewels which Garrick's widow had presented to Kean were listed in the catalogue of Kean's belongings sold by auction a year after his death. Extracts from this catalogue are illustrated on the following pages. As may be seen, among the books was a Shakespeare First Folio; valued today, by Sotheby's, at some £4,500, it sold for £1 6s. od, which was five shillings more than the price paid for Garrick's 'star and garter' (worn by Kean as Richard III), but considerably less than the sum the auctioneer got for a dressing-gown Kean had worn as Macbeth—that went for a handsome five guineas.

This splendid collection of curiosities and valuables came from Kean's private retreat, a cottage on the island of Bute, to which he used to retire when he wanted to be out of the reach of colleagues and the public. The journey must have taken nine or ten days by coach and boat. In the early nineteen-fifties, when Donald Wolfit and his wife Rosalind Iden were touring Scotland, they crossed to Bute to pay their respects to the cottage. Rosalind made me a very charming drawing of the gateway with its four stone pillars, on which Kean had placed sculptured heads of Shakespeare, Massinger, Garrick and himself.

On the following pages are some extracts from the catalogue of Kean's possessions sold by auction after his death, and ranging from a magnificent silver-gilt vase, ice pail and cup presented to Kean by his fellow actors to commemorate his first performance as Sir Giles Overreach, to a chainmail petticoat and four large deal packing cases. The very bed in which he died was put up as a raffle prize (page 182).

A CATALOGUE

Of the following

Unique Selection of Valuables

Of the late

EDMUND KEAN, Esq.

Culled especially

FROM HIS COTTAGE IN THE ISLE OF BUTE,

And removed for peremptory Sale, viz. the

Magnificent Gold Cup,

Of elegant form, chaste design, and elaborate workmanship, presented on the 24th day of June, 1816, by Robert Palmer, Father of the Drury Lane Stage, in the name of the Committee and Company of Performers, in testimony of their admiration of his transcendent Talents. This Cup may be considered a most interesting Theatrical Document, as the names of the Committee and of the Ladies and Gentlemen forming the Company, with an appropriate Inscription, are engraved upon it; also, the

SNUFF BOX PRESENTED BY LORD BYRON,

The Top formed of Mosaic, of a most beautiful description, representing a Wild Boar Hunt;

A SILVER GILT CHASED SNUFF BOX,

From William Bingham, Esq. of Montreal;

The Snuff Box presented by the Covent Garden Performers in 1828;

A GOLD MEDAL, BY THE PHILANTHROPIC INSTITUTION;

Two Silver Sideboard Cups, by E. Simpson, Esq. of New York; a valuable Gold Repeater, Massive Gold Chain; three Gold Seals, Key, and the Snake Ring worn by Mr. Kean; a small

SERVICE OF USEFUL PLATE,

A Liqueur Chest; also a Unique and Interesting

LIBRARY OF BOOKS,

Including many choice Works, several Presentation Copies, all the Standard Works, and a Variety of Plays, with Remarks and Memoranda by Mr. Kean, and many other curious Documents;

Which will be Sold by Auction, by

Mr. GEORGE ROBINS,

AT HIS AUCTION ROOMS, IN COVENT GARDEN,

On TUESDAY, JUNE the 17th, 1834,

At Twelve o'Clock, by direction of the Administrator.

The Collection may be viewed on Saturday and Monday preceding the Sale, and Catalogues had at Mr. GEORGE ROBINS' Offices in Covent Garden.

Alfred Robins, Typ. 29, Tavistock Street, Covent Garden.

THE INTERESTING VALUABLES.

4.10   121   An ELEGANT GOLD MEDAL, beautifully finished, chased border

> *Presented by the Western Philanthropic Institution, London, to Mr. Kean, as a token of respect and gratitude for the kind exertion of his brilliant talents at their benefits in 1824 and 1827, at the Theatre Royal Drury Lane.*

8.18.6   122   A HANDSOME CIRCULAR TORTOISESHELL SNUFF BOX, *with Mr. Kean's crest, the ' Boar,' lined with gold and chased lip*

> *Presented by his Brother Performers as a trifling but cordial acknowledgment of his valuable assistance and most liberal conduct at the Theatre Royal English Opera House, in November 1828, on the sudden closing of Covent Garden Theatre.*

30 guineas   123   A TRULY ELEGANT SNUFF BOX, OF TORTOISE-SHELL, *lined with gold, the top representing a* WILD BOAR HUNT; *vividly and naturally pourtrayed in the most beautiful* MOSAIC WORK, *(symbolical of Mr. Kean's crest;) an elegant gold frame of chased foliage encloses the picture, chased gold border and lip*

> *N.B.—This Box was the Gift of LORD BYRON to Edmund Kean, Esq.*

MISCELLANEOUS ITEMS.

124   The Portrait of MR. MOSES KEAN, uncle to the celebrated actor

125   *An elegant mahogany liqueur chest, brass bound, containing 4 cut glass decanters and 6 liqueur glasses, neatly fitted up*

> *Presented by W. C. to E. K.*

1.1   126   *The celebrated* DAMASCUS SWORD, presented by LORD BYRON to MR. KEAN

> *This sword is considered a very rare specimen of the Damascus blade.*

127   THE MACBETH SWORD, worn by Mr. Kean in this Tragedy, and presented to him by the Gentlemen of Edinburgh; the following inscription is engraved upon it:—

> *This sword was presented to Edmund Kean, Esq. to be worn by him when he appeared on the stage as Macbeth, the King of Scotland, November 1819.*

128   An inlaid TURKISH SWORD, worn by Mr. Kean in the character of Othello

... 'ON THY DEATH-BED'

To the Theatrical World and the Curious Generally

THE BEDSTEAD

on which

EDMUND KEAN, THE TRAGEDIAN

breathed his last.

This relic, once the property of the greatest genius
that ever graced the British Stage, will be

RAFFLED FOR

by 40 Members
at 5 shillings each

at Mr Phillips',
Swan Tavern and Lord Dover Hotel,
Hungerford Market,

on Tuesday Evening next, the 16th inst.
at seven o'clock to the minute.

The Proprietor and Winner to Spend Half a Guinea each.

The Bedstead can be seen on application at the Bar,
by Tickets, Sixpence each,
which may be had in Refreshments.

James Stewart once told me that William Randolph Hearst had bought up the entire contents of the room in which Cardinal Richelieu died. On the bed lay his nightgown and nightcap, and on the table alongside it the breviary he had been reading. . . . I was reminded of the Brecht Archive, where the room in which Brecht died has been preserved intact. He was reading the Daily Telegraph *and had marked with a blue pencil a small paragraph about a British Secret Service agent who had undergone plastic surgery, at his own expense, in order to effect a complete transformation. The operation had gone wrong and he was endeavouring to sue the Foreign Office for compensation. Alongside this Brecht had written, 'Good subject for a play.'*

XI

THE SEASON ENDED

Sacred to the memory
of

THOMAS JACKSON

Comedian

who was engaged December 21st, 1741
to play a comic cast of characters
in this great Theatre, the world,
for many of which he was prompted by nature to excel.

The season being ended, his benefit over,
the charges all paid, and his account closed,
he made his exit in the Tragedy of 'Death'
on the 17th of March, 1796,
in full assurance of being called once more to rehearsal;
when he hopes to find his forfeits all cleared,
his cast of parts bettered,
and his situation made agreeable
by HIM who paid the great stock–debt
for the love HE bore to performers in general.

Epitaph from Gillingham, Norfolk

PROGRAMME NOTE

Mr. MACREADY as VIRGINIUS the ROMAN FATHER.

Every visitor to the theatre—the word 'playgoer', it seems, is mysteriously old-fashioned—will surely add now a personal mosaic of things read, heard, experienced.

Thus (things read) I recall the Swiss traveller Thomas Platter's enjoyment of the jig danced by the company at The Globe, Bankside, 'with extreme elegance,' after the *Julius Caesar* of 1599; a woman in the gallery waking from a dream while Garrick was in one of his tragic parts, and shouting incomprehensibly 'Rumps and burrs!'; Kean's death scene as Richard the Third; Macready at his farewell (1851) entering as Macbeth (with the spurious line, 'Command they make a halt upon the heath') to a tumult of

184

Drury Lane cheering; and Irving's entrance as Hamlet (Lyceum, 1874) with his 'troubled, wearied face displaying the first effects of moral poison'.

Then, things experienced: the first rising of a velvet curtain, seen from the hushed pit of a Theatre Royal; presently *Lear* on the stage; tramcars thudding outside through the winter darkness. A *Hamlet* production improvised in a ballroom near Elsinore on a summer night of tumultuous rain; the joys of great acting, classical, farcical, tragical-comical (we need the categories of Polonius); the players at their meridian, audiences at theirs; the sound of the word, what Shaw called the 'irresistible, impetuous march of music'; a world of voices, figured satin, a silver tempest, a noon-cannon boom, or a ringdove's *roucoulement*.

We have shown simply a vision of the humours and tragedies of the theatre, its excitements, oddities, splendours, the masters and eccentrics, the lords of misrule, the actors and listeners, the singers and the silences, the great London houses and the holes-and-corners of the pomping folk, not just places where, said St John Ervine, 'melancholy men and misunderstood women sit and twiddle their souls.' A famous twentieth-century editor once chose to call his weekly drama criticism *Theatre and Life* until someone wrote to him, 'Surely they are the same thing?' and he confessed 'Indeed, they are', and changed the title. Let me refer you back to Bernard Miles's preface: to 'the suspicion that the whole human story is a kind of play, a tragi-comedy in many episodes with script still being written in the wings.'

Our gratitude now to all who, in a score of ways, have helped to compose and to present this book.

J. C. Trewin

P.S. W. Davenport Adams issued in 1904 *A Dictionary of the Drama* which, alas, never got beyond its first volume, A–G. At random from it:

> '*Elfie; or, The Cherry Tree Inn.* A drama, in three acts (1871) by Dion Boucicault. Bob Evans, who loves Rosie Aircastle, is accused of robbing the inn; but the crime has really been committed by his rival, Deepear, disguised in a waxwork mask which has been made by Sadlove, a waxwork showman, in the likeness of Bob's face.'

Life? Well, why not!

INDEX

References to illustrations are given in italic numerals.
Reference to captions are marked *cap.* in parentheses.
Authors' names are given in Roman type, in parentheses, following play or book titles.

187

. . . then these goodly Pageants being done, every mate sorts to his mate, every one bringes another homeward of their way verye friendly.

Philip Stubbes (1583)

New Theatre-Royal in Covent-Garden,

This prefent MONDAY, FEBRUARY 24, 1783,

KING LEAR.

King Lear by Mr. HENDERSON,
Glofter by Mr. HULL,
Baftard by Mr. AICKIN,
Kent by Mr. CLARKE,
Albany, Mr. DAVIES, Cornwall, Mr. THOMPSON,
Burgundy, Mr. HELME, Phyfician, Mr. BATFS,
Gentleman Ufher by Mr. WEWITZER,
And Edgar by Mr. LEWIS,
Goneril by Mifs PLATT,
Regan by Mrs. WHITFIELD,
And Cordelia by Mrs. ROBINSON.

Being her firft Appearance in that Character,
To which will be added, The NEW PANTOMIME, called

LORD MAYOR'S DAY;
Or, A FLIGHT from LAPLAND.

The PANTOMIME will end with a REPRESENTATION of

The Lord Mayor's Show on the Water.

AFTER WHICH (FOR THE TWELFTH TIME) WILL BE A

NEW HISTORICAL PROCESSION

Of the SEVERAL COMPANIES, with their

RESPECTIVE PAGEANTS.

And the CHIEF MAGISTRATES belonging to

The CITY of LONDON,

FROM ITS FOUNDATION.

The Scenes, Machinery, and Decorations, both of the Pantomime and Proceffion, in-
vented and defigned by Mr. RICHARDS; and executed by Him, Mr. Smirk,
Mr. Hodgins, Mr. Catton, and Others.
The Whole of the NEW MUSIC compofed by Mr. SHIELDS.
BOOKS of the SONGS, with an Explanation of the Proceffion, to be had at the Theatre.

Tomorrow, (For the Firft Time) a New Comedy, called

A BOLD STROKE FOR A HUSBAND,

With A NEW PROLOGUE, EPILOGUE, SCENES, and DRESSES.

And THE QUAKER.

Praise for *Entrepreneurial Marketing*

If you're unconvinced that marketing makes or breaks entrepreneurial ventures, you'll change your mind after reading this book. The Internet, global distribution, and consolidation all create new challenges and opportunities for today's entrepreneurs. The authors offer sound advice and the same kind of solid direction you would pay hundreds of thousands of dollars to buy from a consulting firm. I've used many of these techniques, with Len Lodish's help, to grow our business from 5 percent of the market to over 50 percent.

> —Ralph Guild
> Chairman and CEO, Interep

This book is filled with valuable and productive concepts, methods, ideas, and paradigms. These concepts have been an important contribution to Synergy's performance—four consecutive appearances on the Inc. 500 List and a compound growth rate of 80 percent to current profitable revenue in excess of $20,000,000—all from initial capital of less than $100,000. A must have for entrepreneurs.

> —Mark Stiffler
> Founder and CEO, Synergy, Inc.

Finally! A practical, hands-on guide to marketing for startups. This step-by-step handbook gives an entrepreneur a clear, real-world roadmap for generating attention and excitement around their business. I only wish I had a book like this when I started Half.com!

> —Joshua Kopelman
> Founder and President, Half.com

This book's cost/benefit approach to entrepreneurial marketing has helped me to acquire profitable customers at less than 1/30th of the cost of my competitors who have recently gone out of business. If you want to succeed and have limited resources, this book is required reading.

> —Ken Hakuta
> Founder and CEO, Allherb.com, Dr. Fad, and Marketer of the Wacky Wall Walkers

ENTREPRENEURIAL MARKETING

Lessons from Wharton's
Pioneering MBA Course

LEONARD M. LODISH

HOWARD LEE MORGAN

AMY KALLIANPUR

John Wiley & Sons, Inc.

New York • Chichester • Weinheim • Brisbane • Singapore • Toronto

To our best venture partners, our spouses who have supported us in so many ways for most of our lives—Susan Lodish for 35 years and Eleanor Morgan for 33 years. We love you.

      —Leonard M. Lodish and Howard Lee Morgan

To the two people I love most in my life—my adopted Mom and Dad.

        —Amy Kallianpur

Contents

Preface

Marketing, more than technology, is most often the reason for the success or failure of a new venture. Yet there are few detailed guides, and fewer serious studies, on what does and does not work when dealing with entrepreneurial situations. This book is designed to help today's many entrepreneurs make the best use of their time, money, and effort in growing their businesses. The book is itself the product of entrepreneurial marketing thinking. There is a target market that has a need for help that we hope to provide. We have seen no books that combine conceptually sound marketing concepts and paradigms with practical guidance on how to apply them in entrepreneurial situations.

This book has a very pragmatic objective. We are not trying to deliver a complete compendium on marketing or on entrepreneurship. We cover only marketing concepts, methods, tactics, and strategies that can add value to real entrepreneurial ventures as we move into the next millennium. We have been guided in our thinking, not only by our practical experience with dozens of companies, but also by a newly completed survey of the Inc. 500 companies done jointly by the authors and *Inc. Magazine*. These results, detailed here for the first time, provide new insights into what types of marketing programs and channels are used in diverse business settings. The survey contrasted a representative sample of the Inc. 500 winners in 1999 with a sample of entrepreneurs in the Pennsylvania area who represent more "normal" entrepreneurs. We will outline the differences between the Inc. 500, and non-Inc. 500 groups as we discuss the concepts in each chapter. The survey results are described in Appendix B.

We take very seriously the constraints that entrepreneurial firms typically have. They are limited in (1) financial resources,

(2) people to help with any nonproduction-related research or analysis, and (3) time. While bigger, older companies may have the luxury of waiting longer for their marketing and sales strategies to produce results, the entrepreneurial company has to worry about the short term. For most entrepreneurs, without a short-term cash flow, the longer term is impossible.

Origins

This book should be the best of both the academic and practical approaches to marketing issues. It comes from the intersection of both approaches. The book got started as a by-product of the Entrepreneurial Marketing course which Len Lodish developed at the Wharton School of the University of Pennsylvania where Amy Kallianpur was a doctoral student and a teaching/research assistant. Len Lodish has over 30 years of applying marketing and strategic thinking to entrepreneurial ventures and of consulting with major packaged goods manufacturers such as Procter & Gamble and Pepsico on improving their marketing productivity. In the class, MBA students worked in groups to develop marketing plans for entrepreneurial ventures they were possibly starting. Along with the instructors' comments on how marketing could be used to help entrepreneurial ventures, the students were exposed to successful entrepreneurs who spoke and answered questions. In the five years since the course began, 25 entrepreneurs have come to share their experiences. A favored presenter in each semester was Howard Morgan who has more than 25 years experience with over 30 high-tech entrepreneurial ventures, as a consultant, director, executive, and financial resource.

The Importance of Marketing for Entrepreneurs

Marketing is of critical importance to the success of most entrepreneurial ventures. Compared to other business functions, marketing has been rated as much more important to the new venture's prosperity. Fourteen venture capitalists who backed more than 200 ventures rated the importance of business functions to the success of the enterprise. The marketing function was rated 6.7 on a scale of 7.0, higher than any other business functions. In-depth interviews with the same venture capitalists concluded that venture failure rates can be reduced as much as 60 percent using pre-venture marketing analysis.

As part of the preparation of the 1997 Inc. 500 list of the fastest growing private companies in the United States, the CEOs of those companies were asked to outline their greatest weaknesses and strengths. Note that sales and marketing strategies are perceived as their biggest strengths compared to other strategic assets:

	Strength	Weakness
Sales and marketing strategies	145	19
Managing people	112	89
Financial strategies	53	75
Information technology	28	19
Product innovation	12	2
Other	59	35

Marketing is the tool that the entrepreneur needs to help a product or service be perceived as more valuable than the competition by target segments. Marketing strategies and tactics help guide the development of products and services that the market wants, help target the firm's offering to the right customers, get the product or service to the customer, and help insure that the customers perceive the incremental value of the offering better than the competition and will pay for the added value.

Marketing is important, not just in its traditional role of aiding in developing, producing, and selling products or services that customers want. Marketing can also help the firm recruit the best people, and at least as important, help to raise money to finance the venture. Just as marketing can help in exchanges with customers, it can also help in guiding recruiting efforts to make sure that targeted prospective employees perceive added value compared to competition and are motivated to become new employees. As we will see later, the capital raising problem is also assisted by marketing paradigms, strategies, and tactics. The trick is to realize that capital raising really involves marketing a different product—equity or debt in the entrepreneurial venture—to different sets of target markets (e.g., venture capitalists, "angels").

Marketing in the Next Millennium—The Pervasive Web

The Internet has been one of the most explosive growth phenomena of our times. In just four years, stock trading on the Internet has grown from zero to more than four million accounts. The success of specialized retailers such as Amazon.com in bookselling, N2K in recorded music, and software.net in software has shown that direct one-to-one marketing to consumers, on a 24 hours/7 days per week basis, can lead to success.

Getting visibility and name recognition as one of more than two million domain names now requires a major marketing effort or creative, leveraged approaches. The Web is important for its ability to connect an organization not only to its customers, but also to its suppliers, investors, and any other stakeholders who have an interest in its operations. Each such connection is an opportunity for marketing and promotion, and for the building of a brand. An entrepreneur ignores the Web at his or her peril. This book describes how to leverage the Internet across the various constituencies.

Challenges of the Next Decade

There are a number of key challenges to any organization that will operate over the next decade. Globalization, corporate consolidation, ecological issues, increasing sensitivity to privacy and data ownership issues, and new governmental regulation must all be considered when designing marketing efforts.

Marketing across national boundaries creates challenges that once could only be profitably managed by large companies. Since the Internet immediately puts your product and service information at the fingertips of the world, it is important to be ready for the global customer from day one. In addition, you must be prepared for competition from very far away, for on the Internet, no one cares if you're next door or halfway across the world, as long as the goods or services can be delivered in a timely, reliable manner. An executive in Australia said he routinely orders his books from Amazon.com, since they arrive in Australia within 48 hours, often months before the Australian bookstores get the same books.

Continuing merger and acquisition growth, and the increased number of strategic alliances are altering the competitive structure of many industries. This creates opportunities for some entrepreneurial ventures, and problems for others. Many new Internet ventures have been bought, often for large amounts of money, just to acquire their customer bases. Hotmail, started as a free e-mail service, was purchased by Microsoft for more than $200 million so that they could have access to the eight million members. Similarly, Excite bought MatchLogic for their ability to target advertising to users. Once these purchases were made, smaller competitors often found that their value shrunk rapidly, since there were no other obvious acquirers.

Other key issues for entrepreneurial marketers in the next millennium include the changing demographics, values, and expectations of the population. In the developing world, the boomer generation will begin retiring in the early 2000s. At the same time, the lesser developed populations are beginning to acquire technology and consumerism. China, India, and other parts of the world offer growth opportunities, but require closer cooperation with government, and better understanding of different cultures than most U.S. ventures have shown. Entrepreneurial ventures can take the lead in taking advantage of these new opportunities.

The key to any marketing is an understanding of "*What* am I selling to *whom?*" Chapter 1 addresses this question. After covering positioning and targeting, we cover developing, selecting, and evaluating new products and services. We then cover the important pricing decisions that entrepreneurs must make and need major help with. We then help the entrepreneur to make decisions on the main elements of the venture's marketing mix-channels, rollout, sales management, promotion and viral marketing, and advertising. We next show how entrepreneurial marketing can help hire the best people and raise capital productively. Finally, we conclude with guidance on building strong brands and strong companies that will endure.

LEONARD M. LODISH
HOWARD LEE MORGAN
AMY KALLIANPUR

Acknowledgments

This book is the result of the Entrepreneurial Marketing Course that Len Lodish teaches in the Wharton School MBA program. In addition to the invaluable help and wise counsel of Howard Morgan and the expert assistance of Amy Kallianpur, there are many people who have helped the course and this book.

The Wharton MBA students who participated in the class for the past five years have been inspirational to us all. The entrepreneurs who have either spoken to the class or helped the book with sharing their real world experiences have been invaluable. A partial list of those entrepreneurs includes: Mark Stiffler of Synygy, Inc.; Craig Tractenberg, the franchise law guru at Buchannan, Ingersol; Gary Erlbaum of David's Bridal and other ventures; Eric Spitz of Trakus, Inc.; Mel Kornbluh of Tandem's East; Bob Tumulow of Rita's Water Ice; Steve Katz of many ventures; Jim Everett of Country Junction; Bill Gross of Idealab; Alan Markowitz of many ventures; Ralph Guild of Interep; Ken Hakuda of Allherb.com; Dwight Riskey of Frito Lay; Barry Feinberg of many ventures; Chuck Holroyd and Mike Perry of IndyMac Bank; Barry Lipsky and Mort David of Franklin Electronic Publishing; and Gerry Shreiber of J&J Snack Foods.

The Wharton Global Consulting Practicum has also been a source of rich entrepreneurial experiences of foreign companies entering the United States. This book has benefited from the insights of Therese Flaherty, Guri Meltzer, Shlomo Kalish, Ron Waldman, and David Ben Ami of that program as well as all of the MBA students and faculty in Israel, Chile, and Mexico.

Many colleagues at Wharton, Michigan State, and other academic institutions have helped with concepts, methodologies, and paradigms. John Little, Pete Fader, Magid Abraham, Gerry Eskin,

Abba Kreiger, Jerry Wind, David Reibstein, Russ Palmer, Terry Overton, Erin Anderson, C.B. Bhattacharya, David Aaker, Robert Nason, and Irwin Gross have been very helpful. The participants in Wharton's Executive Education Sales Force Management program have also contributed many valuable ideas and insights. Thirty years of experience working with Information Resources, Inc. has helped Len Lodish with significant learning about how consumers react to advertising and other marketing mix elements.

Many entrepreneurs have helped Howard Morgan with practical lessons from the schools of hard knocks and of great wisdom. Bill Gross, Larry Gross, Marcia Goodstein, and Bob Kavner and the rest of the staff at idealab! have provided an intensive course in entrepreneurial marketing and the time to work on this book. Jim Simons, John Wilczak, Marvin Weinberger, Josh Kopelman, Phil Shires, and many others have broadened his horizons on overall strategy and guerilla marketing techniques and tactics.

We want to also thank Charlene Niles and the staff of *Inc. Magazine* and Ian Mac Millan, Greg Higgins, Mark Dane Fraga, and the staff of the Wharton Entrepreneurial Center and Wharton Small Business Center for making our survey possible and helping with its administration.

CHAPTER 1

Positioning, Targeting, and Segmentation

Positioning and segmentation are the real core of what makes the entrepreneurial venture work or not work. All of the venture's important decisions and tactics are critically dependent on these basic decisions. A key question is:

What am I selling to whom?

Positioning is how the product or service is to be perceived by a target market compared to the competition. It answers the question: "Why will someone in the target market(s) buy my product or service instead of the competition's?" An equivalent question is: "What should be the perceived value of my offering compared to the competition's?"

Segmentation answers the question: "Which is (are) my target market(s)?" Entrepreneurial ventures typically begin life with one product or a small line of related products. The answers to these positioning and segmentation questions are not easy, but are crucial to

1

the venture's success. Two related concepts of management strategy must be considered to most productively answer the positioning question. These include the venture's *distinctive competence,* and its *sustainable competitive advantage.* Once the positioning decision is made, the entrepreneur can tackle all the other marketing-related decisions. If the other marketing decisions are made before the positioning and targeting is defined, there is a danger that the venture will not be perceived in the market as well as it could be. The sequence of decisions for an entrepreneurial venture is summarized in Figure 1.1.

This book is organized like Figure 1.1. We first discuss the positioning, targeting, and segmentation decisions and their relationship to competitive strategy. We then cover how all of the marketing-related decisions should be made in light of the positioning and segmentation decisions. Please keep in mind that the real decisions are not made in as logical a manner as might be implied by Figure 1.1. There should be constant feedback and adjustment of the positioning and segmentation decisions as other elements of the marketing mix are evaluated, tested, and implemented and as the competition and environment change and evolve.

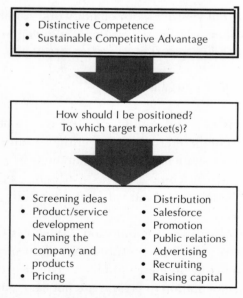

Figure 1.1   Market oriented strategy and tactics.

Distinctive Competence and Sustainable Competitive Advantage

Sustainable competitive advantage is the Holy Grail that most entrepreneurs continually pursue. If a way can be found to continually be ahead of competition, then the venture will probably return higher than normal returns to its owners. Being ahead of competition means that the venture can more easily sell more, and/or charge higher prices, and/or have lower costs than "normal" firms. Let's look at competitive advantage from an entrepreneurial marketer's point of view. As you will see, the entrepreneurial marketer's point of view is the customer's point of view. Your competitive advantage is why the customer or potential customer will more likely buy from you than from your competition. If you have succeeded in developing a competitive advantage that is sustainable from competitive encroachment, you are creating sustainable value.

Distinctive competence is how some people refer to the advantage that is the source of the sustainable competitive advantage. If the advantage is sustainable, then your venture has something that is difficult for your competition to emulate and must be somewhat distinctive to your venture. What are sources of distinctive competence for entrepreneurs that might be sources of sustainable competitive advantage? Creative entrepreneurs seem to be finding new distinctive ways to get customers to prefer them to the competition. Here are some of them:

- Many companies use technology to obtain competitive advantage. Patents and trade secrets are weapons to keep the competition from imitation. For software companies, source code for their products is a key competitive advantage. Priceline.com has a patent on their method for having consumers try to name their own price for goods and services. This is a great source of sustainable competitive advantage.

- Other companies may rely on excellent design, perceived high quality, or continual innovation, as distinctive competencies.

- Others will use excellent customer service by loyal employees who have adopted corporate service values. Southwest

Airlines is an excellent example of a venture that differentiates itself from competitors with both excellent customer service and technology for scheduling and turning flights around. Many consumers fly Southwest, not only because it is economical, but because it is fun. Many other airlines have tried to imitate Southwest and have been unsuccessful.

- Reputations and other differences in customer perception of products, services, and companies can be extremely valuable sources of sustainable advantage. If consumers perceive you as being a preferable source, they will be more likely to choose your products or services. Dell's service reputation as well as its business-to-business salesforce have succeeded in getting many customers to perceive them as a trustworthy, reliable resource for computers and related equipment and services. As a result, Dell has also been difficult to compete with.

All of these are ways that entrepreneurs search for sustainable competitive advantage. They relate to how customers choose one product or service versus another. Key positioning and segmentation decisions are intertwined with why customers will choose you versus your competition. Thus, the positioning decision is best made to leverage the distinctive competence of the venture. We first discuss a related key strategic decision: Which customers are you targeting with your positioning?

Segmentation and Targeting

The positioning and segmentation decisions are typically developed together. Although we will take them one at a time, we consider the interrelationships as we go. Conceptually, segmentation is a process in which a firm's market is partitioned into submarkets with the objective of having the response to the firm's marketing activities and product/service offerings vary greatly across segments, but have little variability within each segment. For the entrepreneur, the segments may in many cases only number two: (1) the group we are targeting with our offering and marketing activity and (2) everyone else. The targeted segment(s) will be related to the product/service offering and the competitive strategy of the entrepreneur.

There are some very important questions that need answers as part of the selection of target market segment(s).

The most important question is: *Does the target segment want the perceived value that my positioning is trying to deliver more than other segments?* Sometimes targeting may involve segments who differ on response to other elements of the marketing mix, however most smaller, entrepreneurial ventures differentiate target segments on the value they place on the differential benefits they perceive the firm to deliver. If a firm can target those people who value their offering the highest compared to the competition, it has many benefits including better pricing and higher margins, more satisfied customers, and usually a better barrier to potential and actual competition.

Almost as important to profitable segmentation is the question: *How can the segment be reached? And how quickly?* Are there available distribution or media options or can a self-selection strategy be used? Are the options for reaching the segment cost effective? Can enough of the segment be reached quickly enough so that you can be a leader before competitors (particularly on the Internet) can target the same segment?

Another question is: *How big is the segment?* If the segment is not big enough in terms of potential revenue and gross margin to justify the cost of setting up a program to satisfy it, it will not be profitable.

Other questions to keep in mind include: *What are likely impacts of changes in relevant environmental conditions (e.g., economic conditions, lifestyle, legal regulations) on the potential response of the target segment? What are current and likely competitive activities directed at the target segment?*[1]

Virtual Communities—The Ultimate Segment?

The Internet has fostered thousands of virtual communities. These are made up of groups of people who are drawn together online by common interests. Just as enthusiasts for certain activities (such as hobbies, sports, recreation) have gotten together in metropolitan areas for years, the Internet lets enthusiasts from all over the world "get together" virtually. The same phenomenon holds for business users of certain software or specialized equipment. Users or potential users like to get together to help each other with mutual solutions to common problems, helpful hints, new ideas, or evaluations of new products that might help the community members. It is much easier to post notices on an online virtual bulletin board than to physically go to a meeting. A virtual community member can interact with his counterparts any time of the day or night and reach people with very similar needs and experiences.

These virtual communities can be an entrepreneur's penultimate segment. In terms of the previous segmentation selection questions, the answers to the first two questions are almost part of the definition of an online virtual community. If your product or service offering is tailored (or as importantly, is *perceived* to be tailored) to the members of a virtual community, then it will be positioned as very valuable to that segment compared to any other group. The size of the segment is easily determined as the size of the virtual community.

The incentives for entrepreneurial companies to get involved with virtual communities are great, but it is not a one-way street. All elements of the marketing program need to be cleverly adapted to the new segmentation environment. The challenges of marketing in virtual communities are summarized nicely by Mckinsey consultants John Hagel III and Arthur G. Armstrong:

> Virtual communities are likely to look very threatening to your average company. How many firms want to make it easier for their customers to talk to one another about their products and services? But vendors will soon have little choice but to participate. As more and more of their customers join virtual communities, they will find themselves in "reverse markets"—markets in which customers seek out vendors and play them off against one another, rather than the other way around. Far-sighted companies will recognize that virtual communities actually represent a tremendous opportunity to expand their geographical reach at minimal cost.

An Entrepreneurial Segmentation Example—Tandem's East

A clever entrepreneur can use target segmentation as a prime reason for beginning a venture. An example is Mel Kornbluh who began a company called *Tandem's East* in his garage in the late 1980s. Mel is a specialist in selling and servicing tandem bicycles—bicycles built for two (or three or four). Mel realized that there was a segment composed of bicycling couples who would appreciate the unique benefits of tandem riding. It is the only exercise that two people can do communicating while they exercise, appreciating nature together, even though they may have very different physical abilities.

When he began his venture, intuitively Mel had very good answers to the set of questions. There were actually two target segments that Mel could target. The first was existing tandem enthusiasts—those who already had a tandem and would need an upgrade or replacement. The other target segment was relatively affluent bicycling couples who had trouble riding together because of differences in physical abilities. The couples needed to be affluent because tandems are relatively expensive when compared with two regular bicycles. They are not mass-produced and do not take advantage of mass scale economies.

At the time he started, there was no one on the East Coast who had staked out a position as a specialist in tandems. Because tandem inventory is expensive and selection is very important to potential buyers, Mel could establish barriers to potential competitors by being first to accumulate a substantial inventory. He was also able to establish some exclusive arrangements with suppliers by being first in the area and offering them a new outlet. Thus, his distinctive competencies, tandem knowledge, a substantial inventory, and some exclusive lines were the source of sustainable competitive advantage.

It was relatively easy for Mel to reach both of his segments. Existing tandem enthusiasts were members of the Tandem Club of America that has a newsletter they publish bimonthly. It was relatively inexpensive to advertise in the newsletter that reached his first segment precisely. Not only did it reach the segment, but also because the readers were already enthusiasts, they paid attention to every page of the newsletter. Over time, Internet user groups dedicated to tandeming also formed. They were also natural vehicles for effectively reaching the segment.

His second segment was also relatively easy to reach cost effectively. Affluent bicycling couples read cycling magazines—the major one being *Bicycling Magazine*. Again, because they were enthusiasts, the target segment paid a lot of attention to even small ads. This segment also attended bicycling rallies and organized rides.

Both segments were way larger then he needed to make the business viable. With very small response rates in either segment, he could afford to pay his overhead and begin to accumulate a suitable inventory. In fact, his advertising costs were significantly under 10 percent of revenues, an extremely cost effective way to reach his segment.

Thus, Tandems East began and flourished by creatively seeing target segments that valued what Mel was selling. The segments were substantial, very easily reached cost effectively, and competitive barriers could be erected.

An Entrepreneurial Segmentation Audit

Appendix A is a segmentation audit that the entrepreneur can use as a checklist to make sure that he or she has considers all elements of segmentation. For an entrepreneur, many of the issues in the audit can cost effectively be answered only qualitatively. However, not considering these issues can cause big problems.

For perspective, our survey shows that 12 percent of the Inc. 500 CEOs did significant segmentation studies, but only 2.3 percent of the non-Inc. entrepreneurs did such studies. So both groups could profit from becoming more sophisticated in their segmentation.

One of the audit's most important issues is: *How well is the segmentation reflected in all the other marketing decisions that the venture makes?* The goal of the rest of this book is to flush out the issues. How does segmentation and targeting relate to all the other elements of the marketing mix for an entrepreneurial venture?

The interrelated positioning decisions to which we turn next are fundamental to segmentation and targeting.

Positioning

Positioning answers the question: *Why should a member of the target segment buy my product or service rather than my **competitor's***? A related positioning question is: *What are the unique **differentiating** characteristics of my product or service as **perceived** by members of the target segment(s)?* The bold words in these positioning questions are crucial for effective implementation. First the word **perceived** must be analyzed. It is obvious that people make decisions based only on what they perceive. Many entrepreneurial firms are happy when they have developed products or services that are *actually* better than competition on characteristics that they know should be important to people in their target market(s). What they forget is that the job is not done until the targeted people actually **perceive** the differences between their product and competition. In fact, on the Internet, many companies try to gain the perception that they're better long before they can deliver on that in reality.

One of the hindrances to effective positioning is that most humans cannot perceive more than two or three differentiating attributes at a time. It is important that the targeted positioning be easy to remember. If there are too many differentiating attributes, the potential consumer can get confused. The entrepreneur's job is to isolate the most important differentiating attributes of his or her offering and use those in all the elements of the marketing mix. In many cases, it is very cost effective to do concept testing or other research with potential consumers to isolate the best combination of attributes (see the concept testing section that follows). In other cases, the entrepreneur can instinctively isolate a good combination of attributes.

Entrepreneurs, who have been successful, may overstate how easy it was to get a good combination of attributes for their positioning. Companies such as Starbucks (just great tasting, excellent quality coffee) or Apple Computer (fun and easy to use) were successful at least partly because of very effective positioning. What has not been documented has been how many entrepreneurial ventures failed (or were not as successful as they could have been) because their positioning and associated target segments weren't very effective. Venture capitalists' estimate that as many as 60 percent of failures can be prevented by better prelaunch marketing analysis. This underscores how important it is to get your positioning right and testing with real consumers that it is right.

A big mistake many entrepreneurs make is to position based on *features* of their product offering compared to their competitors. It's amazing how many entrepreneurs we have encountered who have great ideas that are based on technical features that are somehow better than their competitors. The fundamental paradigm that *customers don't buy features, they buy benefits* has been lost on many entrepreneurs. Even more precisely, customers buy based on *perceived benefits*. Not only does the entrepreneur need to develop the best set of benefits versus the competition; she must also somehow get the customers to perceive these benefits.

In his book, *What Were They Thinking? Lessons I've Learned From Over 80,000 New Product Innovations and Idiocies,* Robert McMath also says that communicating features instead of perceived benefits is "one of the most common mistakes marketers make."[2] He describes a training film in which British comedian John Clease illustrates how a surgeon might explain a new surgical procedure to a patient lying in a hospital bed:

> Have I got an operation for you. Only three incisions and an Anderson Slash, a Ridgeway stubble-side fillip and a standard dormer slip! Only five minutes with a scalpel; only 30 stitches! We can take out up to five pounds of your insides, have you back in your hospital bed in 75 minutes flat, and we can do 10 of them in a day.[3]

The surgeon is concerned only with technical features that he as producer (entrepreneur) is excited over. The customer has very different concerns. All that the customer probably wants to know is whether he'll get better, what his risks of complication are, and whether he'll experience pain.

An Entrepreneurial Positioning Example—the Wharton School

The following example is an excellent example of very effective positioning and entrepreneurial marketing. *Business Week* recently ranked the Wharton MBA program first in the United States for the third time. This rating can be traced to the entrepreneurial marketing thinking and positioning insight of Professor Jerry Wind, a colleague in the Marketing Department of the Wharton School. Jerry headed the faculty-student-alumni-administration committee that developed the new Wharton curriculum in the early 1990s. When the faculty adopted the innovative new curriculum, Jerry was the person who did most of the public relations interviews following the approval.

In every interview Jerry repeated four key phrases over and over. Wharton will train managers who are *global, cross-functional, good leaders, and leveraged by technology.* These benefits were designed into the new curriculum because the school's research showed them to be very valuable to Wharton's various constituencies and not perceived as delivered by the other premier business schools. All of the other Wharton administrators who spoke to the press took their cue from Jerry and also emphasized those four attributes over and over. Because these all were fairly new concepts for business schools to adopt and because Wharton was the first major business school to overhaul its curriculum, all the major business media picked up the story and gave it emphasis. Most of the target segments that Wharton wanted to influence changed their perception of Wharton's position because of this media blitz.

There was a perceptual vacuum on most of those attributes that Wharton was able to fill. Once a perception has been lodged in someone's mind, it is not easily changed. Thus, in the competition among business schools, it has been very difficult for a major business school to capture from Wharton the public's perception of distinctiveness on any of those four dimensions.

There was a lot more to the new curriculum than the four phrases that were emphasized. However, because Jerry is a positioning expert, he knew that the target markets would be able to perceive only a limited number of differentiating attributes. The market research done by Jerry's committee helped them to decide the four most important new differentiating attributes to stress. If the school had tried to publicize all of the new attributes of the new curriculum, the message would have been diluted and the school would not have been able to reach its preeminent perceptual position with its target markets.

Again for perspective, 53 percent of the Inc. 500 CEOs did many positioning studies, but only 26 percent of the non-Inc. 500 did them. One of the reasons behind the Inc. 500 success could be their positioning.

Distinctive Competence, Sustainable Competitive Advantage, and Positioning

Now that we have explored segmentation and positioning, their relationship to the strategic concepts of distinctive competence and sustainable competitive advantage should be easy to understand. The fundamental positioning and segmentation decisions of *What am I selling to whom?* cannot be changed easily. It takes typically more effort to try to change a positioning than to attempt to establish a new one in a vacuum. To change a positioning means undoing one perception and replacing it with another. In the Wharton School example, the school had to develop or have internally strength in areas that would lead to perceptions of "global, cross-functional, good leaders and leveraged by technology." These should be distinctive competencies that differentiate Wharton from its competitors and should be such that they would be sustainable from competitive inroads.

For entrepreneurial companies, the intertwined positioning, distinctive competence, and sustained competitive advantage decisions are the most important strategic decisions made before beginning a new business or revitalizing an older business. The positioning and segmentation decisions are just the public face put on the distinctive competence and sustainable competitive advantage decisions. If the market doesn't value "what they perceive to be the distinctive competence of your firm versus the competition" (another way of defining positioning), then the positioning will not be successful. Furthermore, since it is difficult to change perceptions, the perceived distinctive competence should be sustainable over time. Thus it is crucial to get the positioning reasonably close to right *before going public the first time*. In Chapter 2 we will explore cost-effective ways of getting market reaction to positioning options before going public.

Orvis Company—Excellent Entrepreneurial Positioning

The Orvis Company has done an excellent job of capitalizing on a unique positioning in a very competitive industry. They sell "country" clothing, gifts, and sporting gear in competition with much bigger brands like L.L.Bean and Eddie Bauer. Like their competitors, Orvis sells both retail and mail order. How is Orvis different? They want to be perceived as the place to go for all areas of fly-fishing expertise. Their particular expertise is making a very difficult sport "very accessible to a new generation of anglers."[4] Since 1968, when their sales were less than $1million, Orvis has been running fly-fishing schools located near their retail outlets. Their annual sales are now over $350 million. The fly-fishing products contribute only a small fraction of the company's sales, but the fly-fishing heritage adds a cachet to all of Orvis's products. According to Tom Rosenbauer, beginner fly fishermen who attend their schools become very loyal customers and are crucial to continuing expansion of the more profitable clothing and gift lines. He says, "Without our fly-fishing heritage, we'd be just another rag vendor."[5]

The Orvis positioning pervades their entire operation. Their catalog and their retail shops all reinforce their fly-fishing heritage. They also can use very targeted segmentation to find new recruits for their fly-fishing courses. There are a number of targeted media and public relations vehicles that reach consumers interested in fishing. Their margins are higher than the typical "rag vendor" because of their unique positioning. The positioning is also defensible because of the consistent perception that all of their operations have reinforced since 1968. A competitor would have a very difficult time and large expense to reproduce the Orvis schools and retail outlets. It also would be difficult for a competitor to be a "me too" in an industry where heritage is so important. The positioning and segmentation decisions Orvis made in 1968 probably added close to a billion dollars of incremental value to their venture since that time. That value is our estimate of the difference of Orvis's actual profit since 1968 compared to what the venture's profitability might have been had they just been "another rag vendor."

Positioning, Names, and Slogans

Many entrepreneurs miss positioning opportunities when they name their products, services, and companies. As we will discuss in depth later, entrepreneurs have very limited marketing funds to educate their target markets about the positioning of their products and services. If the names chosen do not themselves connote the appropriate positioning, then the entrepreneur has to spend more funds to educate the market in two ways instead of one. They have not only to get potential customers to recognize and remember their product name, but they also have to educate them about the attributes and benefits of the product that goes with the name. Many new technology and Internet based ventures have been very intelligent and creative in their names that do connote the appropriate positioning. Companies such as CDNow (CDs on the Internet), ONSale (online Internet auctions), Netscape Communications (Internet browsers), @Home (using existing TV cable for home Internet connections), and Reel.com (movie sales on the Internet) make it easy for potential customers to remember what they do and at least part of their positioning. On the other hand, all you know from the name Amazon.com is that it is an Internet company. The fact that it sells books is not evident from its name. Educating consumers needs to be done with other marketing activities.

Some fortunate companies have gone even further by making their names not only support their positioning, but also simultaneously let their potential customers know how to get in touch with them (for example, 1-800-FLOWERS, 1-800-MATTRESS, Reel.com). Some entrepreneurs have registered Internet locations that will be valuable to others who have not yet realized their value. These entrepreneurs intend to sell those locations to the companies who will find them valuable. These fast-moving entrepreneurs have already taken Internet sites for all of the potential political candidates for the U.S. presidential election in 2004.

If the name of the company or product is not enough to position it in the customer's mind, then the next need is for a slogan or byline that succinctly and hopefully memorably hammers home the positioning. If the positioning has been done well, then a slogan or byline can in many cases fairly completely communicate the appropriate attributes. One good example is Alan Marcus & Co. They advertise with very small space ads in the *Wall Street Journal* with their slogan and byline always the same. The ads always begin with "America's Largest Fine Watch, Diamond, and Jewelry Discounters" and have "Elegant Price Cutters since 1973" below the company name. Nothing else really needs to be said to communicate what the company does, who the company is, and why people should buy from it. The positioning inherent in these two bylines is a good example of concentrating on only the few, most important, attributes to stress in order to position the company. BMW has been using "the Ultimate Driving Machine" for many years to differentiate itself as a performance automobile. Michelin uses "Because so Much is Riding on Your Tires" to try to differentiate itself as better on the safety attribute for tire buyers.

Just as brevity and simplicity are valuable in positioning, they are also as valuable in slogans and bylines. The slogan that goes with a company or product name should be one that can be retained for quite a long time, as long as the positioning will be in force. Robert Keidel proposed other ground rules for effective slogans: Avoid cliches (e.g., "genuine" Chevrolet, Miller); be consistent; use numbers, but have them backed up; be brief; take a stand; and make it distinctively your own.[6] All of these rules are consistent with our effective positioning paradigm and make good sense.

Summary

Each venture must answer the *What am I selling to whom?* question before it can create successful marketing strategy and tactics. Segmentation selects the subgroup(s) of all consumers to whom we think we should sell our products. Positioning tells members of the segment why they should buy our product or service, vis-à-vis any competitors. The positioning and segmentation decisions are intertwined with strategy decisions about distinctive competence and sustainable competitive advantage. The Internet creates the opportunity for the address (URL) to be of great service in positioning, since the name (e.g., reel.com, or etoys.com) can be both descriptive and informative.

CHAPTER 2

Selecting, Developing, and Evaluating New Products and Services

Most entrepreneurs have at least one product or service concept in mind when they begin planning their venture. In this chapter, we describe some helpful methodologies and concepts and codified entrepreneurial experience that can help screen new product and service concepts. We also describe cost efficient methods for getting marketplace and channel participants to help both improve the design and gauge the potential sales outlook for the idea. The idea is to try to conserve scarce resources by developing and implementing only ideas that are likely to make significant entrepreneurial returns. After discussing screening and concept testing for existing new product ideas, we then review some very interesting research that helps the entrepreneur choose a better battlefield to enter, if she has the option of choosing different kinds of products or services to consider for her venture.

Evaluating Specific Venture Ideas—Concept Testing

Every product or service idea has to be wanted by some market segment more than competitive products or services in order to obtain sales. Very simply, if customers won't choose your new product or service over the existing product or service, then you won't succeed. It is amazing that so many entrepreneurs do all kinds of analyses of costs, patent protection, possible competition, and market potential (if every one who could use one of my widgets bought one, we would have sales of $5 billion!) What they don't do is get actual reaction from real customers to the product or service concept. The entrepreneur just doesn't know all of the factors that the end customer will consider when he evaluates the new product or service. As we discuss in Chapter 5 on distribution channels, it is also very important to get channel intermediary reactions to the concept as well. Before we describe methods for getting customer and intermediary's reactions and suggestions for product improvements, we provide an example of how valuable these methods can be.

Trakus: the Value of Concept Testing

An MIT MBA, Eric Spitz and two high-tech MIT undergraduates founded Trakus, Inc. in 1997. The company was originally named Retailing Insights to reflect their initial product concept. They were going to do Videocart right using the latest technology. Videocart was a computerized shopping cart that was developed and introduced in the early 1990s. The cart would know where it was in a store and let the shopper know about specials and other useful information that depended on the cart's location in the store. So if a shopper were in the cereal aisle, the screen on the cart would show the cereal specials for the day. The cart could also show advertisements for cereals when the cart was in the cereal aisle. To keep shoppers' attention, the cart had a number of useful consumer functions. These functions included locating items in the store, getting a number for the meat or deli line remotely and being paged when your number is ready, providing recipes and store location for all of the recipe's items, local news, and so on.

The original Videocart venture failed because of poor execution. The carts were not recharged or repaired on a timely basis. Thus, when a consumer went to take one, the odds were that the cart would not function well. Word of mouth among consumers and the early store sites became negative so no new stores wanted to put the carts in. From a public market value at one time over $300 million, Videocart Inc. failed and declared bankruptcy in the mid 1990s.

Eric's team was going to do Videocart right using all the new technology. Instead of FM transmitters for location in the store, they had developed an indoor version of the GPS global positioning system to use. They would be able to identify the shopper's frequent shopper card or name and pull information from the Internet. Thus, the shopper could put their shopping list in at home and it would be available electronically at the store. The carts would be of value to store operators because they would get more customers to patronize their stores. The retailers would also be able to sell promotion opportunities on the cart to the manufacturers just as they did in their weekly circulars. This was a significant profit opportunity for the retailers. To advertisers, the computerized shopping cart was the perfect opportunity to reach the consumer at the most important point—just as they were making their actual purchasing decision. The new Videocart was going to be much cheaper than the original because of the lower costs of new technology. On paper, the venture looked terrific. Eric obtained $50,000 seed money from an angel investor. The angel investor requested that before the team spend any money on product development, that they concept test the idea to both of the customer groups that would need to buy the idea. These were the retailers who needed to subsidize putting the carts in the stores in return for promotional funds they would get, and the advertisers who were to pay for advertising on the carts.

The team developed a very compelling description of the new generation videocart, which included all of the benefits that either the retailer or manufacturer would obtain. They even had a neat simulation of how the system would work and what the cart's screen would look like that they put on their laptop personal computers. They showed this to retailers and manufacturers and at a given price asked how likely they would be to buy into the carts. After asking the purchase intent question, they also asked a number of questions about what manufacturers and retailers liked and what they disliked about the cart concept. The answers the team received were not very encouraging. For retailers, the cart's previous bad reputation was a big barrier. Retailers were very apprehensive to try another version of a product that had a terrible reputation. This implied that the team would have to establish extensive beta sites (at the venture's expense) to prove over a long term that the carts would work and would provide the benefits the team anticipated. Not only that, but retailers were also very frugal and were very reticent to commit their own funds to investing even partially in the carts. The retailers were used to having manufacturers pay for most new innovations as a way of getting or improving their shelf space and in-store position.

For the manufacturers, they were only willing to pay for advertising on the carts if the carts would demonstrate that they actually had an incremental effect on the manufacturer's sales in the stores. Not only that, but manufacturers also required significant scale to justify their infrastructure to support the new advertising medium. That meant that Eric's team would have to be in a significant fraction of all of the U.S. supermarkets before the manufacturers would begin to commit significant advertising and promotion funds to the medium. It did not take much rough calculating to determine that the cash investment required to reach a break even (if a break even were at all possible) would be huge. The probability of convincing venture capital or angel sources to invest that kind of money was very low. Eric's team was discouraged for a couple days by the results. However, they had most of their angel's seed money left and lots of technical skills in the areas of GPS location, communications, and digital signal processing. After the bad concept testing results sunk in, the team had a brainstorming session where they generated and evaluated a number of product ideas that would leverage their distinctive competence as they viewed it.

The outcome of that brainstorming session took the team in a very different, but much more profitable direction. Eric, a sports nut, conceptualized a product concept that the rest of the team said could be accomplished technically. They were going to put little rugged transmitters on athletes (in their helmets or on their clothes) and put receiving antennas in a few places in the stadium. They could then determine in real time, digitally, where every athlete on a team is, record it, and process that data to generate new valuable statistics, and display the information virtually immediately. The information would include speed and acceleration of each player and real time location of each player. If you know the weight of two players and their acceleration the instant they collide, you can easily calculate a "hit" gauge. This hit gauge would be a valuable addition to the broadcasting of football or hockey. The broadcaster could also analyze any plays by showing the digital picture of the replay and associated speed and acceleration statistics and processing the digital data to illustrate good or poor performance of some players. The digital, real time data and information would also be perfect for "broadcasting " the games over the Internet.

The team concept tested this idea similarly to the way they had potential customers evaluate the videocart. They developed a simulation of what the system might look like and presented it to members of potential market segments that might be interested in the system. They also changed their name to Trakus, Inc. to reflect their new orientation. The segmentation and decision process that would be used by each segment was much more complicated for the new Trakus sports product. There were teams, leagues, players associations, coaches (who could use the system for training), advertisers, agents, Internet sports companies, and so on who all could contribute to or influence Trakus' market reception and potential revenue. Before they exposed the concept to all of these market participants, they applied for patents on their ideas to give them some protection after they exposed them to the market.

In contrast to the lukewarm reception they received for Videocart, the Trakus concept "rolled the socks up and down" of almost all of the people they interviewed. The biggest concern anyone expressed was whether the team could actually develop the product and have it work reliably. At the time this is being written, Trakus has raised over $4 million from angels and a venture capital firm. They are on schedule to introduce the Trakus system at the Fleet Center for the Boston Bruins 2000–2001 hockey season. They have already demonstrated that the system can track 12 players in real time and just need to ruggedize the system for a production version. Recently, Trakus was identified by *Inc.* magazine as one of the 10 "hottest" new companies of 1999 and by *Fortune* magazine as one of 10 high potential, new high-technology companies.

If the Trakus team had not concept tested their original Videocart idea and had gone ahead to develop and implement that concept, it is not certain that they would have failed. However, given their concept testing results, the odds of having a huge success were low. On the other hand, the concept testing results were used the way they should have been used—to screen an idea before a lot of resources were spent on it. The concept testing caused the team to "go back to the drawing board" and generate other product ideas that could best leverage their unique skills and abilities.

The team deserves credit for interpreting the concept testing results in a rational manner. Human nature goes against rational interpretation of valuable, but negative information. When the team had organized itself and made its mission to "do Videocart right," it was very difficult emotionally to receive and rationally process information that said that the market did not want a new Videocart nearly as much as the team thought they did. The U.S. culture seems to reinforce these emotional reactions to negative, but valuable information. It is not seen as "macho" to decide to give up on an idea, admit you were wrong, and go on to make the best of what you have left. Especially in an entrepreneurial venture that is typically started with the product/service idea as the main motivation for the team to get together, it is very difficult to admit that the initial idea may not be as profitable as the team first thought. As we describe how to do concept testing for entrepreneurial ventures, keep in mind that it is a challenge to use the concept testing results rationally.

Concept Testing

Concept testing is a research technique that checks whether the prospective purchaser and/or user of a new product-offering bundle understands the product/service idea, feels that it answers a need, and would be willing to purchase and/or use it. Concept testing is basically a set of procedures in which potential customers are exposed to a product or service concept and are asked for their reactions to it. Next we discuss in detail how to perform these procedures most advantageously for entrepreneurs.

The technique can also help to improve the product-offering bundle by understanding problems and/or improvement opportunities that are perceived by the potential consumers. Its primary purpose is to estimate customer and/or intermediary reactions to a product-offering bundle before committing substantial resources to it. Concept testing forces the entrepreneur to expose the idea to the people who will have to receive perceived benefits from it, and to make sure that these people do perceive the benefits. If done well, concept testing and associated procedures can provide a number of important benefits to the entrepreneur, including:

- Identifying likely product failures and limiting the amount of resources spent on ideas that the market does not perceive as helpful.

- Separating good ideas from poor ones and supporting resource allocation to those ideas that the market does want.

- Supplies suggestions for improving the product-offering bundle to make it perceived as more useful to the market participants.

- Generates rough price-sales volume demand curves for new product-offering bundles (see Chapter 3). Well-designed and well-executed concept testing can provide estimates of how the demand for a product will change at alternative price levels.

Because concept testing is best at estimating consumer reaction to the product-offering bundle *before* they actually use it, it works for estimating a new product or service trial, but is not very effective at estimating repeat purchases for goods. The experience with the physical product or service bundle and whether it delivers on its implied promise will be the most important determinant of whether the customer purchases the product again. Thus, concept testing is more useful for estimating trial rates for frequently purchased products and potential sales for consumer-durable products as well as business-to-business durable products. However, even for durable products and business-to-business products, if the initial customers are not satisfied, they will tell other potential customers that the product is bad. Word of mouth can be the biggest help and also the biggest problem for entrepreneurs, depending on whether the initial users are satisfied that the product meets their expectations. The entrepreneur should keep in mind that concept testing can only help estimate revenue *assuming that the product meets the customer expectations* when the customers actually use the product or service.

Concept testing can be a very productive tool for the entrepreneur. It can be done relatively quickly at a relatively low cost. It is also a very flexible technique. A number of ideas can be handled in a single study, as well as the evaluation of different versions of the same basic product-offering bundle. From a cost/benefit viewpoint, concept testing is usually a great value for the entrepreneur. We next discuss some "nuts and bolts" of concept testing and then discuss what concept testing doesn't do, that is, some of its limitations.

Doing Concept Testing—the "Nuts and Bolts"

To use concept testing productively, the following questions must be addressed:

- What kind of information specifically should be collected from respondents?
- What should be in the concept statement?
- What are the best modes of data collection?
- Who should be exposed to the concept?
- How should the questions be asked?

We'll take each of the previous questions in order.

*What Kind of Information Specifically Should Be
Collected from Respondents?*

The most valid information you could gather from a respondent is
to *actually ask for and receive an order* for purchase of the product
based on the concept statement. We discuss these *dry tests* when
we discuss modes of data collection. If you can not realistically
perform dry tests, then the next most valid information is *purchase
intention*. Purchase intention is an indication of how likely the respondent would be to buy the product, after they were exposed to
the concept. The usual scale that is used to scale purchase intention is: Definitely would buy, Probably would buy, Might or might
not buy, Probably would not buy, and Definitely would not buy.

It is risky to interpret purchase intentions absolutely; especially
any answer except Definitely would buy. The exposure of the concept will typically sensitize the respondent to the product concept
and may bias them to tell the perceived source of the concept test
what they feel the concept tester wants to hear. People want to "be
nice." The purchase intent question also implicitly assumes that the
respondent has been exposed to the product, has understood the attributes of the product, and is able to find the product available in
the channel that the respondent would use to buy the product.

To counteract the "be nice" bias, include somewhere in the concept test a comparison of the new product with some existing product it might replace. Equivalently, some respondents can respond to
a concept that describes the existing product in the same form as
the new product. The purchase intent scores on the existing product can then be a base from which to compare the intent scores on
the new product. For example, if product A is an existing product
and product B is the new product, both products would be described by a concept statement as shown below, and purchase
intent would be collected for both products. The fraction who "Definitely would buy" can be compared for A and B. If B has 20 percent
more intent to "Definitely buy," then it is reasonable to assume that
if consumers are aware of product B, understand its attributes, and
can find it distributed, then B could reasonably sell 20 percent
more than A. Some researchers will take a small fraction, around 30
percent of the "Probably would buy" into their calculations by

adding 30 percent of the responses to the "Probably would buy" box, to the responses for the "Definitely would buy."

To counteract the other awareness and distribution limitations, the researcher should multiply the fraction of the market that the concept test says would buy by at least three estimated reduction factors, all fractions less than one. The first factor, f1, is the fraction of the target population(s) that will be aware of the new product. This will depend on how successful the marketing plan is for the product. The second factor, f2, is whether those who are aware will understand and perceive the attributes and benefits of the product as well as those who were exposed to the concept in the concept test. This reduction factor, f2, also depends on the success of the marketing plan. Finally the third factor, f3, reflects the odds that members of the target market(s) will be able to easily purchase the product where they would expect to find it. Multiplying the concept test purchase intent fraction by f1 times f2 times f3 will reduce the purchase intent number to one that is much more reasonable and more predictable of in-market performance.

For example, let's assume a concept test was executed to a representative sample of potential customers in our target market and that 30 percent of those responding indicated they would "Definitely buy it." To be conservative, we'll assume that none of the people who said "Probably would buy it" will eventually buy the product. We must multiply the 30 percent by f1,f2, and f3 to reflect awareness and distribution limitations. Based on our introductory marketing plan, we'll assume that 40 percent of the target market will become aware of the product (f1 = 40 percent) and that only 30 percent of those aware will perceive the benefits and attributes as well as those exposed in the concept test (f2 = 30 percent). Further, based on how much of our category volume is sold in stores which plan to carry our product, we assume that 60 percent of our target market will easily be able to find the product where they will expect to purchase it (f3 = 60 percent). Thus, if we multiply the 30 percent by 0.4 times 0.3 times 0.6, we obtain 2.16 percent, an estimate of the percent of the target market that might make an initial purchase of the product. Different assumptions for these reduction fractions can be used to test for sensitivity of sales forecasts to these assumptions.

Other questions can aid in both improving the actual product and the way it is described to potential consumers. These questions should be asked *after* the purchase intent question. The purchase intent question is meant to measure the attraction of a concept after the potential customer has been exposed to the concept, not after the potential customer has been asked many questions about the concept that normally heighten his interest in the concept.

Questions about how well potential consumers understood the concept and what they liked and didn't like about the product are usually very helpful. The likes and dislikes can be very useful in improving either the product or the way the product is described. The respondent should be able to "play back" the products attributes and benefits, as they perceived them after having been exposed to the concept statement. The respondents could also answer questions about how interested they are in the product—extremely interested, somewhat interested, and so on. If many respondents are extremely interested, but relatively few express high purchase intent, then perhaps the price used in the concept test was too high.

Depending on the product and its target market, other questions can be asked about situations for which the respondent sees the product as useful, or problems the product might solve. If the respondent can tell which products the new product might replace, this is also helpful. Answers to these questions can be valuable for improving the marketing materials for the product's introduction.

Some people put price response questions into the concept test by asking *the same person* purchase intent questions *at different price levels in the same concept test*; for example, "How likely would you be to purchase the product if it were $140, $130, $120, or $100?" The respondent would give a separate response for each alternative price level. *This procedure is extremely biasing and should be avoided.* The respondent assumes that she is "negotiating" with the concept tester and gives very biased results that are not usually indicative of how the respondent would actually react if she were exposed to the product at different price levels.

The right way to include price response in a concept test is to include *one price* as part of the product's description. *Each respondent* is exposed to only one price as a descriptor of the product. However, *each respondent* can be exposed to *different prices* than other respondents. As we'll see later with some examples, price is a very psychological attribute and can have a big impact on how potential consumers perceive a product or service. This procedure insures that the potential consumer sees only one price, the same way the person will see the product in the real market.

What Should Be in the Concept Statement?

The concept statement should as closely and realistically as possible mimic how the respondent would be exposed to the product and its attributes when the product is actually introduced. Most concept statements look like product brochures or print ads. The concept statement typically also includes where the respondent could expect to buy the product or service, and all the benefits that are part of the positioning plan. As discussed, the price of the product is one of the attributes that should be an integral part of the concept statement. Figure 2.1 shows a concept statement for one product from a new novelty diaper line that has university and sports team logos on them. To be realistic, the concept test should be done in each of the possible target market segments with the specific logo for that segment as part of the concept description. One of the possible market segments was alumni of the University of Pennsylvania. The concept is slightly disguised to protect confidentiality.

What Are the Best Modes of Data Collection?

The entrepreneur wants to have the respondent exposed to the concept in a manner as close as possible to how they would be exposed in reality. There are limits and trade-offs of costs versus validity of the concept test results. If you would use a print ad or direct mail piece to introduce your product, it is not very expensive to "dummy up" some sample ads as part of the concept statement and then to expose people to those adds. These kinds of concepts are most validly exposed through personal interviews with the respondent either at her home or at her place of work. Depending on the segmentation targets, it sometimes is cheaper and not less valid to use centralized locations like malls. Telephone interviews can be very cost effective for concepts that are

Product Concept: Futurewear is a line of designer diapers, which feature university and professional sports team logos. One of the diapers has the University of Pennsylvania "Penn Quaker" logo, both on the tape and bottom ("tush") of the diaper. This diaper is made of premium materials and is functionally equivalent to a good disposable diaper. It is a fun, novelty item, which will typically be purchased as a gift (i.e., baby shower, Christmas) rather than as an everyday item by parents. The diapers will be white, packaged in a very nice gift box of 19 that also has the Penn Quaker logo, and be priced at $11.95. The diaper will be available at most stores that have other University of Pennsylvania logo merchandise, as well as Web stores that sell baby merchandise. What a nice, fun way to help a loyal Penn alumnus start his or her child show their support of Penn! The perfect gift for anyone who is a Penn supporter!

Figure 2.1 Logo diaper concept statement.

easily understood over the phone and may be advertised on radio when they are introduced. Sometimes a combination of mailing, e-mailing, or faxing the concept statement can be combined with telephone interviews. These combinations can be very cost effective and for many products and services do not lose much validity compared to in-person interviews.

It is usually cost effective to contract with a local market research firm to actually field the concept test. They have experience in getting with the right people and can help with the actual test design. However, if they tell you to do something that contradicts the major points in this chapter, then you should change suppliers. Depending on your time versus resource constraints, it may be possible to use students at nearby universities who are studying market research. However, if they use your product as a class project, it may take two or three months to get results. Commercial firms can turn around some concept tests in a few weeks.

For products that will be sold or promoted with the Web as a primary marketing tool, concept testing can very easily be done directly on the Internet. In fact, depending on one's ethics, it is very feasible to "dummy up" online ads and/or product descriptions, and *actually ask for the order online*. When respondents actually start the order process, you then can explain to them that the product is in development and that you were testing market place reaction. You could then send them some kind of a gift as a token of thanks and apology, and put their name on a list of those who will get the first chance to buy the product when it's ready. This *dry test* as direct marketers call it, is the most valid way of getting real consumer demand for a new product or service. Such dry tests are often used in countries where questionable marketing practices are more widely accepted; in the United States, this mode of assessing reactions may raise ethical concerns. The Web is not the only place dry tests can and have been used. Direct response marketers have been using dry tests for years. Depending on which media vehicles they use for advertising, they have to consider that they are prematurely letting their competitors know their new product plans. Dry tests with direct mail are much easier to hide than dry tests in radio, television, or print.

Who Should Be Exposed to the Concept?

If your positioning and segmentation planning are complete, then it is obvious that decision makers and decision influencers of the target segments should be exposed to the concept. In concept testing, it usually pays to be inclusive with possible target segments. If you are doubtful about a target segment, it makes sense to concept test some members to help decide whether to include the segment in your plans. The cost of concept testing is typically small compared to the foregone profits of missing a possible segment.

For business-to-business products and some complex and/or expensive consumer products, you must be careful to interview all of the possible influencers of the purchase decision. For example, you are considering introducing a new angiography product to hospitals, you should interview not only the physicians who would use the product, but hospital administrators who would need to approve the purchase as well as nurses who might influence how the product were to be used. For high-involvement consumer purchases like appliances, computers, and telecommunications equipment, there may be many possible decision influencers that need to be tested. For example, for computers and telecommunications equipment, many consumers turn to "experts" whose opinions they request before they make purchase decisions. It is very important for the entrepreneur to seek out and interview these experts.

If the entrepreneur does not know the decision process in her target markets well enough, before performing the concept testing, it makes sense to do some qualitative questioning of market participants to find out how these type of decisions are typically made. Questions such as "Would you consult anyone else before making a purchase decision?" or "Who else would have to approve this decision?" can be very enlightening.

Concept Testing Channel Members

In Chapter 6, we discuss concept testing for channel members as being as important as for the end purchasers. However, concept testing with channel members *is no substitute* for getting systematic end user reaction to a product. In the book *The Silicon Valley Way*, Elton Sherwin Jr. describes a disguised, but real company, The Palo Alto PC Company, that neglected to concept test the end purchaser and solely relied on the results from the distribution channels.[1] This company had been successful designing and building small, good looking, premium-priced notebook PCs and selling them through a strong network of distributors.

As Palo Alto PC began designing their fourth generation notebook, they did a cursory survey of their largest distributors. They assumed, and their distributors confirmed, that "Customers want it even smaller."

The new Palo Alto PC was a hit with the media. Its innovative keyboard made it both small and cute. Unfortunately, few customers bought it. Sales plummeted. It turns out that executives wanted longer battery life, brighter screens, and thinner PCs—but not smaller keyboards.[2]

Distributors are very good at reacting to the aspects of the product that affect how well they will "push" them—the mark-up, the terms, the logistics, the end-user marketing program, and so on.

They also can sometimes tell you what *they think* their customers will want. However, as this example points out, there is typically no substitute for getting end-user reaction to concepts.

How Should the Questions Be Asked?

Concept testing for entrepreneurs typically involves either *monadic* testing (a person gets exposed to only one concept) or *paired comparison* testing (a person is exposed to a pair of concepts).

Monadic testing should be used when you seek a detailed uncontaminated reaction to a concept. It is typically better to monadic test when direct competitors are hard to identify. Monadic tests also work better when there is little external search for alternatives prior to purchasing.

On the other hand, when there are direct competitors already in the market, it can be useful to also do a *paired comparison* evaluation of the new product versus others. If there's enough time, the paired comparison can be done after the monadic evaluation. The paired comparison purchase intent can be asked as "Which would you prefer to purchase, Product A or Product B?" Here also a scale can be used, just as it was in the monadic purchase intent: Definitely prefer A, Moderately prefer A, Toss-up, Moderately prefer B, Definitely prefer B.

As we discussed, this comparison evaluation helps to ground revenue predictions in what you know about existing products. For example, if your new entrepreneurial product is preferred by 20 percent more people than existing product A, you know that its potential is to sell even better than Product A. This is only a *potential,* however. The above caveats on any purchase intent measure are also salient here (e.g., awareness, understanding the product benefits, and finding the product in distribution).

Concept Screening

Getting reactions of potential purchase influencers can be very helpful, not only after one product concept has been determined, but also to help *screen* candidate product ideas before much work or resources have been spent on them. For this screening application, *card sorting and evaluation* is sometimes cost effective. Simply give the respondent several product descriptions, each on a card or a separate sheet. The respondent can sort them into a rank order and can rate each idea on either a semantic (excellent, good, fair, poor, etc.) or numeric scale. For consumers over about 35 years old, the movie *Ten* has made it very easy to use 1 to 10 scales for marketing research.

Using the Web for Concept Testing—CarsDirect.com and Goto.com

Many times, the reactions of consumers to concepts are biased by their inability to really understand what would be offered. The Web allows for certain concepts to be tested in a live manner, with direct validation or refutation of the basic concept. When CarsDirect.com was started, there was a lot of skepticism about whether or not people would actually buy big ticket items sight unseen on the Web. Rather than do a lot of focus groups, screening, and so on, these entrepreneurs elected to do a quick test on the Web.

With less than a week's work, they put up a site that offered "Cars at invoice price." The pricing was already widely available on the Internet, and a small number of pages were put up inviting the user to search for the car they desired, and submit an order on the Web. Once their order was received, a phone call was made to verify that they were serious, and a deposit was taken, and the car delivered.

When the test site was ready, CarsDirect.com bought the top listing for the cars keyword at GoTo.com, to direct some traffic to the site. Over the course of a single weekend, four cars were ordered. The company bought them at retail prices and subsidized the difference between that price and the invoice pricing that had been advertised. For less than $20,000, they had proven that people would buy very large ticket items on the Web. After that, several million dollars was invested to build the successful Web site that sold more than $250 million worth of cars by the end of 1999.

Similarly, with GoTo.com, a search site that charges for higher position in search results, there was great skepticism that either consumers or advertisers would use it. The company put up the site, and verified that advertisers would give us credit cards and pay for their ads. None of the cards was actually charged in the first

month, since it was merely a concept testing experiment. The refined version created a public company worth several billion dollars.

Caveats for Concept Testing

Even though concept testing is typically very valuable in terms of
cost/benefits for entrepreneurs, it has a number of limitations that
constantly need to be kept in mind:

1. As discussed, if the product or service does not deliver the
   benefits promised in the concept, the revenue predictions will
   never happen. The more costly, risky, and high involvement
   the product is, the more important is the experience of the in-
   novator and early adopter users. If this experience is worse
   than the benefits expectation of the concept test and the expectations of these "lead users" based on the introductory
   sales and marketing material, then the product will be severely
   penalized.

2. Changes in the product between the concept test and the
   product's introduction will cause possible changes in consumer reactions.

3. Sometimes R&D and production cannot execute the product
   exactly as promised in the concept test.

4. If the concept test has not been tested in a very realistic way,
   respondents may overstate their preferences in order to "be
   nice" to the interviewer. It is human nature to tell someone
   what you think they would like to hear. Thus, respondents may
   say they like the product, but not buy it when it actually comes
   on the market.

5. Concept testing can only predict initial purchase. It cannot
   predict how many people will use the product regularly, or how
   many will repeat purchase it. For repetitively purchased products, high trial rate alone does not guarantee success.

The Survey Results on Concept Testing and New
Product Testing

Only 33 percent of both Inc. 500 and non-Inc. 500 entrepreneurs
concept tested their first products before they introduced them.

However, 38 percent of the Inc. 500 report that they continually do new product testing versus only 21 percent of the non-Inc. group. Thus at least the Inc. 500 group is learning to be more careful versus the non-Inc. group in evaluating new products before they are launched. However, both groups should be doing more concept testing.

Summary

Concepts testing really amounts to getting systematic direct reactions of market and channel participants to your product/service concept before you spend the time and resources to develop, produce, and introduce it. Historically, traditional concept testing has been able to predict product trial rates within a 20 percent range, about 80 percent of the time for frequently purchased packaged goods. For example, if predicted trial was 50 percent, the product trial rate would be between 40 percent to 60 percent in 8 out of 10 cases. However, today most packaged goods firms do qualitative focused groups rather than systematic concept testing for their new product screening and evaluation. Entrepreneurial firms do not have the luxury of using less than the most cost effective methods.

The details of exactly how and who should be concept tested are not nearly as important *as just doing it!* The most important thing is to get direct reaction, including some measure of purchase intent from members of your target markets. If you don't do that, you *significantly increase your odds of failure* for your new venture. As an added bonus, concept testing can be combined with price testing to help maximize the profit contribution of the new product. We show this in the next chapter. Before we discuss pricing in the next chapter, we will review some very interesting research that helps the entrepreneur choose a better battlefield to enter, if she has the option of choosing different kinds of products or services to consider for her venture.

Finding More Receptive Battlefields

Are there better markets for entrepreneurial survival? Are there characteristics of product/markets that make them more likely to be receptive to successful entrepreneurial activity? Three European researchers analyzed 30,000 new U.S. businesses to find characteristics that were more likely to be associated with entrepreneurial ventures that would survive for ten years or more.[3] The researchers developed measures of three groups of characteristics: the first was customer-buying patterns, the second was competitor's marketing and channel strategies, and the third was production requirements.

Customer-buying patterns were described by the following characteristics: The first was *purchase frequency* which was measured by the proportion of product line which was generally purchased less than once per year compared with products which were purchased frequently. The second was *purchase significance* which was measured by the percentage of the product line which represented a major purchase for the ultimate buyer. The third measure of consumer buying patterns was the degree of customer/distributor fragmentation. This was measured by the percentage of product lines for which there were over 1,000 customer accounts at the manufacturer level.

Competitors' marketing and channel strategies were described by three variables: The first variable was *pull marketing* which was measured by the expenditures on media advertising as a percentage of total sales revenue. The second variable was *push marketing* which was defined as the cost of marketing excluding media spending as a percentage of sales revenue for the product lines in each group. Finally, *channel dependence* was described as the percentage of products which pass through an intermediary before reaching the user.

Production requirements were described by four variables: The first was *labor* versus *capital intensity* which was measured by calculating the ratio of total employees to the total book value of plant and equipment in the industry producing each group of products. The second variable was *employee skill requirements*. It was defined as the number of "high skills" jobs as a percentage of total employees involved in producing the product group. The third variable was *service requirements*. It was calculated as the percentage of products requiring a moderate to high degree of sales or technical service as classified by the suppliers who were surveyed. The last variable in this group was *made to order supply.* It was defined as the percentage of product lines that were made to order based on customer specifications.

They analyzed almost 30,000 independent start-ups for a five-year period ending in the mid-1980s. They performed a statistical analysis of the relationship of survival rates of independent start-ups and the above product/market characteristics. Their main results are summarized in Figure 2.2,[4] which shows hostile and fertile product/market segments for independent start-ups.

The data showed that entrepreneurial start-ups had significantly better chances of survival in two product/market segment types: those that had high-service requirements and those that had low purchase frequency. The high-service requirements results imply that the greater attention to customer needs and flexibility an entrepreneurial start-up can offer can give it an advantage over less attentive established vendors for that product/market segment.

The result that product/market segments which made infrequent purchase decisions are also more fertile is consistent with

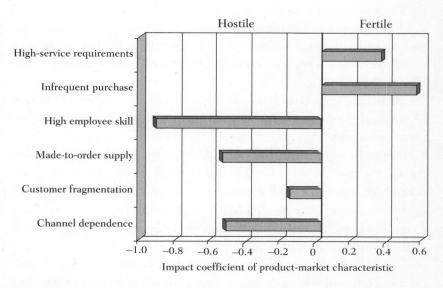

Figure 2.2 The impact of product and market characteristics on the survival of independent start-ups. *Source:* Hay, Verdin, and Williamson, "Successful New Ventures: Lessons for Entrepreneurs and Investors," *Long Range Planning,* vol. 26, no. 5, (1993), pp. 31–41.

other theories of business-to-business marketing. Infrequent purchases typically involve the customer reassessing the attributes of product or service offerings. In this circumstance, there is a higher likelihood of attending to new information and possibly trying a new alternative product offering.

Figure 2.2 also shows four product/market characteristics that an entrepreneur should avoid, all other factors being equal. Those segments that require high employee skill and made to order supply are harder for entrepreneurs to succeed in. These segments may require extensive employee training and big investments in production assets—both luxuries that are difficult for a new entrepreneur to supply. The other two entrepreneurially hostile segment characteristics make it very difficult for the small player to target the segment effectively. Both highly fragmented customer bases and high-end customer dependence on channels make it relatively more difficult for the entrepreneurial marketer to reach her target customers. The Internet makes it easier to reach fragmented customer bases, since geography no longer plays a role, but even on the Web, if the base is too fragmented, the cost of customer acquisition may rise to unprofitable levels.

For corporate "intrapraneurs," Hay, Verdin, and Williamson also report the product market segment types that were hostile and fertile for corporate ventures. The results are summarized in Figure 2.3.[5]

The only segment characteristic common to higher likelihood of survival for both corporate and independent ventures is infrequent purchase. Segments in which a customer is more likely to be receptive to new information are evidently fertile, regardless of the assets that the new venture brings to them. Segments that require high employee skill are also hostile to both independent and corporate entrepreneurs. Evidently, high employee skill is a barrier to entry of established competitors, regardless of whether the new entry is corporate or independent.

The other characteristics differentiate those segments which corporate resources can impact. Pull marketing requires resources for mass marketing and may also leverage the reputation of a corporate parent. Corporate subsidiaries seem to be at a disadvantage when infrastructure to support push marketing is required by the

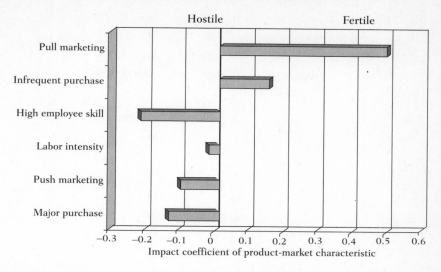

Figure 2.3 The impact of product and market characteristics on the survival of corporate ventures. *Source:* Hay, Verdin, and Williamson, "Successful New Ventures: Lessons for Entrepreneurs and Investors," *Long Range Planning,* vol. 26, no. 5, (1993), pp. 31–41.

segment. Perhaps long periods of experience are necessary to set up effective networks. This experience with the push marketing infrastructure can be an effective barrier to entry.

Even though these results can help an entrepreneur or corporate subsidiary to choose a more receptive product/market to enter, keep in mind that all of the positive and negative characteristics are only effective on the average. Certainly, not every entrepreneurial venture that attacks segments with the fertile characteristics will be successful. The results just show that the entrepreneur or corporate subsidiary will be more likely to not fail or to fail in those segments. These results are not a substitute for the careful concept testing we advocate in this chapter.

CHAPTER 3

Entrepreneurial Pricing Decisions

Pricing is typically the most difficult decision for entrepreneurs. It is also probably the most important since it ultimately determines how much money a company can make. In today's world, you not only have to price products that have significant manufacturing costs, or services with large human elements in delivery, but also intellectual property that can be replicated for essentially zero cost on the Internet. Unfortunately, some entrepreneurs think pricing is easy. These entrepreneurs use very comfortable, precise rules for pricing. These simple rules are usually one of two types— mark-up rules or competitive matching rules. Mark-up rules just take the product's or service's costs and mark them up by a margin percentage. This margin percentage may be standard for the industry, or related to what the entrepreneur is used to, or what she needs to make her forecasted profit at the forecasted revenue for her venture. The competitive "rules" usually have the entrepreneur planning on pricing just a bit lower than competition, or matching their prices. These rules make it very easy for the entrepreneur to make the pricing decision without having to do much work or careful thinking. However, like many things in life, "no pain, no gain." The problem with these "rules" is that they may leave too much money on the table.

Why? Very simply, because other prices may be more profitable to the venture. For example, if my widgets cost $1, and I sell them for $2, a "keystone" or doubling mark-up, why shouldn't I be happy? You haven't asked the proper question: *Of all the possible prices I can charge for my widgets, which price will maximize my profitability over my planning horizon?* If, when I price my widgets for $2, I sell 400,000 units per year, is that the best possible price in terms of total profitability from the widgets over the product's life? Selling 400,000 units at $2 per unit brings in revenue of $800,000. From that revenue product costs of $1 per unit equals $1 × 400,000 or $400,000. This leaves $400,000 as gross margin or contribution to fixed costs and profit due to the widgets.

What would happen to my units sold if I charged some other price? If a reasonable estimate can be made of units that would be sold at alternative prices (the "elasticity of demand"), you can find the price that maximizes profitability over the planning horizon. We will describe methods for getting estimates of demand at alternative prices later, after we show how valuable they can be if they are integrated into the cost structure of the venture. The reason that different customers will pay different prices is that they may have different perceived values for using the products. Let us assume that our widgets would sell the amounts indicated in Table 3.1.

The maximum revenue price is $3 per widget for revenue of $900,000, only $100,000 greater than the original price of $2. However, the contribution is 600,000, 2.4 times the profitability of the original $2 price! However, there is even a better price—the price of $3.50 per widget has a lower revenue of $875,000, but

Price per Unit	Units Sold	Revenue ($)	Cost at $1/Unit	Contribution ($)
1.0	600,000	600,000	600,000	0
1.5	500,000	750,000	500,000	250,000
2.0 (original)	400,000	800,000	400,000	400,000
2.5	350,000	875,000	350,000	525,000
3.0 (highest revenue)	300,000	900,000	300,000	600,000
3.5 (highest profit)	250,000	875,000	250,000	625,000
4.0	200,000	800,000	200,000	600,000
5.0	100,000	500,000	100,000	400,000

Table 3.1 Contribution for Alternative Prices

has a higher contribution of $625,000. This contribution is 2.5 times the contribution that would have occurred had the original price been used. This is an obviously simplified example, but not simplified in isolating how important the analysis of alternative prices is to most entrepreneurial ventures. The impact of the initial pricing decision on the venture's ultimate profitability is typically huge. We'll show some real examples later of what this decision has meant to some entrepreneurial ventures as well as how to estimate the revenue at alternative price levels. However, first it is time to give the quick entrepreneurial marketer's guide to *cost accounting!*

The reason for bringing up cost accounting is that the profitability of pricing decisions depends solely on revenue and *variable costs*. Fixed costs are almost irrelevant in deciding the best price to charge for the product or service. Why? Because if fixed costs, by definition, don't change when the number of units sold changes, they will be incurred *regardless of the alternative price that would be charged*. All of the "contribution" numbers in Table 3.1 should really be contribution to fixed costs and profit of the venture. The $1 cost assumed in the simple example should be only the variable costs to produce, sell, and deliver an incremental unit. Fixed costs that will be incurred regardless of the price will be subtracted from the contribution to estimate the profitability of the widget product. If any constant number were subtracted from each contribution row, the price that maximizes contribution and profit will not change. Thus, fixed costs do not affect the best price to charge for a product/or service. There is only one exception to this rule: If the estimated contribution of the best price is *not enough to cover the fixed costs* associated with the product or service, then the product or service should *not be introduced*.

Getting Price Right Early—It's Hard to Raise Prices Later!

It is even more important to get the pricing done well early in the product's life. If you lower a price over a product's lifetime, no one will complain (except possibly the customers who just bought it at a higher price). However, it is much more difficult to raise a price significantly because you realize the product's perceived value is much higher than you thought. Human nature does not consider such price rises as "fair." If you can convince potential customers that your costs have gone up, that is usually perceived as a legitimate or fair justification for raising prices. Customers do not typically go through such fairness evaluations when they originally see a price for a new product or service. Human nature and fairness arguments take over only when prices are raised. Thus, it is even more important to have your initial price set at a very good level.

However, for many new products, it is usually the innovators who will take a risk on a new product or service. For taking this initial risk, the first customers want (and deserve) special pricing treatment. Sometimes they even deserve to get the product at no cost to try until they are convinced of its value. It is okay for the entrepreneur to give special pricing to these first innovative customers. However, the prices should be structured as *charter customer discounts* or *introductory discounts* from a *regular price* that is publicized as what will be normal after the introduction. This paradigm gives the entrepreneur much more room to determine marketplace reaction and adjust his actually selling prices by adjusting the introductory discount level and time period.

By having a regular price stated up-front, the entrepreneur is free to charge up to that level without generating market perceptions of unfairness. There are some entrepreneurs who have kept introductory prices for over a year after a product has been introduced.

Survey Results on Pricing Methods

The graph in Figure 3.1 shows the survey results of how the entrepreneurs priced their first products and Figure 3.2 shows how they currently price their products. Notice that the Inc. 500 CEOs have learned to use perceived value-in-use pricing much better than the non-Inc. group. Part of the reason for the success of the Inc. 500 ventures is very likely associated with over half of them learning to do perceived value pricing, whereas the non-Inc. group did not learn over time to price more productively.

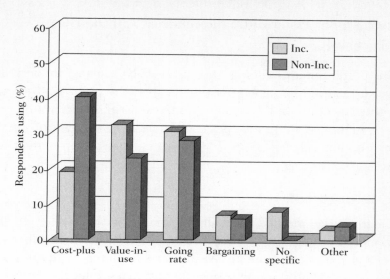

Figure 3.1 How did you price your first product?

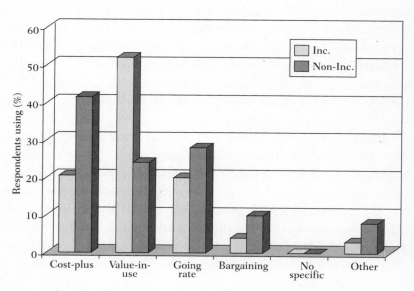

Figure 3.2 How do you price your products currently?

Methods for Determining Revenue at Alternative Price Levels

The entrepreneur reading this is probably saying to herself—"Sure, it would be more profitable to price so as to get the most profit, but how can I get good estimates of the sales I would realize if I charged alternative prices?" There are a number of ways to do this that can be grouped into two categories—in-market and pre-market testing.

In-Market Methods

The in-market method is usually preferable because it is typically a very valid predictor of what revenue would be at alternative price levels. However, it is not always practical to charge different prices for the same product or service in the marketplace. You cannot charge different prices for what is perceived as the same product bundle if market participants will communicate with each other. If one market participant finds out that another participant bought what they perceived as the same product bundle at a better price, they will feel cheated. Even though rationally, they got enough perceived value from their purchase or they would not have made it, psychologically they feel cheated. If they feel that way, they can begin saying bad things about your product. Bad word-of-mouth is very damaging to a new product or service that lives based on customer perceptions. If a potential customer hears bad things about a product from a respected source, it can undermine all the other marketing activities you do.

If the customer perceives the product bundle to be different, then the consumer will not necessarily be upset about hearing that someone else paid a different price. For example airline seats or concert tickets will be priced differently depending on when the customer decides to buy them or exactly where they are located. We will discuss more about yield management and other methods for charging different prices to different segments for different product bundles of the same physical product later in this chapter.

However, there are circumstances where it is highly unlikely for market participants to become upset. These are products or services that are purchased individually and usually not discussed very much among consumers or products whose prices may be difficult to compare because they are customized to each potential customer. Many product/market combinations can be tested in market. For example if one of your primary marketing vehicles is personal sales and your product price is somewhat dependent on the potential customers characteristics, it is relatively easy to evaluate market reaction to different price levels. Have each of the salespeople involved in the test use different price levels for every nth potential customer on which they call. For example, if there were three alternative price policies to test, then every potential customer would be exposed to one of the three different pricing policies, and each customer would have a $\frac{1}{3}$ probability of being exposed to each policy. As long as it's pretty difficult for the potential customer to compare the pricing algorithm actually used by your salesperson, it will be difficult to compare prices across different potential customers. Thus, even if two customers do talk who have been exposed to different pricing algorithms, they will not be likely to find out that they actually were quoted different pricing options. For example, if the pricing of software is developed based on a fixed charge for organizational training, another charge for installation, and another set of charges per "seat" or installed computer terminal, then it becomes difficult for two firms who have different needs to compare prices.

The Perfect In-Market Price Testing Vehicle

Because purchasing is done individually on the Web, and each person can be exposed to a different, customized Web site, the Web can be an extremely effective and valid price-testing device.

The Internet offers one of the best vehicles for market and price testing ever invented. Immediate feedback, large sample sizes, and live customer reactions make it much more efficient and valid than focus groups or limited city tests. Idealab! will often test banner ads and pricing by using 1 to 5,000 banners to drive viewers to specific pages on a site, keeping cookies to track their behavior, and then examining the followthrough once they have reached a site.

With utility.com, a provider of deregulated electric power in a number of states around the United States, the pricing and messages were honed through a series of tests. The vice president of marketing first stated that he thought they needed to offer 15 percent off to get customers to switch from their existing supplier. Perhaps, they could get away with only 10 percent off if they chose "green" (environmentally clean) power. There were a number of skeptics which led to the company using a test.

After testing a number of different banners to get the best colors, animation and messages, they tested offers of 5 percent to 15 percent off, each leading to a page that offered 0 to 5 percent additional if you signed up right away. The results were non-intuitive. The offers that drew the most people to the site were 7 percent off and 11 percent off. They were significantly higher draws than 15 percent off or 10 percent off. Once at the site, the best additional offers were 0, 1, and 3 percent off.

The best combined action came from a 7 percent offer to get visitors to the site, where they were offered 3 percent off for immediate signup—a total of 10 percent off. Green versus nongreen power had only a very small effect and is now offered as an option on the signup pages. Without the testing, the company would have used the "instinct" of 15 percent, with both higher cost and lower effectiveness.

The cost for the test was under $5,000, since off-peak banner advertising can be purchased very inexpensively, and it only takes several thousand tests to make it work.

Survey Results on Web Price Testing

Neither group in our survey do as much Web price testing as they probably should. Only 6 percent of the Inc. 500 and 7 percent of the non-Inc. group do much price testing on the Web. Perhaps their products are not suitable for such price testing, but more than likely, they are both missing out on an opportunity.

Premarket Methods—Pricing and Concept Testing

Our discussion in Chapter 2 of concept testing before a product or service is introduced, mentioned that it could be used as a very effective vehicle for estimating the relative differences in sales that would occur at alternative price levels. The basic idea is very simple. Part of the concept description of the product or service is the price. If you want to concept test four alternative prices, then have every concept description have only one of the four pricing alternatives, with each respondent being exposed at a .25 probability to one of the alternatives. So every fourth concept test will have the same price. The estimates of number of units that would be bought at different price levels can be calculated in the same way as any other concept test. What is very valuable to the entrepreneur is to analyze the resulting revenue implications from the alternative pricing policies.

Since any biases of the concept test would be constant over the four different prices, the relative differences in response of one price versus another will usually be quite valid. For example, if the concept test results indicate that 40 percent more widgets would be sold at a 20 percent lower price, that percentage difference will be the same regardless of what the base absolute sales of the widgets would be. Regardless of whether the actual sales of the widgets in market would be 1,000 units or 10,000 units at the base price, the estimate of 40 percent more units that would be sold at a 20 percent lower price should be valid.

A Price-Concept Testing Example

A small, non-U.S. manufacturer (who we will call ABLE) of faucets for kitchen sinks had been selling one model of faucet through a major do-it-yourself retailer for two years—and just barely breaking even, if all of the costs associated with the faucet were taken into account.[1] The manufacturer, ABLE, wanted to see if they could convince the retailer to change the retail price from $98 to a higher price, enabling ABLE to raise the wholesale price to the retailer. As part of a larger study, a paired comparison concept test was administered in the retail store to customers who were about to buy a kitchen faucet. The customers were asked to choose which of two alternative faucets they would rather purchase and provided concept descriptions of each. The concept statements included a picture of the faucet and all of the descriptions of the product features and/or benefits that were on the respective faucet boxes. In the large do-it-yourself retailers, the box on the shelf was the major way in which the customer was able to evaluate alternative products prior to making a purchase. The box's perception on the shelf is very important in most mass merchandisers. Each concept statement also had a price associated with it. Each customer that was tested received a concept test with one of four alternative prices for the ABLE faucet—$98, $127, $141, or $160. The other faucet they were given to evaluate was constant throughout the test. It was the major seller at the retailer with a price of $141. An example of part of the concept test survey is shown in Figure 3.3, where the ABLE faucet is B.

Twenty-five percent of the people received the ABLE faucet concept description priced at $98, a different 25 percent received the ABLE concept priced at $127, and so on. The competitive faucet was always constant and priced at $141. The results of this part of the concept test are shown in Figure 3.4.

From the results, demand seems to go down very significantly at prices over $98. It falls from 40 to 5, a drop of 85 percent. If this pricing option was the only alternative ABLE could pursue, it would not make sense to raise the faucet's price. However, some

---

1. Looking at the photos and descriptions below, how much do you think each of these faucets sell for?

A. _____   B. _____

- Pull-out spray for hard to reach places
- Adjusts from aerated stream to powerful spray
- Can be mounted without deckplate to accommodate accessories
- Easy do-it-yourself installation
- Water-saving aerator
- Washerless, one-piece cartridge
- Lifetime limited warranty

- Pull-out spray
- European design faucet
- Matching deckplate
- Easy installation
- Flexible connector tubes
- Ceramic disc cartridge/washerless design
- 20-year limited warranty
- Solid brass construction

If the price for Faucet A was $141 and $98 for Faucet B, which would you purchase?

Figure 3.3   Feature-Oriented Concept Test.

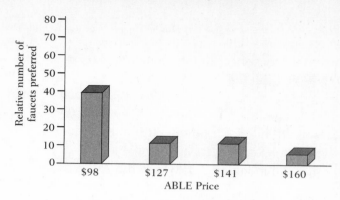

Figure 3.4   ABLE Faucets Concept Test.

entrepreneurial marketers looked carefully at the ABLE box. They observed that the product description on the box was all stated as product *features* as opposed to product *benefits.* For example, flexible connector tubes probably don't mean very much to the typical faucet buyer. However, if the feature was translated into a benefit such as "flexible connector tubes to fit into tight spaces under the sink," it might have more value to a potential purchaser. How many potential purchasers would know the benefit associated with the feature "ceramic disc, washerless cartridge"? How much more valuable is "ceramic disc, washerless cartridge design eliminates leaks and ensures maximum control"?

Price Response Depends on Perceived Value

To estimate the impact on price response of describing the product on the box with benefits versus features, another cell was added to the concept test described in Figure 3.3. Half of the respondents saw a benefits-oriented concept statement while the other half saw the original feature-oriented copy. The concept statement for the benefits-oriented box is shown in Figure 3.5.

The benefits-oriented box copy was also shown to different respondents at one of the same four alternative price levels. The concept test was not only able to estimate the response of the new box copy at the four alternative price levels, but also to compare the *benefits*-oriented copy versus the existing *features*-oriented copy for the box at the different price levels. This is because the

1. Looking at the photos and descriptions below, how much do you think each of these faucets sell for?

A. _____   B. _____

- Pull-out spray for hard to reach places
- Adjusts from aerated stream to powerful spray
- Can be mounted without deckplate to accommodate accessories
- Easy do-it-yourself installation
- Water-saving aerator
- Washerless, one-piece cartridge
- Lifetime limited warranty

- Pull-out spray for multi-purpose use
- European design faucet
- Matching deckplate to cover sinkholes
- Easy step-by-step installation instructions
- Flexible connector tubes fit in tight spaces under sink
- Ceramic disc cartridge/washerless design eliminates leaks, ensures maximum control
- 20-year limited warranty
- Solid brass construction for long life

If the price for Faucet A was $141 and $98 for Faucet B, which would you purchase?

Figure 3.5   Benefits-Oriented Concept Test.

control faucet was the same for all 8 versions of the concept test—two copies times four different price levels. The results for the responses to all 8 versions of the concept are shown in Figure 3.6.

Keep in mind that the concept test biases, whatever they are, are not typically going to affect any one cell of the eight test cells versus any other. The results add a lot of value and are a wonderful illustration of how important perception is to price response. They also illustrate how valuable it is to help the consumer understand product benefits that are associated with certain features. First, notice that *just by describing the product with benefit-oriented statements on its box, sales would double compared to the current box's feature-oriented statements.* Twice as many respondents chose the ABLE product versus its major competitor when it was described by relating the features to their consumer benefits. The benefits-oriented description added considerable perceived value to the customer. Approximately the same number of faucets would be sold at $160 (a 60 percent higher price) for the benefits-oriented box copy compared to the original features-oriented

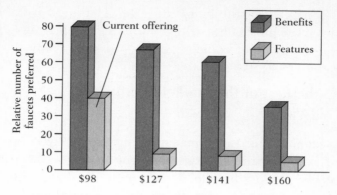

Figure 3.6 ABLE Faucets—Demand estimates.

copy. Thus, just *changing the box copy to a benefits orientation added over 60 percent to the perceived consumer value of the same physical faucet!*

The other cells in Figure 3.4 are also quite valuable—both to ABLE and to the retailer. Notice that demand goes down much less severely for the benefits-oriented copy as the price goes up, compared to the existing features-oriented copy. When the retailer evaluated her costs and profit alternatives, the $141 price made the most sense if ABLE were to raise its wholesale price for the redesigned benefits-oriented box. At $141 with the redesigned box, the concept test shows a true win-win-win situation. ABLE gets to significantly raise its price to the retailer. The retailer sells more units of ABLE's faucets. The consumer gets a faucet that they would value at $160 for $141. Everyone is happier. It doesn't always work this way, but when it does, it is very gratifying to true entrepreneurial marketers.

Survey Results on Pricing, Concept Testing, and In-Market Testing

Of the Inc. 500, 50 percent have done some concept testing at different price levels versus 33 percent of the non-Inc. group. Of the Inc. group, 33 percent has done some in-market price testing versus 30 percent of the non-Inc. group. Here again, more than half of even the most successful ventures are not pricing as potentially profitably as they could.

Pricing, the Rest of the Marketing Mix, and Perceived Value

As the example illustrates, managing pricing really is highly dependent on how well the entrepreneur manages the *perceived value* of her product bundle. This perceived value is affected or can be affected by *every* element of the firm's marketing mix. The price itself can be a big driver of how potential customers will perceive your product-offering bundle.

Price and Perceived Value

Sometimes, a price that is too low, particularly for a new product, can have a big impact on how valuably it will be perceived. Our next example crystallizes this phenomenon. When one of the authors was in graduate school, his professor had started an entrepreneurial company to manufacture and sell educational kit machines for helping to understand how the binary logic and arithmetic of computers worked. The machines were composed of lights, wires, and switches, so that binary arithmetic and logic could be simulated by series of light bulbs being either on or off. The first kit machine in the entrepreneur's line was the red and blue MINIVAC 601, priced at $79.95. The entrepreneur had three target market segments for the MINIVAC 601—home hobbyists, high schools and colleges, and computer and technology companies (for training their employees on how computers worked). The product did very well with the first two market segments. Home hobbyists bought the product at consumer electronic stores and some high-tech hobby shops. Many colleges and some upper socioeconomic high schools also bought the MINIVAC as an educational aid. However, no one in the third segment, the corporate sector bought the product. The entrepreneur interviewed some target customers to try to find the problem. He found out very quickly. The typical description of the MINIVAC by the corporate types was "Oh, that—it's just a toy!"

The entrepreneur was creative and he listened carefully. He also understood intuitive marketing. His next product was the same basic kit—with the switches upgraded to higher tolerances and the machine color changed from blue and red to gunmetal gray. The name was changed to the MINIVAC 6010 and he increased the price from $79.95 to $479. The MINIVAC 6010 sold very well to the corporate segment at $479. The $79.95 price was too low for the corporate buyers to take the product seriously. At such a low price, it had to be a toy and was not serious. The color and packaging of the original MINIVAC 601 amplified that perception. By changing the color, name, and packaging, and most importantly the price, the entrepreneur was able to change the perception in the corporate segment. The impact on his bottom line was just amazing! The price you put on your product offering, by itself, creates a very important part of the perceptual position.

Pricing of Intellectual Property

One of the most difficult things to price is something that has essentially no cost associated with another copy—intellectual property. On the Internet, much of what is being sold is information; once created (especially in electronic form), multiple copies can be recreated for no cost.

In physical goods, the price is most often related to the cost of producing the item, including some amortization of the intellectual property (research and development) used to create the design, as well as the raw materials and processing cost to turn those materials into the item for sale. Gross margins of 60 percent to 80 percent are not uncommon in high-tech industries, so that an Intel chip that sells for $300 may have a cost (including marketing, R&D and production) of $50 to $60.

The marginal cost of providing news reports on Yahoo is effectively zero. The gross margins on the product are often above 95 percent, with the small cost of goods being associated with maintaining the servers that hold and transmit the information. How then, should one select the pricing?

One price that has often been successfully used on the Internet is *free*. Give away the intellectual property so that people will come to a Web site and see the advertising, or take advantage of e-commerce opportunities. Most of the stock trading operations provide research reports and other products that way. E-Trade, DLJ Direct, Wit Capital are all examples. They also price their actual services—stock trading—as close to their real cost as possible, with only Schwab making a profit on the transaction costs.

Hotmail, ICQ, and other "virally marketed" services are all vehicles that provide a free service, which is purely communications or other nonphysical products, so that they can direct advertising and marketing to the users.

There are some groups that can successfully charge for intellectual property, usually through some form of subscription pricing. The *Wall Street Journal* online is one of the most successful subscription based services on the Web, with a $69.95 per year price for people who do not also get the print edition, and a lower price for those who are already print subscribers. The *New York Times* charges $9.95 per year for access to their Crossword puzzles online, getting a dedicated audience to whom they can also e-sell. And playboy.com is an extremely successful subscription site, where those so inclined pay annually for the ability to access photos, editorial material, and chats about sexually explicit material.

What Else Can Impact Price Response?

Anything that can impact the perception of your product's offering bundle can impact the price that potential customers will be willing to pay. Very simply, if the customer does not perceive that the value he perceives more than justifies the price, he will not purchase. We use the term "product's offering bundle" here as we do in other places in this book in the widest interpretation possible. It includes anything that the customer can perceive impacts the value they get from the whole experience of buying and using your product or service. The first time the potential customer comes in contact with your firm or product or service, they begin to get impressions that will affect their value perception of the offering bundle. If it was an advertisement, did it connote the right positioning? If it was an e-mail, did it come across consistent with a high value positioning?

When a customer or potential customer calls in to your firm, is the phone answered in a manner consistent with a high value perception? If potential customers get put on hold for very long, they will get bad perceptions about how fast your firm might react to any problems that need to be corrected. If the phone people are not polite, considerate, and genuinely helpful to the caller, the firm and its products perception will suffer.

An Example of Price Being a Symptom of Bigger Problems

A 100+ year-old shipping company was concerned that they were losing business to competition and that their margins were continually being squeezed by what they thought was increased competitive price pressure on their routes. The firm retained a market research consultant who interviewed some of their customers and potential customers. The consultant found a number of problems that influenced how customers or potential customers perceived the firm and its product-offering bundle. One pervasive problem was that the firm's telephonic interface with customers was appalling compared to competition. If someone called into a regional shipping office to either ask about a price quotation or what the status of a shipment was, there were many instances when the phone just rang and rang and was never even answered! The increased price pressure the firm was facing was not brought about by competition, but more by the reaction of their potential customers to the perceived value decline in the product-offering bundle. The appalling telephone interface was just one example of the problems with customer treatment at the firm. Only after the customer sales and service operations of the firm were completely redesigned from the ground up, would the company be able to command what it considered reasonable prices.

Other chapters have shown how all the elements of the marketing mix can affect perception that then affects price response. All of the channel management decisions affect how the end customer will perceive your product-offering bundle. The environment your product is in when the customer sees it can have a large impact on its perceived value. The same product will have a higher perceived value if the consumer sees it at Tiffany's rather than at Wal-Mart. The dynamic management of distribution channels we describe in the channels chapter has as its major objective to achieve high contribution margin and prices. Once a product has been sold at low-end channels, it typically cannot be sold at premium prices at the higher end channels.

Perceived Value in Use for Business-to-Business Products

A key way that an entrepreneur can market new products and services to businesses is to show the target business that they will be more profitable if they adopt the entrepreneur's new product or service. If the potential customer *perceives* that his business will be more profitable if your product/or service is used, then they will likely buy it. The key word here is *perceives*. If the customer understands and believes that your product can make the production, service, or delivery process more efficient or more valuable to the customer's customers, then the entrepreneur can make a nice sale. To use this value in use positioning, the entrepreneur must understand how the potential customers will want to calculate the value in use of the entrepreneur's new innovation. If there are certain measures that an industry uses to indicate efficiency or productivity, they will probably feel more comfortable if they see the new entrepreneurial innovation with data on that measure.

How does all of this relate to pricing? According to Irwin Gross of the Institute for the Study of Business Markets at the Pennsylvania State University:[2]

> "Customer Value" is the hypothetical *price* for a supplier's *offering* at which a particular customer would be at overall economic *break-even* relative to the *best available alternative* to the customer for performing a set of functions.
>
> "Customer Perceived Value" is a customer's *perception* of his/her own "customer value."

While customer value can never be known precisely, it is a very useful idealized construct, similar to a "perfect vacuum" or a "frictionless plane" in physics.[3]

The best pricing situation occurs when there is a perceived win-win situation. The buyer perceives that including the price of the new product from the entrepreneur, he or she will have higher "customer value" when adopting the new entrepreneur's product. The entrepreneur in turn makes much higher profit margins than normal because of her understanding of how to create perceived value better than her competition.

Your competition may not be as treacherous in many business-to-business situations as it may first appear. The concept of really going into depth to understand perceived customer value is not that common. According to Gross, who has studied business-to-business markets for over 20 years: "Customers spend more effort to know supplier's costs than suppliers spend to know customer's values."[4] A really effective entrepreneurial marketer will spend her scarce time and resources to understand exactly how her target market participants develop perceptions of customer value and what methods are best for changing those values.

There are typical components that make up perceived customer value for new entrepreneurial product offerings. These can be grouped into product value, supplier value, and switching investments. According to Gross, the product value is the relative benefits delivered by the product itself, independent of the supplier, while the supplier value is the relative benefits delivered by the supplier, independent of the product itself. The switching investment is the costs and risks involved with the transition from the current practice to the implementation of the new alternative.[5] All of these benefits, of course, are *as perceived* by decision makers in the target market. Gross has categorized components of attributes that affect perceived customer value, dividing them into attributes that impact perceptions of immediate customer value versus those that will impact expected customer value in the future. Table 3.2 outlines the attributes that can impact perceived customer value.

A good entrepreneurial marketer will do whatever is necessary to make sure that her offering's perceived customer value is higher than her competition. She will understand the components that are important to the members of the target market. She will then make sure her product offering and all of the marketing elements that support it are doing the best job possible in

	Immediate	Expected
Product	• Product performance • Durability • Serviceability • Downstream performance • (Current risks)	• New technology • Product flexibility • Follow-on products • (Long-run risks)
Supplier	• Supplier performance Delivery tech, sales, services, etc. • (Promotional values, services)	• Supplier relationship • Technology access • Security of supply • Strategic • (Supplier power)
Switching	• New capital • Training • Transitional quality • Communications	

Note: Parenthesis indicate negative attributes.

Table 3.2 Attributes Affecting Perceived Customer Value

positively impacting the value perception. As Table 3.2 shows, it is not just the product/service offering itself that needs to be impacted. It's also much of the supporting services and impressions that the entrepreneurial venture leaves. The salesforce, the marketing communications, the channels used, the product packaging, the product's name, the service package, and so on, all are part of what can impact perceived customer value. For business-to-business markets, real entrepreneurial marketing can enable much higher prices than competition.

The SAS Institute, Inc.—Very Effective Management of Perceived Customer Value

The SAS Institute, Inc. has become the world's largest privately held software company by creatively and uniquely applying many of the concepts in this chapter. The Institute provides data warehousing and decision support software to target markets in business, government, and education. The end result of this entrepreneurial marketing is a very unique software pricing strategy. All SAS Institute software products are licensed, not sold. According to their brochure: "SAS Institute's pricing strategy is designed to foster

Win/Win relationships with our customers which lead to building productive long-term partnerships."[6] The Institute is not shy about the objectives of their pricing policy. "The strategy is to establish pricing consistent with the value received by SAS software customers, as they implement mission critical applications."[7]

The SAS Institute pricing model is unique among major software vendors. The other vendors typically sell a software purchase along with a maintenance contract. Their customers buy each new software release and have the option to pay ongoing fees for technical support. These other software vendors, typically public, or with objectives of going public, want to maximize the short-term revenue they obtain with each sale. The suppliers of investments for software vendors in the financial markets do not necessarily let the software firm's price for value over time as SAS does.

The SAS Institute license model has the customer pay a first year license fee and an annual fee to renew the license. According to SAS, the annual license model provides the customer with a number of valuable benefits:

- Low cost of entry (typically less than fees paid for entering a purchase/maintenance model)
- Rapid return on investment (ROI)
- The most current release
- Technical support
- The most current documentation
- All updates during the license period

Customer's investments are protected by ensuring that they always have the most up-to-date technology.[8]

The customer is never locked in to more than a one-year commitment to SAS. The company must then be perceived by their customers as continually providing excellent technical support and on-going enhancements to the software. If the customers do not perceive they are getting value from SAS, they can go elsewhere. The customers can also easily add or delete components of the SAS software as their needs change over time. SAS even comes out and says in their own literature that: "The strategy is to establish pricing consistent with the value received by SAS software customers as they implement mission critical applications."[9]

Let's compare SAS's pricing model to the typical enterprise software company. The typical company sells its software once, with a very big sales effort. They then charge annual ongoing maintenance fees of 15 percent to 18 percent of the initial purchase price. These maintenance fees sometimes include updates and improvements to the software. Is this pricing consistent with the customer's perceived value? Not really. The customer should receive increasing value as the software becomes implemented and tailored to the customer's specific situation and as it is improved and updated over time. The perceived value to the customer of software will almost always be higher after a successful implementation than before it. If the implementation is unsuccessful, then the reverse situation would hold. Because of these risks, customers are not willing to pay up-front as much for software as they would pay if they had continual successful experience to value. The amount the typical enterprise software company can charge up-front is thus less than the discounted present value that the customer would pay over time under the SAS Institute rental plan.

SAS's job becomes keeping its customers continually delighted so that they will continue to pay the relatively large yearly license fees. SAS does that very well. They renew 98 percent of their customers annually! Thus, 98 percent of their revenue is recurring. This is an astonishing statistic for any software company. They also have used their recurring revenue as a base for expansion. The latest public statistics available show revenue in 1997 of $750 million, more than double that of five years earlier.[10] SAS also has enough gross margin to spend over 30 percent of revenue (*revenue, not profits!*) on research and development, to enable them to provide software improvements that continually delight their customers.[11]

The SAS customer value orientation and their pricing model which captures more of that value than competition is supported by a superb employee group that is in turn supported by very marketing-oriented employee policies. SAS treats its employees in ways that foster excellent long-term performance and high loyalty.

Some of their policies include 32-hour work weeks, onsite day care, unlimited sick leave, and a fully supported gym on premise. In an extremely competitive market for software talent in the Raleigh Durham research triangle, SAS has a turnover rate lower than 5 percent compared to over 20 percent for many competitive software companies.

Why don't other software companies emulate the value-oriented pricing model of the SAS Institute? We can only speculate. One reason may be that too many U.S. companies (and their financial backers, including public shareholders) are too short-term oriented to pass up one time purchase prices for a longer term, but higher value rental revenue stream. The other reason may be lack of courage to look a customer in the eye and ask for a legitimate percent of the perceived value that your software is delivering. We hope that more entrepreneurs will be encouraged by the SAS Institute example to not be afraid to set pricing policies to receive some of the perceived value they are creating.

Summary

We began the chapter by showing how often cost-based or competitive-based pricing rules may be "precisely wrong." We showed that a "vaguely right" approach is to attempt to charge the price (or prices) that maximize the entrepreneur's profit return over her planning horizon. It also is very important to get the initial price level at a good level, because it is much more difficult to raise prices over time than it is to lower them. Next, we described methods for in-market and pre-market (concept testing) for determining the potential relationship between alternative prices and the sales revenue that those prices would produce. The Web is the perfect in-market price-testing vehicle for many products.

We then showed a number of examples of how the price you can and should charge is intertwined with all the rest of the elements of the marketing mix. The marketing mix and the product offering bundle all effect the perceived value for the potential customer. This perceived value in turn affects the price the consumer is willing to pay. For a consumer product, we demonstrated how a change in the product description on its box would double the

sales of the product. The box described valuable consumer benefits as opposed to the older box that described product features.
We showed how perceived value in use affects the price response
of business-to-business products. We concluded the chapter with
the example of the SAS Institute's unique marketing mix and pricing structure that captures and creates more perceived customer
value than competitive software customers. Our survey results
show that the Inc. 500 CEOs price more productively than the
non-Inc. group, but both groups could probably improve by adopting more of the concepts in this chapter.

CHAPTER 4

Public Relations and Publicity

Public relations include any publicity for your product or service that is perceived by the public as not being paid for. This differs from advertising that is perceived by the public to be paid for. As we will see, publicity is not really free. It does not happen by chance, but is the result of entrepreneurial activity and resources allocated to it. Public relations can be extremely valuable because, when used successfully, it may be perceived as much more credible than any paid advertising by your target market. The Merck and Company, Inc. Clinoril™ case shows how valuable public relations can be.

A Public Relations Success Story

Clinoril was a Merck prescription drug for arthritis that was one of a number of nonsteroidal anti-inflammatory arthritic drugs introduced a number of years ago, before any pharmaceutical firms did any direct consumer advertising or public relations. At the time of product launch, Walter Cronkite was still the dean of national television newscasters, one of the most trusted public figures. His version of the *CBS Evening News* was the clear broadcast news leader and had been for many years. As it happens, the day Clinoril was launched, a public relations freelancer retained by Merck luckily got to Walter Cronkite's staff with a news release about the launch of the product. It was a slow news night and Walter Cronkite decided to do a story based on the news release. What came out on the news broadcast was Walter Cronkite saying something very close to: Merck and Company today introduced a new wonder drug for arthritis called Clinoril.

The viewer response to that announcement was unprecedented for any pharmaceutical product. Literally thousands of people called their doctors to ask them about this new arthritis wonder drug—Clinoril that Walter Cronkite announced. Merck's first year sales of Clinoril were more than four times their forecast. They credited all of the additional sales to the 30 seconds that Walter Cronkite devoted to a very credible announcement of their product launch. Doctors were pressured into prescribing the product by consumers who asked for it. Consumers got a very good (actually over-inflated) perception of how good the product really was. Clinoril was not a "wonder drug," but if Walter Cronkite said it was, many people perceived it. Merck's news release did not call it a "wonder drug." That was the Cronkite's news staff's interpretation. The value to Merck of that 30 seconds on the *CBS Evening News* was probably in the hundreds of millions of dollars.

This Merck experience was the beginning of all of the direct-to-consumer advertising and public relations that now routinely occurs with the launch of new prescription drugs. The mass media impact on consumers for prescription drugs can be huge. Viagra is a recent very successful public relations campaign. We next discuss the crucial role of public relations and publicity in product launches and roll-outs.

The Role of Public Relations for Entrepreneurs

Before people can buy your product or use your service, they have to know it exists, and how to get to it. Even more importantly, they should feel that they are going with a winner, if there is a choice among products in the category. Proper use of public relations and publicity (as Clinoril did) can provide this "winner" feeling far faster, and at much lower cost, than a big national advertising campaign—one that an entrepreneurial company may not be able to afford.

In the Internet world, the key driver to quickly gaining leadership in a new category is the creation of "buzz"—the feeling that you are the winner. Netscape, Yahoo, Microsoft, and others have all been beneficiaries of this. Gaining the mind share of a user—so that he routinely tries your Web page before a competitor's, quickly translates into market share. As Ann Winblad, general partner of Hummer Winblad Associates, and an extremely successful venture capitalist has said, "It's the cheerleader approach, where you tell the world that we're the winner even before the game has started, which is successful in the Internet space." EPinions, for example, went with a very high profile *New York Times Sunday Magazine* story, long before their site launched. The article made it seem as if the management team was experienced, the best and the brightest, and that they were certain to be the leader in shared opinions. The fact that About.com had thousands of users and millions of page views doing the same thing did not stop ePinions from making its claims. The perception of leadership quickly becomes the reality. When Netscape first made its browser available, Spry, Quarterdeck, and Spyglass all had products in the marketplace—some of which were technically superior. But a concentrated public relations campaign, coupled with guerilla marketing tactics that we discuss in Chapter 9, got tremendous coverage in the trade press—which declared Navigator as the browser to beat. And it soon had the overwhelming market share to make the perception a reality.

Gaining the Perception of Leadership

How can you achieve this perceptual edge? First let us understand how most users make their decision on which Web site to visit, which high-tech product to buy, or which complex, hard-to-understand product they should buy. Generally they ask someone they trust—an information gatekeeper in their organization or personal life, or they read a trusted source in a newsletter, trade or general publication. Thus, the key to gaining the perceptual edge is to influence the influencers, or gatekeepers. And where do the gatekeepers get their knowledge? From a smaller set of influencers whom they trust. It is like a pool, where a stone thrown in the center creates waves that ripple outward, growing ever larger in diameter, until they reach the shore. You need to reach these groups:

- Gurus (e.g., key industry insiders, respected authorities)
- Influencers (e.g., key trade and business press, respected experts, or experienced users)
- Decision makers (key bellwether buyers)—those who can say yes
- Naysayers—people who can say no along the way
- Mass buyers—the masses who mainly follow what they perceive as the winning trend

In every industry, a few insiders are considered the industry experts or gurus. They are generally the ones quoted in *Business Week, Forbes, Fortune,* and the *Wall Street Journal* when key industry events occur. Often, they publish high-priced newsletters and run invitation-only conferences for CEOs of industry companies. In the Personal Computer industry during the 1980s and 1990s, Stewart Alsop, Esther Dyson, and Richard Shaffer filled this role. As the decade closed, Bob Metcalfe has taken over for Alsop, Chris Shipley and David Coursey have expanded into the space, and Dyson and Shaffer have each added personnel to help run their newsletters and conferences (Table 4.1). But reaching these players, and being covered in their newsletters or appearing at their conferences, creates some immediate buzz both with key industry buyers and partners and with key venture capitalists who can fund your entrepreneurial venture.

The telecommunications, semiconductor, database software, and applications software sectors all have additional gurus, letters, and conferences. And the same holds true for biotech, energy, and every other field we have examined. At the core of the industry are a handful of influencers, who spread the word about new ideas, products, and services, along with their opinions. These opinions are usually dispositive of success or failure in the first year after launch.

Release 1.0—Esther Dyson, Kevin Werbach

Computer Letter—Dick Shaffer

DemoLetter—Chris Shipley

Softletter—Jeff Tartar

Agenda Conference—Bob Metcalfe

PC Forum—Esther Dyson

PC Outlook, Network Outlook, Enterprise Outlook—Dick Shaffer

Internet Showcase—David Coursey

Demo Conference—Chris Shipley

Investment Conferences—Morgan Stanley (Mary Meeker), CSFB/DLJ (Jamie Kiggen), Goldman Sachs (Michael Parekh)

Table 4.1   PC Industry Gurus, Conferences and "Must Read" Newsletters

After the gurus come the influencers—editors and writers at the key mass trade and business publications in the field. In the computer world, the Ziff Davis publications (*PC Week, PC Magazine,* etc.), and the IDG *Infoworld* and *Computerworld* newspapers have the broadest reach among decision makers. You must be sensitive to the lead times of each publication, to maximize the coincident coverage of your story. That is, if you want to launch a new product in May, you need to meet with the longer lead monthly magazines two to three months in advance of when you want the story to appear, with the weeklies two to three weeks prior, and with today's daily e-mail "zines" (online magazines), a few days before the news should hit.

For products with a consumer focus, the key mass columnists can provide tremendous boost in product launch. Walt Mossberg, personal technology columnist for the *Wall Street Journal,* can make or break a product with an early review. He receives hundreds of requests each week, and has policies for filtering that good public relations agencies understand. He demands, and usually gets, to be the first to publish about your product. He likes to have them significantly in advance so that he can actually work with them and provide feedback. When Franklin Electronic Publishers and Starfish Software were launching REX, Mossberg was brought in almost a year prior to launch—under appropriate embargo agreements. His input on the early betas was invaluable in making a better product. His review at the launch was a key factor in early product sales, and in helping the visibility of a product that had very little advertising dollar spending.

Newsweek's Steve Levy, *Business Week*'s Steve Wildstrom, and *PC Week*'s Michael Miller and John Dvorak also have earned the respect of their readers with their insightful reviews. It is necessary to view these influencers not just as targets for getting a message out, but as highly knowledgeable users who can help to improve the design and feature set of a product or service. Clearly, in today's world it is not only the print press, but television, radio, and the Internet that must also be attended to. It was, after all, the Internet's Matt Drudge who broke the Lewinsky story rather than *Newsweek,* which held it while awaiting further confirmations.

With the plethora of cable channels has come an opportunity for companies to provide short (30 second to 2 minute) video new releases (VNR) which are often picked up by local news or specialized cable services. The impact of such a piece shown on television, often with a voice over by the local news or science reporter, should not be underestimated. When MetaCreations announced its Power Goo consumer image funware, the VNR was picked up by dozens of stations, and sales were noticeably increased. CNN *Science Today* often does reports on products of interest. Miros Corporation's face recognition system appeared on the *Science Today* cable program, and Web site page views grew by thousands of page views for the seven-day period after the showing.

Reaching the decision makers is best done with focused direct marketing, and with special events, which are described in Chapter 9. But the more general positive buzz you can get with a product, the less likely the naysayers are to voice negative—against the crowd opinions.

Spokesperson/Evangelists

One of the key tasks for a public relations effort is to help one (or at most two) people in the company create personal one-to-one relationships with the gurus. Most often the CEO and chief technical person are the ones who should build and nurture these relationships. They require visiting the gurus on "press tours," getting them prerelease (beta) software or hardware, and oodles of technical support to ensure that any product usage goes smoothly. You should understand that this is a two-way street; the guru can't be a guru without being in on the latest product entries, and everyone likes to know a secret, or be in the know a little earlier than the next person. Often, if the relationship can be built early enough, the gurus can contribute to making the product more user friendly—and by having an emotional stake, are more likely to help declare the product a winner.

The evangelists who meet with the press need to be personable, knowledgeable about the company and its products, and sensitive to what can and can't be said regarding fund raising without triggering legal obligations in the case of public companies, or concerns about "hype" in private companies. It is important not to lie to the press or influencers—although spin is certainly acceptable and common. One of the biggest mistakes is talking in the "hoped for present" tense (i.e., "Yes, the product can do xxxx," when it can't). It's also important to plan the pitch in a way that is respectful of the available time of the person being wooed. Some training in public speaking—of the type that Power Presentations of San Jose provides to entrepreneurs going on a road show—can be very helpful in correcting typical mistakes. The wrong body language, too much hesitation when responding to questions, and other problems can leave a mistaken impression on the guru. Remember, in most of these cases, first impressions last.

The overall company and product pitch should be planned for at least three lengths: the "elevator story," the 15-minute demo, and the 30 to 45 minute road show pitch. The elevator story is meant to be told in the time it takes to go a few floors next to someone in the elevator—typically 30 seconds to two minutes. It has to convince them that they should want to hear more. There are some iconic ways to do this, the most popular current one being "We're going to be the Amazon.com of . . ." eToys, for example, was planned to be the Amazon of toys and is achieving that goal. But this pitch needs to have some differentiation. "The REX has almost the same functionality as a Palm Pilot in a credit card size device, and synchronizes with your laptop by being a PCMCIA card."

The 15-minute demo should be just that. No more than a minute or two to introduce the speaker and company—naming any credibility enhancers (advisory board members, directors, investors), followed by a demo that ideally allows for the person being briefed to get hands on with the product. Most of the gurus in high tech are gadget nuts at heart—they are the epitome of early adopters—even where, like Walt Mossberg, they try to put themselves in the mindset of the more average user. This puts the evangelist, be he CEO or CTO or just plain Marcom person, in a position of preaching to people who want you to succeed. But they need to make the product vision their own, so that they can preach it to others.

Finally, if there is lots of time available, a slide show (Power-Point or equivalent), which can be quickly tailored to the specific audience, should be prepared. This should include sections on company history, financing, product rollout plans, advertising plans, partnering deals (quite popular with Internet companies), and, of course, the product itself.

Figure 4.1 shows how many hours per month our Inc and non-Inc. CEOs and their other managers spend on public relations in a typical month.

Linkage to Fund Raising

For those entrepreneurial ventures that are also raising money (almost all of them), the public relations efforts serves two purposes—helping the product to be perceived and perform as a winner, and helping to fuel the fund raising. An additional set of influencers reach this community, and there is a feedback effect of strong venture capital support on the core gurus and influencers. A Kleiner Perkins funded venture has the credibility of one of the most successful partnerships behind it, and gurus take its investee company claims with somewhat less skepticism than those of an unknown company. For this field, David Bunnell of *Upside Magazine*, Rafe Needleman of *Red Herring*, Jason Calconis of *Silicon Alley* magazine, and Jonathan Weber of the *Industry Standard* have risen to the top ranks. Having the company mentioned prominently in these publications has helped get audiences not only with influencers,

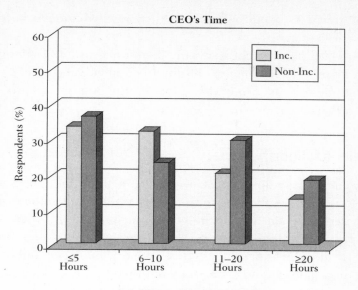

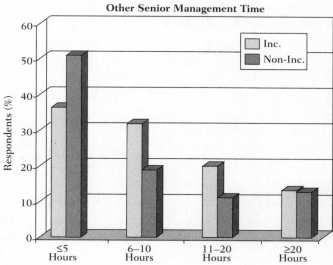

Figure 4.1 Time spent on public relations per month.

but also with targeted high-profile customers who might have otherwise waited.

Similarly, having the company mentioned in *Red Herring* may open doors that have been closed. Since most venture capitalists want to be seen as riding with a winner, the buzz which proclaims that acts like perfume to the investor.

Public Relations Agencies

There is always a lot of controversy about the value that a public relations agency can bring to the table. Many small companies believe that they can get to the gurus and influencers themselves, and that the often-sizable cost of using an agency may not be worthwhile. Our experience is that, properly managed, public relations fees gain you a tremendous multiple on your investment in them, as long as your expectations are properly set at the outset. The agency provides three basic functions:

1. Creative—helping to define the message

2. Execution—getting the message out

3. Rolodex—knowing who to go to, and having the ability to get them to listen

While there are dramatic quality differences among agencies with respect to how they perform the first two functions, it is the third that distinguishes the top few agencies from the next tiers. Many of the very top agencies (Alexander Oglivy, Cunningham Communications, Connors Communications) have become very selective about taking on clients, and very expensive—in much the same way as successful lobbyists offer access to the right people as part of their value added.

Creating the positioning and its associated message in a form best suited to reach the various types of audiences is mainly a task for the company's top management. The agency can and should, however, guide the words and "spin" of the message so that it tells the story in a memorable, quick manner. With MetaCreations, the message became "The Visual Computing Company," which tied together product lines in consumer and professional graphics. The second part of MetaCreations message was "leading edge user interface," using Kai Krause as the spokesperson and creative genius. As the public relations groups (both internal and external) found, it is sometimes hard to manage genius.

Once the press releases, press kit, and evaluation or demo software and hardware are created, the execution phase begins. The best agencies have good mailing lists of editors and other influencers. Each company must create their own contact lists, and maintain them internally so that they can continue follow-up even if they switch agencies or bring the function in house. Agencies often have direct access to public relations Newswire, Business Wire, and so on to get a story out there quickly. They are also more likely to know who has recently been assigned to which specific beats in the various periodicals, and which stock market analysts are willing to see nonpublic companies.

Measuring the effectiveness of public relations is something that should be done in as quantitative a manner as possible. A good clipping service can let you measure how many column inches of print, and radio or television air time, the public relations efforts have generated. One firm had a spreadsheet with the posted ad rates of most of the key periodicals, which allowed them to translate column inches into the equivalent cost, if they had run those inches as paid advertising. While not a perfect absolute number for value, it is quite useful if tracked over a period of time, and gives at least some handle on the advertising alternative. When possible, a good lead tracking system can be used to tell which mentions led to actual calls, Web site visits, or customer e-mails. At some companies, purchases are tracked all the way back to these types of leads—showing again the true value or the public relations effort.

As with most hiring, interviewing and reference checking are key in selecting the public relations firm. It is imperative to check out the work they have done for similar customers. Call the CEO or marketing counterpart and ask how easy they were to work with. Be specific about the staff that will work on your account—some junior people will normally be assigned, but make sure the supervisor is someone you trust, and will actually be on the account. Too often, the name partners at these firms are mainly out marketing, not performing the actual work—although they will argue that they're keeping the influencer relationships strong, from which your company benefits.

Timing Is Essential

The sequencing and timing of the public relations effort is crucial to getting maximum bang for the marketing dollar. Ideally, you are creating a crescendo that begins with buzz about the company, moves on to create buzz about the specific product, gets industry gurus and key influencers talking off the record about the product, and culminates in a blizzard of press coverage led by the daily mass and trade press, and followed up over each of the next two or three months with additional stories in the monthly magazines, radio, and television.

PayMyBills.com began as a project at the Wharton School and was entered into their annual business plan competition. As the judging proceeded, and the plan made it into the final eight, a leading Internet firm decided to fund it as a full-fledged business. The cofounders were brought out to idealab!'s Pasadena headquarters, and told that they had 60 days in which to launch the company and the business. The business plan competition provided the opportunity to get some buzz about the company. Since major media covered it, articles appeared in the *New York Times, Philadelphia Magazine*, and other locations. This helped the company in its initial hiring and fund raising.

The founders moved into idealab! on May 19. Ten days later, they had hired 10 people, mainly through a job fair and contacts on the net, that had heard of them through the articles, and the Industry Standard Internet online newsletter. Three weeks later, idealab! used the buzz to raise more than $4MM for the company at a much more favorable valuation than would have been possible without the public relations. The Alexander Oglivy agency, which has a long relationship with idealab!, was hired to get a fast-track product launch. They created an interview schedule for trade press, business press, and radio that focused on a product launch date of July 19 (slipped from an original July 4 target). Meetings were held with the *Wall Street Journal*, *LA Times*, *PC Magazine*, and others, for a focused print exposure at the launch.

In addition, spot radio was purchased in several cities, including advertising on the Howard Stern show for the first two weeks after launch. All of this orchestration led to a number of interviews, lots of customers, and acknowledgment as the leading player in this new field. This occurred notwithstanding that the two competitors, PayTrust and CyberBills, had been in existence much longer, but had not quite launched and were staying in stealth mode. By taking the aggressive route to public relations and product launch, PayMy-Bills.com tilted the playing field, and is now reaping the benefits.

As a counterpoint, if you are going to be that aggressive, you have to deliver. Boo.com, a luxury apparel site funded by Bernard Arnault of LVMH, orchestrated the public relations campaign and got the company buzz, but repeated delays in launching the site (more than eight months late), caused people to be skeptical. When it was launched, it was so slow and painful to use that the company will have negative public image to overcome as it improves the site.

Summary

"On the Internet, no one knows you're a dog," says a famous New Yorker cartoon showing a dog at a keyboard. No one knows your company exists either, unless you take the proper steps to gain the perception, and then deliver the reality of leadership. This is just as true for other non-Internet businesses as well.

Using the above techniques for public relations to work through the various circles of influencers is many times the best way to quickly have that perception created. This perception of leadership will help not only in selling the product or service, but also in hiring and fund raising for the entrepreneurial venture.

CHAPTER 5

Entrepreneurial Distribution Channel Decisions

Nowhere has technology had a bigger potential impact than in the standard functions that used to be considered under "distribution decisions." Distribution encompasses all of the activities that need to be performed so that your product's "offering bundle" is transferred productively from you the entrepreneur to the customer who will buy and benefit from the offering. The offering bundle includes not only the entrepreneur's product or service, but all of the ancillary parts of the bundle that help to mold the perception of the end customer. Packaging, how the product is placed on the shelf, what the clerk says and knows about the product, the end user price, how the end customer is treated when she has a problem or a question before or after purchase, and how easy it is for the end customer to evaluate alternative product offerings, are all just some examples of ancillary parts of the offering bundle. The choice of which intermediaries are involved between the entrepreneurial venture and its final customers and how these intermediaries are managed has a big impact on the offering bundle.

The distribution decisions are now much more complex than they were even 10 or 15 years ago. The alternative ways for the different parts of the offering bundle to be "distributed" have been increasing at a very rapid rate. In this chapter, we give the entrepreneur some conceptual structure to generate and evaluate new, creative and possibly productive distribution options. We describe a number of options that other entrepreneurial firms have been able to use effectively. We also show methods for evaluating the options in terms of their impact on the perceived offering bundle to the entrepreneur's target segment(s). Figure 5.1 puts the macro logic of distribution channel decisions covered in this chapter in perspective.

To help you make some good distribution decisions, we first look at the required functions any distribution system must perform. As shown in Figure 5.1, these functions are (1) reassortment/sorting, (2) routinizing, and (3) facilitating search. We next

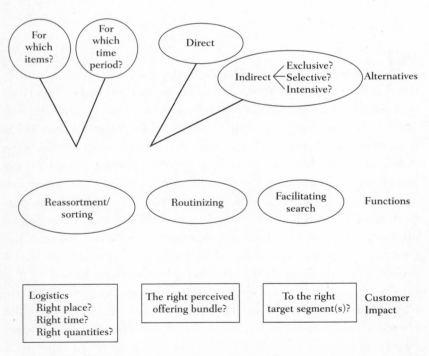

Figure 5.1 Entrepreneurial distribution channel decisions.

use the example of offering music directly over the Web to concretely examine how the distribution channel decision can significantly influence how the end consumer perceives your offering. We then look at options that need to be considered as part of the affect of the distribution channel decisions on the perceived offering bundle. These alternatives include direct or indirect or franchising. For indirect distribution, we also consider the alternatives of exclusive, selective, or intensive distribution. We examine the very important dynamic aspects of distribution channel distributions. Over the life of a product, the appropriate channel may change significantly. For franchising, we look at two points of view: (1) Should you offer a franchise for your venture? and (2) Should you buy a franchise to start your venture? We then examine what happens when the channel perceives you as competing with them when you didn't before—channel conflict—and provide some guidelines for managing and anticipating such conflict. We conclude with a plea to do concept testing with channel members in order to determine if your assumptions about their reactions to your actions are valid.

Required Functions of Any Distribution System

First, physical distribution will always need to be performed. The product or service somehow has to get to the end customer or end consumer. It should be the right *product* or *service* at the right *place* at the right *time* in the right *quantities*. Along with physical distribution, distribution strategy also impacts the offering bundle that the end consumer sees. The offering bundle can be a critical element of your success as an entrepreneurial venture. Who the consumer is and what the consumer perceives when she is making her evaluation and purchasing decision should be the embodiment of your positioning and segmentation strategy.

Distribution intermediaries (e.g., wholesalers, jobbers, retailers, value-added resellers) possibly can be used to perform some of the required functions more efficiently and/or more profitably to the entrepreneur. Pitt, Berthon, and Berthon outline three basic functions that intermediaries can perform to improve the productivity of a distribution channel:[1]

1. Reassortment/sorting
2. Routinizing transactions
3. Facilitating search

Reassortment/sorting refers to all of the typical intermediary activities that need to happen for physical distribution from a producer that likes to supply relatively large quantities of a relatively small assortment to an end consumer who will typically want relatively small quantities of a large assortment of offering bundles. These activities may include arranging the products, sorting them into groups that are relevant to consumers, aggregating goods from different suppliers, breaking bulk by providing the right, smaller quantities to the end customer, and putting together new packages of goods from different suppliers. Your supermarket is an example. Somehow from a Procter and Gamble who ships a container of toothpaste to a central distribution point or to a wholesaler, the goods get on the shelf for you as a consumer to compare with other competitive toothpastes on the same shelf.

Routinizing transactions are activities that standardize products and services and automate transactions so that bargaining is not needed for each small transaction and it makes it easier for the end customer to compare alternative offerings. In some instances, resupply of products is completely automated so that orders are entered and products replenished when inventories reach a certain minimum level.[2] For example, there is a complete electronic connection between Wal-Mart cash registers and the Procter and Gamble (PG) logistical and production system. When the sales at the Wal-Mart cash register indicate that store inventory of a PG product is in need of replenishment, the PG system is notified and production and shipping is initiated at the optimal time. There are no negotiations between PG and Wal-Mart for each replenishment. There is implicit trust that neither party will take advantage of the other.

Not only large firms can take advantage of automated resupply. Penguin Software is an entrepreneurial venture that supplies Linux based servers with installed software for businesses. Penguin sells on the Web and has an outsourced manufacturer who actually puts together the servers. Penguin has an automated linkage with its

manufacturer so that as orders are entered on the Web, an automated request is generated to the manufacturer. The customized
servers are then shipped to Penguin so that the software can be installed. Penguin keeps little inventory.

Facilitating search is the classic aid by intermediaries to make
it easier for sellers to find buyers and to make it easier for buyers
to find their best alternative product or service to purchase. The
traditional retailer puts products from different suppliers on the
same shelf so that the consumer can make a less uncertain purchase than he would if he didn't have the alternative products
right in front of him. In general, intermediaries can reduce uncertainty for both buyers and sellers. A good intermediary can help an
entrepreneur do a better job of understanding and responding to
customer needs, and can simultaneously help consumers to be
surer that their purchases will indeed satisfy their needs.

It is clear that the Internet is becoming a major influencer of
how this search process is being performed. The search function
is made to order for the Web. The Web has spawned a number
of ventures that have used its capabilities to make search more
effective for matching needs of buyers and sellers. These would
include eBay, Carpoint, eCost, Mysimon, and Verticalnet as examples. In all of these sites, the consumer can evaluate many alternatives on criteria that she dictates. She can sort potential
purchase options by any criteria she chooses (e.g., cars by horse-
power and then economy).

Evaluating Distribution Options—Disintermediation

Technology is making more alternatives available for the entrepreneur to consider for fulfilling the discussed functions. The distribution of products whose physical makeup is digital is being
revolutionized by the Internet. It is now feasible (and some musicians have begun to do this) for an artist to produce a digital
recording and distribute it directly to consumers over the Web (or
for an author to directly publish a novel as did Steven King). For
music, *disintermediation* (replacing traditional channels and going
direct) is replacing a record company, record distributor, rack job-
ber, and retailer with a direct artist-customer relationship. If the

customer knows which recording of which artist they want, direct distribution may be very attractive.

It would seem at first blush, that all artists should jump aboard the disintermediation bandwagon and distribute their music directly. They would not have to pay all of the middlemen their cuts, and would be able to establish a direct relationship with their customers. This direct relationship would enable all kinds of activities to create more value (and thus make more money eventually). The artist could create loyalty programs to reward and encourage his best customers. The loyalty rewards might include special seats for concerts or special memorabilia. The artist could also reward current customers for referring new customers with similar added-value offers. However, the disintermediation decision is not this simple. There are other sides to this story.

First, how will consumers find out about the artist's Web site? Many Web sites are spending tens of millions of dollars to get people to their sites. Does it make sense for each artist to go it alone to try to get customers to his or her site? Second, do all potential consumers know they want a particular artist's song(s) or do they want to listen to a number of options before they make a purchase? Some consumers may also be concerned about the quality of the digital recording they will download. How do they know it's of high enough quality? What about consumers who are not able to play digital music or to receive digital music over the Web? Should they be ignored? These are just some of the myriad of issues that need to be considered in developing a distribution strategy. The entrepreneur's decisions on distribution can be at the same time the most difficult and the most important decisions she makes when launching a new business.

All of the functions described must be evaluated before choosing a distribution option. If the entrepreneur has really done her homework on the positioning and market segmentation issues, then the distribution options to be evaluated may be self-evident. However, as technology and the environment change the characteristics of existing options and generate new options, the entrepreneur has to constantly review these options. Let's look at our digital music example in more depth to illustrate some of these issues.

Does the artist have her segmentation determined? Is she trying to reach a very small cult group, or does she want to add value to a larger market? The answer to the targeting question will have a very big impact on the distribution strategy. However, the strategy decision is even more complex. How do the members of the alternative target groups want to buy music? Even if the cult group is the target, the direct Web site may not be appropriate. Do the "cult" consumers know where the Web site is? Do they have the technology available to download and play digital music? Do they want to buy music over the Web? How will they be reached? All of these issues can at least be evaluated by concept testing distribution options as part of the offering bundle that is concept tested by consumers before the entrepreneur makes this decision.

The distribution decision is the one that has the most impact typically on market segmentation. With the distribution channel, the entrepreneur can implement plans with more than one target segment, if the plans are cost effective. Conceptually, it makes sense to use the distribution channel(s) that are preferred by each of the target segments. Consumers will typically find it pretty easy to tell you where they would go or look to try to find your new product or service. If it is consistent with your desired positioning and cost effective, then multiple distribution options for multiple segments may make sense. However, another big issue comes up that needs a different evaluation methodology. How will existing and parallel distribution channel members react to the new direct offering?

The existing distributors may get very upset if you try to eliminate them. If they are powerful, they may severely impact your music sales through traditional channels, if they become upset with you. They may refuse to carry music that is also available directly in digital form. If you want to sell your music on classic CDs and tape as well as on the Web digitally, then you will need to have the cooperation of these distributors. To add even more complexity, if you use some distributors, they may conflict with other retailers and distributors, for example, Web-based versus store-based. Issues of channel conflict in which two intermediaries perceive themselves as competing needlessly can be big problem sources for entrepreneurs.

A whole set of other issues comes from your positioning. Your positioning should be embodied in the offering bundle that ends up being shown to the end customer. A good distribution strategy enables your offering bundle to be perceived by the end customer as you have planned. The distribution decisions can greatly impact how the end customer perceives you. Does the end consumer need to make a choice among a number of alternative artists, or do they feel okay just evaluating your offerings? Do they want to choose among different forms to buy the music (e.g., digital downloads, compact disks, digital audiotape)? How will they want to evaluate the options? Will they want to listen to everything? Will they want to read or hear unbiased reviews of the music before they buy it? How will they prefer to pay for it? Is credit card number on the Web acceptable? What about shipping? How fast do they want their music, if it isn't downloaded? How long will they wait for a digital download?

What typically happens is that the entrepreneur never gets exactly the optimal offering bundle by the distribution system she has assembled. She makes tradeoffs of less than optimal offering bundles versus the costs of the available distribution options. She is trading off potential revenue from getting the offering bundle perfect versus lower costs from less than perfect distribution options. If she has done a good job with her concept testing with target market participants and of considering the important concepts in this chapter, she should be able to make productive decisions on these distribution tradeoffs.

Distribution System Design—Direct versus Indirect

The disintermediation example of using the Web to distribute music directly to consumers is only one example of direct distribution. Similar to manufacturers' representatives and your own salesforce, distribution options can run the gamut from direct to indirect systems in which there are many layers of middlemen who handle your goods before they are bought and used by the end customer. The entrepreneur is making different tradeoffs depending on how direct or indirect her distribution system is designed. Some impacts on the business effected by distribution options include fixed and variable costs, efficiency versus effectiveness of contacts, amount of control, mass coverage versus targeting ability, and level of customization provided to the end customer. Table 5.1 lists some of these tradeoffs as a function of whether the distribution system is direct or indirect.

Because distribution intermediaries typically take title to your goods and then mark them up, or else take a fee for each item they handle, their costs are typically mostly of *variable* nature. They do not usually charge the entrepreneur for the fixed costs of their operations. However, some intermediaries do have minimum quantities that they may handle—effectively imposing some fixed costs. On the other extreme, direct distribution typically involves *fixed costs* for warehousing, billing, and other administrative costs. Fixed costs add more *risk* to the venture because they will be incurred regardless of what level of sales actually occurs in the market place. Variable costs lower risk because they are only incurred when sales are made. So direct distribution typically entails more risk than indirect distribution. However, that lower risk comes with other attributes that may or may not be worth lowering risk.

Indirect distribution is typically more *efficient* in terms of physically getting goods from the entrepreneur to the final consumer. By combining your product or service with other products and services, the middlemen are able to more efficiently perform the kinds of functions described above. However, the middleman also takes some *control* over the offering bundle and may not provide the offering bundle that is best for your product, because he is combining your product with others. When the entrepreneur is more in control, he will be able to portray his product in the best way he can—this is typically more *effective* in adding perceived

Indirect	Direct
Variable costs	Fixed costs
Efficiency per contact	Effective per contract
Control	Control
Coverage	Targeting
Customization	Customization

Table 5.1 Indirect versus Direct Distribution Options

value to the offering bundle. The added control also enables direct distribution options to develop a more customized offering bundle for each potential customer. The indirect distributor will not typically have the flexibility, or ability to make changes for each customer because the indirect distributor has to keep the needs of all of his products in his offering bundle strategy.

Distribution Exclusivity Alternatives

Many entrepreneurs do not even consider distribution exclusivity options. They assume that they should use the same channels in the same way as everyone else in their industry. Options regarding exclusivity are not considered nearly as often as they might be by entrepreneurs. The exclusivity options vary by how selective your distribution channel is and how it may vary over time. The two extremes are exclusive distribution and intensive distribution. In the middle is the selective distribution option. Exclusive distribution gives a retailer or other intermediary the exclusive right to sell your product in a defined "area" for a defined time period. Area used to mean geographical area—such as a country or metropolitan area. However, areas in cyberspace can also be exclusive to one or a select few "e-tailers." Selective distribution gives the right to distribute your product to some entities in a defined area, but limits the number to a select group. Intensive distribution lets anyone who wants to distribute your product. There are a number of tradeoffs that the entrepreneur needs to evaluate when she considers her choice of distribution channel exclusivity. First, as with almost all entrepreneurial decisions, creativity in terms of options is crucial. Exclusivity is just a subset of the distribution options that should be generated and evaluated as part of the venture initiation process. Table 5.2 shows elements of the tradeoffs that are involved with different levels of distribution exclusivity.

Exclusive Distribution

The exclusive distribution option has a number of advantages that most entrepreneurs do not realize. The first advantage is that it is usually easier to sell into a distribution channel if you are able to offer exclusivity. Exclusivity adds value to your offering bundle to most intermediaries. Using the Internet as an example, if you can

Exclusive	Selective	Intensive
Possible easier sell in Higher control	Resellers compete Less reseller loyalty	High coverage Convenience
Higher margins for all		Lower control
Less competition at point of sale		Less push to the end consumer
More push to the end consumer		More mass pull needed
Less coverage		More coverage
More association with channel members' attributes		Faster sales cycle possible
Possible guaranteed minimum sales		

Table 5.2   Distribution Exclusivity

offer your product to only one Web site for resale, then that Web site operator does not have to worry about any price competition from other Web sites. This price competition is made easier on the Web by the robots that automatically find the lowest price for purchasers among the competing sales sites on the Web. Not only can you sell the product easier with exclusivity, but also in many cases you can extract valuable benefits for a struggling entrepreneur. Typically exclusivity is negotiated with either some payment in advance for it, or some guaranteed minimum sales quantities that the distributor will have to sell in order to retain the exclusivity.

Information Resources, Inc.—Funded by Exclusivity

In the early 1980s, John Malec and Gerry Eskin had developed a potentially valuable way to help major packaged goods companies evaluate the incremental revenue impact of changes in their television advertising. They were able to fund their venture by offering exclusivity to their potential customers at a time when they were having trouble getting funding from traditional sources. They had developed and patented technology to use to target cable television viewers in smaller markets without access to television signals over the air. Their concept was to put boxes on the top of cable household television sets, and to put computer systems into the "head end" where the cable system got the microwave programming signal. This technology would enable Information Resources to have viewers of the same television show on cable get different advertisements than the other viewers of the same show.

This ability to target ads was combined with a consumer panel of households who were given cards that were scanned at all of their area's food and drug stores. The Behaviorscan® system was able to very validly evaluate television advertising changes by performing the changes in an experiment where the experimental groups were matched by prior purchases of the brand and category. The matching of the experimental groups was done with the household panel data that was collected every time the household made a purchase at any of the food or drug stores in the metropolitan area.

The Behaviorscan concept was very attractive to many packaged good's advertisers, because it was the first way they had seen to validly get a handle on the productivity of their very large television advertising expenditures. For example, if one group of matched households were given 50 percent more television advertising for a brand than another group of matched households, the experiment was designed so that all other possible effects on sales were controlled for, and a valid measure of advertising productivity—its incremental impact on revenues—could be obtained.

Information Resources leveraged the interest of these major packaged goods firms to fund their development. Before they had any of their markets instrumented, Malec and Eskin presented their design and patents to the major packaged good's firms. They offered *category exclusivity* in return for up front payments that would pay for the development and implementation of the instrumented market technology. The packaged goods marketers were so worried that their competitors would get a competitive edge, that Malec and Eskin were able to fund their development *without any* outside funding. At the same time, Malec and Eskin were actually having problems getting funding from traditional sources. Exclusivity to potential customers turned out to be a very creative, extremely cheap, way to finance the venture.

Evaluating Channel Exclusivity

By giving exclusivity, you enable the channel member to associate your product more closely with the channel member's other products. In many cases, this can be a win-win situation for both parties. If the positioning of your product is consistent with that of other products the channel member carries, then your product will reinforce the positioning of the other products and simultaneously benefit from the association. For example, many upscale products will have exclusive retailers in each geographical area who are "authorized" to sell their product exclusively. Even the adjective "exclusive" has been used to describe this kind of product. "Exclusive," very high priced watches and certain high-end designer fashions are examples of products that use exclusivity as one of their distribution leverage points.

If a channel member has exclusivity, she will typically have more motivation to "push" the product to the next level of distribution, or to the final consumer. "Push" involves promotion, distribution attention (e.g., shelf space, display in store, advertising). Because she has exclusivity, the channel member can push the exclusive product and not worry about a competitive channel member capitalizing on the "push" by selling the "pushed" product without paying for any of the "push expenses." On the other hand, if the exclusive product is very attractive to consumers, advertising the exclusive product may get new people into the channel member's business and cause them to buy other products while they are there. Some very powerful retailers have begun to understand the value of having unique, high-perceived value products on an exclusive basis. Home Depot, for example, has a number of products made especially for them that can bring in new customers or cause existing customers to come visit the store more often. Home Depot's exclusive line of dehumidifiers was very well rated by a consumer magazine and thus brought new customers in. Home Depot did not have to share those new customers with any competitors because of their exclusive arrangement with the manufacturer.

Because of the lack of interchannel competition, the margins on exclusive goods are usually higher, not only for the channel members, but also for the manufacturer. The manufacturer typically has some more control over what the channel member does with her product if she has an exclusive arrangement. In many cases, the exclusivity contracts will not only have guaranteed minimum purchase quantities, but also stipulations about how much and what kind of "push" will be performed by the channel member.

However, the granting of exclusive distribution is not a one-way street.

If you give an exclusivity contract for a long period, you may end up at the mercy of the channel member to whom you have given exclusivity. During the contracted exclusivity period, as long as all of the exclusivity contract provisions are being observed, you may have very little leverage over the channel member. This happens often when an entrepreneur enters a foreign country using a full service importer/distributor. These importer/distributors typically assume all responsibility for the product once the container leaves the entrepreneur's country. The entrepreneur is typically not very knowledgeable about the sales potential and/or the potential perceived value of her offering to the end consumers in the foreign country. The importer takes advantage of this by negotiating a contract that has a competitive price that the importer pays for your product, but does not specify the price or other marketing mix elements that the importer will use in his country. There are also typically annual minimum purchases that are required to retain the exclusivity. The agreements can be very long in duration 10 to 20 years, or even lifetime. The importer/distributor is thus free to do whatever he wants with the product as long as he buys his minimums from the entrepreneur. Sometimes, the importer will second source an inferior version of your product to distribute along with your product and unfairly leverage your brand equity. In other cases, the importer will develop a competing version of your product and limit his competition to the minimums he has to sell of your product.

One author has been working with foreign companies entering the U.S. market for over 20 years, including a number of Israeli firms. A number of Israeli firms wanted to enter the U.S. market and found someone in the United States who spoke Hebrew. That person became the exclusive importer/distributor and told the Israeli firm that "standard practice" was to have very long exclusivity terms—20 to 30 years in many cases. The Israeli firms lost millions of dollars in opportunity costs because of the treatment of their exclusive distributors for whom they had no operational recourse. Many American entrepreneurs have had similar experiences when they attempted to enter other countries—especially those with very different languages and culture. Just as it makes sense to generate and evaluate a number of alternatives for other elements of your marketing plan, it is at least as important for the distribution channel decisions.

Before getting into long-term exclusivity agreements, you should know your market, how the product offering should be perceived, and have some reasonable ideas about its perceived value and pricing options. The long-term exclusive distributor is crucial to your business—it's like a marriage. You should check out all alternatives and be sure of the ethics of your chosen distributor, if you choose the exclusive route.

Item Exclusivity

Some firms use exclusivity by item to help lower price competition between competing channel members or competing retailers. They will make small differences between models and give retailers or channel members exclusive rights to one model for a geographical area. This exclusivity by item does not help as much with all of the advantages of exclusivity in Table 5.2. However, in a number of industries, it has become the way most firms go to market. For example, the medium and high-end furniture manufacturers will have different models that are exclusive to different retailers in a U.S. metropolitan area. The biggest advantage the furniture retailers see from this tactic is that their potential customers cannot easily compare prices from one local dealer to another. Now that furniture is beginning to be sold on the Internet, it will become even more important for local retailers to attempt to insulate themselves by having exclusive items.

Intensive Distribution

Intensive distribution is the opposite extreme in the options described in Table 5.2. Anyone who wants to carry your offering is encouraged to do so. The objective is to be everywhere the end customer might be and possibly buy your product offering. Impulse purchases such as candy, snacks, and so on are typically well suited to intensive distribution. However, in order to be successful, the consumer needs to know your product is there and perceive its value. The product needs to be pulled off the shelves by the customer compared to all the other competitive products. The classic, non-entrepreneurial way for that pull to happen is for a company to spend millions of dollars on advertising and promotion. As entrepreneurs, we know better ways. Our chapters on advertising, promotion, and public relations cover creative cost-effective ways to pull products through intensive (and other) distribution channels. One of the most creative ways to use intensive distribution is with *fad* products.

Wallwalkers

Ken Hakuta was the master user of intensive distribution to support his launch of "Wacky Wallwalkers" in concert with the rest of his ingenious, creative marketing plan that he executed in the mid-1980s. Because of the amazing demand built up by his fortuitous national public relations "Blitzkreig," every store in the United States wanted to sell Wacky Wallwalkers. Wacky Wallwalkers were exactly what their name hinted. They were little plastic octopuses that if thrown against most walls, would slowly walk down the wall, one leg over the other. Every retailer wanted to sell Wallwalkers after they were featured as the "newest fad" on the *CBS Evening News*.

Ken knew that time was of the essence and that he should take advantage of the extraordinary consumer demand by getting as many Wallwalkers into as many storefronts as possible as fast as possible. He was aware that cheap knockoffs would soon arrive to compete, even though he had an "exclusive license" from the Japanese manufacturer. To accomplish mass distribution as quickly as possible, Ken authorized toy and novelty distributors to sell his product to the trade rather than have his own sales and distribution team. The distributors had the entire infrastructure in place to quickly get the product to all of the retailers who were demanding to be part of the Wallwalkers action. Ken gave an additional mark-up to these distributors to compensate them for their part in the distribution chain. He thus made less on *each* Wallwalker that he sold than he would have earned had he used his own sales and distribution system. However, he correctly estimated that his total number of units sold would be much higher with the indirect distribution system. The total profits he earned by selling over 200 million Wallwalkers in less than one year were much higher than he would have earned had he struggled to develop his own sales and distribution system. He also was able to capitalize on the consumer demand before the knockoffs were able to become a big factor.

The use of intermediary sales and distribution resources was appropriate for Ken for another reason. He correctly viewed Wallwalkers as a product with limited life and did not plan to follow Wallwalkers with any other products targeted at similar mass-market customers. If he were planning a long-term business where retailer relationships were going to be important, than more direct contact between Ken's people and the mass retailers would possibly make sense. He was right to view Wallwalkers as a once in a lifetime opportunity. He made "tens of millions"[3] of dollars on the Wallwalkers—not bad for a year's work and virtually no assets before he started!

Selective Distribution

Selective distribution is in the conceptual middle between exclusive and intensive distribution. Here, some, but not all, resellers are authorized to resell your product and/or service. By not allowing everyone to carry your product, you retain some control as to how it will be resold. The control mechanism is the implied threat to take away the product from those resellers who do not follow your rules for your product. You also may have a higher say in how the end consumer may perceive you. The selective distribution option is best if it is integrated with the rest of the marketing mix to underlie a sound positioning and segmentation plan. Brooks Sports found a way to compete with Nike that includes selective distribution as an important, integrated element of its marketing mix.

Brooks Sports—Integrating Selective Distribution with Effective Positioning and Segmentation

When Helen Rockey came to Brooks in 1994 after 11 years at Nike, Brooks was a mess. Brooks had been successful during the running boom of the late 1970s, but in the 1980s they tried to chase Nike.

They expanded into other categories like basketball, aerobics, and baseball, and signed big name athletes like Dan Marino and James Worthy to sell its $70 shoes.[4] Brooks, like Superscope (discussed below) had committed the classic error of trying to move down the prestige of distribution channels to maximize revenue. According to *Forbes:*

> But in trying to become a mini-Nike, Brooks was stretched too thin. When business began to slow, it began using cheaper materials and selling its sneakers at rock-bottom prices to discount retailers like Kmart, which sold them for as little as $20. Brooks lost credibility with joggers, and between 1983 and 1993 it lost some $60 million. "I don't think I really knew what I had gotten myself into," Rockey says.[5]

Helen developed a completely different marketing strategy to differentiate Brooks from the rest of the competition. She went back to Brooks' running heritage and decided to be perceived as the shoe for serious running enthusiasts. This revived positioning and implied segmentation dictated all the elements of her new marketing mix, including distribution. This new strategy was consistent with what was left of Brook's distinctive competence—relationships with Far-East suppliers, design capability, and a new CEO who herself was a running enthusiast.

The best outlet for the newly positioned Brooks line was the specialty running stores that catered to the running enthusiasts. Helen had to make her product attractive, not only to the end purchaser, the running enthusiast, but also to the specialty running store retailers. She did that with all the elements of her marketing mix—especially her product and pricing, and very selective distribution. She first limited the Far-East suppliers from 20 to the 3 best at producing high quality shoes and redesigned the line to be attractive to serious runners. She next boosted the suggested retail prices significantly—to as high as $120. The margin to the running specialty stores was about 45 percent. This was a good margin for the stores—as long as the prices were not undercut by other retail competitors. This is where Brooks' selective distribution was critical. Helen had to control all of the retail outlets to ensure that no one was undercutting each other. She did this by ensuring that only specialty running shops got the shoes and that the discounters were not able to carry the line. In the beginning of the repositioning, she had personally visited the major retail specialty running stores to convince them that she really was dedicated to having a brand that both Brooks and their partner selective retailers would make very good money on.

The other elements of Brooks' marketing mix also supported the new segmentation and positioning. Their salesforce helped their retailers to run running clinics and trained the retail salesforce about how to get the right shoe for the store's runner clientele. Brooks also had an extensive and professional presence at the major running trade shows. There are no more celebrity endorsements. Instead the company has over 200 competing runners who are given free shoes. These runners are icons within the serious running community.[6] Because the target segmentation made mass media unnecessary, Brooks was able to take advantage of media that reached its target audience very efficiently. Brooks spends less than a million dollars per year in niche publications like *Runners World* and *Running Times.* This reinvented positioning and segmentation has been very productive for Brooks. According to *Forbes:* "Brooks' sales have been growing at a 30 percent clip for the past 4 years and should hit $100 million by next year (2000). Operating income (net before depreciation, interest, and taxes) last year (1988) topped $4 million, from $3 million in 1997."[7] Some brands may not be suited for intensive distribution. Brooks was one of them, as it was developed over time. Brooks does not have the potential to out compete or out muscle Nike or Reebok. However, it does have the potential to make a lot of money for its entrepreneurial owners if they continue to understand its limitations and have a marketing mix (including selective distribution) consistent with its revised positioning and segmentation.

Value-Added Resellers

Many business-to-business products are marketed through a form of selective distribution. They often will form relationships with *value-added resellers* (VARs) who bundle their product with other products and services to solve their customer's problems. The conceptual logic that supports a decision to use VARs is very similar to that of evaluating manufacturers' representatives as a sales mechanism. The VARs value added is their relationships with their customers and the other synergistic products and services that they may bundle together to solve customer problems. Many technical products that need to be used together with other products in an integrated solution are best marketed through VAR, selective, indirect distribution channels. For some component product categories, the end customer does not expect to buy directly from the manufacturer, but wants to buy an integrated solution from a VAR. In those categories, the VAR can almost become the end customer to the entrepreneurial manufacturer. The entrepreneur's job is to understand the needs of the VAR and provide more perceived added value than competitors.

Nice Systems—A VAR Example

Nice Systems, Ltd. is an entrepreneurial company started in Israel that has used the VAR channel all over the world to grow from less than $10 million in 1991 to over $100 million in 2000. Their major product line has been integrated digital recording and quality control systems for telephonic voice applications. These are systems that digitally record phone or other voice sources and provide technology so that the customer can easily search for and access conversations that were recorded over time. The markets for Nice Systems' products include call centers, trading floors, air traffic control, and public safety and security. Even though the product is very similar, or even identical for each of these markets, Nice has wisely chosen to have selective distribution with different VAR partners in each market. For trading floors, Nice has authorized firms like British Telecom, Siemens, IPC Information Systems, and so on. For call centers, they have associated with Alcatel, Aspect Telecommunications, Rockwell, Lucent Technologies, and so on. In each of these markets their objective is for the VAR associates to integrate the Nice Systems products into their total communications offerings to their target markets. Nice could not have grown nearly as rapidly nor have as good a base of business had they not utilized a VAR strategy. The drawback to the strategy (if there is one) is that Nice must make sure that its offering bundle is not only attractive to the end customers in the call centers and air traffic control centers, but also attractive to their VARs as well.

Selective distribution is very important if aspects of the place the product is bought are important to the perceived value of the entrepreneur's offering bundle. The entrepreneur can use the concept testing procedure to check whether the potential customer views the product offering any differently if it is carried in one store versus another. If a product is described as available at Sharper Image or Neiman Marcus, it will be perceived differently than if it is described as available at Wal-Mart and Kmart.

Preservation Hall Jazz Bands—A Selective Distribution Example

Alan Jaffee, the entrepreneur who founded the Preservation Hall Jazz Bands in New Orleans understood the importance of selective distribution in determining how his product offering was to be perceived. He founded the Preservation Hall Jazz Bands by personally finding old Dixie Land jazz stars and rehabilitating them and caring for them so that they could recreate Dixie Land jazz as it was in its hey day. His objective was to have the Preservation Hall Jazz Bands perceived as art, not just as entertainment. To ensure that potential consumers received the correct perception, Mr. Jaffee only let the bands perform in venues that were perceived as mainly artistic as opposed to entertainment. For example, the bands would perform at the Tanglewood or Wolftrap music festivals, but not at stadium rock or jazz concerts. If they performed on television, it was on the Bell Telephone Hour, not on a weekly variety or entertainment show. For those readers who saw the Preservation Hall Bands perform in the late 1980s or early 1990s, Alan Jaffee was the rotund white man playing the tuba in the all-Black band. Their home venue, Preservation Hall on Bourbon Street, New Orleans, also reinforced their artistic, authentic positioning. The "hall" is very simple with benches for the audience to sit on, with no alcoholic beverages served. You are supposed to go to Preservation Hall to listen to Dixie Land Jazz and appreciate it as an art form. Their home venue, their venues on the road, and their media appearances all support and are synergistic with that positioning. Alan Jaffee did marketing at Gimbels Department Store before he founded Preservation Hall, and that may have prepared him to position his "offering" so well.

Dynamic Distribution Management

Many entrepreneurs need to understand that distribution channels can sometimes be more valuable if they are changed over time. This is true especially for product lines that continually have innovation and change a lot and/or have new products or models that are introduced. The distribution channels need to change because the prestige you want to associate with your newest and most innovative product may be very different from the prestige you are able to associate with an existing product. If the existing product has been sold for a length of time and is no longer considered as state of the art, it will not command as much prestige and status as the "newest and most advanced." Consumer electronics and fashion items are those for which changing distribution *by item* over time is often an excellent strategy. If you can associate the high prestige items with the high prestige distribution channels, and the lower prestige items with the lower prestige (and typically lower margin) distribution channels, you can often create win-win situations for both you and the distribution channels.

The reason this item change over time works has partly to do with examining the needs and values of the various types of channel members. The high-end channel members (Sharper Image, Bloomingdales, Hammacher Schlemmer) want to sell exclusive, high perceived value items. They do not want to sell the same items that the lower end, mass market channel members (Wal-Mart, Kmart, etc.) sell. The high-end retailers do not want to have to compete on price with the same item in a lower end, lower margin store. The high-end stores perceive that their better service and the store ambiance justify higher markups than their mass-market competitors. They also do not sell the kind of mass volumes that the lower end stores do. This also justifies their higher profit margins because their fixed costs are higher per unit of sales.

The lower end channel members have just the opposite set of needs. They would like nothing better than to be able to sell the same items that the high-end stores do. They want to advertise that they have the same items as the high-end stores, but for less. Managing the delicate balancing act of the different channel hierarchies is a real challenge for many entrepreneurs. However, with careful planning and a bit of *chutzpah*, an entrepreneur can successfully manage these conflicting channel priorities. We cover two examples next—one of an entrepreneurial company Superscope, Inc. that mismanaged the balance of their distribution channels and Franklin Electronic Publishers that has managed the process very well for 12 years.

Superscope, Inc.—Couldn't Achieve Balance

In the late 1980s, Superscope, Inc. bought the right to the Marantz label for high fidelity components. When Superscope bought them, Marantz was a premier manufacturer of very high-end audio components—tuners, amplifiers, speakers. Marantz's distribution was consistent with their high-end image. They had a very selective distribution channel—only the most prestigious and best audio/video "consultants"/dealers in each metropolitan area of the United States. The Marantz business had good profits, but was not very large in terms of sales volume. The Marantz positioning and pricing limited their target market to the high-income audio file market segment. With a limited, but very profitable target market, Marantz was growing with the high-end audio market—around 10 percent per year.

Superscope was not satisfied with the growth potential of Marantz. They reasoned that the brand's perceived value was so high that it could sell much more if its distribution were broadened and its advertising budget increased. When Superscope talked with mass-market retailers and distributors, they got big intentions of purchasing and promoting the Marantz line. Retailers like Wal-Mart and Kmart or Circuit City would like nothing better than to get a very high-end, high-gross profit product line. Their modus-operandi would be to discount the list price to build volume and sell very large numbers of units. They might even use the Marantz line as a loss leader to build store traffic. They reasoned that middle market consumers would love to have an opportunity to buy high-end products at a good discount.

Superscope thus began a very ambitious program to sharply increase the sales of Marantz by significantly broadening the line's distribution. They began offering the line to the mass-market retailers. They encouraged them with coop advertising programs to advertise Marantz in their weekly circulars and newspaper inserts. Most of the circulars of retailers like Circuit City or Kmart advertise temporary price reductions and other kinds of special pricing. Initially, the sales results of the increased distribution program were extremely strong. For the next two years, Superscope's Marantz sales volume more than doubled and their corporate profits were up even higher because of economies of scale. Superscope was a very hot stock in New York for about a year.

Then things began to unravel. The high-end, exclusive retailers got very upset that they were being undercut on price and out promoted by the mass retailers. The high-end clients were very sophisticated and were willing to go to Kmart to buy for much less what they used to buy at the high-end specialty retailers. So the high-end retailers began to lose business. What did they do? The high-end specialty retailers began refusing to carry Marantz and changed allegiance to other audio equipment makers who would respect the selective distribution to only high-end specialty channels that would not compete with each other on price. For a while Superscope did not care about these distribution losses, because the high-end business was more than being made up for by large orders from the mass retailers. However, once the majority of the high-end retailers stopped carrying Marantz, its cachet and prestige began to really suffer. The high-end retailers began to bad mouth Marantz as "the cheap brand" that was being sold through Kmart. The mass marketers began to also shy away from paying good wholesale prices for Marantz because it began to no longer fly out of their stores as it used to. This wholesale price pressure made a big impact on Superscope's profit margins. Superscope then decided to increase their profit margins by making Marantz offshore at much lower costs and somewhat lower quality. This manufacturing change held up Superscope's profits for a time, but it also added even more fodder for the high-end "Marantz Bashers" who created much word-of-mouth about the decline in Marantz quality. The mass-market retailers then began to cut back their orders because the consumer demand for Marantz was deteriorating. Superscope's volume began to drop precipitously. They tried to introduce a line of Marantz "Gold," made domestically, that would only be sold in the high-end stores. The high-end stores turned Superscope down flat because they felt betrayed by their Marantz experience. They would not trust Superscope not to do the same with Marantz Gold that they did with Marantz. Superscope is no longer in business and the Marantz name lost most of its former value.

Superscope made a number of mistakes. They did not create long-term value for any of their distribution and retailing channels. They used the Marantz reputation partially built by the high-end retailers to hurt the same high-end retailers when they broadened distribution to price oriented competitors. They lost the trust of the high-end retailers by not treating them with the exclusivity that they rightfully expected. They lowered the quality of the brand as they lowered the prices. They sacrificed their long-term positioning and perceived value for a short-term big revenue and profit spike. Their short-term thinking killed the company.

Franklin Electronic Publishers

Franklin Electronic Publisher's core business is handheld reference products like dictionaries, thesauruses, wine guides, and so on. Over the years, Franklin has had a spotty record with other product lines, but they have continually been able to slowly grow and make good returns on their core product line. Their dynamic distribution channel management by item is a big part of their long-term success with this core line. They use a tried and true formula to provide a win-win situation for all of their channel partners—from the high-end Sharper Image and Bloomingdales to the lower end Wal-Mart and Kmart. They give each of them what they want without alienating anybody. Sharper Image and other high-end catalog retailers, as well as the high-end retailers and e-tailers, all want exclusivity to the high end for items that they sell. Sharper Image does not get too upset if Hammacher Schlemmer sells the same new Franklin translator at the same price. However, if Kmart or the Damark catalog are each selling the same item at 30 percent lower *at the same time as the Sharper Image,* the upper-end retailers get very upset.

Franklin handles this conflict by *cycling its items* through the distribution channels over time. Their newest models get very selective distribution to the high-end retailers for about six months. They then are released to the mid-level retailers, like Radio Shack, Macy's, and so on for another six-month period. After that period, the items are released to the mass-market retailers, the Wal-Marts' and Kmarts. If Franklin has its plan working perfectly, they have new items every six months to feed into the channel to replace the items that have been released to the next prestigious levels. When they release the item that has been at Sharper Image for six months to the next level, they should have another brand new item to take its place. Sharper Image and other high-end retailers are happy because they are always the first to have the newest and most advanced items that they can price at high margins because of their very selective distribution. The mid-level retailers are also relatively happy because they get to carry items at a discount that had just been in the Sharper Image at higher prices. The lower level mass-market discounters are also happy because they get to carry items at a further discount that had just been in the department stores and other mid-level retailers at higher prices.

Franchising: Still Another Distribution Option

Many entrepreneurs have used franchising to accelerate their revenue growth. However, as is the case with all distribution alternatives, franchising is better for some product/market situations than for others. We first describe what franchises are and which types might be useful for entrepreneurial ventures. We then evaluate the advantages and disadvantages of the different types and how a decision to offer franchises should be evaluated. We also look at franchises from the point of view of buying a franchise because more entrepreneurs consider buying franchises as a way to get their venture started than any other business form. We next consider the unique conflicts that occur between franchiser and franchisee and how they might be managed.

Different Types of Franchising

A franchise is usually permission or a license granted by the franchiser to the franchisee to sell a product or service in an agreed-upon territory. Franchising is typically a continuing relationship in which the franchiser provides assistance in organizing, training, merchandising, systems, and management in return for payments from the franchisee. Franchises are a big part of business in the United States. Approximately 1 in 12 businesses is a franchise and $1 trillion in revenues come from franchises.

The different types of franchises depend on what rights are licensed to whom. Different forms of franchising are cropping up all the time. The following forms are examples of those that have been used by entrepreneurs. These forms are not mutually exclusive. Many franchise forms can have elements of these different prototype forms:

1. *Manufacturing Franchise.* Here, the franchisor provides the right to a franchisee to manufacture a product using the franchisor's name and trademark. The most prevalent examples of this form are soft drink bottlers. Other examples include companies who manufacture private label goods that have a retailer's label on them and firms that manufacture fashion apparel under license to a designer label. The Callanen Watch company (now a division of Timex, Inc.) had a license to manufacture watches under the Guess™ label.

2. *Manufacturer-Retailer Franchise.* In this form, the manufacturer gives the franchisee the right to sell its product through a retail outlet. Examples of this form include gasoline stations, most automobile dealerships, and many businesses found in shopping malls.

3. *Wholesaler-Retailer Franchise.* Here, the wholesaler gives the retailer the right to carry products distributed by the wholesaler. Examples of this form include Radio Shack (which also manufactures some of its products), Agway Stores, Health Mart, and other franchised drug stores.

4. *Business Format Franchise.* This is the most popular form and includes elements of the other forms. It is typically more all-inclusive. Here, the franchisor provides the franchisee with a name, an identity, and a complete, "proven," way of operating a business. Examples include Burger King and McDonald's fast-food outlets, Pizza Hut and Dairy Queen restaurants, Holiday Inn and Best Western hotels, 7-Eleven convenience stores, and Hertz and Avis car rentals.

From the Franchisee's Point of View

For the franchisee, these franchise forms can be very helpful for some entrepreneurs who want to start a business, but may not have the vision, creativity, resources, or skill to start a completely new venture. All of the forms provide for the franchisee to benefit from the market power of large-scale advertising and marketing expenditures. These large marketing budgets typically come from the collective resources of all the franchisees. Many franchises also enable franchisees to band together and buy products and supplies at better prices then they could as individual entrepreneurs. Probably the biggest value of these franchises is the brand name value and equity that has been built up over, in some cases, many years by the franchisor. The different forms may also add unique advantages.

For manufacturing franchises, the franchisee may get a well-protected market that they have exclusively. Many manufacturing franchises may also permit the franchisee to obtain licenses from more than one company. For example, the Callanen Watch Company also had a license to manufacture Monet brand watches. Having multiple licenses can lower risk levels for franchisees, especially for items that may go in and out of favor. For Callanen, if the market for Monet watches was waning, perhaps the Guess brand could take up the slack.

The business format franchise adds a number of benefits to the franchisee that has little business experience. The best business format franchises have encapsulated all the relevant knowledge and experience of the franchisor into training and operating systems that take most, if not all, of the guess work out of operating the franchise. McDonald's is famous for its "Hamburger University" that trains its franchisees in all elements of running a successful outlet. The franchisee basically gets to leverage on all the other experience of other franchisees and the franchisor in the past. The franchisee is helped in setting accounting procedures, facility management, personnel policies, business planning, and actually starting up. Most franchisors also help with outlet location and help arrange financing. Many business format franchises are in businesses like fast food, and convenience stores that are not very sensitive to business cycles and can make it easier to weather a poor economy. This franchise form is also available for a wide range of prices. Some business format franchises can also be operated from home-like aerobics instruction or direct marketing of cosmetics.

The typical advantages of becoming a franchisee include:

- Lower risk of failure
- Established product/service
- Experience of franchisor
- Group purchasing power
- Instant name recognition
- Operational standards assure uniformity and efficiency
- Assistance in setting accounting procedures, facility management, personnel policies, and so on.
- Start-up assistance
- Location assistance
- Help with financing arrangements
- Power of national and regional marketing

However, there is another side to being a franchisee. Many readers of this book want to be entrepreneurs at least partly in order to be their own boss. All of these franchise benefits come at the cost of sacrificing much autonomy. For most franchises, the franchisee has little, if any control over the product/service they sell, or the marketing decisions on advertising, public relations, or location. It may be impossible, for example, to drop or add products that may be more or less suitable to the particular needs of your market area. Local public relations may be under the franchisee's control, but with constraints from the franchisor. The franchisees may have a cooperative governing organization that decides on national advertising and promotion policies together with the franchisor. Each franchisee is limited to one vote in these organizations. There are also usually very strict rules and regulations on all aspects of operating the business.

Aside from autonomy, there are other typical disadvantages of becoming a franchisee. You pay for the privilege. There usually is an initial franchise fee, ongoing royalty payments as a percentage of revenue, as well as a percentage of revenue to a cooperative marketing fund. The marketing fund is administered by the cooperative franchisee-franchisor organization. These fees are all "off the top." The franchisor gets paid before the franchisee may make any profits. The franchise agreements may also impose restrictions on selling the franchise if things go badly, and may also restrict how the business may be passed on to your heirs. Because the business depends on the franchisor's success, there is also a risk that the franchisor may fail. Visible franchisor failures recently have been Arthur Treacher's Fish & Chips, and Boston Market.

Disadvantages of buying a franchise include:

- Payment of an initial franchise fee
- Ongoing royalty payments "off the top"
- "Off the top" payments for cooperative marketing fund
- Cannot add or drop products unilaterally
- Little say on national marketing policies and tactics
- Must conform to operating procedures—even if you have a better way
- You depend on the franchisor for much of your success
- Some large franchisors have failed

- May be restrictions on selling the franchise
- May be difficult to pass the business to your heirs

Besides considering all of the benefits and disadvantages, before selecting a franchise, the potential franchisee should carefully read the "Uniform Franchise Offering Circular" (UFOC) for each franchise being evaluated. The U.S. government requires this document. It contains the information that typically is needed to make a well-informed decision about the franchise as well as some not as useful information. The UFOC document is much like a prospectus that is required as part of an initial public offering for a company's securities. Its major purpose is to keep the company making the offering from getting sued by people who buy the securities (or in this case the franchise). The lawyers thus make the issuing company disclose any possible risks that the franchisee might be taking when they buy the franchise. Because of this bias in the way the document is written, it should be read in a special way. If one took all of the possible risks the lawyers put in these documents literally, you would not buy any franchise or any new public security. The lawyers get paid to invent risks to worry about. Most of the risk stuff is "boilerplate" that can be found in most of these documents. There is, however, much very important information in the UFOC that is crucial for evaluating a franchise. Table 5.3 highlights the important information in the UFOC that should be scrutinized before entering into a franchise agreement. Because there are many "fly by night" franchisors around, it really pays to do your homework before buying any franchise. The UFOC can be very helpful. *Under no circumstances should you buy a franchise without scrutinizing the UFOC.* Some franchisor sales people can be over zealous. From the franchisees point of view *caveat emptor* (let the buyer beware!) is the point of view that is necessary.

From the Franchisor's Point of View

Advantages for the Franchisor

Franchising is a distribution option that should be considered by more entrepreneurs. Many of the aspects of franchising can be very attractive.[8] Franchising enables rapid expansion without large investments by the entrepreneur. The alternative ways of expanding

Business experience of the franchisor and its affiliates

Qualifications of franchisor's directors and managers

Any lawsuits against the company and/or managers

Any bankruptcies of the company and/or managers

Initial franchise fee and other initial payments

Description of all required continuing payments

Any restrictions regarding purchasing from the franchisor or its affiliates

Any restrictions on the quality of goods and services that the franchisee can use

Any financial assistance available from the franchisor

Restrictions on goods and services the franchisee is permitted to sell

Restrictions on customers with whom the franchisee may deal

Territorial protection for the franchisee

Conditions under which the franchise may be:

1. Repurchased
2. Refused renewal
3. Transferred to a third party
4. Modified
5. Terminated by a third party

Description of training programs provided

Description of involvement of celebrities or public figures in the franchise

Financial statements and history of the franchisor

Basis of potential franchisee earnings projections made by the franchisor

Percentage of franchisees that have achieved the projected results

Names and addresses of other franchisees to contact for their point of view

Statistical data on:

1. Present number of franchisees
2. Numbers projected for the future
3. Number of franchisees terminated
4. Number of franchisees repurchased by the franchisor

Copy of the franchise contract

Table 5.3   Important Information for the Franchisee in the UFOC

involve both selling equity and losing some control, or borrowing money, which adds leverage and may encumber some assets. When the entrepreneur successfully franchises, she effectively leases a sliver of the business and in return receives the franchisee's capital, energy, and entrepreneurship. The more rapid expansion that franchising enables may allow the franchise to take advantage of some scale economies. Large networks mean collective buying power. Franchisees can compete with other chains because they can buy in larger quantities and vendors recognize and reward the franchise's growth. Franchisees often also set up their own advertising and promotion cooperatives to obtain scale economies.

The scale economies also increase the ventures access to real estate. Single location businesses have difficulty obtaining access and credibility with mall developers, leasing agents, and limited access locations such as stadiums and contract food feeding operations. These landlords are looking for name brands and consumer recognition, as well as repeat leasing in multiple locations. Franchising eliminates these entry barriers.

The "employees" that become franchisees are typically highly motivated to succeed because their own money is on the line. For most entrepreneurial companies, recruitment, retention, training, and retention of great managers are key to successful expansion. The best managers are typically hard to retain unless they are offered equity. Franchising gives managers their equity with their own investment. The franchisees' investment is always at risk. This causes commitments of time and energy that typically cannot be bought with a salary. If particular skills are needed for the operation of the venture, franchisees can also be sources of highly skilled employees.

As discussed, the franchisor typically gets paid "off the top" as a fraction of revenue and also gets an initial franchise fee. This is typically a more predictable cash flow source than profits from an owned business. Thus, the franchisor can make profits, even if her franchises may not be profitable. It is this inherent conflict between the franchisor's incentives versus the franchisee's that causes some of the questionable and unethical franchises to arise. Conflicts between franchisees and the franchisor also come from this potential conflict of interest. Franchising works best when the entrepreneur has a proven business model that can be replicated in different areas or venues, and in which both the franchisee and franchisor are better off financially than they would be if they were not together.

Franchises are typically easier to sell than the equivalent business that is not franchised. Think first about a traditional business with 50 managers with hundreds of employees in 10 cities with 100 leases. Contrast this with a franchise business that has 10 managers responsible for 50 franchisees with 100 locations. The franchise business is more attractive for an outsider to buy and becomes an easier exit strategy than a traditional business.

Disadvantages for the Franchisor

There are also drawbacks to franchising. To attract many franchisees and generate good long-term word-of-mouth, the franchisees should do well financially. These franchisee profits are sometimes sacrificed when the franchise form is chosen. If the entrepreneurial venture is really best suited for franchising, the franchise fees should more than make up for these foregone profits as returns on resources invested in the venture. Because the franchisees are independent businesses, the franchisor has only the control given explicitly by the franchise agreement. The franchisor is thus banking the image and positioning of his franchise on the franchisees. The franchisor cannot just fire those "employees" who do not keep up the firm's image and positioning. This is the same conceptual problem that users of independent sales representatives also have. It takes constant vigilance and many programs to convince the franchisee partners to handle the image and positioning as if it were their own—which it really is. Successful franchises have reduced the fundamentals of operating their businesses to a cookbook, or operations manual. Their training programs succeed in transmitting the founder's intended positioning through the franchisee to the ultimate consumer.

The franchisor also must put in suitable systems and controls to ensure that the franchisees pay the correct amount of ongoing franchise fees based on revenue of the outlet. When in doubt, the franchisee would rather report lower revenues. In many franchises where large amounts of cash change hands, this control problem can be very big.

The franchisee and franchisor will typically have different incentives for pricing. For the franchisor who gets paid as a fraction of revenue, maximizing revenue becomes the objective. For the franchisee, profits are the objective. The franchisee may want to raise prices in order to increase profits at the expense of lower revenues. These pricing conflicts add a constant level of tension to many franchises.

As a franchisor, it is not as easy to change the channels of distribution because you no longer own them. Your franchisees will get very upset if they think you are going into another channel of distribution that may compete with the franchisees. For example, GNC franchises natural food and herbal remedy stores around the world. GNC has not been able to successfully use the World Wide Web as a distribution channel because their franchisees rightfully objected to the company competing with its franchisees. This is just one example of a *distribution channel conflict* that needs to be managed and planned for very carefully. We discuss management of these conflicts later in this chapter.

Another potential disadvantage of franchising is that you may be creating a new set of competitors that learn the business through your franchise and then replicate the operation under another name. In this case, it is very important for the franchisor to maintain brand positioning, image, and other proprietary assets that would make it difficult to replicate the franchise under a different name.

Rita's Water Ice—A Successful Franchising Venture

Rita's Water Ice is an entrepreneurial venture that has succeeded very well using the franchise form. They have been able to leverage the benefits of the franchise form and minimize the impacts of most of the disadvantages. Robert Tumolow, a retired Philadelphia fire fighter, started Rita's in the summer of 1984. Bob and his mother, Elizabeth, experimented with various new recipes for Italian Water Ice—an ethnic summer refresher that was very popular in Philadelphia. Their first store was opened in Bensalem, Pennsylvania, a suburb of Philadelphia, in May 1984. According to Rita's Web site, "the response was overwhelming—people really seemed to love it. Word of mouth spread like water ice on a hot summer sidewalk."[9] The next year Bob's brother John Tumolow joined the business and in 1987 they opened their second location. In 1989, the company made the decision to franchise.

For a small entrepreneurial venture begun with little capital, franchising made sense from a resource requirement point of view. Rita's could not afford to rapidly expand to more stores without going out and raising equity capital. Each franchisee invests between $135,000 and $242,000 initially to start a new Rita's outlet. That investment includes an initial franchise fee, finding and leasing a site, constructing the store layout, equipping the store, and working capital. At the end of 1999, Rita's has approximately 225 outlets in the Northeast and Florida. The capital needed to open all of those outlets at minimum would have been $100,000 per outlet or 225 × $100,000 = $22.5 million. In 2000, the Tumolow interests held all of the Rita's assets privately and had not had to take in public funding to expand. In addition, the firm took in over 200 franchise fees from each newly opened franchise. They also get an ongoing 6.5 percent of the gross sales of each franchisee. Their sales are proprietary. However their Web site says that Rita's sold over 30 million water ice cups in 1999. If we assume that their total sales per water ice cup (including pretzels, and other products) is $1, then the total gross sales across their system might be close to $30 million. Since Tumolow gets 6.5 percent of $30 million in sales, that is $2 million. That's not bad annual revenue. The franchisees also have to contribute 2.5 percent of revenue to a collective advertising fund. If we assume that the initial franchise fee covers the costs of selling and starting up franchises, and that the cooperative advertising fee really covers the Rita's corporate marketing budget, then the $2 million of ongoing royalties that Rita's collects is probably very profitable. Franchising was a very good distribution channel choice.

Rita's also developed a very smart way to collect their ongoing franchise and collective advertising fees, without having to audit or monitor their franchisee's sales. They just add a charge of 9 percent (6.5 percent royalty fee + 2.5 percent advertising fee) of the calculated gross sales for each gallon of Rita's mix that is shipped to each franchisee. The only way franchisees can get around paying the royalty would be to buy their mix from another supplier. All

Rita's personnel need to do for control is to spot check to make sure that each outlet has only Rita's authorized mix in use. Many franchisors must put in elaborate control systems to make sure that they are getting the right amount of ongoing revenue-based franchise fees.

Another constraint for expansion of company-owned stores was the ability to find, retain, and motivate real competent help to run the stores and serve customers. The stores were not open all year—just in the spring through early fall. (Most people don't crave water ice in the winter in the Northeast United States.) As hard as it was to get restaurant and fast-food employees, it was even harder if you weren't going to be open all year. An unwritten requirement for getting a Rita's franchise is that family members want to work in the outlets. One of the neat benefits of owning a Rita's franchise was that the franchisee and his or her family only needed to work during the late spring through early fall. The franchisee had the late fall and winter to relax. Rita's was not only selling franchisees a business. They were also selling a lifestyle.

Rita's, like most franchises, had two (at least) target markets it needed to satisfy to be successful. The first was the ultimate consumers who bought the water ice experience at its outlets. The second target segment was the franchisee who must invest in many cases their life savings to buy a Rita's franchise. It is not inexpensive to sell franchises. The first few franchises were sold by word-of-mouth to customers at company-owned stores who really liked the Rita's product. However, to expand to areas outside of metropolitan Philadelphia, Rita's had to get its franchise offering bundle exposed to potential franchisees. In any new area, the first Rita's to open was a company-owned store. This company-owned store attempted to replicate the original Philadelphia experience, using word-of-mouth to expose customers both to the end product at the Rita's outlet, and also to the possibility of becoming a franchisee. Just as most business-to-business products need a salesforce to help close the big sales, Rita's required a franchise salesforce to follow up and close all of the leads that came into the new areas.

Like most franchises and other distribution channels, it is very important for the franchisor to continually manage the channel relationships so that each franchisee continues to perceive the value proposition that it is getting from the franchise relationship. Rita's, like most successful franchisors, attempts to have franchisees perceive themselves as members of Rita's extended family. If you as a franchisee perceive yourself as a "family member" of a very successful family, then many conflicts between franchisor and franchisee don't crop up. Franchisees who perceive themselves in this way are going to be the best source of positive word-of-mouth for attracting new franchisees. Good entrepreneurial marketers know that word-of-mouth is the most powerful, cost-effective marketing lever a venture can have.

Rita's franchise has been able to counter one possible disadvantage of franchising in the best way. Rita's is not very worried about its franchisees opening up competitive outlets for a very simple reason. According to Bob Tumolow, Rita's CEO, the average Rita's has almost twice the revenue of competitors in the same area.[10] This is because the product's reputation, the expanded product line (including gelati and crème ice), and the cooperative marketing campaign have created perceived value for consumers that is much higher than Rita's competition. Rita's has been able to create a win-win situation in which *both the franchisor and the franchisee are better off with each other than they would be if they were not together.* This synergy objective should be the essence of not only effective franchise management, but also effective management of all distribution channel relationships.

From franchising, we next turn to a different aspect of channel management—how to manage and anticipate channel conflict.

Managing and Anticipating Channel Conflict

Entrepreneurs can get in major trouble if their channel members perceive the entrepreneur as beginning to compete with them when they had not been competing before. Channel members are used to relating to their competitors and usually consider it "part of the game" to compete with their channel counterparts. For example, the specialty running stores that sell Brooks running shoes are used to competing with each other on the basis of service, location, and assortment, but typically not on price. If Brooks were to try to sell directly to runners and bypass the retail channel (using a catalog or the Internet), its retailers would get upset and many would probably stop supporting Brooks. The retailers would feel that the implicit rules by which they had been operating had changed without their consent. Understandably, that gets them very angry.

Managing channel conflicts leverages all of the marketing concepts we discuss in this book. The entrepreneur needs to define roles for every channel member that are not conflicting and easily understood. These roles should be consistent with the venture's segmentation and the offering bundle that is appropriate for each segment. The benefits that are added by different channel partners will not be valued the same by all of the target segments. The channel partners will end up making the most money if they are matched with the segments that value the channel partner's benefits the highest. The channel partners also want to perceive that they are being treated fairly—which means being adequately compensated for the value that they add.

There is a big difference between channel conflict management at the beginning of a venture and when the entrepreneur wants to change the rules in the middle of the game. When a venture is beginning, the channel members should understand their role and any potential conflicts before they become a partner. If the entrepreneur has done his job well of marketing the role of the channel member, and the channel member signs up, there usually will not be any conflict problems. As long as the channel member perceives that his role has not changed and that the entrepreneur has not done anything to change his role or competitive situation, he will feel that he is being treated fairly. Human beings are comfortable when their expectations are fulfilled and not changed. However, if the entrepreneur wants to change the roles of the channel members after all the expectations have been fulfilled, there can be very big problems.

For example, when vineyards began to supply firms like Virtual Vineyards that sold wine directly to consumers over the Internet, the existing distributors and brick-and-mortar retailers became incensed. They pressured state legislatures all over the United States to outlaw alcohol sales over the Internet. So far, Florida, Georgia, and Kentucky have made it a felony to ship alcohol directly to consumers and at least 17 other states prohibit such sales.[11] Rumors also go around that some distributors will refuse to support those vineyards that sell over the Internet. These distributors felt that the Internet e-tailers jeopardized their positions as exclusive representatives of vineyards in each state. If the e-tailers were already part of the picture when the distributors were signed, it would not have been a problem for the vineyards. Depending on the strength of the distributors and their importance to the venture's success, the entrepreneur may have to creatively pacify the existing distribution partners to change or update the channels. The Internet will be causing many entrepreneurs to creatively deal with channel conflicts as they try to leverage the Internet's benefits.

The best alternative is if the entrepreneur can restructure the roles of all the distribution partners so that every member of the channel becomes more productive and adds more value. This is the best win-win scenario. Herman Miller, Inc. seems to have found this win-win scenario in the way it has restructured its distribution channels to take advantage of the Web to target a new segment.[12] Herman Miller's core business is selling its sleek, ergonomic premium cubicle office furniture systems to major corporations under big contracts at volume discounts. According to *Sales and Marketing* magazine,

> The emphasis is on *big*. The company's network of more than 250 contract dealers typically nab five-year purchasing contracts to configure, deliver, and install millions of workstation components to thousands of a single customer's employees. They also go to extraordinary lengths to serve those customers. Dealers reupholster furniture, reconfigure workstations as needs change, move employees' workstations to new offices, and provide ergonomic consultations.[13]

These big dealers are not able to sell ones and twos of chairs or workstations very economically. The burgeoning small office-home office (SOHO) market was not being served well by the big partners

Herman Miller had for their core business. To serve the SOHO market, beginning in 1994, Herman Miller put a few items in Office Depot and other retailers targeted at that market segment. In June 1998, Herman Miller introduced its full-fledged online store targeted at selling to the SOHO segment. Before Herman Miller management communicated with its core dealers and released its programs to help its core dealers using the Web, the dealers were furious. When the Web site was first started, the dealers' perceptions were very different than Herman Millers. Because Herman Miller had not done the appropriate marketing with their dealers, the dealers assumed that Herman Miller was out to directly compete with them. Herman Miller, to their credit, quickly realized they had a problem and began an intense program of communicating to the dealers that the online SOHO customers were a very different market segment from the major corporations in their core dealer market. They also communicated to the dealers that the same underlying configuration engine of their Web site was also available to help corporate customers more easily and efficiently deal with their Herman Miller partner dealer. The site was designed so that corporate customers, through their own customized Intranets would be able to develop their own configurations and price them in a much more efficient and productive manner. The dealers would still handle this corporate Intranet business, but it would lower their costs significantly.

"But even if they don't go after new business, the system will significantly lower operating costs, because information only needs to be entered once," says Gary Harmsel, senior vice president of distribution. "A dealer's average operating expense level runs in the 16 percent to 18 percent range, and this system can help [him] lower it to 12 percent. If you can take six points out of your operating expenses, pass some of that on to the customer, but also keep some for your future investment purposes, it's a win for everyone."[14]

Sometimes it is not possible to segment your market clearly so that different channels can be used for the different segments. If you are changing channels, to go on the Web and sell direct for example, it may be the best policy to make your existing channel your partner in the new channel. Ethan Allen is typical of many ventures that have been selling through very selective retail distribution and decided that the Web was too big of a potential channel to ignore. Ethan Allen owns 25 percent of its bricks-and-mortar retail outlets. The other 75 percent are independently owned and operated under license. To use the Web effectively and to not alienate their licensees, Ethan Allen had no choice but to make their licensed retailers partners in their Web operation. If they had opened up an independent Web operation, their retailers (to whom Ethan Allen is their sole supplier) would have been very upset with the new competition. The Ethan Allen CEO, M. Farooq Kathwari, made the only reasonable decision under the circumstances. "In exchange for a cut of the Internet revenue, the store owner would deliver much of the merchandise, accept returns, and handle the minor repairs often needed when furniture comes out of the crate."[15] Stores were also to be encouraged to make contact with people in their area who visit the Web site and express an interest in having decorating help.

Kathwari also realized that his dealers needed to correctly perceive the new role of the Web in their partnership with Ethan Allen. Before the Web site was launched, he met personally with each of the dealers (in groups) to explain to them how "We'll do this in a partnership. . . . We don't want to bypass you."[16]

For established ventures with existing exclusive distribution, it is very difficult to bypass them without doing something like Ethan Allen. On the other hand, if Ethan Allen did not have well defined territories for its dealers, the above partnership would have been very difficult to implement. However, if Ethan Allen had multiple dealers in an area, then the dealers would be used to competing with each other, and adding a Web competitor would not have been seen as such a direct threat to each dealer. Auto companies, for example, are not having as much trouble dealing with Web retailers for this reason.

Survey Results on Channels

Of the Inc. 500, 38 percent are integrating the Web with bricks-and-mortar operations versus only 13.9 percent of the non-Inc. group. Of the Inc. 500 47 percent are doing e-commerce on the Web versus only 23 percent of the non-Inc. group. Here again in their channel decisions, the Inc. 500 CEOs seem to be farther along in adopting productive paradigms.

Concept Testing to Channel Members

If the entrepreneur uses all the concepts and paradigms in this chapter and decides on her "optimal" distribution strategy and tactics, she still may not be successful. If the distribution channel members you have chosen won't do the part you expect, then the plan and venture may fall apart. It is at least as important to get channel members' reactions to your new entrepreneurial product(s) or services, as it is to get the reactions of the ultimate consumers. Just like consumer concept testing is best when the consumer is exposed to the product in the most realistic manner possible, concept testing to the channel members is completely analogous. The channel member should be exposed to your concept as realistically as possible. A brochure mock-up and descriptions of all the services you will supply to the channel member should typically be part of the concept. You also should let the channel member know explicitly what functions you expect him to perform as well. All tentative prices and terms should also be shown. If you have done concept testing with customers of this channel member, it can be helpful to summarize those results as part of the concept. Consumer concept testing results can be powerful arguments for convincing a retailer to carry your product.

The channel member should answer a similar type of question to that the end consumer is asked. "How likely will you be to buy and carry this product or service?" "What do you like best about this concept?" "What about the concept could be improved?" If the channel members are all "extremely likely" to buy and carry your product, then you can feel very confident that the distribution channel plan will work as you hoped. On the other hand, if your offering excites only a small fraction of the channel members, you have problems that need fixing before introduction. Just as testing a product with real consumers can give the entrepreneur excellent feedback that may be very different from her logic and planning, the concept testing to the channel members can be even more valuable. There may be aspects of your offering bundle that you never even considered that are very important to the channel members.

Summary

The concepts, options, and examples in this chapter are designed to encourage entrepreneurs to give the attention, creativity, and resources to the distribution channel decisions that they deserve. The creative juggling of different items for different time periods juxtaposed with decisions on direct, exclusive, selective, or intensive distribution can make big differences in how the entrepreneurs' offering is perceived by his or her target segment(s). These differences in perception can have large impacts on the venture's ultimate profitability. Just as with the end customer, concept testing the offering with channel members is typically a very cost-effective way to "reality check" all of your major distribution plan assumptions.

CHAPTER 6

Product/Service Rollout

The most crucial time in the marketing of a new product or service is the initial rollout. Since first impressions last, it is essential for an entrepreneurial venture to successfully launch its product. In fact, in the world of Internet mania, the difference between an initial rollout being a success or a dud can mean literally billions of dollars in market capitalization. Much can be learned even before the launch of a new idea, using a beta test to gather feedback and jump start the customer acquisition process. This means choosing the most appropriate reference accounts, gaining those reference accounts, getting the press onboard, and ironing out the bugs in the several months, weeks, or in Internet time, days before a formal product launch. Most importantly, it means getting great referrals from delighted, influential reference accounts.

Reference Accounts

In selling software (or any product that the potential user sees as possibly risky), nothing helps as much as strong reference accounts. For customers to believe your advertising or promotional materials takes a great leap of faith. For them to believe what they hear from other experienced users is merely an act of trust that those users have no incentive to lie about your product's virtues and faults. Reference accounts provide for an organized word of mouth campaign, so that when the press and key targeted accounts need to hear from noncompany sources, there are users to call.

The benefits to the company from a good reference account are great—credibility with peers of that account, spokespeople to talk with the press, and examples to use in advertising and public relations. To gain these advantages, the reference accounts themselves need to be provided with benefits of their own. These often take the form of reduced pricing (at least for a long initial period), increased training, and far greater and more responsive support than later customers may find (although hopefully the product's bugs will have been ironed out and less support will be needed).

Sometimes, the benefits are important enough to make a deal with a customer that otherwise pains the CFO of the start-up. In the 1970s, an MBA student at Wharton who had developed a time-shared computer program to automate the trust accounting process for banks started what became the SEI Corp. He wanted to commercialize the software and an associated support service for bank trust departments to use. His competition during that time was in-house accounting machines and manual calculations for the most part. Without his product (called Trust-Aid), when IBM declared a dividend, someone manually had to go into each different trust account to enter that event so it was accounted for correctly. Conceptually, adopting Trust-Aid should have been a very easy decision for any bank based on very high value in use. However, as the student quickly found out, no bank was going to put its "family jewels"—its trust accounts—onto a system that no one else had shown to be reliable and to actually work. He asked his teacher, one of this book's authors, for advice. The advice was simple: "You need to get a very credible reference account, and even if you have to give the software and service away for free, it'll be worth it." That is exactly what the student did to get his first customer. He gave it free for over a year to his first "customer." He was not very happy about not having any initial revenue for a year, but it was probably the only way the company (now with a market cap in the billions) would have gotten started.

It wasn't until that first customer had run the system for nine months without using the old manual system as a back up, that the student got his first paying customer (at still, reduced "charter rates"). The first customer was really only a credible reference after he had put his trust department "family jewels" in the care of the Trust-Aid software and service and had stopped using the old manual system. Even when the reference account had both systems running (with Trust-Aid running very successfully), he was not a credible or convincing reference site until he had demonstrated his own faith in the software and service.

Choosing Initial Reference Accounts

For those products or services that are very innovative or likely to be perceived as "risky," the choice of who to get as initial reference accounts can have a huge impact on how fast (or whether) the product is adopted by the market. For Trust-Aid, if the initial reference account had been a bank that other banks looked to for guidance on new technological innovations, the sales progress of Trust-Aid would have been much faster.

In most markets, there are individuals and entities that are known as early adopters and leaders in technology application. If these leaders are first to adopt your product, then the going will be much easier than if your first reference accounts are not respected as leaders. The medical market is probably the best defined in this dimension. For most new prescription drugs or new medical devices, who the first users are is crucial to whether they may become successful. Doctors have a "pecking order" of prestige and respectability. They will be much more likely to try a new innovation if it is first adopted by the physicians they perceive as highly influential in their field.

General Electric has been very successful in the MRI and CT Scanning businesses, not because they've had the best technology, but because they've had very strong relationships with the most influential doctors, hospitals, and health centers. The most influential people in the market always test their new machines. It is very hard for a competitor to enter the U.S. market with a new machine because most of these influential and respected early adopters are associated with General Electric (G.E.). For example, Elscint, an

Israeli-based competitor of G.E. with arguably better technology, has not been able to make a major dent in the U.S. market, because they have not been able to get the most influential people and institutions in the market to sacrifice their long-term relationship with G.E. G.E. has been doing all the right things to continue to cement their relationship with the highly respected market innovators. G.E. supports their research and conferences, puts them on advisory boards, and so on.

The Beta Process

Most products go through many revisions between the concept and final versions. The changes are often stimulated by real user feedback to the engineering and product management teams. The process that helps this to happen is the beta process. The terminology is in common use in engineering hardware and software areas, where the first versions of a product are called "alpha" versions, the first versions that can go to customers for testing are called *beta*, the almost final versions are called *release candidates*, and the final versions are called the *released product*.

At each stage, successively more users and/or customers have the product in use and are making comments to the product management team. This process is normally run by and of benefit to the engineering department. Properly managed, however, it can be a great help to the marketing of the product.

In today's Internet world, beta users provide the buzz discussed in Chapter 4, and amplify the presence once the service is launched openly to the world. Where beta testing was usually limited to a few customers, or a few dozen, there are now cases where the number of beta users is in the tens of thousands. Microsoft Windows 95 had over 100,000 beta users, and Netscape Communicator usually has a beta version and a shipping (frozen) version available for download most of the time.

When a customer agrees to join a beta program, they usually agree to spend some minimum amount of time using the product, to respond to questionnaires about the features and benefits of the product, and to be available for calls from the press or other customers. In return, their questions and problems should be dealt with at high priority, and they can gain visibility to their peer groups as thought leaders, and the psychic income of seeing their name in print in interviews and articles about the product.

Choosing the right customers is very important since they will not only influence the press, but provide the most cogent feedback at a key time when the offering may still be changed. Customers whose needs are not aligned with a majority of intended users could skew product features in an undesirable direction. In the software world, beta customers are often chosen from existing users of previous products. Such customers are already predisposed to a company, and can get the extra benefits of additional support and relationships to help if they have problems with any product.

On the Web, many offerings are completely new, and there is no customer tradition. In this case, one should make a list of the key target customers—be they Fortune 500 companies, Inc. 500 new comers, consumers of certain demographics, or others. One then networks into a decision maker who is willing to listen to the benefits of a new product, and convinces her that her company will benefit from being a first mover—not only through discounts, but also through having a several month advantage over any competitors. For consumer sites, there may be specific discounts, and the ability to say "I've been there first."

iExchange.com, a site that permits people to share stock market advice and rates them on the accuracy of their predictions, needed to beta test for two reasons. The first involved the usual issues of making sure the programming was properly done and that the servers could handle the loads. Second, in order for the site to be attractive to general users, there needed to be enough predictions, about enough stocks, to give interesting content to new users. As an idealab! company, iExchange.com first called on all the people in the idealab building (about 150) and asked them to post recommendations. The incentive offered was free pizza and T-shirts. After two weeks of building several thousand recommendations, these people were asked to virally expand the beta test to their friends and family members, by sending them e-mails promising prizes for their entries.

During this beta period, users were periodically asked for comments about the user interfaces, their interactions, and their overall comments about the site, including look and feel, mission, and effectiveness. Their movements through the site were tracked with software that could show each successive click and determine when they were leaving the site. All this information was fed to the product managers and developers each day, and changes were made to improve the length of time and number of page views per visit, as well as the overall performance of the site.

As you reach the later stages of the beta process, it is important to have critics, as well as friends, test the site or the new product. People with a real need and use for the product will provide a less filtered set of responses than those who are merely friends doing a favor. It is often the harshest critic who provides the spark for a feature change that turns her into a fan—and makes the site that much better for all other users.

For B2B products or services, finding initial customers may be more difficult. One has to convince them to try something that may not succeed, and hence could leave them stranded if they are not careful. And the growth may be much slower. This is why it is so important to choose influential innovators and early adopters to be the initial customers. It also is critical to market to them in the best way.

Marketing to the Initial Customers

Because the initial B2B customers will be those who are innovators and should be influencers, they may need to be marketed to differently then the more mainstream customers. It is very useful to ask the potential lead customers how they prefer to be treated. We have found that in some industries that are normally served by distribution intermediaries, such as resellers or manufacturers' representatives, that the innovators would prefer a different relationship—at least in the beginning. The innovators know they may be taking a risk in trying a new product or service. To mitigate that perceived risk, these innovators want to deal directly with the company without going through intermediaries. If you are dealing in such a situation, it is important to treat the customer the way she wants to be treated. You may have to either hire a direct salesforce if the number of innovative initial customers requires it, or as the entrepreneur, you and other senior managers may assume the sales role directly.

Geoffrey Moore, in his excellent book *Crossing the Chasm*, also recommends a small, top-level salesforce as a way to deal, in particular, with those innovators he terms "visionaries,"[1] to manage their expectations during the sales and initial usage process.

> Because controlling expectations is so crucial, the only practical way to do business with visionaries is through a small, top-level direct sales force. At the front end of the sales cycle, you need such a group to understand the visionaries' goals and give them confidence that your company can step up to those. In the middle of the sales cycle, you need to be extremely flexible about commitments as you begin to adapt to the visionaries' agenda. At the end, you need to be careful in negotiations, keeping the spark of the vision alive without committing to tasks that are unachievable within the time frame allotted. All of this implies a mature and sophisticated representative working on your behalf.[2]

This salesperson's role does not stop when the sale is finally closed. She must also make sure that whatever happens, the initial client's expectations are exceeded. The referral of these initial users is what the business will live on. If this initial salesperson is not a senior manager, this person should have direct authority from the CEO to do whatever is necessary to exceed this customer's expectations.

A very successful Israeli high-tech company had established a very nice North American business selling products and services to call centers through VARs and large equipment vendors. They had a different new product targeted toward security departments of large firms. The firm originally planned to use the same type of sales and distribution to introduce the new security product— VARs and large equipment vendors. However, after interviewing the potential innovators, the company had to change their initial marketing plan. The innovative potential initial customers were not receptive to dealing with intermediaries. They wanted to deal directly with the company. The company used their senior managers as direct salespeople and began a very successful rollout of its new, innovative, security product. If they had not asked their initial target customers how they wanted to be treated, they would have had significant problems in penetrating the market.

Partnering for Rollouts

When Intel or Microsoft announce a new product, they release a list of companies that are "supporting" the new platform or processor. These partners help validate the eventual success, and hence make it easier for a large company customer to take a chance. Once they know that others will be using it also, they feel less afraid of being left stranded, or of being unable to convince the supplier to fix the product if it isn't working.

Smaller companies can also improve their chances of success on a product launch, by including the testimonials of a number of key strategic and tactical partners in their announcement.

When Metastream.com prepared to launch its new Metastream 3D format, which allows low bandwidth streaming of 3D content on the internet, it wanted the credibility that strong partners bring to a new effort. Two months prior to launch, a concerted effort to sign up partners, who could participate in the launch event, was undertaken. Microsoft, Intel, and AOL all had an interest in seeing 3D proliferate on the Web. For Intel, it meant a need for more processing power, for Microsoft, a leg up for its Internet Explorer 5.5 browser, and for AOL, better e-commerce. In addition, a number of companies that wanted to use the technology on their Web sites, including Nike, Sony, and CBS, all agreed.

Each of the partners got strong press exposure, the ability to add to their own leadership and forward thinking images, and early use of the technology. MetaStream.com, because it was linked with such powerful partners, got coverage in the *New York Times,* on CNBC, and other prime media venues that probably wouldn't have covered the story, or featured it, because of the names associated with the launch.

The business development and technical organizations, rather than the straight marketing and salesforces, had to make the introductions and connections to the partners, since those organizations had to be convinced that the technology would succeed before they could approach their own marketing and public relations operations. The lead time for such endorsements is longer—typically two to three months—and it pays to create the relationships between your company and possible partners even sooner.

Summary

A strong product rollout can set the tone for success, and dramatically reduce the time needed to gain customer and market acceptance. Planning for this requires sufficient time prior to launch, choosing the best reference accounts, treating them well, and sufficient feedback from a well run beta program. Rolling out a Web site, or Web-based business, can be done more rapidly, but still requires testing and trials to see how consumers react to each piece of the Web site.

CHAPTER 7

Entrepreneurial Sales Management

All the elements of the marketing mix should be derived from the marketing driven strategy of the entrepreneurial organization. The salesforce decisions must be consistent and derived from the positioning and segmentation decisions that are the core of strategy. In particular, the positioning and segmentation usually imply a role for the salesforce in the marketing mix as part of the product's position and as a mechanism for implementing part of the market segmentation targeting.

For example, the Tandems East firm uses the owner, Mel Kornbluh, as its prime salesperson. His perceived expertise and experience with tandem bicycles, and willingness to satisfy customers are the bulk of his offering to potential customers. He also performs part of his firm's targeting functions by asking qualification questions during his first interactions with potential customers. On the other hand, some e-commerce companies have no role for personal sales in their marketing mix. Amazon.com customers have no interaction with any human salespeople when they make their purchase evaluations. However, the information and very personalized software Amazon.com has developed imitates what might happen if a customer went into a good bookstore and

133

asked an experienced salesperson for information and recommendations. Dell Computer uses a mix of online sales and personal sales depending on customer preferences. Some Dell customers feel more comfortable interacting with a real person and value the salesperson's perceived problem-solving ability. Some bigger Dell customers feel that they deserve special prices and/or have special circumstances that need a personal touch.

The question the entrepreneur needs to answer is: Given my positioning and segmentation strategy, what perceived value needs to be added by a personal salesforce in order to most productively implement the strategy? If your thinking has been clear and your research has been good in the segmentation and positioning process, the role of the salesforce is usually obvious.

Once the role of the salesforce has been determined, then the other salesforce decisions are easier to make. This chapter will follow the logic as outlined in Figure 7.1.

The Role of the Salesforce in the Marketing Mix

Your creativity is really the only limitation to alternative ways a salesforce can possibly contribute to your perceived product offering. There are a number of traditional roles that the salesforce may fulfill. The salesforce may find leads and qualify those leads

Figure 7.1   Entrepreneurial salesforce issues.

to determine if they would get value from your offering. These roles can obviously be fulfilled by other marketing mix elements such as the Web or direct mail. You need to evaluate what will work best for your venture. Possibly experimentation would make sense to test some of the options.

Other salesforce roles impact how the potential and current customer may perceive your offering. Many salesforces are consultants to their customers. They solve their customers' problems by recommending appropriate products and possibly showing the customers how to use them. The apocryphal stories of medical equipment salespeople helping with medical operations are actually true. The best medical equipment suppliers have as a key asset well-trained salespeople who know at least as much as the orthopedic surgeons about how to use their equipment. The salespeople are a big part of what the surgeons are buying.

Similarly, in the financial services marketplace, the salesperson can provide a big part of the perceived value of the financial firm's product offering. Stockbrokers may in fact be what many customers perceive they are buying when the brokers are performing advisory services. For this reason, many customers will switch brokerage firms when their broker moves to a different firm. The customers perceive more value from their broker than from the firm's research and investment products.

The salesperson may also negotiate prices with customers as in the traditional auto dealership. Other roles include following up after the sale to make sure that the customer's expectations are exceeded and to solve any problems that arise by being an advocate for the customer with the entrepreneurial venture. In general, a good salesperson-customer relationship can generate trust and loyalty that can be a very important, competitive advantage.

In the age of electronic commerce, many firms are finding that the role of their salesforce needs to change. For VWR Scientific Products, the salesperson in many cases no longer actually takes orders. She used to drag around catalogs and order forms and would sell replacement and new laboratory supplies and equipment. She would also keep the customer apprised of the order status. All of that work is automated. That salesperson makes a sale by convincing her client to go to the VWR Web site to place an order, rather than to a competitor's. The VWR salesperson's role is most importantly to build customer trust and loyalty. The salesperson helps to customize each client's VWR Web site to reflect corporate agreements or negotiated pricing. Most importantly, the salesperson is on site to help if any problems occur and to give personal service. As Mark Quigley, a VWR regional sales manager said, "We still like to give personal service. . . . The customer still likes to see a body."[1]

The most obvious and very important role of the salesperson is sometimes neglected. Someone has to ask for the order and close the sale. It's amazing how many entrepreneurs forget that many customers will not part with their funds without a salesperson asking them for the order. Based on the logic of Figure 7.1, once the role of the salesperson is determined, you need to examine whether you want to outsource the function to representatives or hire your own direct salesforce. In our survey, 82 percent of the Inc. 500 CEOs had a direct salesforce versus 56 percent of the non-Inc. group. Of the Inc. 500 group, 12 percent used an indirect salesforce versus 9.3 percent of the non-Inc. group.

Should We Outsource to Representatives or Go Direct?

Many entrepreneurs (and larger corporations also) neglect to even evaluate the option of outsourcing part or all of their sales function. In many circumstances, an independent representative can fulfill the salesforce role better and more efficiently than can a direct salesforce. Before we look at some of the tradeoffs, we should quickly outline what representatives are and what they are not.

Typically, manufacturer's representatives (Reps) are independent companies that sell on a commission basis and bear all of their own sales expenses. They are generally a local or regional entity with a defined territory that they cover. They generally do not carry competing lines and their representation contracts with their principals are not usually guaranteed for a long term. Their role is to either replace or in some cases, supplement the direct salesforce. Reps are not a substitute for a distributor, however. They do not hold inventory or take title, invoice or ship, or take credit.

The decision on whether or to what extent to use reps depends on tradeoffs of a few advantages and disadvantages reps bring to the table. These advantages and disadvantages have to be interpreted in terms of the role the salesforce should play in the positioning and segmentation of the company and its products. Let's first look at the advantages.

Rep Advantages

The assets reps have are relationships with their customers. In many cases, they have been providing their customers a number of products for many years. The good reps have achieved positions of perceived trust and reliability with their customers and understand their customer's needs very well. The rep may be able to achieve synergy by bundling your product with other products she's already selling. Also, because of the economies of combining products, a rep can typically call economically on smaller buyers or call more often on a single buyer than can the typical direct salesperson. Because their asset is their customer relationships, reps typically are more permanent and have less turnover than direct forces. Reps also pay more than direct salespeople and may retain their salesforces longer. Reps are also likely to be pretty nimble, sales focused, and very conscious of their sales costs. Reps also add a lot of flexibility—their low overhead, almost all variable costs make it easy to forecast sales costs, and provide downside cost protection if revenue is lower than anticipated. It is also much easier to terminate reps than an internal salesforce.

Rep Disadvantages

However, reps also have disadvantages: Because they have many masters (principals) whose products they must juggle, getting focus on your product may be difficult. The reps may also be too diversified to devote appropriate attention to the subset of their accounts that find value in your products. Some products may not have existing rep networks that are appropriate for your product. In other cases, the really good reps may already be taken by a competitor. The biggest tradeoff that needs to be evaluated, however, is the loss of control that is part of being with a rep.

The Control Issue

When your firm directly employs the salesperson, theoretically you can direct the salesperson to do whatever you wish. However, in actuality, there's a continuum of realized control that depends on the kind of compensation and supervision system the entrepreneur chooses (Figure 7.2).

Figure 7.2 underscores the relation between compensation method and the ability to control the salesperson. If your salespeople are on a straight commission with a low or nonexistent base salary, they will also not be easy to control. If you suggest a salesperson compensated by commission do something she does not feel will add to her commissions, she will not want to do it. The rep is even harder to control because she has many masters and possibly conflicting activities she can do for each principal. On the other hand, if you pay the salesperson some kind of base salary, you can expect him or her to do some noncommission activities in return for his or her salary.

Control is important depending on the product positioning and segmentation and the appropriate role of the salesforce. If your salesforce plan requires activities that have unspecified payoff, then rep organizations (or straight commission) are probably not appropriate. If you have a product that requires single-minded dedication, then a rep may not be appropriate, but straight commission might be a viable option.

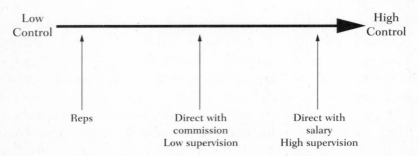

Figure 7.2   Control continuums.

What Situations Favor Direct versus Rep?

A very interesting study by Anderson[2] analyzed how 13 firms in the electronic components industry decided on the rep versus direct decision in 159 different sales district/product combinations. These companies had a broad range of products from commodities to new, innovative, glamour products. The companies used reps when in doubt between rep and direct and they used reps for the normal, nondescript sales situations. However, there were many situations in which companies went direct, including:

1. Situations where it's difficult to evaluate the salesperson's results "by the numbers," for example:
   a. Measures of sales results are inaccurate.
   b. It's difficult to assign credit for the sale because of multiple influences on the customer.
   c. Performance means much more than current sales, for example, there are long-term implications to short-term sales.

      One example of these situations might include selling pharmaceutical products to managed care organizations. Since independent doctors who may belong to more than one managed care organization may prescribe drugs, the influence of the managed care organization may be tenuous. However, if a drug is not one that is preferred by the managed care organization, it may be more difficult for some of a doctor's patients to fill a prescription for your drug.

2. Situations where product and applications knowledge are difficult to learn, important, and/or complex. These include:
   a. Highly complex, unusual, or difficult to understand or explain products.
   b. Highly complex, unusual, or difficult to understand or explain applications.

      Mainframe computers, enterprise software, consulting, and corporate legal services are typically this type of situation. The "rainmakers" of legal and consulting firms are the firms' direct salesforces.

3. Situations with highly confidential information in which sales-people come to learn sensitive information about their company and customers.

4. Situations where support activities are critical, for example, marketing research, trade show participation, after sales service, engineering support before the sale.

Choosing Reps

The decision on which reps to choose is very important and should not be taken lightly. What you are buying with the rep is market reputation, relationships, and positions with complementary products. There are two criteria to tradeoff when choosing a rep. The first criterion is the rep's market position—is he or she top in the market or does he represent the less attractive products? The second criterion is whether the rep will have enough resources and use them to push your product or service versus the other products he sells. The best reps may not take enough time to push your new product, especially if the new product is small compared to the reps' current line. On the other hand, if your new product is really innovative and valuable, it may be used by the rep to gain more access to his target accounts by introducing accounts to a new, valuable product.

How can you efficiently get the information to make these tradeoffs? The way is similar to other recommendations in this book. *Talk to market participants.* Specifically, as part of the concept testing for a new product or service, ask also about which reps the target market prefers to buy from. Most market participants are quite willing to recommend people they prefer to buy from. Finding out how well the rep will push your product, if you choose him or her, is not so easy. Finding out how excited a rep firm will be with your product is comparable to finding out if the end customer will buy your product. Concept testing can be very helpful. You should interview rep principals from alternative rep firms and show them your product, tentative sales aids, and any possible advertisements for the product. You want to present your product to the rep in its most positive light. Then monitor the rep's reaction and compare across all the reps you interview. Your ideal rep is one that is very excited about how your product will help the rep's business, and a rep who is highly valued as a resource by the marketplace for your product. The entrepreneur's judgment after having talked both with alternative reps and with a sample of market participants should provide a very productive rep choice.

An important caveat: The rep choice is crucial to the financial viability of many businesses and should not be taken lightly. Above all, choosing a rep should *not* be done opportunistically. *Do not choose the first rep that approaches you.* It is almost always very productive to invest some time and money to find the best rep. Even when time and money are very scarce for the entrepreneur, it makes sense to get information *from market participants* before making a decision like choosing a rep that has very long-term and pronounced effect on your venture.

Effective Rep Management

If you have decided to use reps, they will not be successful without you thinking very carefully about how they will be managed. Reps are another group that needs marketing attention. Just like the end customer, you need to understand what makes the rep tick—what her objectives and goals are and how your product offering can add perceived value for the rep. Anderson, Lodish, and Weitz studied how 71 independent reps actually allocated their time to their principals' products.[3] They found that, in general (and no surprise) reps allocated time to maximize their commission income from their principals. However, reps also deviated from solely resource allocations that maximized their commission income to favor principals who they perceived had similar goals, good communication, and mutual trust. Reps also favored principals who had active involvement in the rep's activities. The authors' findings imply some specific tactics that help obtain more of a rep's attention:

1. Make your products easier for the rep to sell. Make its price/ perceived value better for the end user. Provide sales training for reps. Develop and implement promotions toward the end user that the rep can use to make his job more efficient.

2. Increasing commission rates will increase the sales effort toward your product, but it will have diminishing returns.

3. Reps favor products that are synergistic with other products in the rep's portfolio.

4. Principals should develop very trusting relationships with their reps.

5. Principals should improve communication through recognition programs, product training, consultation with the reps, as well as by informing reps of plans, explicitly detailing objectives, and providing positive feedback.

6. Principals that have a hands-off approach to reps lose time for their products.

7. Even interfering in the management of the rep with negative feedback results in greater time for your product.[4]

Rep Management and the Perceived Value Proposition

The struggling entrepreneur should be noticing that many of the above tactics cost either money (e.g., end user promotions, sales training), or margin points (e.g., improving the price/value relationship, increasing commission rates). If you have an excellent business plan that has a positioning strategy that succeeds in creating incremental perceived value to the end user compared to the competition, then you should have room to share some of that value with your outsourced intermediaries in the channel.

Franklin Electronic Publishers, Inc. manufactures electronic handheld reference tools—spelling correctors, dictionaries. For the past 15 years, they have successfully used reps to sell their product in the consumer electronics channel. Especially when they began as an entrepreneurial company with little resources, but a new unique product, the Spelling Ace spelling corrector, reps were a crucial part of the marketing plan. Because the Spelling Ace was able to be sold to the consumer at prices that gave very good manufacturing margins, Franklin was able to share some of those high margins with their reps and their retailers. The reps got very good commissions for selling the products and the retailers got better margins than

Entrepreneurial Sales Management   143

comparable products that competed for scarce shelf and display space.

This Franklin example underscores the importance of including all elements of the marketing mix as part of the initial business plan. The positioning and segmentation decisions have a big impact on the viability of the venture partly because they have a big impact on what is possible for other elements of the marketing mix. The management of reps is only one element in which the positioning and segmentation decisions have a crucial impact.

Personal versus Telephone versus the Web and other Nonpersonal Sales

It is not obvious that a personal salesforce is appropriate for all situations. The telephone, the Web, and other activities may be more efficient for accomplishing needed tasks in the marketing and sales process. The entrepreneur should first determine the tasks and activity that are required for each step in the sales process. Then she should evaluate the costs and the benefit of alternative ways to accomplish those sales tasks. Tables 7.1 and 7.2 show the evaluation of two alternative sales processes for a venture. Table 7.1 evaluates a field sales-oriented sales process and Table 7.2 evaluates how the same process might be accomplished by telemarketing instead of field sales. These are disguised real examples.

Sales Activity	Prospects Remaining	Delivery Vehicle	Elapsed Time (wks)	Activity Cost ($)	Total Cost ($)
1. New lead	100	Mail/telephone	0	25	2,500
2. Literature fulfillment	100	Mail	1	10	3,500
3. Quality prospect	100	Telephone	2	15	5,000
4. Initial meeting	30	Field visit	4	200	11,000
5. Follow-up call	20	Telephone	5	15	11,200
6. Demonstration	10	Field visit	7	250	13,700
7. Proposal	5	Overnight service	8	100	14,200
8. Additional follow-up	3	Telephone	12	50	14,350
9. Approval/purchase	3	Telephone	16	10	14,380
10. Postsale follow-up	3	Telephone	20	30	14,470

Table 7.1 Field Sales-Oriented Sales Process

Sales Activity	Prospects Remaining	Delivery Vehicle	Elapsed Time (wks)	Activity Cost ($)	Total Cost ($)
1. New lead	100	Mail/telephone	0	25	2,500
2. Initial literature	100	Mail	1	10	3,500
3. Quality call	100	Telephone	2	15	5,000
4. Second literature	30	Mail	3	10	5,300
5. Consult/sales call	30	Telephone	4	25	5,800
6. Payback worksheet	20	Telephone	6	5	5,850
7. Configuration call	10	Telephone	6	10	5,950
8. Proposal	5	Overnight service	8	100	6,450
9.–12. Additional follow-up	3	Telephone	12	100	6,750
13. Approval/purchase	3	Telephone	16	10	6,780
14. Postsale follow-up	3	Telephone	20	30	6,870

Table 7.2   Telemarketing-Oriented Sales Process

In Table 7.1, the entrepreneur has estimated the sales funnel for her typical personal sales process. Starting with 100 prospects, she estimates how many will remain after each stage in the process. For example, of each 100 prospects who have been qualified, 30 will remain as prospects after the telephone qualification call. She also estimates the elapsed time for each activity and the costs of each activity. It is usually pretty easy to get good estimates for the timing and costs of the various activities and sales calls. The most difficult estimate is the success rate for each activity, that is, what fraction of the people in the funnel will proceed to the next stage. For example, above there is an assumption that 5 out of 10, or 50 percent of prospects will ask for a proposal after a demonstration. Before one begins their business, it will be pretty difficult to get good estimates for that kind of response percentage. However, once the business is going, it is conceptually easy to measure these percentages by keeping track of the number of people in the funnel at different stages, their treatment by the sales process, and the fraction who go on to the next stage after each task is performed. The challenge is to keep track of the data in the middle of launching a new product or service.

Notice that in Table 7.2, there are different activities in the telemarketing oriented sales process. The funnel also has different costs and different fractions progressing from stage to stage.

However, if the assumptions are reasonably correct, for this case, the telemarketing oriented sales process will be much more efficient for accomplishing the sales process. The personal sales approach may convert more prospects per 100, but it costs over 50 percent more to get each completed sale. Only if the number of prospects is very limited does it make sense to use a personal sales approach for this example.

What these examples should illustrate is how important it is to determine all of the stages of the sales process, and then to estimate the costs and benefits of performing them by different vehicles. In many cases, it will be very difficult to construct funnels like Tables 7.1 and 7.2 with no sales experience. What then makes sense is, as you begin your operations, to *experiment* with the sales process alternatives that make a priori sense. As the sales process is performed, keep track of the number of prospects in the funnel for each stage along with elapsed costs and timing. After a suitable length of time, you should be able to infer which approaches to the sales process are most efficient and use those on an ongoing basis.

It is very important to evaluate many options for accomplishing the sales process. Not every prospect should necessarily be put through the same sales process. Some market segments may respond differently to different sales processes. Depending on the costs and potential value, in many cases, it makes sense to experiment with different sales processes for different market segments. Again, depending on the circumstances, some potential prospects may wish to choose the sales process that they prefer.

Indymac Mortgage Holdings has developed technology to automate the underwriting and risk-based pricing process for home mortgages. The technology is being distributed and sold in two ways to capitalize on two types of consumers that the Indymac management has defined: low tech + high touch, and high tech + low touch. The first segment is much more comfortable with a personal intermediary to help them apply for and go through the home mortgage purchase process. So a mortgage broker (personal salesperson) sits with the client and types information about the proposed loan and the loan applicant. Within 5 minutes, the

Indymac e-MITS system comes back with an underwriting decision and a price for the mortgage that has been uniquely determined for the potential purchaser based on his or her credit history, and so on. The system also prints out right at the computer, all of the closing documents that will be needed for the loan to be closed.

The same e-MITS technology is used in Loanworks.com, the direct to consumer Web site that Indymac has introduced for the other high tech + low touch segment. The Web site performs almost the exact same functions as the technology available on the Web for the mortgage brokers, but it is presented directly to consumers who feel confident enough to apply for and close on a mortgage without relying on a mortgage broker intermediary. These customers get to pay less for their mortgages because they are not paying the sales commissions for the mortgage brokers.

Many other creative entrepreneurial marketers have also realized that one sales/distribution system may not fit all of their customers. Just as product and service offerings should be tailored to the needs of market segments, so should the sales and distribution process that is a part of what the end consumer finally perceives. Barnes and Noble did the same thing as Indymac. They sell the same books at stores with personal assistance and over the Web at BarnesandNoble.com. Their competitor, Borders, did not take advantage of this segmentation opportunity and lost much potential business to Amazon.com and BarnesandNoble.com.

Salesforce Size, Deployment, and Organization

If you have decided to use a personal salesforce, a number of questions quickly surface. How big should the force be and how should it be organized and deployed? The conceptual answer to these questions is easy. A salesforce is like any other investment the entrepreneur makes. If adding resources to the salesforce is the most profitable place to use the scarce capital, and if the use is more profitable then putting the money in the bank, then the funds should be added to the salesforce. Funds should be added until it is no longer the most profitable place to put capital. The salesforce is the right size when the "last person added" brought in more of a return on investment than any other investment opportunity.

In many cases, the appropriate salesforce size can be dictated by the market segment(s) that are being targeted and the costs and incremental benefits associated with the role of the salesforce. In many cases, a salesperson is a necessary part of what the channel expects from the entrepreneur. For example, if you expect to sell through retailers such as department stores or mass merchandisers, these firms have expectations about terms of sales and service from their suppliers. As a small, entrepreneurial organization, you will not typically be able to change the customary way in which other suppliers have set the retailer's expectations. Interviewing buyers from the retailers as well as salespeople (or reps) who service the retailers can get you enough information to roughly estimate the sales time associated with the various activities that are required by the potential customers. You can then also estimate the incremental revenue associated with those activities. It's then straightforward to calculate the marginal revenue and marginal costs of this salesforce activity.

For other sales situations, it makes more sense to evaluate the activities by estimating directly the impact of sales calls on the revenue of clients and/or prospects. For example, what would happen to the revenue of a typical customer of type A if we called four times per quarter instead of twice? This kind of question should be asked for alternative levels of salesforce size and deployment levels that you are evaluating. Once the revenue associated with the alternative levels of sales efforts has been estimated, then the incremental revenues and incremental costs can be applied to roughly determine the appropriate salesforce effort to use toward each type of client and prospect.

There are three ways to estimate the sales response to alternative call frequencies. Judgment of the salesperson along with her manager (who may be the entrepreneur) has been shown to be better than deploying salespeople without considering sales response to different levels of call effort. By evaluating judgments of the sales impacts of different call effort levels to different segments of accounts, it is straightforward to allocate time to those segments where it adds the most incremental profit contribution, and then continue to add time to that segment and/or other segments until the incremental return does not justify the salesforce costs. Before the business begins operations, judgment is probably the only way to determine the best salesforce size along with some guidelines on deployment over account segments.

Survey Results on Determining Salesforce Size

The Inc. 500 CEOs gravitated toward two methods—47 percent used forecasted sales and average revenues per salesperson and 35 percent used gut-feel. Of the non-Inc. group, 16 percent used both of these methods. Only 5.9 percent of the Inc. 500 and none of the non-Inc. group used forecasted incremental revenues to compare with incremental costs.

Naturally Occurring Salesforce Experiments

Once the venture has begun and the sales process has begun, the entrepreneur can evaluate any naturally occurring experiments that may have happened. These naturally occurring experiments happen when different accounts in the same segment get different amounts of sales effort. If the entrepreneur has planned her information system to keep sales as well as salespeople call reports, she can evaluate to what extent different levels of salesforce effort have seemed to cause sales changes. The problem with this procedure is that the salesforce may be choosing who to spend more or less effort on within a segment based on other factors such as prior relationships or specific knowledge about that account's situation. The analysis may attribute sales changes to the wrong causes. The most accurate, unbiased estimates come from the third way of getting sales response to alternative levels of sales effort—experiments.

Instead of letting naturally occurring changes happen to salesforce effort levels on accounts, it can be very valuable to *randomly assign* different levels of effort to different accounts within a segment. If there really is a random assignment of different levels of sales effort to accounts, then other possible causes are mitigated by the randomization. The same concerns and issues for designing experiments that we describe for advertising decisions are also appropriate for salesforce experiments (see Chapter 9).

Deployment with Limited Salesforce Size

Many entrepreneurs do not have the luxury of evaluating many different levels of salesforce sizes and appropriate deployment levels as we described. They are very limited in resources and cannot afford to have many salespeople. In these cases, it is crucial to "skim the cream." Using the judgmental method described above, the entrepreneur must only spend her salesforce effort where it contributes the highest amount of incremental revenue and profit contribution. However, keeping track of the sales effort and associated incremental sales generated from it, can be an excellent way to show a source of financing what to expect if more resources were made available for increasing salesforce effort.

Travel costs and entertainment expenses also need to be considered when the size and salesforce resource decisions are made. If the location of some accounts will necessitate extra trips, then these costs should be prorated over the accounts to be called on during the trips. The salesforce organization decision will also impact travel costs if it means that different people will be calling on different accounts in the same geographical area.

Salesforce Organization and Travel Costs

Salesforce organization generally relates to markets and geography. The trade-off of most alternative organizations is conceptually simple. Is the specialization of sales effort achieved by having salespeople specialize in one or more market segments more beneficial to the firm than the increased costs associated with the specialization? The increased costs of segment specialization are typically travel costs and the opportunity costs of time spent traveling. For small entrepreneurial companies with their own salesforces, the organization that is appropriate is usually obvious. If there is only one target market, then a geographical sales organization is the only reasonable option. A geographical sales organization has territories that are geographically determined, with each salesperson covering accounts in one territory. If there is more than one target segment, another possible organization is to have a salesforce for each segment. Each segment salesforce then would have its own geographical organization. It would then be possible to have more than one salesperson covering the same geographical area with each salesperson calling on accounts in different segments. The more specialized the salesforce is, the larger geographical area each salesperson's territory will cover.

Compensation

Matching Incentives

If you remember one idea from this salesforce chapter, it should be this one: People (and especially salespeople) do what they think will make them the most money for the time they spend at their jobs. Your compensation system should make sure that you and your salespeople have *matching incentives.* If you both are trying to do the same thing, then it's difficult to get into situations in which your salespeople do the wrong thing. The appropriate compensation also depends on the role of the salesperson. For example, if the salesperson has some control over the price she charges, then the compensation should have the salespeople negotiate as good a price as you, the entrepreneur, would negotiate. Auto dealers are classic examples of this type of compensation. The salespeople at most car dealerships who negotiate a price with each consumer have a commission that is based, not on the sold car's sale price, but on the gross margin (sale price – variable costs) for the car. If the commission were on just the sales price, the salesperson would likely be selling cars to maximize revenue by selling more cars at the lowest price she could quote.

This same argument is very pertinent to situations in which your salesforce is selling more than one product. If each product has quite different contribution margins, you want the salesperson to be incented, not on revenue, but on contribution margin (revenue – variable costs). In these multiproduct situations, the entrepreneur does not have to actually share her gross margins with the salesforce. All the salesforce needs to know (and have incentives based on) is the relative profitability of one product versus another. The entrepreneur can have sales compensation based on points for each product. The points just need to be proportionally correct; that is, if product A has 4 points per sales dollar, and product B, 2 points, then product A should have twice as much gross margin per sales dollar as product B. The salespeople don't have to know the exact margin figures to allocate their effort to where they will get the most margin per hour of their time. Many firms have not compensated their salespeople in this way and have foregone some profit by not treating revenue differently from different products. In extreme cases, firms have given sales awards to the top revenue producing salesperson. After some analysis, it was determined that that person was actually *losing money* for his company. He was selling products that were not profitable after his sales costs were considered.

The salespeople will visit customers who are perceived to be most likely to value the products they can sell. If the salespeople are trying to find accounts that will most likely buy the products with high contribution margin, then the salesperson and the firm have matching incentives and the salespeople will naturally gravitate to the accounts that will be most profitable for the firm.

Outback Steakhouse—Perfectly Matched Incentives

Outback Steakhouse has been very successful in an extremely competitive restaurant industry. One reason for their success is how they compensate their store managers. Each store manager invests $25,000 in "his or her store." For that investment, they get 10 percent of the profits that store generates. These store managers report to regional managers who have made similar investments in return for a piece of their region's profits. The incentives here are matched perfectly. These managers will try to use the resources in their control to maximize their income—that is exactly proportional to the income of the Outback Steakhouse Corporation. By maximizing their income, the managers are simultaneously maximizing the income of their "parent" corporation. This compensation scheme is a very creative blend of some aspects of franchising with corporate control. If the managers leave, there are prearranged values for buying back the manager's equity interest in the restaurant.

Incentives versus Control versus Time Horizons

The Outback example points out one concern about matching incentives. Profit can be short term or longer term. You as an entrepreneur may have different time horizons in mind than members of your salesforce. Even if you both are trying to maximize profits, a salesperson may want to maximize short-term profits, whereas you, the entrepreneur may be more concerned with longer-term profits and building the value of the company. Some salesforce activities may be very helpful to long-term profits, but take away from short-term profits. These include market research and call reporting. Our experience is that it is easier to have some portion of the fixed component of the salesperson's compensation specified as payment for these kinds of activities. You thus tell the salesforce that they are being paid to do market research and/or fill out call reports. Most salespeople will not see the value to their future income of these kinds of activities and need to perceive that they are being directly paid to perform them.

It is important to set these expectations at the beginning of the relationship. If the salesperson is told when he is hired, that part of his base salary is for call reports and other paper work, he will feel that this becomes part of his job for which he is being adequately compensated. The base salary can also be used as a way to control the salesperson to do activities that may not be maximizing his short-term income. You may want the salesperson to call on some accounts that will not be ready to buy now, but you need their feedback for the next generation product or service design.

Just as our discussion of reps had control as an issue, the same issues occur in compensation. The more straight commission you have, the lower your control. Our experience has shown that for many businesses, it makes sense to have some element of base salary as a justification for requesting the salespeople do activities that may not be maximizing their short-term commission income. Many of the suggestions throughout this book for continually experimenting with different elements of the marketing mix will be thwarted if the salesforce will not cooperate. By its nature, experimentation will show that some activities are more productive than others. You don't want your salesforce to feel that they are being penalized if they happen to be in one experimental treatment that doesn't perform as well as another treatment. You need to set these expectations at the outset of the relationship. You should tell new salespeople that they are joining an entrepreneurial, adapting, learning, and continually experimenting organization. By their nature, some experiments will work better than others will, and the salespeople should expect that. If you couch their base salary as compensation for these learning and experimental activities, you will avoid possible problems later on.

Compensation for New versus Existing Customers, a Possible Festering Problem

Many entrepreneurs will start their businesses with a straight commission salesforce. This option has the lowest variable costs. If more than one product is involved, the commission rate should be proportional to the gross profit margin of each product. However, another phenomenon is happening with straight commission salesforces that most entrepreneurs don't realize until it has begun to affect their growth and profitability. By then, it is typically too late to solve easily.

If the commission is high enough, and the product potential large enough, a straight commission sales incentive plan can result in amazing salesforce effort and motivation—up to a point. The first salesperson to sell your product will typically work hard to open up many accounts in her territory. She will view this as an opportunity to be entrepreneurial and develop these accounts as her "own little business." However, in her mind she has an idea of what she needs to make in order to "make a good living." Once the salesperson has gotten the territory to the point where her commissions generate this "good living," the salesperson will then tend to coast with her established accounts and protect them from any management gerrymandering.

It is usually much easier to maintain accounts than to get new ones. The straight commission salesperson will get to a point where she will be content to just maintain her current accounts and not spend much effort generating new accounts. The above scenario has been validated as typical by over 1,000 sales managers that have attended the Wharton School's executive program in salesforce management.

One solution to the problem is to have different rates of commission for generating new accounts then for maintaining the business. The commission rate would thus be higher for the first year's business with an account and lower on succeeding years. Alternatively, some firms will have a different commission rate on sales until last year's level is reached and a different level on sales higher than last years.

The Shadow Broadcasting Services

The Shadow Broadcasting Services story, in which one author (Lodish) was a minority investor and advisor, provides examples of a number of the concepts we discuss in this book. Not only are the salesforce compensation issues faced by Shadow illustrative of the discussed concepts, but the business model and product offering decisions applied some of this book's other paradigms.

Shadow's Initial Business Model

Shadow Broadcast Services began as an entrepreneurial organization in New York and Chicago. The business model at first was to gather traffic information using planes, helicopters, police scanners, part-time drivers, and cell phone messages from citizen volunteers. This information was then synthesized, cross-validated, and then broadcast from Shadow's studio to a radio station over high-quality communications lines. Even though Shadow's announcers were remote to the radio station, to the radio listener the Shadow announcer sounded just like he was at the station. The Shadow announcer could banter with the disk jockeys, and participate as a member of the station's broadcast team. Depending on the station, the Shadow announcer could either say he was giving a "Shadow Traffic" report, or be reporting from the "WXXX Traffic Center." One Shadow announcer could be the traffic reporter for a number of stations. Depending on the frequency each station wanted to broadcast traffic reports, a Shadow announcer could handle as many as 10 stations.

The beginning business model was borrowed from Shadow's main competitor, Metro Traffic that operated in over 30 major U.S. markets, almost as a monopoly in the traffic business.

Shadow's beginning business model was to barter the traffic reports for advertising time in the traffic reports that Shadow would sell to advertisers. The Shadow advertising was typically a 10-second spot read at the end of the traffic report along with a lead in. The lead in was typically something like "this report brought to you by Chrysler." Shadow obtained most of its revenue from selling advertising time.

The attractiveness to stations of Shadow was that they didn't have to gather and report their own traffic information. Shadow took advantage of economies of scale by sharing the gathering and reporting costs over a number of stations. However, the way revenues actually occurred showed very insightful entrepreneurial marketing thinking. Another way Shadow and its competitor could have generated revenue was by selling the traffic reports to the stations for cash. There were very different perceptions of radio station managers and Shadow of the value of the 10-second spots that Shadow ended up selling. To stations, they did not feel that they could get much value from selling 10-second spots, when all of the other advertising time on their stations was sold to advertisers in units of 30 and 60 seconds. Stations were also becoming part of big, highly leveraged entities that were valued by the financial markets in terms of multiples of their broadcast cash flow. Cash flow was "king" to most radio station general managers. Thus, paying out cash had a high negative value to most station managers. They would much rather pay for the traffic reports with bartered airtime that they felt they would have difficulty in selling.

Another variable to this perceived value calculation is that to the advertiser, 10-second advertisements were perceived as much more valuable when they were broadcast on a network of stations in an area versus on one or two stations. The 10-second traffic ads were great for announcing temporary promotions or very simple announcements of new features or items. Timeliness of the traffic ads as well as being able to reach large numbers of people quickly was potentially very valuable to advertisers. Shadow was able to deliver a network of stations in a city that an individual station could not match. Thus, what Shadow was bartering to the stations had different perceived value to each party—Shadow and each radio station. Both parties perceived that they were getting better value than the other side in the barter deals.

Another factor that helped Shadow in the beginning was some research they had by chance come across. This research showed that listeners paid more attention to traffic broadcasts than to any other element of a radio show. The research was actually done by a firm that was trying to determine listener preferences for all program content—mainly different music and disk jockey patter, and so on. The firm would play recordings of yesterday's radio program and ask respondents to turn a dial to indicate how much attention they were paying to what they were hearing. The dial went from 1 to 10. The researcher could then monitor the average attention "paid" to various elements of the station's programming. For different disk jockeys, their patter would get scores of anywhere from 2 to 9, the music would also get highly varied scores from 1 to 10, and the normal 30 or 60 second commercials would typically get low scores of 1 to 3. The news, weather, and sports segments were moderately well attended. Scores ranged from 3 to 8 depending on the content. The amazing thing to Shadow was that *yesterday's* traffic report always got an attention score of between 8 and 10! Because most radio listening is done in the car, evidently most listeners are conditioned to pay attention to the traffic reports as they come on. It was useful for the Shadow managers to know that their medium was likely to work for advertisers much more efficiently than the typical radio spot.

An interesting aside—over time, some of the stations began to perceive the high value of 10-second ads delivered with traffic information. These more entrepreneurial station managers started to keep some of the traffic spots to sell themselves and began to charge Shadow and Metro fees for the privilege of providing traffic services to their stations. The differences in perceived value of the 10-second spots acted like many other competitive advantages, they lose value over time if not enhanced in some way.

Shadow's Subsequent Business Model

Shadow management innovated the Shadow product in two major ways. Both innovations had much to do with entrepreneurial marketing thinking about differentially perceived value to different market segments. The first innovation was a response to the increased cost pressure the radio stations were facing. One source of costs was their gathering and reporting of local news, sports, and weather. If Shadow used its already existing infrastructure to not only gather and report traffic information, but also to gather and report local news, sports, and weather, it could do it at a much lower cost per report than could a typical station. Some Shadow announcers would do traffic on one station, local news on another, and sports on still another. Shadow also bartered the new news, sports, and weather reports for 10-second spots instead of selling them to the stations. The stations again perceived this as lower end cost compared to paying for the service. To Shadow, it gave them an even bigger, higher reach network to sell to advertisers with lower incremental costs for the inventory. Because the infrastructure for reporting news, sports, and weather was already in place, the incremental costs per spot of advertising inventory from providing the newer services were lower.

The second innovation did not work out exactly as anticipated, but was pretty valuable. A major expense to Shadow was the helicopters used to gather and report the information. Not only were the helicopters expensive (over $300 per hour), but also they could not be used in inclement weather—just when you really need them. Shadow management evaluated the costs and benefits of installing remote controlled video cameras that could zoom in to observe all the major traffic arteries in a city. If the cameras could replace helicopters, it seemed that the payback on the camera investment would be less than six months! A bonus was that the cameras were to be available 24 hours per day, seven days per week. The cameras would also be useful additions to the television news programs that had started broadcasting reports prepared in Shadow's studios. The cameras were installed and the use of helicopters curtailed.

Over time, the camera additions did not create as much cost reductions as hoped for. The radio stations were reluctant to diminish their number of helicopter broadcasts because of reactions from their listeners. Radio listeners wrongly perceive the helicopters to be the most accurate source of traffic information and prefer to listen to stations that broadcast reports directly from helicopters. An expensive educational campaign was required to convince radio listeners of the better information provided by cameras. Before they made the camera investment had Shadow concept tested the camera innovation with a sample of radio listeners, they would have been able to better plan for the real costs that were associated with the camera program. In planning product/service changes, it is very important to evaluate whether to concept test the changes with all segments and stakeholders who might react to the change.

After about a year, Shadow's major competitor copied these innovations. However, this just increased the profits of both competitors by increasing the size of the market and lowering the acquisition costs of advertising inventory.

The Shadow Salesforce Role and Compensation

The radio stations did not want to add another competitor when they took on a traffic service. Almost all stations stipulated that the advertisers that the traffic service obtained for their network should not overlap with either the radio stations current advertisers or any advertisers to whom the radio station had made a recent pitch. The stations were told that the money for traffic ads would come from different budgets than for traditional spot radio advertising—things like promotion funds, or coop vendor funds.

The shadow salesforces' role was pretty difficult. They were charged with convincing nontraditional radio advertisers to use a new kind of ad (10-second) in a new submedium (within live traffic reports) in a new network. This role is quintessential missionary selling—taking the gospel out to convince new people to convert. In order to attract and motivate the best people for this role, Shadow and Metro paid pretty big draws against commission and pretty high commissions (around 10 percent) on revenue. The really effective salespeople were making several hundred thousand dollars per year. However, many salespeople could not accomplish the job adequately and were asked to leave.

After a few years in the first two cities, New York and Chicago, Shadow managers began to see the "coasting" phenomena set in on some of the best, most experienced salespeople. Once these salespeople had gotten enough accounts so that the commission on those accounts gave them the standard of living to which they aspired, they cut down severely on their new account prospecting and spent whatever time was necessary to maintain the revenue (and commission) from their current accounts. They also spent less time selling, but maintained their income and even improved their standard of living because they had more leisure time. Maintaining revenue from current accounts typically requires less sales effort than getting an equivalent amount of new business. This was definitely true for Shadow.

To improve the situation, Shadow changed its compensation to a higher commission rate for the revenues from an account for its first year (over 12 percent), but a lower commission rate on succeeding year's revenue (less than 8 percent). Theoretically, the commission rates for new versus existing business should be roughly proportional to the effort required for each task. In this way, the salesperson should be indifferent to spending time with current accounts or trying to penetrate new accounts. A compensation system like Shadow's new one helps to control the "coasting" problem. If the salesperson coasts and just services existing accounts, she will get a lower income level. As the reader might have forecast, convincing the experienced salespeople to adopt the changed commission plan was very difficult. The salespeople rightly were concerned that their initial expectations to which they had agreed had been changed. A number of the experienced, best salespeople had performance problems adjusting to the new arrangement. They had to work hard again!

When Shadow expanded to other cities, management initiated the tiered commission plan from the beginning—paying a higher commission for the first year of revenue and lower on succeeding years. It was no problem to get salespeople to buy in to the scheme when it was introduced *at the beginning* of their relationship with Shadow. In fact, the better salespeople were able to accelerate their compensation growth. If they ended up "coasting," they at least did it at a much higher revenue level and had to work harder to keep a compensation level. Hindsight and experience in the newer markets convinced Shadow management that it was much more productive to *introduce the differential commissions at the beginning.*

Salespeople, like any other person (or buyer of something), are much more satisfied if their experience matches or exceeds their prior expectations, than if they are told to change their expectations in the middle of an experience. This is one example of using marketing thinking to manage more than your relationships with customers. Your salesforce also needs to be approached with careful marketing thinking. Just as it is crucial to manage the buyer's expectations when you or your salesforce sell your product or service, it is also just as important to manage your employee's expectations when you "sell" them on working for your company.

Survey Results on Salesforce Compensation

The Inc. 500 group was much more likely to use productive techniques mentioned previously. Figure 7.3 shows the percentage of the survey respondents who used different compensation and motivation methods.

The Inc. 500 CEOs are much more likely to have different compensation for new versus different business and different commission rates for different products. The most striking difference

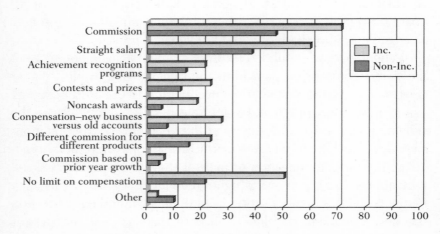

Figure 7.3   Salesperson compensation.

between the groups is that 50 percent of the Inc. 500 firms have no cap on what their salespeople can earn, versus only 21 percent of the non-Inc. group. We have heard of no entrepreneurs who report that their salespeople work harder when their compensation is capped.

Recruiting, Training, and Retention Strategies

Once you have made all of the planning decisions about your salesforce, recruiting the right people is a very difficult job. Chapter 10 on hiring looks at this process as another marketing problem to solve. For most entrepreneurial ventures, you will not be able to have the luxury of training raw recruits from scratch. You just won't have the time or available resources to train them. Raw recruits won't have the market contacts to "hit the ground running." Thus, most initial salesforce hires will come from other companies that have operations in markets related to yours. Chapter 10 discusses entrepreneurial approaches to this hiring/marketing problem.

Training of the salesforce will be very idiosyncratic to the role of the salesperson in your marketing mix and the role of the salesperson in the "product offering bundle" that you offer. As a small, entrepreneurial company, you will typically do better with someone who already knows how to sell. Your job is to make sure that this person knows your product inside and out and how the market will benefit from the product. Anything you can do to help the new salesperson to learn about the buying process at her customers and prospects, the competition, and any other meaningful parts of the positioning of your offering bundle will usually be beneficial.

When to not retain salespeople is a decision that is not made nearly as well as it should be by entrepreneurs (and other managers as well). There is a tradeoff to be made that most managers and entrepreneurs rarely consider. If they have a limited sales budget and/or limited prospects on which to call, then they have a limited size of salesforce to deal with. One way to possibly improve sales productivity is to fire lower performing salespeople and replace them with new recruits who might prove to be higher performing. The tradeoff is costs of hiring and training plus the "burn in" time of the new recruit, plus the chance that the new recruit may also not be very good. In the only analysis we've seen of this phenomenon (on navy recruiting salespeople), the answer was clear. The venture was keeping mediocre people when they would have been much better off "raising the bar."

Summary

In this chapter, we discuss concepts and paradigms that have been demonstrated as useful for entrepreneurial marketers. This has not been a complete compendium of management techniques for sales-forces, only those that have been demonstrated to help entrepreneurs. We have shown entrepreneurial ways to handle the rep versus direct issue, and how to decide which functions to do in person versus which sales functions to handle impersonally. We have described methods for improving salesforce productivity by analyzing alternative options for salesforce size, deployment, and organization. We then discussed compensation options and proposed some criteria for more productive compensation and motivation systems. Shadow Broadcast Services was used as an example of not only a good compensation system, but also entrepreneurial thinking about its product positioning and perceived value to its different market segments. Shadow also exemplifies how much easier for the entrepreneur it can be if he or she gets the compensation system correct in the beginning, and manages employee expectations appropriately.

CHAPTER 8

Promotion and Viral Marketing

Whereas public relations or advertising can get people to hear about your company or product, promotion gets your product itself in front of the customers, channel intermediaries, or the press. It also may provide some temporary inducement for taking an action—like buying or trying your product. Promotion is usually considered to be paid activities or events that provide inducements to customers to do something. However, the delineation of which activities should be called promotion, public relations, or advertising is becoming blurred. As long as we help the entrepreneur with productive activities to market and sell a product, we will not worry about what the activities are called. You can get products in front of the consumer in several ways. This chapter will discuss direct marketing promotions, viral marketing, event marketing, and other guerilla marketing techniques that entrepreneurial companies are likely to use. Please keep in mind that all of these techniques must first and foremost solidly reinforce the positioning and target segmentation decisions that underscore all of the tactics that a successful entrepreneur should use. *If any tactic will jeopardize the perception of your product held by your target market, do not do it!*

Give It Away

Giving free samples of products has been a promotion tactic for a long time. If the lifetime value of the customer that is obtained by the promotion is greater than the cost of the promotion, then it may make sense to give it away. The more repeat purchases the initial customer will make and the less likely she will switch to another product, the higher the lifetime value. For products with high switching costs, free samples to get them started may be very productive.

That's the reason pharmaceutical companies give physicians free samples to get their patients started on certain medications. Many of those drugs are used for the patient's lifetime and the drug's lifetime costs can easily run into thousands of dollars. As long as the drug works, and there are no averse side effects, the physician is not likely to change the medication and the patient is also not likely to ask for a change.

In the new Internet world, giving the product away has also become a key, long-term strategy, not just a short-term promotion. Even a trial bottle of shampoo should be justified by the long-term value of the customer versus the total cost of producing and distributing the sample. We discuss the lifetime value concept in more detail, however, just because it's free, doesn't mean it's cheap. Users have also become savvier about accepting free software, and understanding what it may cost them to operate and maintain it. The Open Source software revolution has spawned companies like Cygnus Solutions, whose slogan is "Making free software affordable."

Netscape popularized the current Internet craze for giving away software by making its Navigator browser software freely downloadable for nonprofit users, and downloadable for 90-day trials for other personal or corporate use. After Netscape had achieved 90 percent market share, Microsoft made their Internet Explorer browser completely free—forcing Netscape to do the same for their browser. Once all of the key competitors had free as the price tag, it became almost impossible for anyone else to enter.

The Netscape strategy actually had two parts to it. The first was to encourage usage among the college and university students who had high-speed access to the Internet within their dorms and schools. The word-of-mouth generated by this group spread rapidly to their professors, who, as consultants to industry and sources for the press, were able to certify that Netscape was the winner. At the time it was launched, Spry, Quarterdeck, and Spyglass all had licensed versions from the University of Illinois National Center for Supercomputing Activities (NCSA), where the original Mosaic had been developed. Netscape had also realized that if they captured the space on the user's desktop, they could turn that into later revenue (monetize the users, in today's Internet terminology), by selling advertising and other items on their home page, which most browsers pointed to when the program was started. And, the user base would drive the corporations to believe that Netscape's winning position translated to their Internet servers, for which large sums could be charged.

The Lifetime Customer Value versus Acquisition Cost

As with any direct marketing, be it direct mail, electronic mail, telemarketing, or door-to-door sales, you have to compute the value of each customer acquired over some lifetime (with appropriate discount rates), versus the cost of acquisition. This value should take into account that some customers will leave. The opposite phenomena also should be considered—that for many innovative products or services, initial customers may influence other potential customers to join. See the viral marketing discussion that follows. In today's public markets, the value can also be inferred from the stock market "proxy valuation" for each customer. Thus, AOL has been valued the way that cable television systems are—at so many dollars per customer served, even though it takes years to realize that value.

Microsoft has chosen to follow the give-it-away-free strategy, with a small twist. It is only given away to those who have other Microsoft products—with the minor exception that they have free IE browsers for Unix and Macintosh operating systems. In addition, they bundled a free Internet server with Windows NT (now Windows 2000), to add value to that system, and, the Department of Justice contended, to keep pressure on Netscape by denying them some of the server revenue. Fighting free Navigator with free

IE has enabled Microsoft to regain 30 to 40 percent of market share for the browser, which also translates into market share for their mail systems Outlook and Exchange.

But giving software away on the Internet is not a simple task. If something becomes popular, you need to be prepared for hundreds of thousands of downloads each day. This requires servers and infrastructure, some of which can be outsourced from such companies as downloads.com or software.net.

Giving Free Trials

Making it easy for a user to try a software product or Internet service is a key factor in creating demand. If several software products perform similar functions, users will stick with the first one they learn, since perceived switching costs are high. It is important to get them to install and use your new service, come to your Web site, and so on. They need to play with the user interface and learn your offering's benefits, so that they can make the purchase or switch decision.

America Online (AOL) achieved their large user growth by carpet-bombing the United States with diskettes (and later CDs) so that users could install and try 10 hours on their service. Even though they had far lower market share in the online world than CompuServe (which they later bought), or Prodigy (which had been supported by IBM and Sears—using Sear's technological prowess and IBM's consumer marketing skills), their market research showed that if they could get people to log on and try some of their online communications (chat, message boards, and e-mail), they could turn them into subscribers. But people who were not already online could not download software to get online. They decided to direct mail diskettes with the installation kit, and later to not only bind them into trade and general circulation magazine, but also to have barrels of diskettes available at many consumer stores and outlets.

The key was their knowledge that every user who logged on for their 10 free hours was equivalent to approximately 25 percent of a 3-month customer, and about 15 percent of a "lifetime (42-month)" customer. Since those revenues were (at the early days) $9.95/month, the value of a person who actually used the disk to log on was close to $100.00. The cost of the package was around $1.00, so even a 1 percent to 2 percent trial rate could yield very profitable results. In addition, the stock market valuation of AOL, as a multiple of the number of subscribers, was several hundred dollars (today it's over $1,000 per subscriber). So in terms of market capitalization and the ability to use that value to raise money for marketing programs, a much smaller trial rate was valuable to AOL. In fact, it has been such a successful promotional vehicle that its use continues to this day.

Getting the disks to the users en masse was costly, so AOL went searching for an even cheaper method—having all the software preinstalled on new PCs. Until Microsoft created the Microsoft Network (MSN), AOL got most major vendors to put all the software for an AOL trial on the computer in return for a bounty for each subscriber who lasted three months. This was a win-win for both AOL and manufacturers such as Dell, Compaq, and Gateway, since AOL also provided (in the pre-Web days), good support forums that could cut down on end-user support calls.

Free trials are not just useful for software. They also may be a valuable tool for other products and services as well. The physician free samples discussed are one example. For products whose benefits may be difficult to describe, providing free trials may be an effective marketing tool. The *Investor's Business Daily* newspaper has been using free two-week trials quite effectively for a number of years as a new business generator. They believe that all the benefits of their paper are best perceived by actually reading it and that it is worth it to make it very easy for their target customer to experience those benefits.

Viral Marketing

The rise of the Internet and the Web has given rise to even faster and cheaper forms of promotion, and the term *viral marketing*. In a viral situation, each user tells his or her friends to download the software, because it will enable them to communicate or work together. Thus, each new user "infects" many of his friends with the product, and an exponential growth can be achieved.

The best-known product of this category is ICQ ("I seek you") which made instant messaging available on the Web. Instant messaging had been one of the most attractive features on AOL—it permits a user to see if a friend is simultaneously online, and if so, to pop up a message on the friend's screen and get a response in real time.

ICQ required Web users to download a piece of software, which took several minutes on normal modems, and to register their e-mail and alias information with ICQ. Within a year, they had over a million users and have grown in three years to more than 15 million users. As AOL moved into the Web, they purchased Mirabilis, ICQ's Israeli parent for almost $300 million, and continued to operate it. All this before ICQ had figured out how to monetize their users.

An equally successful viral marketing campaign was started when one of the Draper Fisher Jurvetson venture capitalists backing Hotmail asked them to put "Get free e-mail with Hotmail" as a tag line on every message sent out by a Hotmail user. Within less than a year, the company had several million users, and was sold to Microsoft for several hundred million dollars. Having not only every user, but also every use of their system be an advertisement for themselves was an extremely cheap way to spread the word. The marginal cost for increasing each e-mail transmission by less than 50 characters was so close to zero as to be almost immeasurable. The marginal return from an extra customer was several hundred dollars in market capitalization when the company was sold.

All of these successful viral marketing and free offer examples are consistent with the positioning and target segmentation of their firms. For example, AOL is targeting the masses with a position of being fun and easy to use. ICQ is almost the embodiment of that positioning.

When Do Giveaways Work?

Clearly, not every product or service is suitable for the "free" strategy. The four key elements needed to make it an efficient way to build customers are:

1. Low product cost
2. Low switching cost

3. Easy distribution
4. Relatively high lifetime customer value

Any software product, by its nature, has low cost of goods. Especially if the documentation is presented online, the marginal cost of reproduction is at worst the cost of a CD-ROM (under $1.00 in volume), and at best the cost of maintaining FTP or Web servers from which potential users can download the software and documentation. Services, such as AOL or other Internet Service Providers, have a cost less than 10 cents per hour. Offering 10 free hours may cost less than $2.50. And many software providers have "crippled" versions, which only work for a limited time period (usually 30 days), a limited number of uses, or have certain functions disabled (can't save files). Software.com, whose PostOffice program is one of the most successful e-mail servers, allows people to use the software for up to 10 user accounts free of charge.

Free trials have long been used in other media, even where cost is high, as long as the customers are well qualified (have a large lifetime value). Bomardier will give you a free trial ride on a corporate jet to convince you of the FlexJet program's benefits. To qualify for the trial, however, you have to do more than send an e-mail.

A key factor in deciding whether or not viral marketing can work is the cost to the user of switching to the new product or service. In the Internet world, this can be equated to the amount of time (or number of forms) a user must spend to set up his new account, software, and so on. For example, there are a large number of portfolio management sites, which keep you updated on your stock holdings. For someone with two or three stocks, the setup is usually very fast—but for users with extensive holdings, who may be the best customer targets, this can often take a half hour or more. This often leads to the good driving out the best, that is, the first reasonable solution a user adopts may be good enough to keep him or her from switching to a better, even much better, solution.

One can help this problem by automating the switch or minimizing the user work necessary to perform such a switch. Jump.com, for example, which offers automated Web-based calendaring, created a synchronization program to import Palm Pilot or Franklin REX data. If a user already had a calendar program running, they merely had to point Jump to their data file, and it would populate its databases without the user having to reenter data. Similarly, portfolio management programs should be able to read Quicken files so that the user doesn't have to do data entry, and can see the value of the new service.

Broad giveaways may often reach too many uninterested users, so it is important to try and target the campaign to maximize the conversion ratio, that is, the number of users who move from trials to real (paid) users. AOL initially distributed disks within computer user magazines, since those were the people who were able to go online. After the success with that target group, disks were mailed to lists of people in the right age/economic demographic—whether or not they had a computer.

Finally, the AOL product was bundled with as many computers as possible. The computer vendors, such as Dell, Compaq, and others were induced to include the AOL software and free trial offer by being paid a bounty on users who actually stayed with AOL for at least three months. In some cases, those bounties were $25 to $50, and the cost to the vendors was a megabyte of software being loaded on an otherwise mostly empty drive during the burn-in phase of production. AOL's success drove others, such as Prodigy, Earthlink, AT&T Worldnet, and most notably, MSN the Microsoft Network, to adopt the same tactic.

Event Marketing

Everyone loves a parade. The excitement of an event can create good feelings about a product or service and lead to a time-focused set of articles and press interviews that generate the all-important buzz about the new idea. Even a small company can generate a large amount of hoopla through a well-planned event—often enough to sound like a much larger company to the customers and competitors. The goal of event marketing is to have the press use editorial ink and space to promote a product, rather than paid advertising. And the press can not only write about the features and functions of the product, but also about the level of excitement surrounding the launch—which will often convince skeptical users to try it.

The Microsoft Windows 95 launch is one of the best examples of event marketing. Not only did Microsoft host some key events at their Redmond, Washington, headquarters, they also held major promotional events around the world, including Sydney, Australia, London, and New York. The press coverage of these events dwarfed the advertising spending that was going on in the initial launch phase, and made most of the general public, as well as computer-oriented consumers, aware that something major and new was happening. Microsoft, unlike a small entrepreneurial venture, also had the wherewithal to continue the press through advertising expenditures post launch.

While product public relations can be gained from event marketing, so can general corporate image and view. The current trend to paying for the naming of football stadiums (3COM Park, Qualcomm Stadium), and post-season games (the IBM Aloha Bowl) is meant to associate the corporate name with certain images. This is not an option open to small start-ups, although advertising on the Super Bowl, as hotjobs.com did in 1999, does tie a sports event and a marketing event together. However, hotjobs.com was the only Web site to advertise on the Super Bowl in 1999, and got a lot of free press as part of its participation. In 2000, however, more than 20 different Web companies advertised on the Super Bowl. The only press that the great majority of these Web sites got was about how much money they wasted by advertising there.

Industry conferences offer some of the best opportunities for event marketing. The key influencers and press representatives are usually present, as are many potential customers, distributors, and agents (not to mention competitors). Getting noticed above the clutter of exhibit booths and trade press ads may not be easy. Events can be as small and simple as the press conference, where company spokespeople announce a new product and invite the press to listen, or as elaborate as the big evening parties and entertainment events.

MetaCreations Corp. was a small computer graphics software company with some interesting new products. It was searching for a method of getting lots of press attention at Comdex—the country's largest trade show—with only a small amount of money in the bank. John Wilczak, the CEO, decided to hold a large party (500 key people from the industry) at a location like the Hard Rock Café or House of Blues. He created the Digital Media Players Party, which would let several companies, including MetaCreations, showcase their newest technologies by having demo stations around the nightclub. The cost for throwing the party was a little over $250,000 that the company didn't have. Wilczak called on some of the biggest players in the industry—Kodak, Adobe, and so on, and sold them on being "sponsors" of the party. As sponsors, they would pay a fraction of the cost $25,000 to $50,000, and get an allocation of invitations and demo stations.

When the invitations went out, they read MetaCreations Corporation (big letters) invites you to the Digital Media Players Party, sponsored by (small letters, Adobe, Kodak . . .). This party was held at three to five major conferences a year for the next several years. MetaCreations managed it and got most of the public relations credit, with a net cost to the company of zero dollars. In addition to being able to be identified with the big guns of the industry, and getting the new products in front of the press and influencer community, the fact that it was seen as the entity throwing the party caused most of the customers to assume it was a much larger company than its sales would have indicated. This increase in customer confidence definitely helped the sales effort.

Consumer Events

Not all event marketing needs to be directed at the influencers. There can be great benefit from events focused on end consumers. During the Windows 95 launch, stores such as CompUSA held special midnight launch parties, designed to draw consumer traffic into the stores, so that you could be among the first to get the exciting new product.

Bikini.com, a Web site devoted to the surf and swimsuit culture, holds the bikini.com world tour, sponsored by various large companies, to generate awareness of the site, and to drive traffic to the site. They've used some of the supermodels whose work is shown on bikini.com to judge local contests. Some of these are tied to spring break events in various parts of the country, or in conjunction with other key local events such as college opening weeks.

Winning the Chotchka Wars

Getting your company's name, logo, and message into the mind space of as many people for as long as possible is a major goal of any public relations effort. One way of doing this is with *chotchkas* (Yiddish word for a small freebie)—T-shirts, key chains, coffee mugs, and so on. These are given away at trade shows, fairs, public events. After a typical Comdex show (the largest computer conference with over 200,000 visitors), we come home loaded with half a dozen T-shirts, a few key chains, some mouse pads, note pads, a logoed Swiss Army knife, and so on. In fact, at the past few Comdex conventions, Jim Louderback of *PC* magazine has run a television show displaying the best chotchkas.

Articles of clothing are common types of chotchka—hats, T-shirts, and so on get your message out to only a few people at a time, and are more effective when given to your own employees. The employees are likely to wear them proudly and, if asked about the company mentioned on the shirt, to provide real information. The people working a trade show should be given hats and shirts so that they are advertising the company not just at the trade show booth, but throughout their stay in the trade show location. Customers who get the clothing often give them to their kids, diluting the multiplier value of the gift, although there is goodwill created with the prospect or customer.

For long-term mind share, mouse pads can keep a company's name, logo, URL, and 800 number continually on the desk of current and potential customers. And they have all the contact information at their fingertips, quite literally. In a similar vein, pads of various types, for example, post-it notes, cubes with the logo on the side and top, binders that hold 8½″ by 11″ pads, and so on often last for a long time on the desk, and within the sight lines of the prospect. By contrast, pens and pencils, even with the company's name, phone, and URL, are often kept in a pocket or purse, and hence do not get the number of exposures that a desk item would. If the prospect is a coffee or tea drinker, a large coffee mug or travel mug will also stay visible on the desk for long periods of time.

There are always new items being touted—water bottles in various shapes, fanny packs, Frisbees. Most of these have the same drawback that clothing does—they are not often kept around the office, where they can affect the decision and speed the ability of the prospect to get in contact with the company. In addition, their cost is often high relative to their value.

On the other hand, using a chotchka to get a more detailed prospect form, either on the Web, over the phone, or at a trade show is a time-honored tradition. "Fill this out and get a free . . . ," still works better than a plea without the bribe. Again, items with longevity such as a small flashlight, a key chain, a telephone rest, are better than the classic T-shirt or hat.

Summary

Every day some entrepreneurial marketer is creatively coming up with new methods for getting her product in front of her target market. The examples in this chapter should be viewed as just that—examples, not as a prescription for repeating promotions that were successful in the past. Using the principles discussed here, along with creatively developing something new and unique, is where the entrepreneurial breakthroughs will occur. Your job is to develop a number of possible promotion and marketing options, evaluate their potential incremental revenue and cost, and choose to execute the ones with the highest return on marketing investment. As with advertising, if there is a lot of uncertainty in the evaluation of either incremental revenue or incremental costs, it may be best to test some options before executing them broadly. Also, the entrepreneur needs to keep in mind that all promotion *must* be consistent with the firm's product positioning and target market.

CHAPTER 9

Entrepreneurial Advertising Decisions

Advertising is probably the most misused (and misunderstood) marketing instrument by entrepreneurs (and managers of larger firms as well). As we discuss next, many entrepreneurs and other managers believe that advertising is too difficult to evaluate on a cost-benefit basis. Using many large frequently purchased packaged companies as examples, many entrepreneurs have adopted many of those larger firms' approaches to advertising. These advertising approaches have a number of "rules" that help a firm or its advertising agencies to make some advertising management decisions. Examples of some of these "rules" include:

1. The incremental revenue produced by advertising is not worthwhile to measure, so don't even try.

2. If an area or market segment has x percent of revenues, it should get x percent of the advertising exposures—its "fair share."

3. If you want to achieve a market share of x percent, you must maintain an advertising budget which is greater than x percent of the amount spent by all the competitors in the category.

4. You should pulse advertising expenditures into periodic flights that will cut through all of the competitive clutter.

5. You need at least three advertising exposures on a consumer to have an effect. Any less than three has no impact.

6. Advertising takes a long time to work and its long-term effect is difficult to measure, but it is there.

7. If you believe television advertising works, then more television advertising is obviously better than less.

These "rules" become mental models that many firms use as rules of thumb to make their advertising decision making easier. Many companies have repeated these and other similar rules so often that they have become analogous to a religion. Many advertising decisions are thus made on faith.

Entrepreneurs can't run their businesses on faith. They must allocate scarce capital resources to maximize their value to the venture. Advertising is only one alternative use of scarce resources. Other marketing elements like promotion, public relations, and the salesforce compete for resources with other uses such as working capital, new production equipment, and so on. We will show in this chapter that it *is* possible to evaluate the potential incremental return versus cost for advertising, especially for smaller entrepreneurial ventures. These returns can then be compared with other uses of scarce capital resources to enable the entrepreneur to make the most productive use of her available resources. However, as we will show, these methods for estimating returns are imprecise, but they are the best that can be done under the circumstances. We will show that it is better to be "vaguely right," rather than using rules such as the ones above which are "precisely wrong."

To emphasize how misunderstood advertising is, even by the large "sophisticated" firms, we first show some recently published research that analyzes the incremental sales effectiveness of their television advertising. We then describe methodologies that entrepreneurs can use to make decisions on advertising so as to be able to at least roughly analyze advertising's return and compare it to other uses for the scarce resources.

Even Large Firms Waste a Lot of Their Advertising Expenditures

Two recently published articles provide convincing evidence that even the largest television advertisers can significantly improve the productivity of their television advertising.[1] The study, sponsored by all the major packaged goods marketers, analyzed almost 400 in market, split-cable, year-long television advertising tests using the Behaviorscan® system, a service of Information Resources, Inc.

Behaviorscan is a household purchasing panel comprising of approximately 3,000 demographically representative households from each of six geographically dispersed markets. All supermarket purchases are recorded via scanners and linked to individual household identification to measure precise purchasing behavior.

In addition, households receive all of their television transmissions via cable technology, and advertising can be directed to or removed from individual households on a targeted basis. This capability has allowed the execution of numerous carefully controlled advertising experiments. Media weights, media plan configuration, and many other advertising variables have been experimentally tested using this technology.

The tests that were analyzed were those in which some panelists received a different level of television advertising than others for a year. These tests give very valid estimates of the incremental revenue impact of the tested campaigns. The study showed that only 33 percent of television advertising for established brands was showing a statistically significant incremental sales response to this television advertising. On the other hand, when television ads worked, they produced big volume effects (a mean increase of 18 percent in sales), the effects lasted for a period of over two years, and they emerged surprisingly fast (within six months in most cases). The difference between the ads that worked and those that didn't was mostly idiosyncratically related to the copy that the campaigns used. There were more smaller brands ads that worked, and ads that promoted the status quo did not work as well as ads that tried to change something or impart new "news." "What you say" was much more important than "how much you say it."

A key finding from the research related to the long-term impact of the advertising: If the advertising had an incremental sales impact in the first year, it had (on the average) a long-term impact that doubled its initial year's incremental effect over the next two years. On the other hand, if the advertising had *no* incremental impact in the initial year, it had *no* long-term impact in the next two years. Thus if advertising does not produce incremental sales when it is first run, it is unlikely that it will produce incremental sales in the longer run. Many consumer oriented Web e-commerce sites learned this lesson the hard way during 1999 and early 2000. They spent millions of dollars to "brand" their sites and got little, if any, incremental sales from the expenditures. The research indicates that it is very unlikely that there will be incremental sales in the future that will accrue to those firms as a result of that "branding" advertising.

These 400 in-market tests also cast much doubt on each of the "rules" in this chapter's introduction. All of these "rules" were not supported by the incremental sales response to television advertising shown in the tests.

How Entrepreneurs Can Improve the Productivity of Their Advertising

The advertising decisions are typically categorized as budget (how much should I spend?), media planning (where and when should I place the advertising?), and copy (what should I say?). Many books have been written on how best to make these decisions. However, the entrepreneur does not have the luxury of trying all the different theories (most of which have not been shown to be fully validated to help entrepreneurs make more productive advertising decisions). Instead, the entrepreneur must do the best with what he has—little money and little time. In that spirit, the following methods and concepts should be helpful.

Typically, the entrepreneurial business gets an idea for an advertising and/or promotion campaign from someone (the owner, an employee, an agency, a customer, a friend, or an advisor). The "campaign" is typically a combination of media, copy, and budget. Examples might be: "Let's run ads on the radio to announce our new line of auto accessories," or "Let's put out circulars in the new office building that just got finished with our menu and a coupon for a free drink." Conceptually, what is needed is a way to evaluate whether the campaign will generate enough incremental revenue so that the incremental margin contributed by the incremental revenue will more than cover the advertising and promotion expense. As long as this return is better than other uses for the campaign funds (including other possible different campaigns), the campaign should be continued.

The big problems are evaluating the incremental return of the campaign and generating campaigns that are even better. We first describe concepts and methods for evaluating incremental returns and next discuss methods for improving the campaigns before they are evaluated. We should emphasize here that the procedures to help with these evaluations are not as precise as evaluating some other uses for capital. However, they are the best that the entrepreneur can do in the typical circumstances in which she finds herself. This situation calls for being "vaguely right" versus being "precisely wrong." The "rules" above are examples of the "precisely wrong" way to approach advertising or promotion decisions. These rules are easy to apply and can be calculated very precisely, but they have been shown not to generate campaigns that are incrementally profitable. We next show some ways to handle campaign evaluation.

Evaluating Campaigns—"Vaguely Right" versus "Precisely Wrong"

For many entrepreneurial businesses, the incremental impact of campaigns is obvious, if the entrepreneur is intelligently watching the daily revenues and either consciously or subconsciously relating daily revenues to the advertising and promotion that is occurring. If the business is direct to the customer, she can also ask customers coming in, calling in, or logging on to the Web site, if the advertising or promotion was involved in their decision to purchase. The entrepreneur has to estimate one number to compare to the actual achieved revenue. That number is "what would revenue have been without the advertising or promotion campaign."

This number can be "vaguely" estimated by using combinations of differences in revenue in prior periods and differences in revenues from the area getting the campaign versus the same time periods in other areas which were not subject to the campaign. If the data is available, the best comparison to use for evaluating a campaign is the difference between revenues per week during the campaign versus before the campaign started compared to the same numbers for areas in which the campaign was not used over the same time periods.

For example, if a campaign ran during May only in Cleveland, and sales per week increased by 25 percent in May compared to the prior three months, the first estimate you might make would be that the campaign increased sales by 25 percent. However, the next thing to look at would be: How did a comparable area without the campaign do in May? You could use the rest of the United States as a comparison, or a market you judge to be similar, perhaps Detroit or Pittsburgh. If Detroit was up 5 percent in May, Pittsburgh was up 7 percent, and the rest of the United States was up 3 percent, you could reasonably estimate that the campaign might have increased revenues by about 20 percent more than they would have been had the campaign not run. The big assumption you are making when using such an estimating procedure is that *no other causes were responsible for the difference between the area with the campaign and the other areas*. For example, was something else also going on in Cleveland that might have caused the sales increases—such as competitive activities, weather, public relations activities, and so on. The same questions need to be asked about the areas used for comparisons—the "pseudo" controls for this "pseudo experiment." This kind of estimating and analysis is called pseudo experimentation because there is not random assignment of the campaign to one area versus another. Without random assignment, you can never be sure that there wasn't some other reason than the campaign that was affecting the revenues.

It has always been amazing to see how many firms, large and small, don't take the simple necessary steps to even attempt to determine the impact of campaigns. If they don't keep the data, they can't do any evaluation. If you don't do any evaluation, you can't improve the campaigns or discontinue the ones that aren't working. Businesses should keep track of exactly what is occurring daily in each campaign and put it in the same place electronically as the revenue numbers.

An Example

As an example, a national retailer of consumer electronics thought it was keeping track of its advertising and promotion programs. The way the data was stored could best be described as "market status reporting" (Little 1979).[2] The data was there for managers to find out what they did in each market each day of the week. However, as the data was structured in the computers, it was impossible to do any kind of analysis of the incremental impact of the advertising or promotion programs that the firm ran. An example of how the data looked as it was stored in the computers is in Figure 9.1.[3] After the situation was analyzed, the data was restructured into a spreadsheet that looked like Table 9.1.

Using standard regression analysis, we were able to estimate the incremental sales impacts of the firm's advertising. The software used for the analysis was Microsoft Excel, which is widely available and very inexpensive. If doing statistical analysis is difficult for you, any statistics graduate student at a nearby university could help you out at very nominal costs.

The regression model related each day's total sales to print, radio, and television advertising during that day and each of the prior seven days as well as sales during the same day last year, and the number of stores in operation that day. The analysis was able to show the impact of one dollar spent in a Sunday newspaper insert on incremental sales for each day of the following week (see Figure 9.2).

The analysis was able to estimate the average incremental revenue per $1 spent in all of the media options analyzed (see Table 9.2).

The relative impact of the various media and days of the week were very helpful to the firm in scheduling their next campaigns. They used more television on Sunday and cut back on other print. They did more weekday radio and less weekend radio.

Element: Advertising Schedule   Plan PD: 5   Page:
Accountability: Adv Director   Meeting: Planning   Version: 12/06/89
Market:

Week No. 1	Sunday 8/20/89	Monday 8/21/89	Tuesday 8/22/89	Wednesday 8/23/89	Thursday 8/24/89	Friday 8/25/89	Saturday 8/26/89	Week 1
Holiday								
Event	/—Super Sale—/	/—Back to School ROP—/		/—Endless Summer 8 Page Tab—/			/ 1-Day Sale /	
Activity TY	AM (6X18) 6000; TV 195 Pts.	8000 Radio (100 Pts.) 3000; TV	TV	PM/ (6X18) C; TV			AM (6X18) 7500	
Total Exp. TY	14000	3000	0	0	0	0	7500	24500
Total Exp. LY	8700	0	0	0	0	19644	0	28344
Sales* TY	50	56	43	46	30	42	58	325
Sales* LY	40	56	32	47	25	60	84	344
Sales* BGT								
Sales* HPF								
A/S TY								0.0754

Week No. 2	Sunday 8/27/89	Monday 8/28/89	Tuesday 8/29/89	Wednesday 8/30/89	Thursday 8/31/89	Friday 9/01/89	Saturday 9/02/89	Week 2
Holiday					/—Labor Day BOS ROP—/			
Event	/—End of Month Clearance Sale—/	/—Endless Summer—/			/—Labor Day BOS ROP w/Radio—/			
Activity TY	AM (6X18) 9500		Radio (200 Pts.) 6000; (6X18) C			AM/PM (6X18) 5605		
Total Exp. TY	9500	0	6000	0	0	5605	0	21105
Total Exp. LY	6700	0	0	0	5200	10200	0	22100
Sales* TY	44	38	43	48	35	43	83	334
Sales* LY	54	53	46	55	42	47	72	369
Sales* BGT								
Sales* HPF								
A/S TY								0.0632

Figure 9.1 The original data.

*In $000

Day Number	Day of Week	Sales ($)	TV ($)	Print ($)	Radio ($)
1	Sunday	50,000	8,000	6,000	0
2	Monday	56,000	0	0	3,000
3	Tuesday	43,000	0	0	0
4	Wednesday	46,000	0	0	0
5	Thursday	30,000	0	0	0
6	Friday	42,000	0	0	0
7	Saturday	58,000	0	7,500	0
8	Sunday	44,000	0	0	0
9	Monday	38,000	0	9,500	0
10	Tuesday	43,000	0	0	6,000
11	Wednesday	48,000	0	0	0
12	Thursday	35,000	0	0	0
13	Friday	43,000	0	5,605	0
14	Saturday	83,000	0	0	0

Table 9.1   The Restructured Data

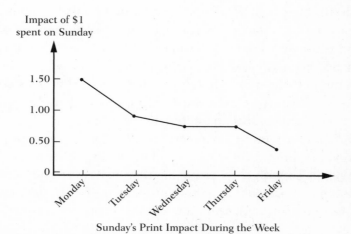

Sunday's Print Impact During the Week

Figure 9.2   Model: Sunday's print impact on Monday to Friday.

TV Sunday	12.07**
Radio during week	5.91*
TV during week	5.27**
Print Sunday	5.06**
Print during week	Non-significant
Radio Saturday	Non-significant
Print Saturday	Non-significant

* $p < .10$
** $p < .01$

Table 9.2 Estimated Incremental Sales Associated with $1 of Advertising

This example utilized naturally occurring experiments to determine the incremental revenue impact of the advertising campaign, after the campaigns had run. The statistical analysis used a multiple of last year's sales in each store as an estimate of what might have occurred had the advertising campaign not been run. A better approach to campaign evaluation is using planned experiments instead of naturally occurring experiments.

"Vaguely Right" Entrepreneurial Marketing Experimentation

The basic idea behind planned experiments is very simple. You want to try a campaign on subsegment(s) of the market and be able to estimate what the revenue would have been had the campaign not been run, by comparing the areas in which the campaign ran to those in which it didn't. To be as confident as possible that your valuation of the campaign is as "vaguely right" as possible, there are five ideal characteristics that an experiment should have. As an entrepreneur, you will not be able to execute perfect experiments, but they don't have to be. The experiments only need to help you go with the campaigns that work best and not spend money on campaigns that are not productive. The five characteristics that you want in designing market tests or experiments are:

1. The assignment of which areas or subjects will get the campaign or the control (nothing different) should be random.

Flipping a coin or throwing dice are fine ways to fulfill this requirement.

2. Nothing else could have caused the results observed except for the campaign you are testing.

3. The results can be logically projected to the firm's real marketing situation in which the campaign would be used.

4. The experimental campaign must precede the sales effects it is supposed to cause.

5. There must be a comparison group that did not receive the campaign or received a different campaign.

The most important characteristic is number one—random assignment. If this does not happen, there is a persistent danger that those exposed to the campaign may in some ways be different from those not exposed.

Evaluation Before Is More Valuable than After

If the evaluation of the incremental revenue attributable to the campaign is not sufficient to justify its opportunity costs, the campaign should not have been run. The funds for that campaign would have been better used in other ways. If the entrepreneur can find ways to evaluate campaigns *before* they are executed in the whole market, then he can only execute campaigns that will justify their expenditures. The *planned experiments* described in the previous section are a very good way to evaluate campaigns using a *sample* of the market instead of the whole market, *before* the campaign is executed for the entire market. The entrepreneur needs to balance costs of the evaluation before the campaign is widely executed versus the value of only executing those campaigns that are very likely to be productive. This balancing act can be very difficult for large consumer packaged goods firms, but for the typical entrepreneur, it is relatively easy. He just has to think about evaluating the campaigns in a reasonable way before they are widely executed.

For any one to one marketing vehicles, such as direct mail, telesales, or the Internet, it is very feasible to test campaigns on selected samples and only broadly execute those that return more than their opportunity costs. For direct mail, for example, it is easy to test a campaign on every nth name on a list, before sending the advertisement to the whole lost. For broader reach media such as radio, television, magazines, or newspapers, more ingenuity is needed. If the firm has operations in more than one metropolitan area, it can test campaigns in some areas, using some other areas as controls. What is very important in these experiments is to match the areas based on forecasted revenues for the test period and to *randomly* decide which areas are the test and which are the control. Flipping a coin or rolling dice to make the choice is perfectly appropriate. The use of chance makes it much more likely that the differences in revenues that are seen in each market are really due to the advertising campaign versus some other reason that caused a person to chose one market versus another. An example of how matched market experiments helped Franklin Electronic Publishers, Inc. to evaluate alternative media and campaigns prior to national role out is shown in Figure 9.3.

The following are excerpts from a presentation which describes Franklin Electronic Publication's advertising test of three alternative campaigns before a choice would be made of which, if any, was to be run. The three campaigns were spot television, cable television, and radio.

Survey Results on Advertising Budgeting

We asked our entrepreneurs how they determine their advertising budgets. The answers showed big differences between the Inc. 500 and the non-Inc. group. Of the non-Inc. group, 65 percent decided advertising budgets based on what the company could afford, versus only 29 percent of the Inc. 500 group. Conversely, 41 percent of the Inc. 500 group used current or anticipated sales and profits versus only 16.3 percent for the non-Inc. group. Finally 21 percent of the Inc. 500 group used these techniques and tried to estimate incremental sales due to the advertising, versus only 5 percent of the non-Inc. group. Here again the Inc. 500 group is more likely to use more productive techniques. But even for them, there is room for improvement.

Improving Campaigns before Testing

Whatever can be done so that campaigns that are developed are more likely to be productive is beneficial to the process. There are a number of steps that the entrepreneur can take to improve the campaigns as they are being developed.

Copy Strategy

First and most important, the entrepreneur must make sure that every campaign that she uses is *supportive* and *consistent* with her *positioning* and *segmentation* strategy. At every opportunity, the entrepreneur should be asking, "Is this campaign going to improve our perception in the direction of our positioning strategy and is it targeted at the right market segment?"

As long as the campaigns are consistent with the strategy, then it's the entrepreneur's job to have the *most widely varied copies* generated and evaluated. Profitable copy generation can be compared to a lottery. The differences in incremental revenues between alternative copies and creative strategies can be very large. Some campaigns can really add large amounts of incremental sales, while other campaigns (with similar budgets) will do nothing or might even hurt sales. Conceptually, the entrepreneur should be generating a number of very different campaigns, evaluate the potential incremental revenue impact of each of them, and only run the best one—as long as the best one is incrementally profitable and pays for its opportunity costs (including being more productive than the current campaign).

However, in reality, it's just not that simple. Managing the advertising process involves a real balancing act for the entrepreneur. A number of advertising management decisions are very interrelated and should be determined simultaneously. These decisions include the answers to the following questions: How many different campaigns should I have generated? How much should I spend for the alternative campaigns? Should I retain an advertising agency? Who else should be tapped to generate new campaign alternatives? Each of these decisions depends on the answers to the other decisions. If one manages a huge organization with plenty of time and resources, it is possible to think

- **Purpose:** To evaluate the impact of advertising on retail movement of Franklin product, especially Franklin BOOKMAN

- **Methodology:** A controlled test will be conducted to evaluate the following:

  1. **$4MM Spot television plan.** If successful, this plan would be implemented in approximately 30 percent of the United States, representing a combination of high impact retail markets and more highly developed Franklin markets, as measured by warranty card returns. It is believed that these markets would yield a 95 reach and a 7+ frequency in the advertised markets. See theoretical plan.

  2. **$4MM Cable television plan.** If successful, this plan would be implemented nationally. Implementation of this plan would yield a 60 reach and a 6.6 frequency in the advertised markets. See theoretical plan.

  3. **$3MM Radio plan.** If successful, this plan would be implemented nationally. Implementation of this plan would run approximately 100 announcements per week.

  The Franklin marketing manager had done a very careful job of developing pay back criteria.

- **Measures of Success**

  To be deemed a success the adjusted unit volume increase within the test markets would need to rise sufficiently to pay back the advertising investment. Based upon current volume, this would translate to an increase of approximately 200,000 units or an 11 percent increase in volume on an annualized basis. Volume increases would be measured across all Franklin volume—not just BOOKMAN.

- **Evaluative Criteria in Reading Test Results**

  Adjustments must be made to data in test versus control to reflect the following:

  • Seasonality
  • Market strength
  • Only portion of entire media plan implemented
  • Translation of national theoretical plan especially in cable markets: buying specs issued to deliver overall reach and frequency and not number of spots. Desired Daypart Mix would include a greater degree of prime and weekend than could be purchased on local cable basis.

- **Payback Criteria by Market**

  Sacramento ($4MM Cable):

  200,000 annual units × 0.72% US / 1.32 Index × 0.60 half the schedule × 0.60 (seasonality index for April/May) / 12 months per year × 2 (May/June)

  Volume increase over two months in Sacramento would have to be 54 units over control.

  Portland ($4MM Spot):

  200,000 annual units × 0.84% US / 1.28 Index × 0.60 half the schedule × 0.60 (seasonality index for April/May) / 12 months per year × 2 (May/June) / 0.85 adjustment for spot only control

  Volume increase over two months in Portland would have to be 77 units over control.

Bakersfield ($3MM):

150,000 annual units × 0.25% US / 1.45 Index × .60 half the schedule × .60 (seasonality index for April/May) / 12 months per year × 2 (May/June)

Volume increase over two months in Bakersfield would have to be 13 units over control. The test design was structured with the three test areas and a control area.

Test Results

The test results showed that the spot television campaign increased sales 66 percent higher than the control, better than the productivity of the cable or radio options.

However, because the number of reporting stories was small and sales per week were small, there was a higher variability than the company anticipated in the sales estimated from the tests. There was still a big probability that was the spot television campaign could have been no better than the control. There was not enough upside for the company to risk its resources on such a risky payoff.

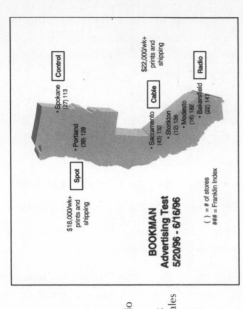

BOOKMAN
Advertising Test
5/20/96 - 6/16/96

( ) = # of stores
= Franklin Index

BOOKMAN Advertising Test
Franklin Weekly Store Movement Data

Performance Summary–Ad Month	Cable	Control	% Change	Radio	Control	% Change	Spot	Control	% Change
Average sales per week–prepost	27.91%	−19.23%	47.14%	4.17%	−19.23%	23.40%	46.75%	−19.23%	65.98%
Sales per store per month–prepost	27.91	−19.23	47.14	4.17	−19.23	23.40	46.75	−19.23	65.98
Sales per store per week–prepost	27.91	−19.23	47.14	4.17	−19.23	23.40	46.75	−19.23	65.98
Sales per point of distribution–4 weeks	27.91	−19.23	47.14	4.17	−19.23	23.40	46.75	−19.23	65.98
Weekly sales per point of distribution	27.91	−19.23	47.14	4.17	−19.23	23.40	46.75	−19.23	65.98

Figure 9.3 Franklin BOOKMAN Advertising Test.

about an "optimally" profitable answer to these decisions. For the rest of us entrepreneurs, the best we can do is a "vaguely" right approach to the process. A discussion of the directional tradeoffs that exist between the alternatives follows.

First:

More campaigns should be created as:

- The cost of generating the campaigns is lower.
- The cost of evaluating each campaign is lower.
- The validity of the campaign evaluation method is higher.
- The reliability of the campaign evaluation method is higher.
- The variability of the sales impacts of the different campaigns that would be generated is higher.

What the entrepreneur is trying to do is only run with the most effective campaign. The more variability there is among the campaigns generated and evaluated, the more likely the best or most effective campaign will be more effective in increasing sales. However, if we chose the campaign that isn't really going to be the best, we will not do as well. Thus, the reasoning for being concerned about the reliability and validity of the evaluation technique. Also, the more costly the evaluation or generation of campaigns is, it's obvious that the profitability of the process goes down faster as we generate and evaluate more campaign options.

More should be spent on evaluating campaign options:

- The more valid and/or reliable the evaluation methods are.
- The more variability in sales success the entrepreneur believes will occur among the campaign options that will be generated.
- The lower the costs of generating and evaluating each campaign option are.

If it is very inexpensive to generate and evaluate each campaign option, and it is likely to be a big impact on revenue from one campaign to the other, and the evaluation is likely to differentiate the best campaign, then it pays to generate and evaluate a lot of different campaign options.

For the typical entrepreneur, the biggest leverage can come from increasing the variability of the campaign options she evaluates. Increasing the variability of the creators of the campaign option does this. The more different are the people and their approaches that create the campaign options, the more likely is it that the best of those options will have more revenue impact. How do you get more varied campaign option creators? Encourage option ideas from everyone who possibly can help in the creative process. Your employees and customers know the business and sometimes can generate very productive ideas. Also many times friends and relatives with whom you discuss your venture can also be a source of creativity.

This reasoning goes against the "standard" way advertising is handled by the entrepreneur. Many entrepreneurs will hire an advertising agency and give them the job of creating and placing their advertising campaign. The agency will do its own creative development and media planning. After the agency has completed its work, they make a presentation to "sell" their campaign idea to the entrepreneur. The entrepreneur either accepts their recommendations or sends the agency back to try again. This approach has been shown to generate campaigns that are not very different from each other in sales impact.

It is much more effective to *separate* the *creative* and *media* functions of advertising agencies. Our logic would imply that more than one creative agency should submit proposed campaigns to be evaluated and be paid for their time. The best campaign among those evaluated would be the one that is broadly executed. If for some reason you have trouble getting more than one creative agency to work for you, another option is to ask for separate, independent, creative teams from one advertising agency to each develop alternative campaigns to evaluate. Then run with the campaign that is evaluated as most likely to increase sales the most.

It is not necessary to have advertising developed only by traditional advertising agencies. Other sources would include freelance people who work part-time for ad agencies, advertising and marketing students at local universities, and art students at local art schools. The conception that artistic production quality for advertising has to be excellent for the advertising to be "great" is not borne out by the existing research. The definition of "great advertising" is where an entrepreneur and the typical advertising professional will differ. The consumer who sees or hears advertising is typically not sophisticated enough (nor cares enough) to be influenced by very subtle artistic touches in advertising. Professionals judge most advertising competitions and awards (such as the Cleo awards). Their judging criteria do not include the sales impact of the advertising. Most of the sometimes large amounts of money that is spent to make advertising (especially television) artistically beautiful is of very questionable productivity.

If you are typical of most entrepreneurs, you are now asking yourself "How can I afford to spend all this money generating and testing alternative campaigns, most of which I'll never even run?" The answer is very simple—you will make more money doing that than with "normal" ways of generating and evaluating advertising. A great advertising campaign that is really effective at increasing sales may be contributing 5 or 10 times as much incremental revenue as a typical campaign. It's worth it to spend money to try to find the exceptionally productive campaigns.

For example, Metacreations Corp. used radio advertising on Howard Stern's radio program to ask listeners to go to their Web site or call an 800 number to order a new software program to manipulating computer images. They let Howard Stern have poetic license to do whatever he wanted to advertise the product. In fact, the advertising cost was cheaper if Stern was free to extemporize his commercials.

This campaign generated more than *10 times* the incremental revenue versus the campaign cost. It was evaluated on a daily basis because it was very simple to watch the big increases in calls and Web site visits every time the "commercial" ran on Howard Stern's show. The campaign was orders of magnitude more effective than any other campaigns the company had run.

Sometimes, it doesn't even have to cost very much to generate productive alternatives. Synygy, Inc. is an entrepreneurial company that does administration of complex incentive compensation plans. They had an advertising agency that they used in the traditional way. The advertising that the agency came up with was run for a period of six months in print media that their target audience—senior salesforce managers and administrators—would read. The objective of the advertising was to bring good leads for their salesforce to follow up. Figure 9.4 shows a typical ad.

This ad campaign brought in from 2 to 5 leads per week either over the phone or to the company's Web site. One of the company's employees (a graphic artist) approached Mark Stiffler, the founder

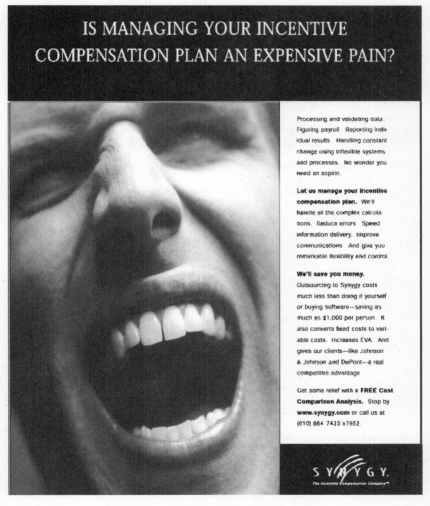

Figure 9.4 The original ad campaign.

and CEO with a mock up of a very different print ad. Mark directed the employee to make it into a print quality ad and tested the ad by running it once instead of the old ad. The new ad is in Figure 9.5.

The ad was so much better than the old ad, that it was obvious by monitoring the inquiries generated that it was orders of magnitude more productive. Synygy began using the new ad exclusively—both in their print media and their direct mail brochures.

Figure 9.5   The new ad.

In the six months that the new campaign ran, inquiries averaged 67 per week! With no change in media budget or media plan, the new campaign was at least 15 times more productive than the old campaign! It was certainly worth the nominal investment by Synygy to test the employee ad! The quality of the new "Tom" ad is probably not wonderful from an artistic point of view. However, *advertising for entrepreneurs is not an art form, it's a way to generate inquiries and sales.*

Media Planning

If the discussion of campaign creative and evaluation was not enough to get the reader's entrepreneurial juices flowing, the next discussion of choosing media should do it. Just as there are big opportunities for increasing revenue with "nonstandard" campaigns, there are also big opportunities for increasing revenues by choosing the most productive among a wide variety of creative media options. The key in media planning is finding the media option that has the most likelihood of generating incremental revenue per dollar spent. We call this "bang per buck" analysis. Again, here the problem is not simple. There are a number of factors that should be considered in generating and evaluating media options. We have been able to distill experience and research over the past 30 years to develop a methodology that can guide the entrepreneur toward "vaguely right" choices.

Again, here the *market segmentation* and *product positioning strategy* of the firm needs to *drive the process*. Any options that are inconsistent with the firm's basic strategy should be eliminated. The media chosen can be an excellent way of implementing a segmentation strategy. One of the reasons for Tandems East's success is the availability of targeted media that reach their target customers very cost effectively. Aside from reaching the targeted segment(s) cost effectively, the media options chosen should also be able to convey the firm's advertising message in an effective manner. For example, even though the audience of *Hustler* or *Playboy* magazine may be very appropriate targets for life insurance products, they would probably not be good environments for the typical life insurance ad. The male reading these magazines is probably not thinking very long-term or is not very receptive to arguments against current pleasure.

The media chosen need to be evaluated not only on who will likely see or hear your ad, but on how potentially effective the option will be in motivating people who will hear or see the ad. Thus, the media options chosen will be directly related to the campaign that will be used. Some campaign options will be more effective in some media options than others. Again, this is not a simple problem. We have developed a relatively simple ranking and evaluation procedure to get right at the basic trade-offs that are essential for evaluating the relative worth of the available options. The methodology considers the relative value of reaching different target market segments, the probabilities of members of each segment actually seeing or hearing the ads, and the appropriateness of the media vehicles as motivators of people who are actually exposed to the ads in them.

Sample Template for Media Evaluation

The first step in evaluating media options is to divide the market into segments that will have different value to you. This is not as simple as it seems, because you will need to estimate how those segments break out the audience of the media options you are considering. Most media audience ratings are typically only broken out by age and/or sex and sometimes other demographic variables. There is a balance between finding segmentation that is relevant to your venture and segmentation that has media audiences available. Sometimes the segments used for the media planning purposes can be as simple as "my target group" and all others. The entrepreneur can then estimate media audiences in the target group for all the options she is considering.

For our sample, we assume that the entrepreneur has divided his target into three segments: younger males with high income, younger females with high income, and all other adults as illustrated in Table 9.3. The next step is to estimate the population of each segment—column A in Table 9.3. Column B answers the question: How valuable to me is reaching a person in one segment versus another? This is an important judgment that will depend on the advertising's objectives, the potential of the segments, and so

Sample Segments	A Segment Population	B Segment Weight = Potential per Person in Segment (Relative)	C = A × B Segment Potential
25–49 Males with income > $35K	2,000,000	10	20,000,000
25–49 Females with income > $35K	2,000,000	4	8,000,000
All others	10,000,000	1	10,000,000

Table 9.3   Segment Data

on. It is a per capita estimate that only has to be done on a relative basis. The numbers in column B could be just as easily 100, 40, and 10 instead of 10, 4, and 1. What is important is the relative judgment of how valuable reaching a person in one segment is versus reaching a person in another. Column C is just the multiplication of Column A times Column B to obtain a segment relative potential.

Table 9.4 describes some of the required numbers and estimates needed for each of the media options that are being evaluated. For our sample, we evaluate four vehicles, one Internet advertising option, a radio ad, a taxi ad on the back of the front seat of a set of taxis, and an ad in a newspaper. It is very important to generate many options to evaluate, even if you have to make

Sample Media Vehicle Options	D Cost/Insertion	E Probability of Ad Exposure Given Audience Membership	F Media Weight = Relative Value of Ad Exposure (Judgment or Experimentation)
City Internet banner ad for 1 week (Internet A)	$100 per week	0.6	1.0
Radio 30-second spot lassic rock station— drive time (Radio A)	$150 per week	0.6	1.5
Taxi seat banners for 1 week (Taxi A)	$ 50 per week	0.8	1.0
City newspaper ad ¼ page financial section (Newspaper A)	$800 per ad	0.3	1.5

Table 9.4   Media Data

rough, "vaguely right" judgments about some of the numbers needed for the evaluation. Creative media options can not only help you sell more stuff, they can position you as different from your competition.

The first column (D) in Table 9.4 is the costs per insertion for each option. The next column, E, is an estimate of the probability that someone who is counted as "in the audience" of the media will actually be exposed to the ad you would run. This estimate depends on how the audience number is determined for each media vehicle. It is absolutely true that your advertising can only work if the potential consumer is exposed to it. Just being in the media vehicles' audience and not seeing your ad does not help. For example, if a person reads the newspaper, but does not see your ad in the financial section, this does no good for your business. Column E estimates the fraction of audience members who will actually be exposed to your ad.

The last column (F) is probably the most *difficult* number to estimate for each media vehicle, but also the most *important*. It answers the questions: How much do I care to have a good potential customer be exposed to my ad in one media vehicle versus another? This number really only needs to be estimated on a relative basis. The best way to think about this estimate is to arbitrarily assign a one dollar value to one media option (A). For the other options, you then answer the question: If it costs one dollar for me to have a good prospect be exposed to my ad in media vehicle A, how much more or less than one dollar would I be willing to spend to have my ad seen instead in each of the other options? In the example in Table 9.4, the radio and newspaper ads are estimated as roughly 50 percent more valuable *per person actually exposed* than the other two media options.

Table 9.5 shows the fraction of each segment that is counted as being "in the audience" of each of the media options being evaluated. The audience numbers come from the syndicated research that is used to estimate who watches, reads, or listens, for how long. The definition that is used by each media option to define "being in its audience" is very important to understand. For example, for television, the definition of audience is typically having the television set in the audience member's household turned on to the channel

Media Vehicle	G 1. High-Income Younger Males	H 2. High-Income Younger Females	I 3. All Others
Internet A	0.04	0.02	0.01
Radio A	0.08	0.06	0.05
Taxi A	0.03	0.02	0.005
Newspaper A	0.25	0.15	0.10

Table 9.5 What Fraction of Each Segment Is Counted as the Audience of Each Media Vehicle Option?

on which your ad appears. Whether the audience member actually watches you ad is a whole other story which is handled by column E in Table 9.4. In Table 9.5, Column G for example, 25 percent of the high-income younger males are estimated to be in the audience of the financial section of the newspaper, but column E of Table 9.4 says that only 30 percent of those audience members actually see the quarter page ad we plan.

The next step in the evaluation is to multiply the total segment potential in column C by the audiences in Table 9.5. The mechanics of this computation are shown in Table 9.6. For each media option, column M is the total audience of each media weighted by the importance of that segment to the firm.

Table 9.7 puts all this together by combining the media audience potential, ad exposure probabilities, and the relative media values. This amount is divided by the costs per insertion of the media to get a relative "bang per buck." In our example, Radio A is most productive, followed within about 17 percent by Taxi A. The other two options are deemed less than half as potentially productive as Radio A and Taxi A.

The template in Table 9.7 for media planning should be used to screen options to then either run in the market place and evaluate, or test in a test market and evaluate. The Franklin Electronic Publications media test described earlier is a good example.

The entrepreneur should continually be evaluating the incremental revenue performance of his advertising options as they are used in the market. Over time, the incremental revenue contribution may begin to decline because of diminishing returns. When this happens, it may be time to try some new options.

Segment	J = G × 20,000,000 High Income Younger Males	K = H × 8,000,000 High Income Younger Females	I = I × 10,000,000 All Other	M = J + K + L Total
Internet A	0.04 × 20M = 800,000	0.02 × 8M = 160,000	0.01 × 10M = 100,000	1,060,000
Radio A	1,600,000	480,000	500,000	2,580,000
Taxi A	600,000	160,000	50,000	810,000
Newspaper A	5,000,000	1,200,000	1,000,000	7,200,000

Table 9.6 Relative Amount of Segment Potential in Media Audiences

$$\frac{\underset{\text{media audience}}{\text{Total potential in}} \times \underset{\text{exposure probability}}{\text{Individual ad}} \times \underset{\text{media value}}{\text{Relative}}}{\text{Media insertion costs}} = \text{A relative "bang per buck"}$$

$$\text{Bang per buck} = \frac{MxExF}{D}$$

Internet A	=	636,000/\$100 =	6,360
Radio A	=	2,322,000/\$150 =	15,480
Taxi A	=	648,000/\$50 =	12,960
Newspaper A	=	3,240,000/\$800 =	4,050

Table 9.7   "Bang per Buck"

Summary

Though this chapter has discussed copy and media separately, it should be obvious that they are very interrelated. Some copy will obviously work better in some media than others. If your copy changes, it means that the media options need to be reevaluated with the new copy and visa versa.

This chapter has introduced a number of nontraditional ways of tackling advertising decisions in a "vaguely right" way. All of these ideas have been tested by entrepreneurs and are also consistent with proven relevant advertising phenomena. The concepts and paradigms are not consistent with the "religion" practiced by many large firms who can afford to treat their resources with less respect than an entrepreneur can. However, it is still paramount that every campaign that you use is *supportive* and *consistent* with your *positioning* and *segmentation* strategy. At every opportunity, you should be asking: "Is this campaign going to improve our perception in the direction of our positioning strategy and is the media plan targeted at the right market segment?"

CHAPTER 10

Hiring Is a
Marketing Problem

The three key items that fuel entrepreneurial growth are ideas, people, and money. We discussed ideas in the previous chapters and discuss raising capital in Chapter 11. All successful companies need a continuing supply of great people to bring their ideas to fruition. Selling to potential recruits is a marketing problem like any other, and many of the same elements need to be considered. Particularly, you should keep in mind that in this chapter we are trying to show how entrepreneurial marketing can help you to hire the best people. There are many other aspects of the hiring and human resources function that are beyond our scope.

Positioning

Great people want to work with winners. One of the key marketing challenges for the human resources (HR) group in a company is to generate the perception that your company is going to be the winner in your product/service space. The same public relations techniques discussed in Chapter 4 can be applied to this dimension. Have the influencers meet the founders and describe the company as a sure winner, and recruits will flock to your door.

People usually like to work in compatible environments. That is, they want to work with people who are more like them than not.

Microsoft, for example, has created the perception that the world's smartest people work there. They use intelligence measures as a key determiner in the hiring process and foster those stories that tell of the "brain teasers" they use in interviews, and the verbal sparring that occurs during Microsoft meetings. As a result, they are able to hire many of the world's smartest folks, not just programmers, but also writers, marketers, salespeople, and so on.

Apple Computer, Inc. has fostered the perception that people who work there "think different" and are not afraid to challenge the status quo. Their consumer advertising campaign and their hiring speeches make the same point. When Steve Jobs was trying to lure John Sculley away from his senior post at Pepsico, he asked, "Do you want to change the world, or just sell soda the rest of your life?" Jobs successfully put forth the message of Apple, in its hiring as well as its operations.

For other large companies, there are specific positioning messages—McDonald's is "everyone's first job," and, as they try to hire more senior citizens, maybe everyone's last job as well. Goldman Sachs, Disney, and McKinsey & Company are perceived as the best places to learn strategic thinking and to become part of the American corporate elite. Procter and Gamble is the place to learn all about brand marketing.

For the entrepreneurial start-up, positioning to prospective employees should be simple and straightforward. They are, after all, going to have to work very long hours, usually for low pay, with most of the rewards coming psychically in the early stages, and through stock options much later. The company's mission and culture must come through in a few sentences or images. Just as important as "the elevator speech" that you should be able to give to a prospective funder, is your firm's first encounter with a prospective employee. The prospective employee should know exactly why your company is a different and better place to work. Use Steve Jobs one-sentence description of Apple as an example.

Segmentation

Almost every market segments itself along certain dimensions. The hiring market is no exception, and is segmented by functional specifications, geography, skill level, and experience level required.

In addition, the risk propensity of applicants causes the more conservative folks to shy away from entrepreneurial start-ups.

Functional segmentation is the seemingly obvious differentiator. You need to market differently to find accounting personnel than manufacturing workers. Yet in the early stages of entrepreneurial companies, each person may have to take on several jobs and functions. The CFO may also run operations, be a purchasing clerk, and work on sales of company equity. It is hard to decide between a candidate with several years of direct experience as a CFO who has come up through the accounting and finance ranks, and someone with the CPA who has also been an operating officer or perhaps run their own business.

Geographical segmentation is an especially difficult one to overcome. There are different lifestyles in Boulder, San Jose, New York City, or Atlanta. People who are attracted to a particular place to live can color the applicant pool for your new venture. It is much easier to find people willing to work all day and night in Silicon Valley than in Atlanta—not that the Georgians are any less productive, just that their culture is built around more family time. Similarly, locating your office where most employees have long commutes (train or auto), puts bigger limits on total time in the office.

Hiring people who have to change locations in a significant way is fraught with risks for both parties. For the applicant, there is great risk that they simply won't like the new location—or their accompanying family members won't. For the company, such employees are subject to the stresses of a young, fast-growing venture on top of the difficult home situation. Infonautics, Inc. found it difficult to recruit people into the Philadelphia suburban area. Even though applicants saw that the housing and school opportunities were far superior to other cities, they remained reluctant, because there were too few other companies to go to if the venture did not succeed. Now, as more Internet companies have located in the "Philicon Valley," it has become much easier to convince potential employees that even if the job that moves them here doesn't work out, there will be ample opportunity for them in their specialty.

With the advent of the Internet, companies can now hire some people who break the geographic boundary limits via telecommuting.

With one or two visits a month to the corporate facility, the telecommuter can retain enough personal contact and credibility for the rest of his or her work which is arriving via e-mail. Hiring telecommuters means marketing to them where they live—on the Net. Jobs.com, Monsterboard, and the other services provide a way to reach this key group of innovative and hardworking technical and creative people.

Experience also segments the marketing job. Entrepreneurial companies often have the luxury of hiring not on the basis of experience, since they are going into business and product areas in which there may be no relevant experience, but more on the basis of "raw" skill. Young MBAs who can serve as Jacks or Jills of all trades may be more responsive to the hiring message of an Internet start-up than someone with 5 to 8 years of experience and career track at a bigger company. But there really is no substitute for experience. The less training a company needs to provide, the faster they can get their product to market.

While some recent, relevant experience is critical, many of the jobs that seek 5 to 10 years of time in related positions are not appropriate for the Internet space. Few people were on the World Wide Web much before the mid-1990s, narrowing the pool of such applicants too severely. What is most important in an entrepreneurial company is the right mix of experienced people, who have some idea how things can be done, with entry-level talent, who know no limits to what can be accomplished.

Building a Team and Corporate Culture

While every hiring decision is critical and needs to be looked at on an individual basis, the collection of early hiring decisions determines what type of team spirit and corporate culture will be created. For a corporation to be successful, it needs to have each of the key personality types as well as each of the critical skills. One needs people who enjoy the detail-oriented administrative tasks, entrepreneurs and visionaries who can work at the 50,000 foot level and not be deterred by small uphill battles that occur each day, people who will grind out the work, and those who can manage and integrate the people and processes of the organization.

Showing a new recruit that the team works together, with common purpose, is a key marketing element in successfully hiring the best. Having the applicants come on days when there are pizza parties or other social occasions is a good way for them to meet many more people than the interviewing schedule permits and to get a sense for the community that they'll be joining in a less pressured manner.

Reaching the Prospects

Traditional want ads and classified job ads are rarely the mainstay of the start-up. Most of the candidates are reached via networking, job fairs, headhunters, and online media. Often, if the publicity surrounding the company is strong enough, resumes will flow in unbidden, from those who want to latch onto the hot new company.

Every employee, from the founder down, must be told to keep watch for any good talent, and encourage them to apply, even when a specific job is not open. Your own employees are great judges of the "chemistry" fit of a candidate, and since one of the keys to successful organizations, and to job satisfaction, is having a best friend at the office, letting people recommend and potentially hire their best friends is a good way to ensure success. Such hires have lower turnover rates and better prospects. They also cost the company far less than standard headhunter fees.

Job fairs are an efficient way to focus your start-up on hiring. Post at local colleges and universities, advertise on the Internet, and hold an open house for 2 to 3 hours late some afternoon (typically 5 to 8 P.M.). This allows those who have jobs to get there and talk with people from many different functional areas in the company. In the idealab! incubators, where there are always 5 to 10 companies, we have held job fairs in which each of these incubating companies, and the other 20 companies we have created that have moved away, sets up a table with a few of their people. As a control mechanism, we only allow each applicant to talk with a limited number of companies—usually 3 to 5. That way, the number of competing offers is limited, and the amount of duplicate processing is cut down. The applicants sort themselves by degree of risk averseness by the companies they choose to talk to, since those that have been in business for years (CitySearch, GoTo.com) get the lower risk takers, and the ones that have started in the past week get the high risk takers.

Networking with local faculty members is crucial to seeing the best talent before it is preemptively taken off the market. If the professors know what you're looking for, they can recommend people to you long before they would think of themselves as being in the job market. One good way to get access to this talent pool is the use of students as interns. There are many well-defined tasks—market research, for example, that can be done by a student or student team during a semester course. This allows the student/prospect and the company to evaluate one another, with no obligations, and without having to make the hiring decision until after you have really seen both the work and work ethic of the candidate.

Pricing

Compensation packages at entrepreneurial companies vary widely. Especially in the first few months of the company's existence, offers may be custom tailored to match the applicant's needs for cash, deferred compensation, equity, and other benefits. The perceived value of a package of salary, options, and perks will vary widely with the age, maturity, stage of life, and relocation status of the employee.

The idealab! formula is to try and keep all salaries below $100K per year in the first 6 to 12 months. To balance this, employees get faster vesting on a portion of their options than is typically industry norms. This is an especially important recruiting tool when dealing with senior people who are leaving highly paid positions, since it ensures that they will have a stake in the company even if their own job doesn't work out. It is much easier for a CEO who is taking a small amount of cash compensation to convince his or her subordinates to stay below the CEO salary level.

Reaching the Prospect

There are many people who play a role in the hiring process, and each needs to be trained in the marketing and sales function associated with recruiting. When the Human Resources person (or department as a company grows) starts out, they should have the mission statement and position description clearly in mind. A key differentiator in entrepreneurial companies, however, is that whatever the position description says, there are likely to be other responsibilities, since there are never enough employees to fill all the roles in a new venture. This message has to be put across to the recruit.

In the army, it is "unit cohesion," the sense of belonging to a small tightly knit group, that makes men and women willing to give their lives to save their fellow unit members. Entrepreneurial companies are also fighting key battles, and unit cohesion is critical. Hence, it is very important to have any potential hire interview not only with HR and the specific workgroup manager, but also with most members of the group in which they'll work. Each of these members has to market not only the company's mission and vision, but also the ethos of their own unit; and has to be convinced that the recruit will contribute to the cohesion and success of the unit.

Programmers each have their own style. Development departments—so important to success in the Internet area—create their own sets of rules and conventions. Making sure that a new entrant into an existing group can work within, and perhaps extend, the group's styles can be the difference between the success and failure not only of the recruit, but of the company. In one open-source software venture, the head of the group was a maverick, who defied most standard programming rules to create a much more efficient e-commerce engine. When hiring for his group, he made sure that he kept a mix of maverick's and traditionalists, so that the creative energy led to productive code, not chaos. This involved meetings and votes among all the existing team members, who ranked each new recruit on several scales, along with an overall "I'd like to work with this person" rating.

Examples

EPinions is a Silicon Valley Internet start-up which is creating a Zagat-type guide to almost anything. They will provide convenient places on the Web for people to input their opinions, will aggregate them and make them available to the Web community. Product reviews, movie reviews, and so on are all in the plan. It was started by a small team who had all done successful start-ups (NetScape, Oracle). They faced one interesting hiring challenge, however. They were unwilling to tell potential recruits about the business plan until after they were hired. This meant having the recruits completely believe in the team, and be excited about working with the team on whatever they chose.

They were able to tell the recruits that there was going to be nothing illegal, no pornographic or gambling related stuff, and little else. What helped was that they could say they were funded by Benchmark Ventures, one of the most successful Silicon Valley backers (eBay, etc.). They could also say that they hoped to launch within six months, so there would not be a long delay in finding out if they could be successful.

Microsoft has grown from 12 individuals in 1978 to over 30,000 today, yet it still considers each hire as carefully now as it did 20 years ago. It has kept a strong marketing effort up both to convince entry-level personnel that Microsoft hires the smartest people, and to convince them that they can still become millionaires when their options vest. The company has very high standards for whom they'll hire as full-time employees. This cachet has also been spread around the college campus recruiters.

Summary

As these examples show and we hope this chapter has shown, hiring and keeping good people needs Entrepreneurial Marketing to make the process as productive as possible. All the concepts we cover in this book for helping improve the interface between the venture and its customers are also important for improving the interface between the entrepreneurial venture and its current and prospective employees.

CHAPTER 11

Marketing and Raising Capital

One of the most important jobs of marketing is to help an entrepreneurial venture show its best side when raising money. In fact, in the world of Internet mania, when profits for many companies may be a distant hope, and the key is customer acquisition and market share, raising capital is a constant and crucial factor in a company's success. In all cases, but especially for Internet companies, investors are most likely to provide funds, at good valuations, to companies perceived as winners that will eventually be very profitable. It is marketing's job to position the company as a (the) winner, leader, and most advanced, world-class competitor in its space. It is also important to be able to create a sense of urgency, to counteract the oft given venture response of "I'll put money in if you have a lead investor." Everyone wants to be the last one in the pool and looks to a lead investor who will commit and help in negotiating the specific terms of the investment deal for all investors. The lead will usually end up with a seat on the board of directors, representing the investors in that round.

The marketing group often plays a key role before, during, and after the fund-raising process. Marketing works with the CEO and CFO in creating the investor presentation. Pitches driven solely by the finance department tend to be too detailed and too dry to generate the investor excitement necessary for a successful sale of stock. Marketing may err too far on the side of hyperbole. Working with investment bankers, lawyers, and others to control the hype tendency, marketing's function is to craft both the "book" (business plan and summary) and the pitch (slide show and presentation) that will be used as the selling documents for a stock offering. Later on, marketing may work with the CFO in the investor relation's function—providing information and the "spin" on that information to the investors, whether public or private. Finally, the marketing department will work with investment bankers.

Product versus Financial Marketing

There are many differences between product marketing and financial marketing, but the similarities are even more numerous. In both, one needs to target the consumer of the goods and services, by working through the chain of influencers and key decision makers, gatekeepers, and naysayers to have maximum impact. In both, getting key benefits understood by all is crucial.

One major difference between product and financial marketing is timing. While the product marketing campaign can often be postponed to coincide with completion of a set of product features, failure to execute financial marketing may mean loss of funds and nowhere to turn—shutting down the business. The key elements of naming, pricing, and positioning still apply, but to the stock, not the product itself.

Naming

It is easier for people to remember who you are, and what your company does, if you have a well-thought through name. eToys, for example, is a name that immediately says toy sales to most consumers—having the name made it easier for investors to remember as well. At idealab!, names may be crucial—in more than one instance the fact that a sufficiently catchy URL was not obtained stopped the investment into the company. The URL for Tickets.com, along with the 1-800-TICKETS phone number, were purchased for a substantial sum to get the benefits of quick consumer and investor recognition and remembrance of the company's business area. Similarly, even though eToys.com also owns toys.com, the use of e before Toys.com gives an investor the idea that this is an e-business—a Web-based version of a more traditional business.

As with any nonfunctional name (e.g., Amazon.com), both product and investor marketing are required to attach the business plan to the name in the minds of customers or investors.

Pricing—Your Venture's Evaluation

Just as product pricing is an art as well as a science, the pricing of offerings in companies is even more so. Once a company is public, and there is a "free market" for its stock, the price will be set in that marketplace. We will come back to this in the discussion of investor relations. In the private markets, there are two types of prices—those set by the buyer (low), and those set by the seller in the face of excess demand (high). What permits a company to get into the latter category is superior marketing.

The key elements that need to be marketed to investors, in addition to the product/service offering, are the people (management team), the financial model, and any strategic relationships that the company may have entered into. Since the investor is buying a fraction of the company, not an instance of the product, it is the expected exit value that is most important. When there is an Internet stock mania, this value may be projected higher by some investors, and lower by others.

As we write this, an idea from a new, untried entrepreneur and group of qualified engineers, marketers, and so on may be worth 30 percent to 65 percent of the equity of a company for an initial cash investment of $250,000 to $2,000,000. With a seasoned team of entrepreneurs, located in Silicon Valley, raising $5 million for 30 percent of the equity would not be unusual. The marketing message around a successful team is clear—"They did it before, they'll do it again." Particularly if the team has either taken a company public, or sold at a good price to a major player (e.g., Cisco), their "product" has a seal of approval.

Segmentation of Potential Investors

The customers for fledgling company stock fall into several categories: angels, venture capital companies, incubators, corporate strategic buyers, or institutional investors. Each has a particular place in the investment food chain and is matched to certain types of companies. By far the largest share of investment funds for new business comes from angel investors. These are friends, family, and retired executives who have extra cash and are willing to take risks and back someone they know. Over 60 percent of the money raised is in this category.

Angels

While angels used to be approached one at a time, the high-tech world has organized this channel, so that it can be more easily reached. Ron Conway, founder of Palo Alto's Band of Angels, manages monthly dinners in which entrepreneurs can present their plan to almost a hundred current and retired high-tech executives. If they like the plan, they can invest from $25,000 to several hundred thousand dollars. And the companies get the network and expertise of senior people at such firms as Hewlett Packard, Apple, Netscape, Sun, and the like. The Band has been so successful that it has spawned a true venture fund, so that the members can participate in more investments with a little less time.

MIT Entrepreneur's Forums are held in several cities, Philadelphia has the League of Retired Executives (LORE) and the Pennsylvania Private Investor Group (PPIG). Los Angeles has the Tech Coast Angels, and the New York New Media Association has the NYNMA Breakfasts. In each of these, members agree to invest at least $25,000 in a start-up each year. They get to make the choice. Negotiating valuation with angel groups is very idiosyncratic, and often results in higher valuations than the venture capital firms would provide.

To get the opportunity to reach these organized angel groups, a company must find a member to sponsor them. Lawyers, accountants, professors, or other successful entrepreneurs can make the introductions for new start-ups that don't already have a link to this community.

Venture Capital Firms

The most visible and helpful investments come from the established venture capital firms. There are more than 4,000 funds that
belong to the National Venture Capital Association, and undoubt-
edly hundreds of others. The typical venture partnership has $50
to $500 million to invest over a three- to four-year period, and as-
sumes that their initial investment will require at least as much in
later rounds. Since the scarce asset of these firms is partner time,
they need to put $2 to $10 million into each deal. (The most recent megafunds are trying to put five or ten times that amount).
Firms such as Benchmark Capital, Kleiner Perkins or idealab!
Capital Partners want to take an active role in helping the investee
companies grow, and provide a *keiretsu* (Japanese for a corporate
family) to help their companies help one another.

The largest venture firms now see tens of thousands of business
plans each year, and fund only a handful (typically fewer than one
per month). How can a company work to maximize their chances
against these 1,000 to 1 odds? First, almost all of the venture firms
only fund plans that have been referred to them by someone they
know and trust. This first screen is extremely important and requires that a company have an advisor (lawyer, accountant, tech-
nologist, professor), who is known to the venture firm. That person
can make a telephone call or send an e-mail that describes the key
business idea or differentiator in a few sentences. If the venture
firm has any interest, they'll then request either a plan or a meeting.
Here the entrepreneur's marketing skills are put to the test. A few
slides and a prototype must tell the story, show how the market
being attacked is large enough to be worth the venture firm's valuable time, and transmit the passion of the entrepreneur to the partners. Venture firms are looking for markets that can get to between
$100 million and $1 billion in a few years, while angel investors can
fund companies that may only do $25 to $100 million.

Incubators

The incubator is a more recent innovation in sources of help, capital
included. idealab!, CMGI, eCompanies in Santa Monica, Softbank's
Mountain View Hotbank, eHatcheries in Atlanta, and Innovation

Factory near Philadelphia are all business incubators, which provide space, infrastructure, and funding to help entrepreneurs get a fast start. Pitching to these incubators is similar to the venture capital presentation, but the business team does not have to be as well-formed. An incubator often provides accounting services, general office services, and some technical consulting to the various companies, as well as overall business advice. Many are funded through industrial development funds, to try and heighten job creation in a particular region.

Corporate Strategic Partners/Investors

Many large corporations have started venture type funds, partly for the financial gains that can be earned, but mainly to keep a strategic eye on new developments in their sphere of interest. Many of the innovations that change industries start in the smallest, rather than the largest companies. Intel, Cisco, even AT&T all have venture funds so that they can benefit from the technologies and business models that new companies have started.

If your entrepreneurial venture has received any visibility at trade shows, in the trade press, and so on, you may be contacted by these groups. They are often brought in as co-investors by the established venture firms.

Exclusivity from Potential Customers

As discussed in Chapter 5, it is sometimes possible to get your future customers to fund the efforts, in a different way than the strategic partners mentioned earlier. In return for limited exclusivity, some companies will make up-front payments sufficient to help you develop and begin marketing your products. These types of arrangements, while rare, are very favorable to the entrepreneurs, since they minimize dilution and maximize the probability of success. Since there is already an interested customer, the feedback in early stages is likely to be highly valuable and can tune the product or service offering to truly match customer needs.

Institutional Investors

Finally, there are hundreds of investment bankers and finders who will try and help you raise money from qualified institutional buyers.

These sources usually want to make large investments ($10 million and up). These investors are willing to pay placement fees. Early stage companies that don't have the large cash requirements may find this market hard to tap.

The Buying Center

Just as every product customer has a set of hoops to jump through, so too do the CFO and CEO when selling the image of the company. For many venture firms or investors, the first test is the analyst or associate who screens the business plan. They are hired to keep too many plans from cluttering the partners' desks or minds, and get points for saying no early. However, they lose double points if a competitor gets a deal they should have bid on. Thus, telling the analyst at Firm A that Firm B is preparing a bid can short circuit the turndown.

After the analyst, the venture firms will often bring in outside "experts" to help them in fields in which they are not knowledgeable. These consultants have their own agendas, along with the formal assignment from the venture fund. It is quite common for them to offer their services directly to the company, after they have made a positive recommendation. They may facilitate the communications between a technically oriented founder and the financially oriented venture capitalist. The company should use their review time as an opportunity to gain valuable competitive intelligence, since these experts have a broader view of the competitive space than most founders.

The Marketing Process for Capital Raising

In the prepublic stage, reaching investors can be done by getting mentioned in the key influencer magazines (and online e-zines) such as *Red Herring, Upside,* and *Wired.* The technologic publications are also a source that many venture capitalists use to try to find deals.

In each region of the country, there are also weekly and monthly business magazines that cover start-up firms. *Crain's New York Business, Philadelphia Business Journal,* and *TechCapital* magazine are examples of publications that can get a young company noticed by potential private (prepublic) investors. After Vindigo was mentioned, more than 60 angels and venture firms called to see if they could participate in the next financing round.

Initial Public Offering

For many companies in the software and Internet world, much of the reason for going public is marketing related. As Jamie Kiggen of DLJ said recently, "The IPO is the premier branding event for an internet company." In fact, the amount of publicity and brand recognition that can be generated by a successful, high-profile IPO is enormous. Planning for an IPO is an arduous task, and the actual road show and offering are several of the most grueling months that a CEO and CFO will ever face. But each meeting and luncheon presentation is selling the company's products, message, and positioning as well as its stock.

The first part of getting the message out is accomplished during the underwriter selection phase. At this stage, the various investment bankers are trying to sell the company on choosing their firm to participate in the lucrative fees associated with the IPO. From the company's point of view, however, this is a chance to familiarize many of the Wall Street analysts who might later cover, or be asked to comment on the company's business and stock prospects.

Too many companies make the mistake of talking to only a small set of bankers. If they want a "first-tier" or "bulge bracket" firm, such as Goldman Sachs, Morgan Stanley, or Merrill Lynch, they may feel it isn't worth their time talking with 10 to 15 smaller players that want to be part of the offering. In fact, just as you wouldn't tell a potential good customer to go away without speaking to him, you shouldn't do the same to the bankers. It is often best to hone the pitch that will be given to the first-tier folks on some of the other firms. Their analysts can constructively criticize the positioning, projects, and passion that your company is using to try and get the highest valuation from these firms. It is common to have one or two smaller, boutique firms, as part of the offering underwriters. More and more, online trading firms such as Wit Capital, e*Trade, or DLJ Direct are also participating. And you can build relationships that may well be needed in later months, after the IPO, if there is any slip in the company's performance.

Just as you wouldn't run a television ad that wasn't professionally scripted and produced, the IPO road show pitch itself requires the same care and professionalism. Power Presentations' Jerry Weissman, whose company helps create road show presentations and then coaches the speakers in dealing with audiences—large and small—in the most effective way, says "[this training] can help add a few dollars to the stock price . . ."

The buyers for the IPO fall into several groups: institutional investors focused on momentum, long-term institutional holders, retail holders, and flippers. A balanced mix of all of these types are needed to have the company's stock in strong enough hands, yet trade enough to be interesting to market makers who support the stock.

Investor Relations

Once the IPO has been completed, a company has to communicate with its investors to keep them informed, and to keep the stock price consistent with the company's performance and promise. While there are a number of firms that can help, in the same way that traditional public relation firms help with product positioning, most companies should have an in-house designee to handle investor queries, provide copies of reports, and coordinate the company's release of information on quarterly basis, as well as it's conference calls with analysts.

The conference call gives the company a chance to present itself to 30 to 100 key influencers each quarter. Many of the analysts on the call will be writing a report or set of comments for their clients—recommending whether or not to buy, sell, or hold the stock. We recommend following four simple rules for these communications:

1. Tell the truth, the whole truth and nothing but the truth.
2. Tell the bad news first.
3. Don't over "spin" the good news.
4. Don't get on the message boards.

While point one should be obvious, the temptation to omit some of the bad news, or to hold back or spin the positive news, can sometimes feel overwhelming. Don't succumb! There is a large group of plaintiff's lawyers just waiting for any misstatements they can use to successfully sue you. (Note "successfully," they'll often sue anyway on bad news, whether or not you've been telling the truth.)

Dealing with bad news is never easy. Getting it out of the way of the market, so that its impact on stock price has been felt, and then allowing the price to recover on good news, is far better than wasting some good news immediately before the bad news comes out. It is also important that everyone gets all the bad news at the same time—avoiding the selective disclosure that could give an unfair market advantage to those who hear it before others. Most companies schedule their press releases and conference calls outside of market hours. Now that the markets are moving toward 24-hour trading, this is becoming more difficult, but it still makes sense to schedule outside the standard 9:30 A.M. to 4:00 P.M. Eastern time window when the bulk of the trading takes place.

Finally, we are also tempted to add some "spin" to good news. A small contract may be touted as a harbinger of much bigger ones, or a move from losses to breakeven may be spun as a major turnaround. It is better to let the investors draw their own positive conclusions.

Over the past few years, there has been a dramatic rise in the availability of information on public companies, which has been good for investors. At the same time, the message board phenomenon has cropped up. On Yahoo, Raging Bull, Silicon Investor, AOL, Motley Fool, and other sites, there are places where "investors" (usually rank amateur speculators) can post any comments they want about your stock. While there are occasional nuggets, most of it is drivel—uninformed, meant to hype or cut the price when a smarter speculator has gone short, or wants to go long. The SEC has been working with the providers to curb the worst of the abuses—outright lies meant to manipulate a stock—but there is still far too much misleading information.

When your Investor Relations executives read these, they, or other employees or officers, may be tempted to correct the misstatements. *DON'T.* Once you start correcting, the public may feel that you have taken on the obligation to always correct them, a task that the company should not, and may not legally, be able to do. False merger rumors, for example, abound on these boards. Companies must say "No Comment" to any questions about unannounced merger activity or, the courts have ruled, they must always respond accurately. This makes it difficult to have secret negotiations, since any leaks would have to be dignified by the company's comments.

You can get help from Yahoo and the other providers if there is harm being done. In one case, a message poster falsely took on the name of the company's CEO. Since Yahoo generally allows anyone to get any unregistered e-mail, they didn't stop this until they were informed of the ruse. At that point, they took away the e-mail address. But the anonymous nature of posting makes it too easy to lie and deceive.

Summary

Each company has its basic product or service, and a separate product called *shares.* Treating the customer base for those shares with the same care and attention as those customers for products and services is crucial to success. In terms of cash flow, most Internet companies take in far more cash in their first five years through financing activities than through product sales.

CHAPTER 12

Building Strong Brands and Strong Entrepreneurial Companies

In previous chapters, we have shown how to tackle all elements of the marketing mix for entrepreneurial ventures. All of these marketing mix chapters had very similar formats. Regardless of whether the decision was pricing, public relations, advertising, distribution channels, salesforce, or product or service design, the format of the decision-making process was similar. The process began with a given positioning and target market and then asked the role of the marketing mix element in furthering the positioning toward the target market segments? Each marketing mix decision process then described various paradigms for developing mix elements that contributed to the incremental revenue of the venture in comparison to the incremental costs of the marketing mix element. Each chapter emphasizes that the marketing mix elements must be justified based on revenue that they contributed over and above the incremental costs of gaining that revenue.

Given this orientation toward incremental revenue and incremental cost, a reasonable question to ask is: Do these marketing mix procedures contribute to the long-term health of the entrepreneurial venture? Are we performing marketing activities for the short-term that help short-term sales for our products or services, but that will hurt the long-term revenue and profit potential of our venture? These are legitimate questions. To try to answer them, we will turn to an expert on brand equity and building strong brands—David Aaker. Aaker has written two books and many articles on how to manage brands for the long term. His most recent book *Building Strong Brands*[1] has as its goal to guide managers in how to build brands that are strong and will endure and prosper over time. We will examine two major concepts that he uses in the book and see how compatible they are with the entrepreneurial marketing approach we advocate. The two Aaker concepts we will examine are: (1) Why it is hard to build brands, and (2) his ten guidelines for building strong brands. To make our examination come alive, we will use an example of an entrepreneurial company that has been very successful in building a strong brand and strong company.

Synygy, Inc.—a Strong, Enduring, Entrepreneurial Company

The company is Synygy, Inc., "The Incentive Compensation Company." Mark Stiffler, an MBA from MIT's Sloan School, founded Synygy in 1991. The firm began as a service to automate the analysis of sales data for pharmaceutical companies. This experience in automating sales analysis led the firm's customers to ask if Synygy could help in managing their salesforce incentive compensation plans. It was a perennial problem for the pharmaceutical firms and their large salesforces. The compensation plans developed by the sales managers were very difficult to implement because of the large amounts of sales data that needed to be processed to tell whether the salesperson had met a quota or what his or her commission or bonus should be. This was the same sales data that Synygy had been analyzing. Most firms were using mostly manual processes that lead to late reports, inaccurate compensation calculations, and salespeople who did not trust the veracity of the numbers on which they were paid. It was a problem that no one had built a business on nor spent much effort against. Many companies were using home-grown systems that were very expensive to build (when all of the real costs were calculated), and very complex to modify if the compensation plan were to change. There was a real need for a more efficient, more valuable approach to the management of compensation plans. Mark and his firm began to develop more and more expertise by becoming the outsourcing vehicle for the administration of plans. They became a group whose expertise grew with each plan they administered. They also developed generalizable computer and information systems to reproduce what their people were doing manually. These systems also were continuously improved. By being very close to their initial customers, they understood how important it was for the plan calculations to be right, but even more importantly to be understandable. The salespeople needed to be able to relate their own actions and effort to how their compensation would be affected. The Synygy team developed over time a series of graphical reports that communicated extremely well to salespeople. Their experience kept building into better and better systems to handle compensation plan administration with a very effective combination of computer systems and expert people. They now do the complete outsourced administration of incentive compensation plans. Since 1991, Synygy has grown fast enough to be on the Inc. 500 list of fastest growing private companies in 1997, 1998, 1999, and 2000.

The only real competition to challenge Synygy (aside from in-house home-grown solutions) has been the recent entry of enterprise software vendors who sell software, but do not provide ongoing plan management services. From its beginnings in the Pharmaceutical industry, Synygy has begun expanding into other industries that employ many salespeople and have incentive compensation as an important part of their plans. As we examine how hard it is to build brands, we will use Synygy, Inc. as an example of a successful strong brand. We will try to understand why Synygy has been able to overcome the obstacles to building an enduring brand and an enduring company.

Why Is It Hard to Build Brands?

Aaker outlines eight reasons that many companies find it difficult to build strong, enduring brands. His orientation is more toward mass-market consumer products, but the concepts are appropriate for any entrepreneur to consider. Figure 12.1 shows these eight reasons.

We shall reinterpret these reasons from the viewpoint of the entrepreneur who is beginning a new venture or has been operating an entrepreneurial venture. The first reason, *pressure to compete on price,* can cause an entrepreneur to make decisions that are counter to building her brand. A lower price, all other things being equal, signals to the marketplace that the value of the product offering is going down also. However, if the perceived value of the offering compared to competition is not going down, then the entrepreneur should not change her price compared to the competition. Many high-tech market categories have price levels that are continuously decreasing as technology lowers costs for all of the players. However, the strong brands within the category will

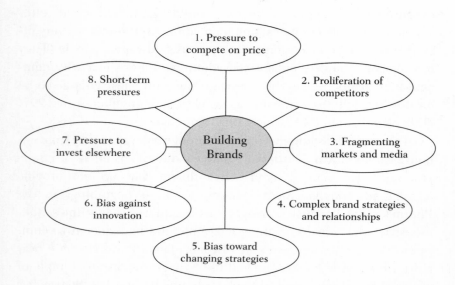

Figure 12.1 Why is it hard to build brands? *Source:* Aaker, David A., *Building Strong Brands* (New York: The Free Press, 1966).

have aspects of their offering that add incremental perceived value versus the competition. This price premium compared to competition based on perceived incremental value is the essence of what excellent entrepreneurial marketing enables. There is no reason to lower this premium unless something else in your marketing mix is changing the perceived value of your offering by the market participants. Dell is an excellent example of a strong brand that has prospered in the face of severe price reductions in its personal computer marketplace. Dell's offering bundle includes several attributes that continue to add perceived incremental value versus their competitors. These attributes include customization of the computer's attributes, simple, easy ordering on the web, an excellent quality and service reputation, and a personal salesforce that has developed a reputation for trust and service in the major business markets that Dell serves. If anything, the price premium that Dell receives is probably increasing over time because the competition has not succeeded in duplicating many of the attributes of Dell's offering that the market values.

Synygy really does not compete on price with anyone for the total outsourcing solution. They do compete with some enterprise software vendors for the software portion of the implementation. However, in order to capitalize on their distinctive competence in complete plan management, Synygy has partnered with their major software competitors to offer the implementation and ongoing administration of the plans using their competitor's software. So, potential customers can buy either a complete solution from Synygy or they can buy software from someone else and pay Synygy to manage the plan. Synygy bases their pricing on a value in use argument. According to a Synygy brochure:

> Don't buy software. Don't build systems yourself. Outsource to Synygy. Synygy's incentive compensation solution costs less than building, maintaining, and running a homegrown system, or buying, customizing, and operating packaged software.
>
> Many of our customers have saved millions of dollars. That's because outsourcing to Synygy increases the top line, improves margins, cuts costs, and improves cash flow by eliminating the huge up-front investment in software and hardware.[2]

The second reason for it being hard to build strong brands, *proliferation of competitors,* always makes entrepreneurial life interesting. However, if you are managing the perceived value of your offering versus these competitors, you should fare well. Also, if your initial positioning strategy is soundly based on your distinctive competence that is the source of sustainable competitive advantage, then you should be ready for proliferating competitors.

Synygy was ready to compete when late in 1998 major enterprise software developers such as Oracle Corp., Siebel Systems, or Trilogy began to offer software to manage incentive plans. Because Synygy's software and operating methods had been continuously improved by their experience and because the operational issues of actually managing the plans on an ongoing basis are so difficult, no competitor has yet challenged Synygy for the complete outsourcing solution. These new competitors are also not finding it easy to finish applications that are referenceable. However, that does not mean that Synygy can sit still. As this is being written, they need to increase their salesforce and public relations presence to counteract the lack of perception that Synygy may have in their target markets outside of pharmaceuticals. They have to be concerned as to how the target markets *perceive* Synygy's offerings as opposed to how much better they actually are. In this situation, word of mouth from satisfied customers is the best weapon Synygy has. As long as Synygy continues to build its distinctive competence and increases its ability to be perceived as adding the most value to its target markets, it may be able to stay ahead of its competitors.

We can combine reasons three and four for why it is hard to build brands for an entrepreneur. These relate to *keeping the positioning of the brand consistent regardless of which media or market that is used* and considering *the brand's relationship to other of the firm's brands.* These reasons should typically not be very salient for most entrepreneurial marketers. Most successful ventures are targeting niche markets, not mass markets, so they should be using very targeted media vehicles and public relations. Most entrepreneurial ventures also have only one brand, their first. In many cases, their brand is their company. As they grow, some of these issues may become more salient.

For Synygy, a key strategic issue they faced was the best way to grow. They could expand their services to existing clients by performing other analyses on the same sales data they used for their incentive plan management. These would help the marketing and sales managers to understand the impact of elements of their marketing and sales decisions. They could alternatively expand their incentive plan management offering to other markets than pharmaceuticals. Both of the options were somewhat consistent with the firm's initial positioning and distinctive competence. However, the potential perceived value and distinctiveness of their incentive plan offering was much higher than the analysis services. Synygy correctly decided to prioritize the expansion of their core incentive plan management offering to other target markets. For their current users, they will do further analysis of the sales data as a value-added service. However, Synygy's marketing budget and sales resources are used primarily toward expansion to new customers and new markets, leveraging their core distinctive competence. The tag line "The Incentive Compensation Company" was adopted after Synygy made this strategic decision to strengthen their company and "brand." If Synygy would have known this strategy decision when they named their firm, it would have been more productive to name the company more consistent with its positioning. However, hindsight is clearer than foresight.

In Chapter 9, we used the change in advertising copy that Synygy recently made that increased their short term advertising productivity by over 15 times. This new advertising copy was still consistent with the basic positioning and segmentation strategies of the firm. The advertising just got the point across much more effectively.

Reasons six—*bias toward changing strategies*—and seven—*bias against innovation*—are issues with which entrepreneurs constantly struggle. For many entrepreneurial companies, the issue of developing a scaleable marketing-sales-business model is very difficult. The really successful firms succeed in developing a way of going to market, and getting and serving new customers that becomes routinized and scaleable, like a formula. The founding entrepreneur no longer has to go to close each sale. The company's positioning and perceived value become known well enough in the market so that sales come somewhat easier. Growth can accelerate quickly when this happens.

However, the entrepreneur can become bored and lose focus. He may want the firm to move into other more interesting products or markets. This changing of strategies can seriously harm the venture; especially if the new products and/or markets are not leveraging the distinctive competence and positioning that have become the heritage of the company. Scarce resources need to be allocated to where they can provide the most long-term value to the firm, not necessarily to the most interesting new idea.

On the other hand, the entrepreneur cannot stand pat with the formula without continuously seeking to improve the firm's perceived value to its customers and leverage its distinctive competence. He must constantly keep ahead of current and potential competition. However, all the innovation should be leveraging the existing positioning and distinctive competence of the firm. If the marketplace needs are changing, then sometimes the positioning and associated product offering needs to adapt to the changing needs. However, the adaptation to the market changes always should be done to leverage the firm's distinctive competence relative to the competition.

Synygy's market needs and competition are constantly changing. We already discussed the new software competition. The market is also moving toward web based systems and applications service providers as new ways to solve information systems problems. The information technology officers at their potential client companies are causing this movement. Synygy is broadening its offering to include different ways of delivering their service. They will provide either a complete outsourced solution, or be an application service provider, or provide just the enterprise software for purchase, or provide the ongoing management and implementation of someone else's software. However all of these options are consistent with its core positioning and leverage their distinctive competence. Synygy knows the "nitty-gritty" of implementing incentive plans to improve their customers' productivity better than anyone. All of their new, broadened offerings are consistent with and leverage that core competence.

The next reason for being hard to build brands, *pressure to invest elsewhere,* may not be as salient for entrepreneurs whose

companies typically have only one brand. The big problem is getting enough to invest in the company's main product offering.
Many new Internet companies are spending on their core brands,
but they are spending it ineffectively. They are not evaluating the
incremental revenue due to the different marketing mix options
they can use.

As this is being written, Synygy is taking steps to significantly
increase its resources to attack some new market segments before
some of their new software competition is able to claim a beach-
head.

The last reason is *short-term pressures*. It is sometimes very
tempting to sacrifice positioning and the brand's perceived value to
do some activity that will help short-term sales and profits. For consumer products, the activities that can cause the most problems are
temporary price oriented price promotions. If these promotions are
not reinforcing the product offering's targeted perceived value,
they can harm this perceived value. If consumers see a brand as always "on sale," it may cheapen its perceived value. Even if such
promotions cause some incremental short-term sales and profits,
if they are not consistent with the positioning of the brand, they
should not be done.

In Chapter 5, we documented what happened to Marantz when
they brought in the discount stores to augment their then high-end
retail distribution channels. The tactic was very successful short-
term, but ruined the company and brand for the long term.

Probably the most common short-term pressure for entrepreneurs in business-to-business markets is from their salespeople to
discount their product in order to "close the sale." Here, if the
customer does not perceive enough incremental value to justify
the normal price, then the salesperson has not done his job, or the
customer is not in the target market. Unless the entrepreneur can
be confident that the "special" price reduction will not become
widely known, then it does not make sense to reduce the price to
"close" this one sale. The other potential customers who would
have been willing to pay the normal price will no longer be willing,
if they learn that someone else has gotten a lower price. Thus, the
price received will trend down to match the "special discounts"
over time and hurt the long-term profitability of the venture. It is
very hard for most entrepreneurs to lose sales, but sometimes it

is the right thing to do, especially if the potential customer will not receive as much value as some other customers. As we show in Chapter 3, a good pricing policy implies that not every potential customer will buy our offering.

Synygy has been able to rapidly grow its business without having to resort to "special" price reductions to get certain clients. They have a given price list to which all companies are subject. Obviously, there are different prices for different numbers of salespeople and for the different levels of service that Synygy can provide.

Can Entrepreneurial Marketers Overcome These Eight Difficulties in Building Brands?

The answer to this question should be obvious. If the entrepreneur has followed the prescriptions in the previous chapters, she will always be building the long-term health of her company and its brands while she simultaneously contributes to the venture's short-term revenue and profits. Every marketing mix activity and in fact, all venture activities must be consistent with the perceived value the firm wants to deliver to its customers and potential customers. The venture must be dedicated to continuously improving this perceived value versus competition by building and leveraging its distinctive competencies and communicating this value to its target markets.

Ten Guidelines for Building Strong Brands

Aaker provides ten guidelines for building strong brands.[3] These are good guidelines for entrepreneurial marketers in general. However, some of them need to be modified to the circumstances in which most entrepreneurs find themselves. The last guideline, in particular, merits significant modification for entrepreneurs:

1. *Brand identity.* Have an identity for each brand. Consider the perspectives of the brand-as-person, brand-as-organization, and brand-as-symbol, as well as the brand-as-product. Identify the core identity. Modify the identity as needed for different market segments and products. Remember that an image is

how you are perceived, and an identity is how you aspire to be perceived.

2. *Value proposition.* Know the value proposition for each brand that has a driver role. Consider emotional and self-expressive benefits as well as functional benefits. Know how endorser brands will provide credibility. Understand the brand-customer relationship.

3. *Brand position.* For each brand, have a brand position that will provide clear guidance to those implementing a communication program. Recall that a position is the part of the identity and value proposition that is to be actively communicated.

4. *Execution.* Execute the communication program so that it not only is on target with the identity and position but achieves brilliance and durability. Generate alternatives and consider options beyond media advertising.

5. *Consistency over time.* Have as a goal a consistent identity, position, and execution over time. Maintain symbols, imagery, and metaphors that work. Understand and resist organizational biases toward changing the identity, position, and execution.

6. *Brand system.* Make sure the brands in the portfolio are consistent and synergistic. Know their roles. Have or develop silver bullets to help support brand identities and positions. Exploit branded features and services. Use subbrands to clarify and modify. Know the strategic brands.

7. *Brand leverage.* Extend brands and develop cobranding programs only of the brand identity will be both used and reinforced. Identify range brands and, for each, develop an identity and specify how that identity will be different in disparate product contests. If brand is moved up or down, take care to manage the integrity of the resulting brand identities.

8. *Tracking brand equity.* Track brand equity over time, including awareness, perceived quality, brand loyalty, and especially brand associations. Have specific communication objectives. Especially note areas where the brand identity and position are not reflected in the brand image.

9. *Brand responsibility.* Have someone in charge of the brand who will create the identity and position and coordinate the execution over organizational units, media, and markets. Beware when a brand is being used in a business in which it is not the cornerstone.

10. *Invest in brands.* Continue investing in brands even when the financial goals are not being met.

The above guidelines are self-explanatory and should be helpful to entrepreneurs as well as the consumer products corporate types to whom Aaker's book is directed. Guideline 6 about the brand system and 7, brand leverage to new products, may be overkill for most entrepreneurs that have one brand that keeps their hands full. Guideline 8, tracking brand equity, should be observed more in spirit by many entrepreneurs. They should remain close to their existing and potential customers to assess how their product offering's value is being perceived. They should put cost effective means in place to check whether the perceived value of the offering is changing over time. Usually, this would be in the form of customer satisfaction surveys as well as getting periodic readings from potential customers on how they perceive the value of the offering versus its competition.

The last guideline needs some modification for entrepreneurs. In fact, depending how one interprets it, the guideline may not be consistent with research we discussed in Chapter 9. The guideline says to continue to invest in the brand even when the financial goals are not being met. We have discussed research that needs to be considered in this investment decision. That research (on television advertising) basically said that *if the advertising didn't work short term, it had no long-term revenue impact.* It also said that *if the advertising worked in the short term, it had a long-term impact that more than doubled the short-term impact on the average.* There is no academic research that says that this conclusion would be any different for other elements of the marketing mix such as public relations or different media. Thus, the key determination that the entrepreneur needs to make is: Does the investment in my brand have an *incremental impact* on the short-term revenue of the product offering? This incremental impact must be determined relative to *what revenue would have been had the investment not been made.* If the brand would be going down if the advertising were not done, and its revenue would *go down less* with an advertising program, then the advertising program has a *positive incremental impact.*

Thus, for entrepreneurs, we would modify the last guideline to read: *Continue to invest in the brand as long as the investment has a positive incremental impact on the brand's revenue.* If your brand marketing investments are not impacting revenue compared to what the revenue would have been without the investment, then it won't help either the long-term or the short-term sales for the brand. The entrepreneurial marketing challenge is to continually find investments in the brand that will have short-term incremental impact. In Chapter 9, we outline methods for managing these marketing investments so that they will more likely have the required impact.

Summary

In this chapter, we have shown how the entrepreneur can simultaneously build short-term revenue and a strong entrepreneurial venture by following the prescriptions in the previous chapters. Entrepreneurs cannot be satisfied to spend money just brand building without having an impact on their revenue. Many advertising and marketing agencies would advocate this unproductive brand building activity. The entrepreneur must resist this advocacy and insist on brand building programs that have an incremental impact. If not, the entrepreneur is throwing her money away with a very high probability. As this is being written, many of the new Internet ventures are throwing away lots of money in "brand building" spending that they have no idea whether is working or not. Effective entrepreneurs should not let this happen. Chapter 9 shows how to manage this process.

CHAPTER 13

Summary and Conclusions

Key Lessons in Entrepreneurial Marketing

The over-riding concepts that pervade every chapter of this book are those of positioning and target segmentation. At the highest level, the market segments into those two groups who give a company money—customers and investors, and those groups to whom the company gives money—employees, suppliers, and channels. Entrepreneurial companies must use the positioning and segmentation concepts for each of these target markets. The decisions on who is the target market and how the target market will perceive the product/service offering versus the competition is the most important that the entrepreneur will make. These positioning decisions should leverage the entrepreneur's distinctive competence and provide a basis for sustainable competitive advantage. All marketing/sales decisions should support and leverage the positioning and segmentation. This implies focus and discipline—characteristics that entrepreneurs sometimes lack.

Because the perception and reaction of the target market to your product offering is so crucial, concept testing or in-market testing of new product or service ideas is almost always a very profitable entrepreneurial investment. In today's Internet world, it can be done relatively inexpensively. Often you can combine concept testing with price testing to obtain estimates of market response to different prices.

You should price your product offering to produce the maximum stream of profits over the product's life. It is easier to lower prices over time than to raise them. The initial pricing policy is a crucial decision. Concept testing alternative prices or in-market testing of alternatives is another generally profitable entrepreneurial investment. Pricing is intertwined with the perceived value in use versus competition for B2B and many other products and services. Thus, pricing needs to be supported by all the other elements of the marketing mix. Pricing decisions are typically not given the attention they deserve.

Public relations activities can result in publicity that is perceived as more credible than paid advertising or promotion. For many markets, creating "buzz" is key and needs to be carefully managed. Timing of public relations activities is crucial in the new product/service diffusion process. Professional public relations firms can be very productive versus learning all of the ropes and making all the trade and general press contacts by yourself.

Distribution channel choices can have a very big impact on how your product "offering bundle" is perceived by your target market. Decisions such as direct versus indirect, or exclusive, selective, or intensive distribution channels need careful evaluation. Concept testing with possible channel partners can be a very profitable way to assist in making this evaluation. You must anticipate channel conflict and manage it creatively. Distribution channel decisions should be managed dynamically over time as the markets, competition, and product diffusion changes.

Decisions on how to roll out your product or service are also very important. Choosing the appropriate reference accounts, gaining them, and generating the right referrals is crucial, especially for technology, B2B products, and the newer, or more disruptive product innovation. Using a high-level direct salesforce (usually including the entrepreneur) can be very productive for these situations.

The salesforce should always be adding and reinforcing the perceived value of your product offering. Many times the salesforce is perceived as part of the offering by your target market. Many of the salesforce decision alternatives (direct versus indirect, deployment, etc.) can be evaluated using in-market experimentation. The direct, personal salesforce should be evaluated versus other options such as telephone sales, or Web sales. There is a big opportunity for both the Inc. 500 CEOs and other entrepreneurs to improve their performance by attempting to evaluate the incremental short- and long-term revenue versus incremental costs of alternative salesforce sizes and deployments. Salesforce compensation needs to match incentives of the salespeople and the entrepreneurial venture. In particular, compensation for obtaining new accounts should usually be different than that for gaining business from existing accounts.

You should resist the temptation to do any promotion, event, or other marketing tactic that will jeopardize your offering's perception in your target markets. Like all other marketing vehicles, these tactics are justified only when the lifetime incremental revenue for the tactic is greater than the lifetime incremental costs attributable to the tactic. Creativity is crucial for these activities and new unique promotional ideas should be sought from very diverse sources. However, before running them broadly, they should be tested and evaluated for their impact on your positioning and on incremental revenues and costs.

Advertising options should be evaluated like other marketing mix elements—incremental revenue produced versus incremental costs over your planning horizon. For advertising, this evaluation may be imprecise, but is almost always better than using out-dated "rules" for managing advertising. In-market advertising testing and carefully evaluating naturally occurring advertising experiments can add much value and productivity. However, the analysis needs to be planned for and the appropriate data gathered and stored so that the analysis can be done. It's best to find very different advertising options by going to creative sources that will be very different from each other.

Many of these marketing concepts and paradigms can be used to hire and retain the best people. Positioning, segmentation, pricing, and marketing mix are all valuable for improving the recruitment and retention processes.

The impact of marketing activities on capital raising can be more important than on incremental revenue for the early stages of many entrepreneurial ventures. Positioning concepts can impact your perception by potential investors as well as your name and all of your other marketing activities. Segmentation of potential investors is also productive. Exclusive distribution contracts may be a low cost source of investment capital.

In our last chapter, we showed how all of the concepts and paradigms for generating and evaluating marketing mix elements by incremental revenue versus incremental costs are consistent with building strong, enduring brands and companies. Everything the venture does should be consistent and support the "offering bundle" perception by the appropriate target segments.

The Best Marketing Decision and Biggest Marketing Mistakes—Survey Results

Table 13.1 lists all of the responses to the open-ended survey questions on the best marketing decision and the biggest marketing mistakes broken out by Inc. 500 CEOs and local entrepreneurs. Let's look at the first four groups of answers—those that had the largest percentage of responses. The contrast between the Inc. 500 CEOs and the other entrepreneurs is striking.

Of the Inc. 500 CEOs, 23.2 percent considered their most important marketing decision (either best decision—16.1 percent, or biggest mistake—7.1 percent) to be related to consistently applying good positioning, targeting, and brand development. Only 5 percent of the non-Inc. group had similar concerns. Similarly, 23.2 percent of the Inc. CEOs (17.8 percent + 5.4 percent) put great importance on hiring professional people for sales, marketing, and public relations who were expert in their target markets. Only 10 percent of the non-Inc. group had similar concerns.

On the other hand, 40 percent of the non-Inc. group (32.5 percent + 7.5 percent) were concerned about getting the right marketing tactics—media, public relations, seminars, brochures, direct sales, and so on. Only 14.8 percent of the Inc. 500 CEOs considered these tactical decisions as their best (8.9 percent), or worst (5.9 percent) decisions. Last, 8.9 percent of the Inc. 500 CEOs thought that getting market reaction before broadly introducing their products was their best marketing decision versus none of the

	Inc. 500 (N = 56 responses)	Non-Inc. 500 (N = 40 responses)
Good targeting, positioning, brand development consistently applied	16.1	2.5
Not being consistent/or effectively positioned	7.1	2.5
Hiring professional for marketing, sales, public relations expert in their target markets	17.8	5.0
Not hiring expert professionals	5.4	5.0
Getting the right marketing vehicles (media, public relations, seminars, brochures, direct sales, etc.)	8.9	32.5
Not getting the right vehicles—not testing alternatives early enough	5.9	7.5
Getting market reaction to new products/services, including market research	8.9	0
Not getting market reaction to new product/services	1.8	10
Using the Web well	5.4	10
Using references sells	3.6	5
Spending too much on marketing and sales	1.8	5
Spending enough on marketing and sales	1.8	2.5
Not spending enough on marketing and sales	1.8	5
Good customer service	1.8	0
Not good enough customer service	1.8	2.5
Using indirect distribution channels including strategic alliances	3.6	2.5
Using trade shows a lot	1.8	5
Using direct marketing a lot	1.8	5
Pricing well	1.8	2.5

*Percentage of Responses for Those Who Answered the Questions—Segregated by Inc. 500 and Non-Inc. 500 Entrepreneurs.

Table 13.1 The Best Marketing Decisions/The Biggest Marketing Mistakes

non-Inc. group. On the other hand, 10 percent of the non-Inc. group regretted not getting market reaction before introducing their products versus only 1.8 percent of the Inc. 500 CEOs.

How do we interpret these results? First, more of the Inc. 500 CEOs have learned how important targeting and positioning are as cornerstones to all of their marketing and strategy decisions. This is the main point of this book. Positioning and segmentation are the drivers of strategy and marketing tactics. Second, more of the Inc. 500 group have learned that it pays to get market reaction to products and services before spending a great deal of money on them. Third, more of the Inc. 500 CEOs have learned that it pays to hire professional help for key marketing and sales roles.

The non-Inc. group is more concerned with getting a magic, short-term marketing tactic that will work, and not realizing how important it is to have those tactics consistently reinforce the firm's positioning and targeting.

However, just because the Inc. 500 CEOs were more likely to understand the basic messages of this book, does not mean that even they can't improve. The survey responses showed plenty of room for both groups of entrepreneurs to significantly improve their profits by adopting the concepts, methods, and paradigms of this book. We hope that this book will encourage other entrepreneurs to adopt them.

The Top Ten Lessons of Entrepreneurial Marketing

We leave you with a simple summary of the top ten lessons you should bring away from this book:

1. Positioning and target segmentation are the key decisions.

2. In-market testing provides the truest indication of perception and reaction to offerings.

3. Price to maximize total profit stream over the product life.

4. Public relations creates buzz with higher credibility than the same dollars spent on advertising.

5. Anticipate and manage channel conflicts—avoiding them means you are probably missing some channels.

6. Marketing may impact raising capital more than sales in a company's early life.

7. Hiring the best talent pays off—market to potential employees with different messages than products.

8. Events and promotions should be used carefully to avoid jeopardizing the primary offering in the target markets.

9. Advertising options should be tested and evaluated—don't be overly swayed by creative material.

10. Positioning and target segmentation are the key decisions (yes, we've said it twice)!

Appendix A

A Segmentation Audit

	Completely Describes Us (A)	Somewhat Describes Us (B)	Does Not Describe Us At All (C)	Don't Know (D)
1. Our business strategies recognize the need to prioritize target segments.	___	___	___	___
2. Our marketing plans include specific plans for each of the selected segments.	___	___	___	___
3. We have specific product and service offerings for each target segments.	___	___	___	___
4. We have detailed information about segments, including:	___	___	___	___
a. Current size of the segment	___	___	___	___
b. Potential size of the segment	___	___	___	___
c. Key business needs of the segments	___	___	___	___
d. Information systems needs of the segment	___	___	___	___
e. Their prioritized needs/ benefits sought	___	___	___	___
f. Their prioritized preference for product and service features	___	___	___	___
g. Demographic characteristics of the segments	___	___	___	___
h. Product ownership and usage	___	___	___	___
i. Competitor's strength in each segment	___	___	___	___
j. Perceived positioning of each competitor by the members of the segment	___	___	___	___
5. We have a process for updating the information on our segments on an ongoing basis.	___	___	___	___
6. Our segments are developed across countries, but recognize unique country requirements and subsegments.	___	___	___	___

	Completely Describes Us (A)	Somewhat Describes Us (B)	Does Not Describe Us At All (C)	Don't Know (D)
7. Information about the target market segments are incorporated effectively into the following strategies:				
a. Positioning	____	____	____	____
b. Product and service offering	____	____	____	____
c. Pricing	____	____	____	____
d. Promotion	____	____	____	____
e. Public Relations	____	____	____	____
f. Advertising	____	____	____	____
g. Distribution	____	____	____	____
h. Salesforce	____	____	____	____
8. We ave an effective process for implementing segmentation research.	____	____	____	____
9. We have an effective process for implementing segmentation strategies.	____	____	____	____
10. We have P&L reports and accountability by segment.	____	____	____	____

Adapted from correspondence of Yoram J. Wind, 1997.

Appendix B

Summary of Survey and Findings

Summary of Survey Findings

1. Company size.

Number of Employees	Inc.	Non-Inc.
< 50	39.4%	90.7%
51–100	24.2	4.7
101–500	33.3	4.7
501–1000	—	—
1001–3000	3.0	—
>3001	—	—

2. Expected revenue for calender year 2000.

Expected Revenue	Inc.	Non-Inc.
< 250,000	58.1%	
250,000–999,999	—	4.7
1,000,000–4,999,999	6.1%	27.9
5,000,000–49,999,999	72.7	9.3
50,000,000–999,999,999	21.2	—
1,000,000,000 or more	—	—

3. Years of operation.

Years	Inc.	Non-Inc.
< 1	—	23.7%
1–< 3	—	18.6
3–< 5	11.8%	11.6
5–< 10	79.4	23.7
> = 10	—	23.7

4. Revenue growth dynamics.

Percent in 1999 compared to 1998.

	Inc.	Non-Inc.	p-value
Mean	61.44%	71.84%	.7932
Standard Deviation	87.16	195.27	

Percent projected for 2000 versus 1999.

	Inc.	Non-Inc.	p-value
Mean	64.97%	79.88%	.5192
Standard Deviation	81.96	115.43	

Average percent growth for the past 5 years.

	Inc.	Non-Inc.	*p*-value
Mean	279.94%	32.81%	.0025
Standard Deviation	427.59	66.48	

5. Frequency of marketing activities.

	Inc.		Non-Inc.	
	Not at All	As Many Times as Possible	Not at All	As Many Times as Possible
Product positioning	17.7%	52.9%	41.8%	25.6%
Segmentation studies	52.9	11.8	60.5	2.3
New product testing	29.4	38.2	39.5	20.9
Prelaunch forecasting	32.4	29.4	55.8	13.9
In-market testing of marketing mix elements	52.9	8.8	69.8	11.6

6. Internet use.

	Inc.		Non-Inc.	
	Not at All	As Many Times as Possible	Not at All	As Many Times as Possible
New product testing	58.8%	5.9%	62.8%	16.3%
Promotion offer testing	50.0	17.7	55.8	4.7
Activities that incorporate the Web with bricks and-mortar operations	23.5	38.2	46.5	13.9
Price testing	64.7	5.9	62.8	7.0
Competitive analysis	20.6	29.4	37.2	20.9
Consumer feedback	29.4	32.4	32.6	20.9
Advertising testing	50.0	8.8	46.5	11.6
Promotion of our products	2.9	67.7	30.2	39.5
Promotion of our company	5.9	88.2	25.6	39.5
Distribution of product/company information	0.0	88.2	20.9	46.5
E-commerce	17.7	47.1	44.2	23.3

7. Pricing of the very first product or service.

	Inc.	Non-Inc.
Cost-plus	17.7%	39.5%
Value-in-use	32.4	23.3
Going rate	29.4	25.6
Bargaining	5.9	4.7
No specific pricing system	5.9	0.0
Other	2.9	4.7

8. Current pricing.

	Inc.	Non-Inc.
Cost-plus	23.5%	41.9 %
Value-in-use	52.9	23.3
Going rate	20.6	27.9
Bargaining	2.9	9.3
No specific pricing system	0.0	0.0
Other	2.9	7.0

9. Did you use concept testing for your *first* product?

   a. 32.4 percent of Inc. companies said yes.

   b. 32.6 percent of non-Inc. companies said yes.

10. Do you typically test your concepts at different price levels before introduction?

	Inc.	Non-Inc.
Always	0.0%	9.3%
Sometimes	17.7	20.9
Never	50.0	67.4

11. Do you test alternative prices in test markets before introduction?

	Inc.	Non-Inc.
Always	0.0%	4.7%
Sometimes	29.4	23.3
Never	67.7	69.8

12. Determining the advertising budget.

	Inc.		Non-Inc.	
	Never	Most of the Time	Never	Most of the Time
What my company can afford	14.7	29.4	7.0	65.1
Current or anticipated sales and /or profits	14.7	41.2	30.2	16.3
Competitors' expenditures	55.9	0.0	60.5	0.0
Market tests	52.9	2.9	58.1	4.7
Analysis of past successes and failures	8.8	26.5	14.0	23.3
Advertising goals	20.6	23.5	30.2	18.6
Forecasted incremental sales versus incremental advertising costs	29.4	20.6	58.1	4.7
Other	0.0	5.9	0.0	4.7

13. Number of campaign alternatives generated for the last ad campaign.

	Inc.	Non-Inc.
0	17.7%	14.0%
1	14.7	11.6
2	8.8	4.7
> 3	20.6	21.0
Average	1.52	1.57
Standard deviation	1.25	1.29

14. Type of salesforce.

	Inc.	Non-Inc.
Direct	82.3%	55.8%
Indirect	11.8	9.3
No salesforce	11.8	27.9
Other	0.0	0.0

15. How did you decide on the number of salespeople needed?

	Inc.		Non-Inc.	
	Never	Most of the Time	Never	Most of the Time
Selling expense as percentage of sales and average cost of salesperson	38.2%	17.7%	27.9%	16.3%
Forecasted sales and average revenues generated per salesperson	17.7	47.0	23.3	16.3
Market response	23.5	17.7	32.6	7.0
Forecasted incremental sales versus sales costs	11.8	5.9	32.6	0.0
Gut feel or judgment	11.8	35.3	16.3	16.3
Other	5.9	2.9	7.0	11.6

16. Salespeople compensation.

	Inc.	Non-Inc.
Commission	70.6%	46.5%
Straight salary	58.8	37.2
Achievement recognition programs	20.6	14.0
Contests and prizes	23.5	11.6
Noncash awards	17.7	4.6
Compensation—new business versus old accounts	26.5	7.0
Different commission for different products	23.5	14.0
Commission based on prior year growth	5.9	4.7
No limit on compensation	50.0	20.9
Other	2.9	9.3

17. CEO's monthly time spent on public relations.

	Inc.	Non-Inc.
< = 5	32.4%	34.9%
6–10	29.4	21.0
11–20	17.7	27.9
> 20	11.8	16.3

18. Senior management monthly time spent on public relations.

	Inc.	Non-Inc.
< = 5	35.3%	48.8%
6–10	29.4	16.3
11–20	17.7	9.3
> 20	11.8	11.6

19. Yearly public relations budget as a percentage of annual revenues.

	Inc.	Non-Inc.
Mean	1.04%	3.5%
Standard deviation	1.23	5.53

20. Yearly marketing budget as a percentage of annual revenue.

	Inc.	Non-Inc.
Mean	5.41%	8.05%
Standard deviation	5.4	7.5

21. Is marketing budget increasing or decreasing over the years?

	Inc.	Non-Inc.
Increasing	82.4%	67.4%
Decreasing	5.9	7.0
Steady	11.8	18.6

22. How confident are you about the contribution of these marketing components to your incremental revenue?

	Inc.		Non-Inc.	
	Very Confident and Confident	Not Confident and Very Uncertain	Very Confident and Confident	Not Confident and Very Uncertain
Salesforce	82.4%	0.0%	55.8%	14.0%
Advertising	35.3	23.5	53.5	9.3
Public relations	47.0	29.4	51.2	9.3
Branding activities	52.9	14.7	23.3	16.3
Trade shows	38.2	17.7	44.2	16.3
Promotions	50.0	20.6	34.9	16.3
Web	58.1	5.9	44.2	18.6
Market research	17.7	47.0	30.2	20.9
Concept testing	8.8	64.7	20.9	34.9

* Findings based on e-mail survey of CEOs of 400 companies on the 1999 Inc. 500 list and mail survey of 250 CEOs from the Wharton School's SBDC network. Results summarized for 34 Inc. respondents and 43 SBDC (non-Inc.) respondents.

Entrepreneurial Marketing Inc. 500 Study

Thank you very much for your interest in our study. Please complete the following form to participate in the study. We would like to assure you that the information you give us will be completely confidential and only data at the aggregated level will be reported. Data on individual companies will never be released without prior written consent from the company concerned.

We are interested in your opinions and application of various marketing concepts, methods, and paradigms. Your answers will be used to help other entrepreneurs to learn from your experiences.

As a thank you for your help, we will promptly send you a summary of the results of this study. We hope you can also learn from the experiences of other entrepreneurs. Please be as honest to yourself in your answers as possible.

This survey takes less than 15 minutes to complete. Please try to complete the whole survey. We really appreciate your cooperation and thank you in advance.

First, some information we will use for statistical purposes only.

1. The size of your company is:
   ☐ $250,000 to less than $1 million   ☐ $50 million to less than $1 billion
   ☐ 50 employees or less   ☐ 501 to 1,000 employees
   ☐ 51 to 100 employees   ☐ 1001 to 3,000 employees
   ☐ 101 to 500 employees   ☐ More than 3,001 employees

2. The expected revenue for the calendar year 2000 is:
   ☐ Less than $250,000   ☐ $5 million to less than $50 million
   ☐ $250,000 to less than $1 million   ☐ $50 million to less than $1 billion
   ☐ $1 million to less than $5 million ☐ $1 billion or more

3. Number of years your company has been in operation:
   ☐ Less than 1   ☐ 5 to less than 10
   ☐ 1 to less than 3   ☐ 10 years or more
   ☐ 3 to less than 5

4. Revenue growth dynamics of our company (i.e., +200%, −50%)

	% 1999 compared to calendar year 1998
	% projected for calendar year 2000 versus 1999
	% approximate average annual growth for past 5 years

5. How often do you conduct the following marketing activities?

	Not at All	Sometimes	As Many Times as Possible
Product positioning	☐	☐	☐
Segmentation studies	☐	☐	☐
New product testing	☐	☐	☐
Prelaunch forecasting	☐	☐	☐
In-market testing of marketing mix elements	☐	☐	☐

6. How do you use the Internet? Please check the appropriate answer.

We use Web-based:	Not at All	Sometimes	As Many Times as Possible
New product testing	☐	☐	☐
Promotion offer testing	☐	☐	☐
Activities that incorporate the Web with bricks-and-mortar operations	☐	☐	☐
Price testing	☐	☐	☐
Competitive analysis	☐	☐	☐
Consumer feedback	☐	☐	☐
Advertising testing	☐	☐	☐
Promotion of our products	☐	☐	☐
Promotion of our company	☐	☐	☐
Distribution of product/company information	☐	☐	☐
E-commerce	☐	☐	☐

7. Let us discuss pricing decisions made by your company. How did you price your *very first* product or service? Please select the most suitable letter from the choices below:

   a. Cost-plus (cost oriented)
   b. Value-in-use (perceived value pricing)
   c. Going-rate (imitative) pricing
   d. Bargaining, price negotiations
   e. No specific pricing system
   f. Other (please specify) _____

8. And how do you price your product currently? Please select the most suitable letter from the choices above: _____

9. For the very first product/service that you launched, did you do concept testing? (Concept testing is exposing the product concept to consumers and asking purchasing intent.)

   ☐ Yes   ☐ No

10. Do you typically test your concepts at different price levels before introduction?

   ☐ Always   ☐ Sometimes   ☐ Never

11. Do you market test alternative prices in test markets before introduction?

   ☐ Always   ☐ Sometimes   ☐ Never

12. Let us now discuss your company's advertising. How do you usually determine your advertising budget? Select the most appropriate answer.

	Never	Sometimes	Most of the Time
Based on what my company can afford	☐	☐	☐
Based on current or anticipated sales and/or profits	☐	☐	☐
Based on the expenditures or competitors	☐	☐	☐
Based on market tests	☐	☐	☐
Based on analysis of past successes and failures	☐	☐	☐
Based on advertising goals and required tasks	☐	☐	☐
Based on forecasted incremental sales versus the incremental advertising costs	☐	☐	☐
Other (please specify) _____	☐	☐	☐

13. Consider the last advertising campaign you ran: (Skip this question if you didn't do any advertising). How many other alternative ad campaigns were generated and evaluated before the one campaign was chosen?

    0 _____   1 _____   2 _____   3 or more _____

14. Let us now discuss your sales force. Which of the following best describes your salesforce?

    ☐ Direct   ☐ Don't have a sales force (please skip the next two questions)
    ☐ Indirect
    ☐ Other (please specify) _____

15. How do you decide on the number of salespeople you need?

	Never	Sometimes	Most of the Time
Based on selling expenses as percentage of sales and average cost of salesperson	☐	☐	☐
Based on forecasted sales and average revenues generated by a salesperson	☐	☐	☐
Based on market response (e.g., inquiry calls per year)	☐	☐	☐
Based on forecasted incremental sales versus incremental sales costs	☐	☐	☐
Gut feel or judgment	☐	☐	☐
Other (please specify) _____	☐	☐	☐

16. How do you compensate your salespeople? Please select all that apply.
    ☐ Commissions
    ☐ Straight salary
    ☐ Achievement recognition programs
    ☐ Contests and prizes
    ☐ Noncash awards
    ☐ Compensation is different, depending on whether new business is being generated or existing accounts are being serviced
    ☐ Different commission rates for different products
    ☐ Different commission rates depending on growth from prior year
    ☐ Salespeople compensation is not limited to a maximum
    ☐ Other (please specify) _____

17. If your estimate, how much of the CEO's time is typically spent on public relations activities per month?
    ☐ 5 hours or less   ☐ 11 to 20 hours
    ☐ 6 to 10 hours   ☐ more than 20 hours

18. In your estimate, how much other senior management time is typically spent on public relations activities per month?
    ☐ 5 hours or less   ☐ 11 to 20 hours
    ☐ 6 to 10 hours   ☐ more than 20 hours

19. Approximately, what is your yearly public relations budget (as a percent of annual revenue)?
    _____ %

20. Approximately, what your yearly marketing budget (as a percent of annual revenue)?
    _____ %

21. Would you say that your marketing budget is increasing or decreasing over the years?
    ☐ Increasing
    ☐ Decreasing
    ☐ Steady

22. How confident are you about the contribution of these marketing components to your incremental revenue?

Marketing research	Very Confident	Confident	Neutral	Not Confident	Very Uncertain
Salesforce	☐	☐	☐	☐	☐
Advertising	☐	☐	☐	☐	☐
Public relations	☐	☐	☐	☐	☐
Branding activities	☐	☐	☐	☐	☐
Trade shows	☐	☐	☐	☐	☐
Promotions	☐	☐	☐	☐	☐
Use of the Web	☐	☐	☐	☐	☐
Marketing research	☐	☐	☐	☐	☐
Concept testing	☐	☐	☐	☐	☐

23. Do you think you have made any *marketing* mistakes while running this business? If so, please describe your biggest *marketing* mistake.

   _____

   _____

   _____

24. Please describe what you think is the best *marketing* decision you have made.

   _____

   _____

   _____

25. I there anything else you would like to add?

   _____

   _____

   _____

To complete this survey, please provide us with the following information that will help us for identification purposes only.

Company name_____

Address _____

City_____ State_____ Zip_____

Phone _____ Fax _____ Your e-mail _____

Company URL (if applicable)_____

Thank you very much for your help.
We will send you a results summary shortly.

Notes

Chapter 1

1. Some of these segmentation questions come from personal discussions and correspondence with Professor Yoram Wind of the Wharton School.
2. Robert McMath and Tom Forbes, "Look Before You Leap," *Entrepreneur,* April 1998, pp. 135–139.
3. Ibid., p. 135.
4. Susan Greco, "Reeling Them In," *Inc. Magazine,* January 1998, p. 52.
5. Ibid.
6. R.W. Keidel, *Wall Street Journal,* June 16, 1997, p. B1.

Chapter 2

1. Elton B. Sherwin Jr., *The Silicon Valley Way* (Rocklin, CA: Prima Publishing, 1998), p. 63.
2. Ibid.
3. Michael Hay, Paul Verdin, and Peter Williamson, "Successful New Ventures: Lessons for Entrepreneurs and Investors," *Long Range Planning,* 1993, 26, no. 5, pp. 31–41.
4. Ibid., p. 36.
5. Ibid., p. 38.

Chapter 3

1. This is a disguised real example from the author's experience. The data have been slightly altered to protect confidentialities.
2. Irwin Gross, Presentation at the Wharton School, March 1999.
3. Ibid.
4. Ibid.
5. Ibid.
6. SAS Institute white paper, "SAS Institute Business Model," 1998, Cary, NC, p. 3.
7. Ibid., p. 4.

8. Ibid.

9. Ibid.

10. Charles Fishman, "Sanity, Inc.," *Fast Times,* January 1999, p. 87.

11. Ibid., p. 96.

Chapter 5

1. Leyland Pitt, Pierre Berthon, and Jean-Paul Berthon, "Changing Channels: The Impact of the Internet on Distribution Strategy," *Business Horizons,* March–April 1999, pp. 19–28.

2. Ibid., p. 20.

3. Jillian M. Marcus, "Eight Legs and an Amazing Feat," Harvard Business School, 1994, Note 394-044.

4. Leigh Gallagher, "Runner's World," *Forbes,* February 22, 1999, pp. 96, 98.

5. Ibid., p. 98.

6. Ibid.

7. Ibid.

8. Some of these advantages and disadvantages come from discussions with Craig Tractenberg, an experienced franchise attorney with Buchanan, Ingersoll in Philadelphia, 1999.

9. Ritasice.com Web site, 1999.

10. Personal communication with Leonard Lodish, 1999.

11. Rochelle Garner, "Mad as Hell," *Sales and Marketing Management,* June 1999, p. 55.

12. Ibid., p. 58.

13. Ibid.

14. Ibid., pp. 58, 59.

15. James R. Hagery, "Ethan Allen's Revolutionary Path to Web," *Wall Street Journal,* July 29, 1999, p. B1.

16. Ibid.

Chapter 6

1. Geoffrey A. Moore, *Crossing the Chasm* (New York: Harper Business, 1995), p. 37.

2. Ibid.

Chapter 7

1. Andrea Knox and Rosland Briggs-Gammon, "No Substitute for Salesmanship," *Philadelphia Inquirer,* May 21, 2000, p. Q1.

2. Erin Anderson, "The Salesperson as Outside Agent or Employee: A Transaction Cost Analysis," *Marketing Science,* summer 1985, 4, pp. 234–254.

3. Erin Anderson, Leonard M. Lodish, and Barton A. Weitz, "Resource Allocation Behavior in Conventional Channels," *Journal of Marketing Research*, February 1987, 24, pp. 85–97.

4. Ibid., p. 95.

Chapter 9

1. L. Lodish, M. Abraham, S. Kalmenson, J. Livelsberger, B. Richards, and M.E. Stevens, "How TV Advertising Works: A Meta Analysis of 389 Real-World Split-Cable TV Advertising Experiments," May 1995, *Journal of Marketing Research*, 32, pp. 125–139; L. Lodish, M. Abraham, J. Livelsberger, B. Richardson, and M.E. Stevenson, "A Summary of Fifty-Five In-Market Experimental Estimates of the Long-Term Effect of TV Advertising," Part 2, *Marketing Science*, 1995, 14, no. 3, pp. G103–120.

2. J.D.C. Little, "Decisions Support Systems for Marketing Managers," *Journal of Marketing*, summer 1979, 43, pp. 9–26.

3. C.B. Bhattacharya and L.M. Lodish, "An Advertising Evaluation System for Retailers," *Journal of Retailing and Consumer Services*, 1994, 1, no. 2, pp. 90–100.

4. Ibid.

Chapter 12

1. David A. Aaker, *Building Strong Brands* (New York: The Free Press, 1966).

2. Synygy Brochure, 2000, Bala Cynwyd, PA.

3. See note 1.

Index